JESUITS AND MATRIARCHS

JESUITS AND MATRIARCHS

DOMESTIC WORSHIP IN EARLY MODERN CHINA

NADINE AMSLER

UNIVERSITY OF WASHINGTON PRESS
Seattle

JESUITS AND MATRIARCHS WAS MADE POSSIBLE IN PART BY A GRANT FROM THE JAMES P. GEISS AND MARGARET Y. HSU FOUNDATION.

SUPPORT FOR THIS PUBLICATION WAS ALSO PROVIDED BY THE CHIANG CHING-KUO FOUNDATION FOR INTERNATIONAL SCHOLARLY EXCHANGE.

THE PREPRESS OF THIS PUBLICATION WAS FUNDED BY THE SWISS NATIONAL SCIENCE FOUNDATION.

Printed and bound in the United States of America
Composed in Minion Pro, typeface designed by Robert Slimbach
22 21 20 19 18 5 4 3 2 1

UNIVERSITY OF WASHINGTON PRESS
www.washington.edu/uwpress

Maps by Jennifer Shontz, Red Shoe Design
Cover illustration: Woodblock print from João da Rocha's *Rules for Reciting the Rosary* (1619). Digital image courtesy of the Getty's Open Content Program.

LIBRARY OF CONGRESS CATALOGING-IN-PUBLICATION DATA
LC record available at https://lccn.loc.gov/2018011124

ISBN 978-0-295-74379-0 (hardcover), ISBN 978-0-295-74380-6 (pbk),
ISBN 978-0-295-74381-3 (ebook)

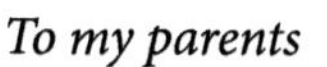

To my parents

CONTENTS

ACKNOWLEDGMENTS

This book is the result of a long intellectual journey that also involved a number of physical displacements. Like any traveler, I relied on many people who acted as guides, hosts, or travel mates. I would like to express my gratitude to all of them, even if space only allows for mentioning a few of them by name.

I had the fortune to be supported by highly knowledgeable and very generous guides. I would like to thank Christian Windler and Sabine Dabringhaus, who accompanied the book from the initial idea to the final manuscript and provided intellectual guidance and practical advice all along the way. Nicolas Standaert and Eugenio Menegon pushed me hard to think about Chinese Catholicism from a women's perspective. Their memorable workshop "The Materiality of Chinese-Western Relations" held in Leuven in 2014 provided me with valuable inputs in a crucial phase of the book's making.

People in many places helped make the journey easier and more fruitful. In Zurich, Wolfgang Behr and Stefan Bumbacher helped to improve my skills in Classical Chinese. Chen Yunü and Chien Jui-yao warmly welcomed me and enthusiastically supported my project during a research stay in Tainan. Christoph Riedweg, his staff, and the *membri* at the Istituto Svizzero di Roma made my research stay in Rome an intellectually stimulating and socially enjoyable experience. Arndt Brendecke and the staff of the Chair of Early Modern History of the Ludwig-Maximilians-Universität helped to make Munich the perfect place for completing the manuscript. Renate Dürr, Jon Mathieu, Barbara Stollberg-Rilinger, and Antonella Romano gave me the opportunity to discuss the project in their seminars. My thanks also go to my colleagues in the Department of Early Modern History at the University of Bern and in the Department of East Asian History at the University of Freiburg—among them Andreas Affolter, Corina Bastian, Tilman Haug, Alexander Keese, Daniel Sidler, Sören Urbansky, Wang Shuo, and Philipp Zwyssig—for many inspiring conversations and comforting words.

Much of this book's journey was taking place in my mind while I was sitting in reading rooms of libraries and archives: the Archivum Historicum Societatis Iesu, the Archivio Storico della S. Congregazione "De Propaganda Fide," and the Archivio della Congregazione per la Dottrina della Fede in Rome; the Biblioteca da Ajuda in Lisbon; the East Asian Library of the Katholieke Universiteit Leuven; and the Bayerische Staatsbibliothek in Munich. In all these institutions, I received the help of knowledgeable and friendly staff. My numerous research stays were made possible by the Swiss National Science Foundation, which granted generous material support from 2011 to 2014.

When the journey drew to a close, Peter Brett and Samuel Weber helped to correct the errors and clumsiness of my English. Stefan Rebenich and Ronald G. Asch read the manuscript and asked critical and thought-provoking questions. Henrietta Harrison offered valuable advice when I started thinking about publishing. Lorri Hagman and Niccole Coggins from the University of Washington Press helped me navigate through the publication process. Two anonymous readers provided helpful comments on the manuscript.

My deepest debt of gratitude is to my family. My parents, Veronika and Roland Amsler, always encouraged me to follow my inner compass and provided loving and often very hands-on support. It is to them that I dedicate this book. Nadir Weber has been my travel mate for many years. It is impossible to say how much I owe to his emotionally supporting and intellectually challenging companionship. Clearly, this book would not have come into being without him. Our children, Valentin and Philomena, keep us busy and teach us the essentials of life. They remind us that it is for the generations to come that historians ponder over times past.

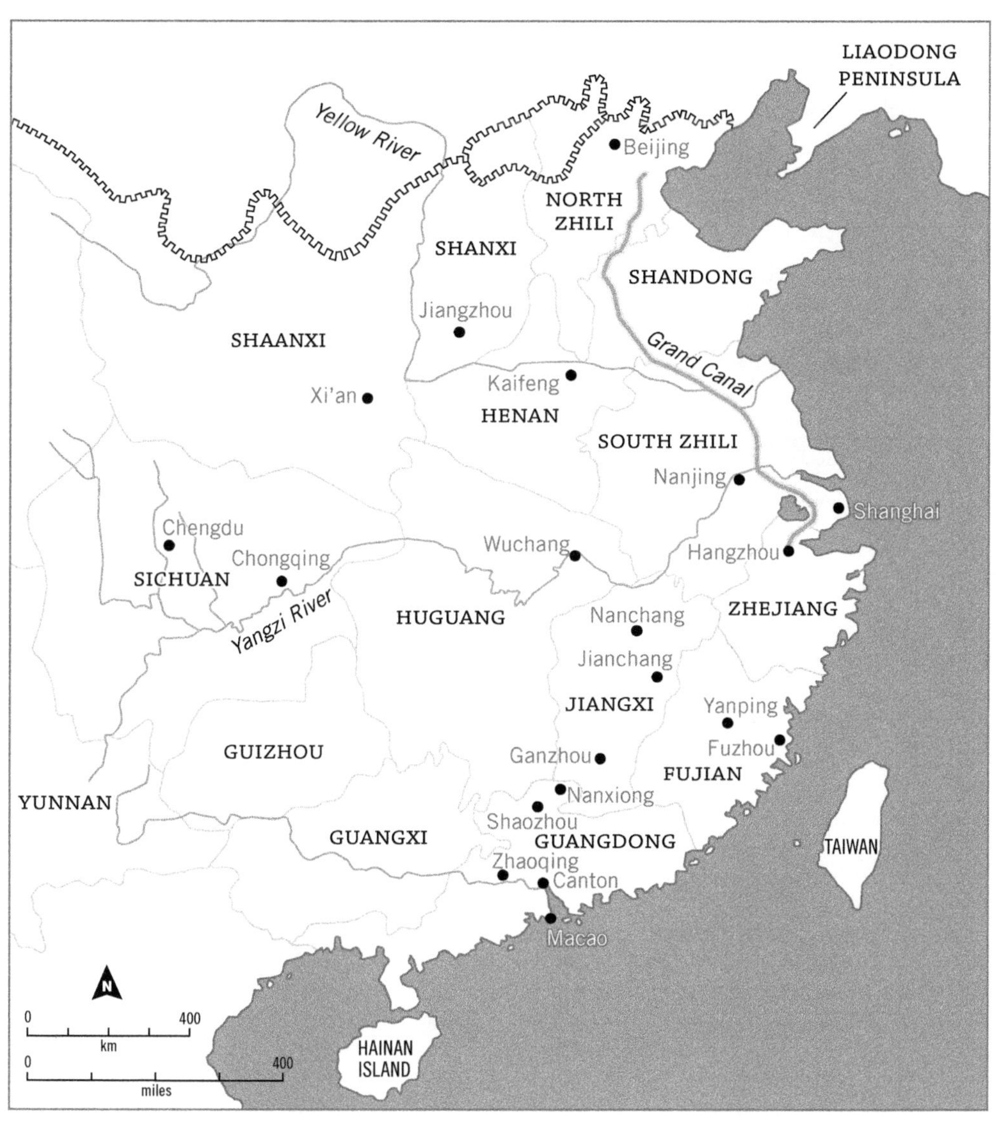

MAP 1. Jesuit residences in China (those mentioned in the book, not all those extant in the seventeenth century)

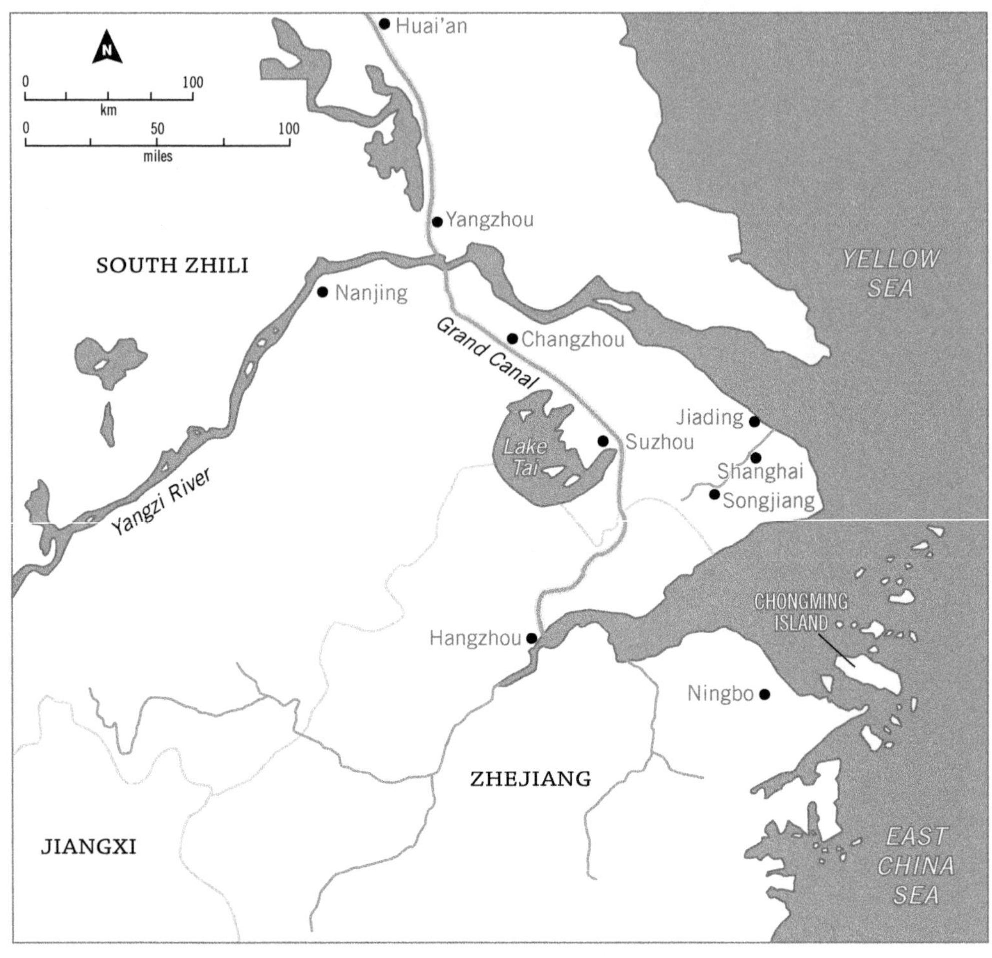

MAP 2. Jesuit residences in the Jiangnan region (those mentioned in the book, not all those extant in the seventeenth century)

JESUITS AND MATRIARCHS

INTRODUCTION

IN 1682 THE FLEMISH JESUIT PHILIPPE COUPLET RETURNED FROM a twenty-two-year stay in China. He arrived in Holland with heavy luggage. Among his many objects were several gifts donated by Candida Xu (1607–1680), an eminent Catholic lady of Songjiang (today part of Shanghai city). The gifts included textiles, such as Mass vestments and altar cloths embroidered by Candida and her daughters; richly ornamented altar vessels made from precious material; and "four hundred volumes in Chinese written by the Jesuit missionaries, the purchase of which was financed by Candida Xu."[1] These gifts were destined for the pope and well-known European churches. Couplet's luggage likely also contained a first draft of a book on the pious life of the China mission's female patron: *The Story of a Christian Lady of China, Candida Xu* (Historia Nobilis Feminae Candida Hiu, Christianae Sinensis).

The Story of a Christian Lady of China was first published in French in 1688 as one of a series of publications instigated by Couplet. Along with the famous *Confucius, the Chinese Philosopher* (Confucius Sinarum Philosophus, 1687) it justified the Jesuits' China mission to a European audience that was by then increasingly unsettled by an emerging dispute between Jesuits and mendicants commonly known as the "rites controversy."[2] It sought to encourage rich European Catholics, especially pious ladies, to emulate Candida Xu in her virtuousness, piety, and generous charity toward the China mission.[3] Like other pieces of early modern European travel writing, it was also intended to provide European readers with what might be called proto-ethnographic information on China.[4] Indeed, *The Story of a Christian Lady of China* would go on to decisively shape historians' knowledge of women in seventeenth-century Chinese Catholicism.[5]

However, *The Story of a Christian Lady of China* raises questions as to whether Couplet's book is indeed a suitable source for historians interested in the role of women in seventeenth-century Chinese Catholicism. In its descriptions of Chinese women it deploys a rhetoric of distance throughout.

"I will say nothing," Couplet wrote at the outset, "about [Candida's] childhood, nor of the fourteen years of her marriage, for Chinese girls and women have so little contact with the world that you see them very rarely." According to Couplet, Chinese women lived "shut away in apartments which are so withdrawn that there is no greater solitude than the one in which they spend the most part of their life."[6] Although Candida had more freedom after she was widowed, Couplet repeatedly insisted that Europeans could hardly imagine the delicacy of the Jesuits' dealings with Chinese women, due to the latter's reclusiveness and modesty.[7]

Was this a prudish Jesuit's attempt to dispel any thought of intimacy between the spiritual father and his female adept? Or was it rather a reflection of the life circumstances of Chinese women like Candida Xu, who was a member of the scholar gentry? If Chinese Catholic women did indeed live as self-contained a life as Couplet suggests, how did missionaries cater to their religious needs? How did Catholic women organize their religious piety, and how did they perceive the "teachings of the Lord of Heaven" (Tianzhujiao) propagated by the Jesuits? These questions are illuminated by analysis of the significance of gendered spatial relations in the Jesuits' mission to seventeenth-century China.

If, up to now, only little has been written about women's role in the Jesuits' mission to China, this is because research on Chinese Catholicism has largely neglected the household as a religious space. The domestic sphere was where, during the seventeenth century, Chinese Catholic women predominantly practiced their religion. Both Jesuit missionaries and Chinese women contributed to this development: while the Jesuits helped to increase the importance of the household as religious space by defining house oratories as women's primary spaces of worship, women used the freedom that the domestic sphere granted them and created their own networks and forms of religious sociability.

The household was the ritual space that Chinese society traditionally assigned to women, who were responsible for domestic ancestor worship, the worship of household deities, the organization of domestically celebrated life-cycle rituals, and domestic seasonal rituals.[8] This gendered division of ritual labor left its traces in Catholic women's religious practices in several ways, furthering women's preference for certain forms of individual piety, shaping Catholic women's ritual communities, and contributing to the emergence of a specific domestic religious culture among women of Catholic gentry families.[9]

THE JESUIT MISSION IN SEVENTEENTH-CENTURY CHINA

When Candida Xu was born, in the first decade of the seventeenth century, commerce, consumption, and the arts were thriving in unprecedented ways in China. The late Ming (ca. 1580–1644) was a period of increased monetization, urbanization, and demographic growth, and it saw a rapid expansion of the printing business.[10] A new, urban culture of consumption was created, and moral and social standards that had been viewed, until then, as timeless started to change.[11] The increased cultural flexibility of the era also extended to Chinese people's piety. People had a strong penchant for syncretism, and new developments within Confucian thinking placed special emphasis on the individual.[12] Some of these developments came to a halt with the fall of the Ming and the establishment of the Qing dynasty by the Manchus in 1644, with the second half of the century experienced by most members of the former Ming elite as a period of deep crisis.[13] Nevertheless, a distinctive Qing culture was only starting to be formed during the first decades after the conquest, so that many of the Ming cultural developments still reverberated until 1700.[14]

The novel developments in sixteenth- and seventeenth-century Chinese society also affected women's lives. Courtesan culture flourished in late Ming cities, and the market in women, on which poor country girls as well as wives changed hands as maidservants or concubines, thrived.[15] Simultaneously, however, growing numbers of Chinese women strove for Confucian feminine ideals. The cult of female chastity made widows commit suicide as a sign of marital fidelity and prompted young girls to keep lifelong fidelity to late fiancés they had hardly ever known.[16] Furthermore, the ideal of female seclusion—derived from the famous sentence in *The Book of Rites* (Liji), "Men and women shall be separated" (Nan nü you bie)—led literati families to accommodate their female members in remote "inner quarters" (*guige*) and caused scholar officials to promulgate new regulations aimed at limiting the occasions on which the sexes mingled in public.[17] While these developments significantly restricted women's sphere of action, trends in the opposite direction were also under way. Ming elite women took advantage of the opportunities granted by the new communicative means of the era. In a cultural environment that celebrated female talent and promoted the ideal of companionate marriage, an increasing number of literate elite women read novels, exchanged letters, and wrote and published poetry.[18] Thus, although Chinese women—and especially elite women—were conspicuously invisible in seventeenth-century China, they simultaneously participated in the semipublic realm of the arts in an unprecedented way.

Of all this, Europeans knew little or nothing at the turn of the seventeenth century. The Ming emperors, who had organized expeditions to South Asia during the fifteenth century, had lost their interest in maritime relations in the sixteenth century. Chinese merchants continued to be important players in the Asian maritime trade. Imperial officials, however, were intent on keeping China uncorrupted by the noxious influence of barbarian lands.[19] When the first Portuguese merchant ships reached South China in the early sixteenth century, Europeans realized that the Chinese were anything but enthusiastic about their arrival. Instead of establishing close trade relations with them, they only allowed the foreigners to stay on a small, rocky peninsula some eighty kilometers south of Canton, imposing strict regulations upon the modalities of trade.[20] From this place—soon known by the name "Macao" in Portuguese sources—missionaries, who had reached this southern corner of China on Portuguese ships, tried to enter China from the second half of the sixteenth century onward. However, they were remarkably unsuccessful in their endeavor. Although some of them were allowed to accompany trade delegations to Canton, no one was allowed to stay in inland China for long.[21] The dream of China's evangelization only started to materialize toward the end of the sixteenth century, when a new ecclesiastical actor entered the stage: the Society of Jesus.

Founded by Ignatius of Loyola in 1534, the Society of Jesus had, from its very beginnings, developed a vivid interest in overseas missions. Already Francis Xavier, one of Ignatius's first companions, had worked as a missionary in India and Japan; he died on a small island off the Chinese coast in 1552.[22] More Jesuit missionaries reached Asia toward the end of the sixteenth century, when the new ecclesiastical order grew in numbers and was fast becoming a principal tool for the implementation of the Catholic Church's reform plans decided upon during the Council of Trent (1545–63).[23] The numbers of conversions were on the rise, particularly in Japan, where the Jesuits had experimented with cultural accommodation, learning Japanese and adapting their outer appearance to Buddhist monks.[24] Inspired by the Japanese model, the Jesuits decided to try to enter China armed with their signature accommodation strategy. In 1579 the Jesuit visitor to East Asia Alessandro Valignano ordered Michele Ruggieri (1543–1607), an Italian missionary stationed in Goa, to come to

Macao in order to learn Chinese. Four years later, Ruggieri, together with his younger confrere Matteo Ricci (1552–1610), moved to Zhaoqing. There the two men, dressed in Buddhist monks' garbs, established the first Jesuit residence in China.[25]

During a period that might be called a long seventeenth century (ca. 1580–1690), the China mission was almost exclusively in the hands of the Jesuits, who in turn were subjected to the Portuguese Padroado, a patronate over all African and Asian missions granted to the Portuguese crown by the pope.[26] Some mendicant friars reached Southwest China from the 1630s onward, and vicars apostolic to China were appointed in the 1680s by the Holy Congregation for the Propagation of the Faith (Sacra Congregatio de Propaganda Fide). However, neither of them posed a serious challenge to the Jesuit monopoly over the evangelization of the Middle Kingdom.[27] From the missionaries' viewpoint, this situation entailed a significant degree of independence from Roman authorities. Despite continued conflicts triggered by the Chinese rites controversy from the 1640s onward, these authorities did not have the institutional means to maintain a firm grip on the distant China mission.[28]

This period was, furthermore, an era when the Chinese authorities were relatively tolerant toward Catholicism. Anti-Catholic incidents did occasionally occur. They included the Nanjing incident (1616–17), during which the vice-minister of the Nanjing Ministry of Rites placed the missionaries and several Chinese Catholics under arrest, and the "Calendar Case" (1664–69), when Johann Adam Schall von Bell was accused of having selected inauspicious dates and places in his function as imperial astronomer, resulting in the exile of the Jesuits in Canton.[29] However, these movements should not detract from the fact that the seventeenth century was a period of considerable growth of Chinese Catholicism, the numbers of converts rising from a few thousands in the 1610s to some tens of thousands in the 1630s and reaching their zenith with approximately two hundred thousand at the end of the seventeenth century.[30]

GENDER RELATIONS IN CHINESE CATHOLICISM

Interest in Chinese Catholicism as a phenomenon of Sino-Western cultural exchange was sparked by French sinologist Jacques Gernet's 1982 book *Chine et christianisme*—a study that rated the Jesuits' mission to China as a failure due to the cultural misunderstanding between the European missionaries and the Chinese. As a response to Gernet, historians have started to unearth evidence of Chinese people's active role in entrenching Catholicism in China.[31] They have shown that the Jesuits relied heavily on Chinese helpers in their evangelical work and that lay institutions were a key element of Chinese Catholic religious life. Drawing on the extensive Chinese documentary records, they have also shown how the Chinese converts' own views on the "teachings of the Lord of Heaven" are visible in their writings.[32] In light of this, several scholars have become interested in Chinese Catholicism as a phenomenon that sprang from intense intercultural interaction between (predominantly European) missionaries and various Chinese actors.[33] Despite this increased attention to Chinese Catholics, however, not much is known about Chinese women who, during the seventeenth century, came into contact with the Jesuits and decided to convert to Catholicism.[34] This contrasts starkly with research on (primarily eighteenth- and nineteenth-century) missions of the Dominicans in Fujian and missions of the Missions Étrangères de Paris in Sichuan and Manchuria, where historians have pointed to the important role of Chinese women.[35]

While the gender perspective was, until now, largely absent from studies on the seventeenth-century Jesuit China mission, historiography on contemporary European Catholicism offers a different picture. Research has shown that the changes triggered by the Tridentine reforms, which were the Catholic response to the Reformation and led to intensified efforts to catechize and control Catholic territories, provided women with new opportunities for piety, but they also restricted religious women's lives by cloistering them in convents.[36] Historians have, furthermore, turned their attention to the Catholic clergy's gendered identity and, in particular, to the Jesuits' attitudes toward women. Studies have shown how the Society of Jesus offered Catholic men an attractive masculine ideal to embrace. They have also shown that the Society's refusal to become entangled with women's religious institutions did not prevent Jesuits from maintaining close contact with (especially) upper-class spiritual daughters, whose spiritual lives were strongly influenced by the interiorized religiosity propagated by the Society of Jesus.[37]

In the same vein, the life circumstances of women in seventeenth-century China are also remarkably well documented. Historians have analyzed how the Confucian norm of gender segregation affected the lives of women of different social strata and have singled out the seventeenth century as a period when women's sphere of influence expanded in gentry families—in spite of the great value attached to female seclusion.[38] Special attention has also been paid to women's involvement with religion. Scholars have pointed out that Chinese religiosity was in many ways closely intertwined with the female sphere and that a focus on women's subculture, rather than on Confucian orthodox discourse, can help to unearth valuable insights into late imperial Chinese religiosity.[39]

Since this study tries to connect the study of women in seventeenth-century China with research on gender relations in post-Tridentine Catholicism, it is important to highlight some basic similarities between Chinese and European understandings of gender during the early modern period. In both seventeenth-century China and Europe, gender was a much more fluid category than in modern societies. Rather than primarily conceived of as a matter of biological sex, gender roles were defined by, and closely interrelated with, family, social, and cosmic orders.[40] That gender relations nevertheless became a contested issue in several of the missionaries' fields of activity was not the result of incompatible notions of what constituted gender. It was due to the fact that, as in many societies, gender relations were essential to the stabilization of power relations and, simultaneously, helped to assess the foreignness and degree of civilization of cultural "others."[41]

Three sets of questions concerning gender relations in the zone of cultural contact created by the Jesuits' missionary activity in China are of concern here. First, how were European and Chinese protagonists' perceptions of the "others'" notions of gender relations shaped by their own society's normative statements on gender, and what was the scope of interpretation in different sources addressing the gender norms of these cultural "others"? Second, what were the implications of cultural encounters for people's gendered identities? The case of seventeenth-century Chinese Catholicism is especially noteworthy for the study of how the Jesuits' masculinity—understood as a prescriptive concept constructed in relation to different forms of masculinities and femininities—was shaped by cultural contact.[42] And third, what was the impact of the Sino-Western cultural encounter on Chinese women's agency? Female Catholic piety can be reconstructed through analysis of the Catholic religious practices of different groups of Chinese women.

SOURCES, GEOGRAPHICAL FOCUS, AND STRUCTURE

Chinese Catholicism is a unique field for the investigation of cultural contact due to its extensive source records. The European-language sources produced by the missionaries are complemented by texts published by the missionaries in Chinese, including catechisms, prayer books, moral tracts, and biographies of saints. Furthermore, Catholicism was also discussed by (male) Chinese authors—both converts and opponents of Catholicism. Taken together, these sources allow for a multi-perspective reconstruction of Chinese Catholicism as a phenomenon created by mutual perception and interaction.[43]

Despite this variety of sources, the most extensive record on seventeenth-century Chinese Catholicism was left behind by Jesuit missionaries, and it is therefore necessary to put these writings and their authors into context. Most of the Jesuit missionaries had entered the Society of Jesus in Europe, where they had studied in the order's colleges. When they undertook the long and hazardous journey to Asia, many of them left Europe for good.[44] Due to the subjection of the China mission under the Portuguese Padroado, the majority of missionaries were Portuguese. Nevertheless, the China mission also saw a considerable number of missionaries of other nationalities—especially Italians, Belgians, and Germans—many of whom played crucial roles in its history.[45] During their sojourn in China they stayed in contact with one another and with their brethren in Europe mainly through written correspondence, much of which has been preserved in European archives.

Many of the missionaries' writings, on which this study draws, are the product of the China mission's organizational effort and administrative work.[46] Within the internal organization of the China mission, three functions had the character of nodes where information was gathered, organized, and forwarded. The Jesuits were subordinated, first, to a (vice-) provincial responsible for the East-Asian missions—and, after the creation of the vice-province of China in 1619, exclusively for the Middle Kingdom.[47] He took care of the flow of information between China and the Roman headquarters, compiling especially the annual letters (*litterae annuae*) addressed to the father general. The mission was sporadically monitored, second, by visitors sent to China by the Roman superiors. These usually wrote extensive reports on their activities and experience in the mission field. Third, the missionaries sought to defend their own interests and clarify internal questions by occasionally sending procurators back to Rome, usually arming them with ample information on the mission in order to substantiate their claims.[48] The mission was connected to the Society's Roman headquarters through these nodes, producing a flow of travelogues, accounts, written correspondence, and annual letters directed toward Europe.[49]

The sources that contain most information on Chinese women's Catholic piety are, perhaps ironically, the annual letters—rather standardized reports sent by the missionaries to the Jesuit superiors in Rome on an annual basis. They were compiled by the provincial of each Jesuit province in order to record the most important events of the previous year, with information usually presented in a strictly geographical structure. Several regulations issued by the Society of Jesus guided the process, regulating the rhythm of writing, the letters' style and content, their circulation, and their compilation.[50] Due to the annual letters' edifying purpose, they mainly contain success stories of conversion and devotion or stories of divine punishment inflicted on "infidels" or undevout Christians. This has prompted historians to question the usefulness of these documents for reconstructing the non-European realities encountered by the missionaries.[51] Despite their edifying nature, however, the annual letters contain much information on how the Jesuits organized and perceived their missions. Furthermore, they often reveal *ex negativo* how non-Catholic practices persisted or reemerged in Catholic communities. To read the edifying stories against the grain can therefore produce valuable insights into Chinese Catholic realities.

To use the available sources in the best way possible, this book includes material on many different Chinese Catholic communities administered by the Jesuits. These were distributed over the vast territory of the late Ming and early Qing empires, stretching from the northern capital of Beijing to the southern merchant hub of Canton, and from coastal Shanghai to western Chengdu (see map 1). It will, however, combine this broad analysis with a more focused study of one particular area, the Jiangnan (literally "South of the [Yangzi] River") region (see map 2). This was not only the region with the densest Catholic presence but was also the most prosperous and culturally advanced region of seventeenth-century China.[52] Owing to this focus, the main sites of cultural contact that this study investigates are urban centers such as Nanjing, Shanghai, Songjiang, and Jiading.[53] Cities were the Jesuits' preferred places of residence and are thus far better documented in their records than rural Catholic communities, which were only occasionally visited by a priest during mission circuits.[54] Although material on rural communities is taken into account if available, the focus of the analysis is therefore on cities and, more specifically, on Chinese Catholic urban households. For, although missionaries moved rather freely within the urban space and made contact with a great number of people whom they invited to their residences, they never made such invitations to women, and they expected female converts to practice Catholic devotion within the domestic realm—a social space that has hitherto been largely ignored by studies of Chinese Catholicism. There are several advantages to a focus on devotional practice within the domestic realm. It helps us understand the ways Catholicism inscribed itself into Chinese family systems and how Catholic households organized their devotion. It also turns our attention to Chinese women's domestic religious cultures, showing them as practitioners of an alternative religiosity and, simultaneously, as active patrons of religious institutions.[55]

The following chapters analyze how the Jesuits adapted their masculinity to Chinese Confucian gender norms and how Chinese women connected with the Catholic religion spread by the missionaries.[56] They will explore the ways in which the Jesuits' accommodation affected their representations of Chinese women, their ministry to women, and Chinese Catholic marriages and how the incompatibility between priestly and Confucian ideals pushed them to find creative solutions in their daily performances. Furthermore, they will show how women made use of Catholic spiritual remedies, how they organized and practiced their Catholic piety, and how they tapped into the Catholic female role model of virginity. Last but not least, they will argue that—in spite of the Jesuits' consideration for the separation of the sexes—Chinese Catholic women's lives were connected with Chinese Catholicism as a whole in many ways.

1 CLOTHES MAKE THE MAN

The Jesuits' Adoption of Literati Masculinity

IN APRIL 1595 THE JESUIT MISSIONARIES MATTEO RICCI AND Lazzaro Cattaneo, who had left their residence in Shaozhou for the southern capital of Nanjing, swapped their Buddhist monks' garb (which Ricci had been wearing for the previous ten years) for the Confucian dress of *xiucai*, scholars who had passed entry-level exams in the imperial examination system.[1] By 1594 Ricci had already started to abandon his Buddhist appearance by letting his beard grow. This was because his Chinese friend Qu Rukui found that Ricci's personality "did not resemble [that of] a Buddhist monk."[2] Qu, therefore, suggested that the missionary let his hair grow and call himself a Confucian literatus. After his change of dress, Ricci ceased to describe himself as a "Western monk" (*xiseng*) and began identifying himself as a "Western literatus" (*xiru*, *xishi*). The Jesuits' change of attire was officially approved by the visitor to East India Alessandro Valignano, who was responsible for overseeing the Jesuits' missions in Asia. In a memorial issued in November 1594, Valignano cautiously interpreted the Jesuits' new accommodation strategy as a merely temporary one, declaring that it seemed wise for them to take on the name, dress, and bodily attire of the literati for a certain period of time.[3] However, what Valignano saw as a temporary necessity soon became the irreversible foundation of the Jesuits' mission in seventeenth- and eighteenth-century China: their accommodation to the Confucian literati elite.

Who, however, were these literati, those scholars whose elegant silk garments Matteo Ricci had preferred to the coarse religious robe of the Buddhist monks? Composed of families of degree holders from whom the emperor recruited his officials, they formed a group at the apex of society. By the seventeenth century, they had firmly established themselves as the sociocultural elite of the Chinese empire. They enjoyed imperial tax privileges, especially regarding the taxation of landholdings. As a result, their families were frequently large landowners and, in some cases, exceedingly wealthy. Many scholar-gentry families were thus able to maintain their social status for several generations, even if they did not produce any degree holders for a considerable length of time.[4] Their prosperity enabled them to participate in prestigious projects such as the renovation of temples, the founding of social welfare institutions, and the improvement of irrigation systems.[5] Even more importantly, it allowed members of the scholar-gentry to live their lives according to the leisurely lifestyle of their peers, spending their time reading Confucian classics, collecting precious antiques, tasting tea, and attending poetry club meetings.[6]

It goes without saying that the Jesuits' adoption of the literati attire affected the social identity of the missionaries in crucial ways.[7] As Matteo Ricci put it, it enabled them to "transcend the boundary that [their] brothers had established [by adopting the] name, dress, and corporeal appearance" of the Buddhist monks and would permit them to converse freely with members of the Confucian literati elite.[8] This was, however, not the only implication of wearing literati attire. The change of dress also entailed the creation of a distinct form of masculinity, combining attributes of the Society of Jesus and the Chinese scholar-gentry. A look at the social mechanisms behind their change of dress, and the effects of this new dress on Jesuit social identity, is useful in understanding how this literati masculinity of the Jesuits was created.

THE LITERATI ROBE: A DRESS IN ITS CONTEXT

Early modern Chinese and European societies shared a common understanding of dress as the primary means for expressing social distinction.[9] The ancient idea that clothing should represent a divinely ordained, stable social order lingered on in both regions throughout the premodern period. In the eyes of early modern authorities, attire served to provide for the "legibility of the world," furnishing the contemporary observer with information about the social, marital, and gender status of every member of society.[10] Sumptuary laws prescribing different dress codes for different social groups were common in early modern China as well as in Europe. Although neither European nor Chinese authorities enforced the laws on a regular basis, they can nevertheless be understood as an attempt to maintain proper social order.[11] The Ming emperors, for instance, proclaimed that the purpose of the dress regulations was "to make the honored and the mean distinct and to make status and authority explicit."[12] Attire was an important means for implementing social distinction (*bie*), a core concept in the Chinese understanding of society.[13] That garments determined social status was also made clear by the Chinese expression "gown and cap" (*yiguan*), a metaphor used to designate degree holders. In Europe the idea that attire marked social distinction was reflected in the popular genre of costume books, works claiming to encompass the entire social world, in all its hierarchical nuance, by depicting its varieties of dress.[14]

There were, however, underlying tensions between early modern discourses on dress and sartorial practice. Economic development and urbanization increasingly ensured that the ways in which people dressed were subject to changes in fashion. This dynamism of early modern sartorial practices gained momentum almost simultaneously in Europe and East Asia.[15] In late Ming China, authorities were powerless in the face of the rapid economic development, something that, paired with the rise of conspicuous consumption among the wealthy elite, gave rise to new textile markets.[16] The increasing diversity and decreasing cost of clothing—developments that, according to one Western observer, outpaced even those in Europe—made the sumptuary laws of the *Collected Statutes of the Ming Dynasty* (Da Ming huidian) a mere paper tiger.[17] These rapid changes in fashion, and unprecedented expansions in the kinds of clothing available, were accompanied by a blurring of social boundaries. It need not surprise us, therefore, that the Shanghai literatus Ye Mengzhu noted a steady increase over the course of the seventeenth century in the number of people dressing in the style of the literati elite. In earlier times literati attire had been worn only by degree holders. Now, by contrast, "those imitating scholar-officials in clothing" merely had to be "sons or brothers of scholar-officials. . . . Scholar-officials also tolerated those who were literate but failed to earn themselves degrees yet borrowed gentry style to distinguish themselves from commoners."[18]

Both the ancient view of dress as a social marker and the new late Ming fluidity of sartorial practice were significant for the Jesuits' change of attire. On the one hand, the close connection between bodily attire and social status made the Jesuits' change of dress a heavily symbolic act, marking a transition to a new social group. On the other hand, the new fluidity of social boundaries greatly facilitated the Jesuits' access to the literati world. The Jesuits' lifestyle lent credence to their claims to be "Western literati," despite their not being members of well-established Chinese literati families. That they had come, in the words of the late Ming scholar Li Zhi, "over one hundred thousand miles to reach China" and had studied the Confucian learning soon attracted the attention of several Chinese literati, who were ready to embrace the foreign missionaries as their peers.[19]

How did the Jesuits' change of attire fit with their European Catholic identity as religious? How was it possible that their mode of dressing disregarded the norm of standardized religious garment—something that mattered deeply to early modern Catholic religious as a marker of corporate identity and a reminder of the religious vow of poverty?[20] In fact, the Society of Jesus differed from most Catholic religious orders whose monastic rules meticulously specified the color and quality of dress.[21] Its founder, Ignatius of Loyola, had abstained from defining a standardized religious habit for the Society. In the "Constitutions," Ignatius stressed that "the Jesuit's dress should conform to the usage of the region."[22] The only limits he imposed on Jesuit attire were his instructions to dress properly and in accordance with the vow of poverty.[23] This sartorial flexibility facilitated the evangelical work of Ignatius's successors. It enabled the missionaries in China to adjust their style of dress several times, exchanging missionaries' cassocks for Buddhist monks' garb, Ming literati robes, and finally the literati dress imposed on the Chinese by the Manchus (who conquered the Middle Kingdom at midcentury).

As an anomaly in the early modern Catholic world, the Society's dress policy fueled the suspicion of its enemies in Europe, who decried the Jesuits' flexibility as proof of a conscious effort at dissimulation.[24] In the Jesuits' mind, however, flexibility in dress was unconnected to dissimulation or inconstancy. It was seen, on the contrary, as an effective means of evangelization, one not interfering with the missionaries' religious vocation. From this point of view, sartorial flexibility could be read as expressing the interiorization of religious norms.[25] This had profound consequences for the ways Jesuits perceived themselves and their social environment. First, it strengthened the individual Jesuit's identification with the goals of the Society.[26] By stressing the interiorization of its values, the Society of Jesus thus achieved a remarkably coherent corporate identity. Second, it also entailed new modes of thinking about cultural difference and cross-cultural communication. Although the Jesuits strictly rejected all things "pagan," they were open to adapting what they perceived as the merely "social" customs of the societies they were evangelizing.[27] Matteo Ricci thus found nothing strange in maintaining that the Jesuits and literati resembled each other with regard to their moral virtue (*virtù*), as morality and religion were, in his mind, distinct categories.[28]

Nevertheless, European Catholic norms of uniformity of religious garments also influenced the Jesuits' Chinese way of dressing. In fact, they developed a particular "Western literati" style of dressing, which straddled Chinese and European cultures and was intended to meet the expectations of both Chinese and European observers. The missionaries attached great importance to this attire as a marker of their adherence to the literati class, but sought simultaneously to maintain a degree of uniformity of dress that would point toward the Society's corporate identity. They preferred dark-colored textiles, reserving bright colors for the collars of their dress only (figures 1.1 and 1.2).[29] This contrasted with the colorful extravagance of the Chinese literati's robes and pointed to the Jesuits' attempt to conform to the Ignatian instruction to dress modestly.[30] Furthermore, it also associated their attire with that worn by their brethren in Rome, who usually wore black cassocks.[31] The Jesuits maintained this preference for plain, dark colors throughout the seventeenth century, retaining it even after adapting to Manchu rulers' regulations regarding dress and hairstyle. An exception was made, however, for those few Jesuits who served the Qing emperor as high officials at court. These Jesuits, among them the famous court

FIG. 1.1. Matteo Ricci wearing an informal literati robe and hat. Oil painting made by You Wenhui (alias Manuel Pereira) after Ricci's death in Beijing in 1610. Chiesa del Gesù, Rome, courtesy of De Agostini Picture Library/I. Moretti/Bridgeman Images.

FIG. 1.2. Nicolas Trigault wearing a ceremonial dress (*lifu*). Drawing made by Peter Paul Rubens during Trigault's stay in Antwerp in 1617. Courtesy of Metropolitan Museum of Art.

astronomer Johann Adam Schall von Bell, wore the more elaborate dress of Qing officials (figure 1.3).

The Jesuits also strengthened their corporate identity by defining the wearing of the literati robe as a privilege reserved for ordained priests. "Our brothers do not use this highly honored dress," Procurator Nicolas Trigault wrote in 1613.[32] One reason for this distinction was the social background of the Society's Chinese lay brothers. Because the Chinese brothers were usually the children of commoners, their adornment in literati robes would have been condemned as an abuse by the literati elite. This may also have been why many missionaries had mixed feelings about the idea of admitting Chinese Catholics to the priesthood, which had been promoted by French

FIG. 1.3. Johann Adam Schall von Bell wearing a Qing official's dress sporting a mandarin square (*buzi*). Copperplate engraving printed in Athanasius Kircher's *China Illustrated* (1667). Courtesy of Universitäts-bibliothek Bern, MUE Gross Xb 7:1.

Jesuits, especially, in the second half of the seventeenth century. When visiting Rome as a procurator of the Chinese mission in 1671, Prospero Intorcetta thus explained to the Propaganda Fide that the church should select Chinese priests from the ranks of the literati. Because these ranks were only attained at an advanced age, he explained, these men would naturally be mature men—something that would only enhance the Chinese priests' authority.[33]

Literati dress, finally, also stressed the difference between the Jesuits and mendicant missionaries, whose Chinese dress slightly differed from the Jesuit Chinese attire.[34] This probably contributed to the impression of many Chinese observers that the mendicants were foreign religious specialists rather than part of the Chinese social elite.[35] However, even more important than these sartorial differences were the differences concerning strategies of evangelization. These became the basis of continuing conflicts between them, culminating in the Chinese rites controversy toward the end of the seventeenth century.

Since the literati robe was a primary marker of the Jesuits' social identity in China, it seems that they used it on a daily basis. This meant that they needed at least two different robes: while they wore simple robes when at home, the missionaries donned ceremonial dresses (*lifu*) for formal occasions, such as visits among officials and "other important people."[36] Besides these interactions with people from the literati class, there were also other occasions during which the Jesuits used the robe in order to benefit from its social prestige. These included the Jesuits' mission circuits in rural areas and informal discussions with Christians.[37] They did not, however, include religious ceremonies, especially Mass, during which the Jesuits wore special liturgical garments. The latter were often made from precious Chinese silks and, in their cut, resembled European liturgical garments (see figure 9.1). They were combined with a liturgical cap (*jijin*), used because bareheadedness was considered a sign of disrespect in China.[38]

ENTERING THE RANKS OF "GOWN AND CAP" (1595–1610)

The Jesuits' change of attire, far from being a carnivalesque disguise, affected the Jesuits' everyday lives in many ways. For, in order to lend credence to their literati identity, the Jesuits also had to adopt the literati's values, habits, and tastes—in short, their lifestyle. In particular, the Jesuits adapted their behavior with regard to three key aspects of literati lifestyle: the literati's concern with refined material culture, their esteem for Confucian learning, and the attention they paid to social etiquette.

Recent studies of late imperial literati lifestyle have highlighted the great importance the scholar-gentry attached to refined material culture. Seventeenth-century Chinese literati used to display their status by means of precious things indicating their wealth, taste, and connoisseurship.[39] The Jesuits partly complied with the literati's enthusiasm for refinement in order to lend credence to their new social identity. In some of their residences, they employed large groups of servants to underline their elevated social status.[40] If they traveled through town, they did not walk on foot, but used sedan chairs carried by bearers.[41] Although the Jesuits' vow of poverty prevented them from furnishing their residences with precious objects such as those that adorned the literati studios in the seventeenth century, their collections of Western curiosities could, at least partially, serve as a substitute. These collections included a wide variety of objects for scientific and aesthetic use. In an incomplete list of Western objects held by the Songjiang residence, Philippe Couplet enumerated "spheres, globes, clock-faces, clocks, mathematical instruments as well as works of glass, crystal, ivory, and enamel; prints and paintings."[42] Objects such as those in Songjiang could not only be shown to curious visitors but could also be presented as gifts to influential friends in order to curry favor.[43] They represented their owners' cultural refinement, belonging to the class of objects that the late Ming scholar Wen Zhenheng (1585–1645) called "superfluous things."[44] In some cases, *europeana* could also be used to directly substantiate one's status claims. With this mind-set Martino Martini, upon hearing in the summer of 1645 that the Manchu army had taken Hangzhou, decided to receive the conquerors by displaying Western books, telescopes, and spheres in front of his residence. In this way he announced himself as a Western scholar offering his services to the new rulers.[45]

The Jesuits' adoption of the literati lifestyle repeatedly provoked criticism from mendicant missionaries. One anonymous critic complained about the lavishly equipped rooms of Jesuit residences. For him their furnishings—complete with beautiful chairs, European paintings, clocks, and "other European gallantries"—were reminiscent of the magnificent apartments of the rich, not those of missionaries subjugated to the vow of poverty.[46] The Jesuits justified themselves with the defense that they only used European objects to evangelize the Chinese.[47] Indeed, the financial situation of the Jesuit mission did not allow for overly luxurious lifestyles. An account book kept by François de Rougemont, who worked in the Jiangnan region during the 1670s, shows that, although the missionary spent some money for purposes of display, his budget was narrowly constrained and vulnerable to unpredictable changes.[48] Tensions between the religious vow of poverty and the refined literati lifestyles may have been more tangible for Jesuits at court than for those who, like de Rougemont, lived in the provinces under financially straitened circumstances (see figure 1.3). Some indication of this may be gleaned from a remark on Ferdinand Verbiest, an appointed official in the imperial bureau of astronomy, recorded by his confrere Louis Le Comte. Le Comte wrote of Verbiest that "his bed, his table, and his furniture were dishonorable for the Mandarin," an apology highlighting tensions inherent in literati Jesuit persona that the missionaries could not entirely resolve.[49]

Even if the Jesuits' adaptation of the literati's material culture caused a real tension between their religious vow of poverty and their new social identity, the literati elite's Confucian learning, and its etiquette, combined well with their European identity as religious men of letters imbued with humanist learning. The Jesuits knew that their mastery of polite Chinese language and of Confucian learning was a necessary precondition for being accepted as peers by the Chinese men of letters (their translation of the term *ru* as "literati" indicates their perception of the scholar-gentry as China's intellectual elite).[50] The Jesuits paid the most careful attention to the study of Chinese language and erudition, from the earliest years of their mission.[51] Not only did they learn standard Chinese (Mandarin), the lingua franca used by literati and officials, but they soon started to focus on the study of the Confucian classics, especially the Four Books (Sishu). A *Plan of Studies* (Ratio Studiorum) probably designed for the China mission by Visitor Manuel Dias the Elder (1559–1639) shows that this was a time-consuming and strenuous process. Four years exclusively dedicated to the study of language included training in spoken standard Chinese and then the reading of texts from the Four Books with fellow Jesuits. The curriculum was completed by two years of study with a Chinese master, selected and paid by the superiors of the mission.[52]

The Jesuits' high esteem for Confucian learning prompted several translations of Confucian classical texts into Latin and the development of a distinct "Jesuit reading" of these texts.[53] The most famous translation was the monumental *Confucius, the Chinese Philosopher*, finally published in 1687 after many unpublished or only partly published predecessors.[54] It made Confucian learning accessible to a European audience for the first time, and it also clearly testified to the Jesuits' reading of this learning as illuminated by the *lumen naturale*, the natural knowledge of God. This knowledge, in their view, had been present in China even before the Christian message had reached this region.[55] Such a reading of these works as rational philosophical texts, imbued with natural wisdom, was facilitated by classical erudition's role in the Society of Jesus.[56] Jesuit learning was heavily influenced by European humanism, whose high esteem for the Greek and Latin classical age strongly resembled the late imperial literati's veneration for Chinese antiquity.[57] The Chinese appreciation of Confucian learning thus struck a familiar chord with the Jesuits, and the missionaries easily integrated it into their humanist scholarly habitus.

Another prerequisite for successful interaction with the literati elite, in addition to a partial adaptation of the material living conditions and the command of the Chinese language and texts, was mastery of its "social grammar." The Chinese scholar-gentry placed a high value on proper ritual (*li*), thought to be crucial for the creation and maintenance of social order. Rituals helped to assign everyone to his proper role (*fen*) and to uphold social distinctions (*bie*).[58] The Jesuits, who had been socialized into the stratified society of premodern Europe, easily understood the importance of proficiency in Confucian etiquette. Matteo Ricci, for instance, recorded how ceremonial practice shifted with the new change of attire, saying that whenever he went to an audience of scholar-officials, he started to use the courtesies of bachelor's degree holders. This ascent in status, he added proudly, was accepted by the Chinese: "The scholar-officials responded to us in the according way."[59] A decade later, when Ricci had settled in Beijing, the missionaries were fully fledged participants in the social life of the literati, part of the incessant *va et vient* of Beijing's educated social elite.[60]

Ricci devoted a full chapter of his diary to describing literati courtesies.[61] Written in a "proto-ethnographic" style, it was probably intended for future missionaries' instruction and could be used by new arrivals as a "how-to" manual. It provided a detailed phenomenology of courtesy rituals, offering, for instance, elaborate descriptions of various styles of greeting:

> The most widespread of their courtesies is to join the two hands and sleeves (which are always very long), and to raise and lower them, standing in front of each other and saying *qing qing*, which is a polite phrase without a specific meaning. When they visit each other, and also when they meet in public, they join the hands as described and lower their heads to the ground. [They bow like this] to each other, often simultaneously, [a courtesy] which they call *zuoyi*. . . . If they want to be very polite, either because they meet for the first time, or because they have not seen each other for a long time, or because there is reason to congratulate or to thank, . . . they kneel down and lower their heads to the ground.[62]

Ricci completed his meticulous account of these ceremonies by describing the sequence of events to be expected during courtesy calls and banquets, something he had been able to study when living as a Western scholar in Nanjing and Beijing.

Literati etiquette also required the Jesuits to observe certain boundaries between themselves and inferior social classes, boundaries established by the rules of social distinction. The Jesuits knew that these distinctions placed them in an entirely different situation from what they had experienced as "Western monks." An anonymous Jesuit writer explained that when wearing the garb of Buddhist monks, considered a "very lowly and miserable people" in China, they had been unable to visit mandarins.

Because Buddhist temples were open to everyone, they could, however, at least receive their visits.[63] Literati Jesuits, by contrast, did not open their residences. Nicolas Trigault, for one, conceded that close relationships with the literati had encouraged them to flee the masses. His insistence on reassuring readers that the Jesuits did not "reject anyone" only highlighted tensions inherent in the Jesuits' accommodation to literati concerns for social distinction.[64] As Catholic missionaries, they aimed at evangelizing the whole population, without "rejecting anyone," a goal not readily compatible with the literati's concern for social boundaries—or with their emphasis on gender segregation.[65]

The Jesuits' adoption of the literati identity not only induced changes with regard to the things they used, the books they read, and the social etiquette they observed. It also affected their social identity as men, their masculinity. How did they perceive Chinese masculine ideals? How did they position themselves with regard to these ideals, and what kind of masculinity did Chinese literati attribute to the missionaries?

GENTLEMEN AND SAGES: PERFORMING LITERATI MASCULINITY

After their arrival in China, the missionaries soon noted how Chinese masculine ideals differed significantly from the European ones with which they were familiar. Their perceptions of Chinese men and literati masculinities were rather ambivalent. Although the Jesuits greatly valued the literati for their cultural refinement and great interest in what the missionaries called "moral philosophy," they described Chinese men as "effeminate" and "feeble."[66] Such depictions may have drawn on a contemporary Chinese discourse bemoaning the overly refined, spiritless masculinity of the late Ming literati.[67] They also drew, however, on ancient European depictions of Asian people. Aristotle had already argued that Asians, because of the hot climate of their countries, were witty but fainthearted and therefore prone to fall into "natural slavery"—a stereotype recurrent in early modern European writings about Asia.[68] Missionaries in China adopted this topos in their writings (even if European authors had more often identified Aristotle's "Asian" with their Turkish archenemy). The Portuguese Jesuit Alvaro Semedo explained, for instance, how the Chinese "lawfully deserve the praise given to the Asian by Aristotle[,] who said that the people of Asia surpass the Europeans in what concerns the spirit, whereas the people of Europe outdo the Asians in strength and courage."[69] Matteo Ricci's equally general, if less positive, view was that the Chinese were an "effeminate and sensual people prone to all sorts of vices."[70] Ricci also observed that Chinese literati lacked interest in warfare and the martial arts, preferring instead—curiously to his mind—the study of books and morality.[71]

The Jesuits' proto-ethnographic writings thus tended to emphasize the otherness of effeminate Chinese masculinities. This, however, was at odds with how the missionaries had themselves adopted a literati identity, a fact requiring intimate involvement with these same masculinities.[72] How did the Jesuits manage to reconcile their masculine self-understanding as European Catholic priests with Chinese literati masculinity? What was their masculine self-representation, and how was their manliness perceived by others?

To answer these questions, it is important to note that seventeenth-century Chinese literati masculinities did not in fact form a single, homogeneous code, but were rather oriented toward different, partly competing masculine ideals coexisting in late imperial Chinese society. These included the young aspiring scholar (*caizi*) with a fancy for elegant poetry and beautiful women, the senior gentleman (*junzi*) with a deep concern for Confucian moral learning, and the sage (*shengren*), an attribute reserved only for a few exemplary men revered for their encompassing moral virtue. The Jesuits were identified, and identified themselves, with two of these masculine models in particular: the gentleman and the sage.

The masculine code most closely connected with the literati dress was that of the gentleman.[73] In Chinese imagery, a gentleman represented the ideal of cultured (*wen*) as opposed to martial (*wu*) masculinity.[74] He represented "the man disciplined by the Confucian norms, from body to language, from manner to dressing."[75] Chinese literature characterized the gentleman as devoted to the common good, observant of the rituals, and embodying the Confucian virtues of righteousness and humanity. His restraint of emotion and sexual desire was considered a precondition for his realization of these moral virtues.[76]

The Jesuits' Chinese supporters understood that, by wearing the literati's attire, the Jesuits could tap into the cultural capital associated with the masculine code of the gentleman. They celebrated the missionaries' concern for modesty and morality as indicating their status as "disciples of the sages," saying that they were, in effect, genuine representatives of the gentlemanly ideal.[77] Catholic scholar-officials spoke out in praise of the Jesuits' gentlemanly virtues, especially after the missionaries had been accused of "immoral behavior" by the anti-Christian scholar-official Shen Que in Nanjing in 1616. Xu Guangqi (1562–1633; *jinshi* [advanced scholar] 1604), in his *Memorial in Defense of Christian Learning* (Bianxue shugao, 1616), thus wrote of the Jesuits: "Their doctrines are completely orthodox; their personal conduct very strict; their learning very broad; their knowledge very clear; their minds completely unsullied; and their views very stable. . . . The reason they have come several tens of thousands of miles to the East is that they heard that there is a correspondence in principle between the doctrines in their own country which seek to cultivate virtue through service of the Lord of Heaven, and the doctrines of Chinese sages which require all men to cultivate virtue by serving Heaven."[78]

Xu's Catholic literati friend, the Hangzhou scholar-official Yang Tingyun (1557–1627; *jinshi* 1592) explained—in an apology titled *The Owl and the Phoenix Do Not Sing Together* (Xiaoluan bu bingming shuo, ca. 1616–22)—that the Jesuits excelled in both wisdom and self-restraint, qualifying them as "selfless and serene scholars."[79] Although Xu Guangqi and Yang Tingyun wrote as Catholics in defense of the Jesuits, and did not therefore represent mainstream Chinese literati opinion, some non-Catholic literati also praised the Jesuits for their gentlemanly behavior. The late Ming eccentric Li Zhi lauded Matteo Ricci as a "most urbane person," who was "most intricate and refined in his interior, and very plain and modest in his exterior."[80] During the early decades of the mission, especially, many Chinese literati echoed Li Zhi's praise of the Jesuits, commending their mastery of Chinese language and etiquette and their concern for morality.

While literati dress signified the Jesuits' gentlemanly masculinity, their long, flowing beards linked them to another masculine code. In China, where men did not usually have abundant facial hair, beards were interpreted as a sign of a man's social and biological seniority. In Chinese mythology they were symbols of supernatural power (*ling*), attained only by divine persons such as Taoist immortals or Confucian sage kings.[81] These symbolic dimensions linked beards to the masculine code of sagehood, signifying a man's perfect completion of moral cultivation and his attainment of encompassing wisdom. According to Chinese tradition, the ideal of sagehood was embodied only by a few extraordinary people. For ordinary mortals, it was unattainable, a utopian ideal.[82]

Although the Jesuits never explicitly referred to the symbolic meaning of beards in Chinese imagery, sources show how they paid utmost attention to this aspect of their appearance. Matteo Ricci started changing his attire not by changing his clothes but by growing his beard. In his writings, furthermore, he particularly stressed the importance of growing beards "as the Fathers in the German province do."[83] Later missionaries also saw beards as a crucial aspect of their appearance. All those arriving in East Asia to enter the China mission started growing beards upon reaching Macao.[84] While Confucian dress indicated the Jesuits' adherence to the scholar-gentry, their beards made them stand out from the crowd, even among the Chinese literati, signaling their proximity to sagehood.

That the Jesuits' beards sometimes provoked powerful responses from Chinese observers is illustrated in an episode recounted by André Palmeiro, visitor of the East Indies, during his journey to Beijing in 1628. A letter of his to the superior general betrays his astonishment at the intensity of Chinese reactions to his long white beard: "Whether I get off the vehicle, enter the inn, stay somewhere, or shorten my beard—at all times people assemble to see me. I do not know whether my looks are unfamiliar or monstrous to them."[85] Palmeiro explained that upon seeing his beard, everyone wanted to know how old he was. Even when his servants lied, exaggerating his already advanced age (he was sixty-two), they were not believed. Only when Palmeiro's attendants said that their master had not quite reached a hundred years were those asking satisfied. "The reason why these men believed that I was so old," Palmeiro wrote, "is because I have a long beard with a very white tip, and since all Chinese imagine that there exist men who know the art of prolonging life, or who through a special fate have a very long life, they thought that I had this fate, and celebrated in me what they wished for themselves."[86]

The Jesuits appreciated the social prestige connected with their beards, but they discouraged people from believing that they resulted from some sort of life-prolonging alchemy, a practice the missionaries condemned as superstitious.[87] Giulio Aleni, in his *Questions and Answers about the West* (Xifang dawen, 1637), therefore stressed how there was nothing supernatural about the Jesuits' beards: "Each region has its own customs, all of which differ from each other. Thus some people have heavy beards, while others have less."[88] Aleni's, however, remained the sole attempt by a Jesuit to demystify the missionaries' beards. Indeed, the missionaries seem to have recognized that they greatly benefited from their beards being seen not merely as a curious foreign custom but as strongly associated with Chinese mythological imagery.

The ideal types of gentleman and sage were both characterized by a concern for moral virtue and sexual restraint. In this respect, they diverged significantly from the ideal of the talented scholar, who represented a radically different type of masculinity. In Ming fiction, he was usually described as a sexually active young man distinguished by poetic talent and beauty.

His fondness for erotic escapades and homosexual romance made him open to excursions to the "pleasure quarters" and sexual relations with servant girls and boys.[89] These practices were strongly disapproved of by the Jesuits. The talented scholar thus represents a masculine antitype from which they wanted to distance themselves as explicitly as possible.[90]

Although the Jesuits made disapproving remarks about the "general sensuality" of the Chinese, they were especially dismayed by one feature of the sexuality that the aspiring scholar represented—his openness to homoeroticism. The fact that catechisms repeatedly condemned "debauchery of sex among men" (*nanse zhi yin*) suggests that the missionaries were confronted with homosexual practices in Chinese Catholic communities.[91] They were shocked by the broad acceptance of homosexual romance in late Ming society. Matteo Ricci, in his diary, deplored the debauchery of the Chinese, which, according to him, made them deserve God's punishment:

> What is most deplorable and most shows the misery of this people is that no less than the natural lusts they practice preposterous ones that are against nature. The latter is neither prohibited by law, nor held to be illicit, nor even a cause for shame. It is spoken of in public, and practiced everywhere, without there being anyone to prevent it. And in some cities . . . there are public streets full of boys made up like prostitutes, and people buy them and teach them to play music, song, and dance. And then, gallantly dressed and made up with rouge like women, these miserable men are initiated into this terrible vice.[92]

Ricci tried to inform his Chinese audience about the inherent "dangers" of homosexuality. He addressed the topic in several Chinese publications intended for a non-Catholic literati audience. His first discussion of the topic appeared in *The True Meaning of the Lord of Heaven* (Tianzhu shiyi, 1603). There Ricci stated that Western philosophers did not even discuss these practices, not wanting to sully their mouths. To make the Jesuits' stance crystal clear, Ricci contrasted homosexuality with the celibacy the missionaries had chosen: "My humble Society's members are like the farmer who retains his seed and does not scatter it in his fields. If you still believe this to be indefensible, how much more indefensible must it be to cast it carelessly into a ditch!"[93]

Ricci addressed homosexuality for a second time when Cheng Dayue, a Beijing publisher and inkstone connoisseur, requested that he contribute some pictures to a publication that provided an erudite literati audience with reproductions of famous or curious images.[94] In *Master Cheng's Ink Garden* (Chengshi moyuan, 1606), one of the four pictures contributed by Ricci showed the men of Sodom blinded by the angels. The accompanying text explained that "in ancient times the people of Sodom gave themselves up to depraved sensuality, and the Lord of Heaven turned away from them. Among them lived one pure man named Lot, so the Lord of Heaven sent his angels to get [Lot] to leave the city and go to the mountains. Then down from heaven rained a great fire of consuming flame, men and animals and insects were all burned up and nothing was left." This time, Ricci contrasted the immoral behavior of the sodomites with the incorruptible behavior of wise men, saying that "the wise man [*zhi*] is happy when amongst good customs, and uses them to strengthen himself; he is also happy among evil practices, and uses them as a sharpening-stone for his own character. He can trust his own guidance in any circumstances."[95] With these lines, Ricci substantiated his claim that he and his fellow Jesuits assumed a place among the wise.[96]

Why did Ricci expend so much energy on rejecting homoeroticism? One reason, as pointed out by Giovanni Vitiello, was that homoeroticism was closely intertwined with homosocial friendship. The Jesuits' rejection of homosexuality was paired with their advocacy of friendship—a notion they wanted to keep strictly separate.[97] Friendship, which experienced a renaissance in late Ming discourse, mattered deeply for Jesuit missionary activity in China, and thus they praised it in their Chinese publications.[98] They wanted to make clear, however, that the friendship they praised did not extend to homoerotic friendship. As Martino Martini explained in *The Search for Friends* (Qiu you pian, 1661): "There are those who love me and those who befriend me. The one who loves me, likes my body; the one who befriends me, likes my heart." He cautioned the reader that vicious behavior ruins friendship.[99] Matteo Ricci, in his treatise *On Friendship* (Jiaoyou lun, 1595–1601), also implicitly warned his audience against "false friends," saying that "if someone makes friends with wicked people, he will constantly see and hear shameful things; he will undoubtedly grow accustomed to them; and he will defile his heart with them."[100]

The Jesuits' rejection of excessive sexuality, as symbolized by the masculine ideal type of the aspiring scholar, was highly compatible with their image as Western literati embodying gentlemanly and sagely virtues. Yet the missionaries' own sexuality, or rather their wholesale rejection of sexual activity, was difficult to reconcile with these masculine codes. The Jesuits' priestly celibacy did, in fact, call their *junzi* masculinity into question, running counter as it did to the Confucian cardinal virtue of filiality (*xiao*).

In Chinese thinking, marrying in order to father sons was a principal obligation that men owed their parents. Male offspring secured not only the continuity of the family line but also that of the worship of ancestors. Mencius's much-quoted view was that "there are three things which are unfilial, and to have no posterity is the greatest of them."[101] From a Confucian viewpoint, therefore, the Jesuits' celibacy, together with their leaving their parents for life in a faraway country, constituted a serious breach of filiality.[102] Chinese literati repeatedly attacked the Jesuits on this point. An anti-Jesuit author from Fujian, the maritime inspector Shi Bangyao (1585–1644), thus criticized Matteo Ricci for having left his family to come to China: "Li Madou [Matteo Ricci] came [to China] alone, traveling by boat over the seas. If his parents die, he does not show appropriate grief by shedding bitter tears. If his parents are buried, he does not cultivate morality by honoring them with sacrifices." Citing Mencius, Shi explained that this behavior was not worthy of being called human, but resembled the behavior of beasts.[103]

The Confucian valuation of biological reproduction not only was intertwined with the concept of filiality but also implied that sexual abstinence was unhealthy and contrary to nature.[104] This was yet another reason why the Jesuits' celibacy was not well received in China, and it resulted in occasional accusations of adultery (sometimes circulating in printed pamphlets) and, in rare cases, even trials. A particularly famous example was that against Niccolò Longobardo, who was unsuccessfully sued for adultery in Shaozhou in 1606. Accused of having seduced a married woman, he was saved only because the woman concerned, even under torture, insisted that she did not know him.[105]

Chinese attacks on the Jesuits' celibacy caused them to expend much energy on justifying their avoidance of marriage and advocating its compatibility with literati virtues. Matteo Ricci began this with an elaborate justification of celibacy in his *True Meaning of the Lord of Heaven.* This apology sought to reconcile celibacy with filiality. Attacking Mencius's dictum that denounced celibacy as unfilial, Ricci suggested that Mencius probably had "received a faulty statement in the transmission" of Confucius's teachings. He ridiculed its content by arguing that "if it really were the case that a lack of progeny represents an unfilial attitude, then every son ought to devote himself from morning to night to the task of begetting children."[106] Ricci suggested, instead, a new, Christian reading of filiality, according to which every man had three fathers: his biological father, his ruler, and the Lord of Heaven. A filial son, consequently, "ought to obey the commands of his most senior father [i.e., the Lord of Heaven—N.A.] even if they run counter to those of his father of lowest rank."[107] Needless to say, Chinese critics were not silenced by this attempted reconciliation of Confucian filiality with Christian thought, robbing as it did Confucian virtue of its ideological core and transforming it into the Christian virtue of obedience to God.[108]

Later apologies for celibacy published by Jesuits complemented Ricci's reinterpretation of filiality with other arguments for sexual abstention. Diego Pantoja's discussion of celibacy in *The Seven Victories [over Sin]* (Qike, ca. 1610–15), for instance, concentrated on the theme of temptation and praised celibacy as the purest form of chastity (*zhen*). According to Pantoja chastity meant to overcome sexual desire. Although it was possible to practice forms of chastity during marriage or widowhood, virginal chastity was seen as the most valuable kind of chastity.[109] Very similar arguments for celibacy were advanced by Alfonso Vagnone in his *Government of the Family in the West* (Qijia xixue, ca. 1625–30). Like Pantoja, Vagnone compared different forms of chastity, stressing the superior value of celibacy to chastity practiced during marriage.[110]

Pantoja and Vagnone also included popular misogynous arguments in their published apologies for celibacy. Pantoja praised the peaceful existence of celibate men, something he contrasted with the tiresome life of heads of household: "Once a man takes a wife, he is trapped. He is no longer the master of himself, and becomes his wife's servant."[111] Vagnone adopted a similar stance, writing that "the famous sage Plato once said: 'If a wise man marries, he is happy. If a wise man does not marry and lives on his own will, he will be even happier.' When someone asked him about the difficulties [of getting married], he said: 'If a man marries, he will only have two peaceful days [with his wife]: The day of their marriage and the day of death.'"[112]

These misogynous statements reproduced a popular European discourse on marriage, which warned husbands against losing control over their wives and admonished them to uphold correct social order within the family.[113] They probably were a somewhat ironic *captatio benevolentiae* that served the purpose of winning the sympathy of a mainly male and married literati readership.[114] As generic topoi, not personal opinions, they did not necessarily reflect general Jesuit attitudes toward Chinese women. These attitudes, as we will see in the following chapter, were characterized by great respect for Confucian womanly virtues and the Chinese ideal of female seclusion.

2 A KINGDOM OF VIRTUOUS WOMEN

Jesuit Descriptions of China's Moral Topography

IN LATE IMPERIAL CHINA, THE SCHOLARLY ELITE'S VIEWS ON, and behavior toward, women were determined by a set of assumptions about gender propriety and space that became decisive for literati Jesuits' approach toward the evangelization of Chinese women. Most importantly, the literati elite were greatly concerned about the maintenance of gender segregation, which required elite women to live a secluded lifestyle. Although the practice of female seclusion was a comparatively recent phenomenon, dating back only to the Song dynasty (960–1279), it was authorized by the most ancient texts from the Chinese classical age.[1] *The Book of Rites* (Liji) referred to the importance of the "separation of the sexes" (*nannü zhi bie*) and prescribed that "men and women should not sit on the same mat, touch one another, [or] draw water from the same well."[2] According to the ideal promoted by this Confucian classic, gender segregation should be so strict that even men and women from the same family would only meet rarely in everyday life. This practice was meant to ensure the maintenance of gender propriety, female chastity, and, by extension, good order in society.

This separation between men and women was tightly connected to yet another dichotomy central to Chinese culture: the distinction between inner (*nei*) and outer (*wai*) spheres reserved, respectively, for women and men. The "inner/outer" binary code was reflected in Chinese residential architecture in a variety of ways. On the one hand, Han houses usually consisted of closed architectural structures centered on one or several courtyards. In European houses the interior was usually intricately connected with the social space of the street, but in Chinese houses the two were clearly demarcated.[3] The domestic realm itself, on the other hand, did not form a homogeneous interior space, but was again structured by the "inner/outer" binary code. As the Neo-Confucian scholar Sima Guang (1019–1086) wrote: "In housing there should be a strict demarcation between the inner and outer parts, with a door separating them. The two parts should share neither a well, a washroom, nor a privy. The men are in charge of all affairs on the outside; the women manage the inside affairs. During the day, the men do not stay in their private rooms nor the women go beyond the inner door without good reason."[4] In residences of the Chinese elite, rooms were arranged according to a complex system. Innumerable gradations existed between the outermost spaces, designated for hosting males, and the innermost space—the women's boudoir.

The boudoir door (*guimen*) demarcated a physically tangible boundary that separated the female space from the male spaces in rich literati households. Recent historical research, however, has emphasized the fluidity of boundaries between inner and outer spheres throughout the Ming-Qing period. It understands *inner* and *outer* as relational terms and the line between the two spheres as a "negotiated boundary," which constantly redefined both separate physical spaces and modes of interaction.[5] People and objects regularly transgressed the threshold of the inner quarters. Maintaining distinctions between inner and outer did not, conversely, always entail a spatial separation, but could also involve bodily practices such as avoiding touch or restraining one's gaze.[6] The question of whether or not contact between women and men was morally sanctioned depended on various factors, such as the age, degree of kinship, and social status of the people involved. Young children under the age of seven *sui* (i.e., eight years)[7] were not expected to respect the separation between the sexes as rigorously as their elder siblings were. Close relatives had more occasions to meet with one another compared to distant family members and people who were unrelated. Families of lower social status, furthermore, did not usually have the financial means to observe the separation of the sexes as strictly as upper-class families did. A humble social background did not, however, prevent people from sharing the elite's ideal of separate spheres. Poor peasant families who lacked the means to maintain separate women's apartments would nonetheless separate the living room from the kitchen using a curtain, thus providing women with a place to retire to when male guests were being received.[8]

Since the gender segregation ideal was embraced by all layers of Chinese society, the respecting of "curtains and screens" (*weibu*)—or the boundaries between female and male spheres—played a vital role in shaping the self-representation of the Han, who claimed to distinguish themselves from their uncultivated, "barbarian" neighbors by dint of their cultivated, well-ordered gender relations.[9] Late imperial Chinese ethnographers often emphasized the otherness of their non-Han neighbors by evoking the ancient Chinese trope of a "kingdom of women" (*nüren guo*), a site of gender inversion and male sexual adventure. This imaginary place contrasted sharply with the Middle Kingdom, which the Chinese represented as a place where cloistered women cultivated the virtue of chastity in secluded apartments.[10]

The literati's valuation of gender segregation and female chastity as a key element of the Chinese social order was, however, paired with a constant fear of the overthrow of this social order by heterodox (*xie*) tendencies within society. Confucian thought thus attached yet another connotation to gender segregation, which was seen as signifying not only Chinese cultural refinement but also Confucian cultural orthodoxy and ritual orthopraxy (*zheng*).[11] Many Confucian moralists were convinced that disorder began to reign whenever sexes mixed. Disregard for gender segregation was perceived as a threat to the politico-moral order and was thought to create chaos (*luan*).[12] The ruling elite's preoccupation with social order made them alert, therefore, to religious doctrines and social movements that promoted gender arrangements differing from the Confucian norm. The government begrudgingly tolerated Buddhist and Taoist doctrines that, although "based on other principles" (*yiduan*), were not perceived as a threat to China's moral order. Nevertheless, the ruling elite constantly suspected the misuse of temples for the public mingling of the sexes, and they acted harshly against "heterodox" religious organizations accused of disregarding proper gender relations.[13]

Popular Buddhist movements, in particular, aroused the suspicion of Confucian moralists.[14] The Buddhist religious community's (*sangha*) notions of family and society differed strongly from those promoted by the Chinese governing elite. The Buddhist monastics' celibate lifestyle was incompatible with the Confucian valuation of marriage and the family, which denounced celibacy as a lack of filiality.[15] Confucian moralists harbored the suspicion, furthermore, that Buddhist celibacy was a mere cover for extramarital erotic romance on the part of the monks, where unmarried men surrendered to suppressed passions, endangering Chinese women's chastity. This suspicion was deepened by the Confucian moralists' opinion that Buddhist monks did not duly respect gender segregation. Buddhist clerics often encouraged female lay devotees to leave their secluded apartments to visit their temples or go on pilgrimages. They also visited the women in their private quarters to expound the sutras to them and edify them with religious talks. These transgressions of Confucian gender boundaries were interpreted by literati as a sign of moral inferiority and thus contributed to the monks' bad reputation.[16]

The literati's fear that women might be led astray by Buddhist monks was one reason why they went to great lengths to prevent women from engaging with pious activities in Buddhist temples. Women were perceived as being especially inclined toward popular Buddhist piety, not least because of the entertainment that temple visits and other communal pious activities could provide.[17] Temple bans imposed by local magistrates were often intended to counter the promiscuous behavior of young women.[18] The frequency with which the bans were issued in the late imperial era can be understood as an indication that officials saw Confucian values endangered by a new wave of lay Buddhist activity.[19] Indeed, so omnipresent were Confucian fears about the degeneration of temples into sites of promiscuity that they were even present in legal texts such as *The Great Ming Code* (Da Ming lü), which imposed severe punishment for sexual promiscuity in temples.[20]

It was precisely because gender segregation formed a core value of the literati elite, and because the Buddhist temple formed, in this elite's view, a potentially dangerous antipode to the morally pure realm of women's inner quarters, that the Jesuits' change of social identity from Buddhist monks to Confucian literati strongly affected their opinions about interactions with women. Wearing the Buddhist monks' garb, the Jesuits had had relatively unrestricted access to Chinese women. Their new literati identity, however, required them to largely refrain from direct contact, especially with gentry women.

Sources show that the Jesuits had a clear understanding of the effects that their change of attire entailed. Nicolas Trigault was the first to remark upon the new attitude toward women that the missionaries' ascent to the ranks of literati had rendered necessary. In the Annual Letter of 1613, he explained that when the Jesuits still wore the dress of Buddhist monks it had been possible for them to interact with women. However, at that time, he wrote, "We were excluded from interacting and conversing with the important and noble men." According to Trigault, this situation had proved disadvantageous for the Jesuits and thus needed to be revised: "When we chose our way to dress, it seemed more appropriate to us to be able to interact with men. We thought that, if we were allowed to interact with men, we would finally also be allowed to deal with women, which [now] actually becomes easier every day."[21] This view of Trigault's—that it was more important to have access to the "important and noble men" of China than to its women—remained decisive for the Jesuits' analysis of their situation in China throughout the seventeenth century. Looking back on the past century of the mission, Trigault's Flemish compatriot Philippe Couplet argued in the 1680s that difficulties in approaching women were a price the Jesuits had had to pay for being able to interact with the powerful. "The first missionaries," he wrote, "wisely judged that it was more important for our Religion to interact with magistrates, literati and family heads than with people who are naturally disposed to piety."[22] In Couplet's view, the social prestige associated with the literati made this trade-off worthwhile.

The transition from monk to literatus not only shaped interactions with women. It also gave rise to a distinctively Confucian representation of China's "moral topography" in proto-ethnographic writing.[23] These works constructed the Buddhist temple and the inner quarter as antipodes—diametrically opposed sites of female immorality and chastity that became constitutive of the Jesuits' representation of Chinese women.[24]

IMMORAL TEMPLES, LECHEROUS MONKS

Missionary representations of China's moral topography, like Chinese literati arguments for Confucian orthodoxy, depicted Buddhist temples and their inhabitants—usually referred to by the Jesuits as "bonzes"—as a prime threat to women's morality and chastity.[25] According to Jesuit authors, temples were places where innocent, pious women were seduced by lewd clerics using their religious lifestyle as a pretext for illicit sexual relations.

This representation is astonishing in view of some striking similarities between the Catholic and Buddhist concepts of religious space. The two religious traditions both distinguished lay practitioners from clerics and established special places where the latter could dedicate their lives to pious activities. They both also developed different kinds of consecrated spaces, with Buddhist temples and Catholic churches usually dedicated exclusively to worship and the monasteries of both traditions permanently inhabited by monks and nuns. These apparent similarities between the Catholic and Buddhist social roles and spaces were matched by similarities in ritual and even doctrine, both religions aiming at man's salvation.

In view of these similarities, it is hardly surprising that the Jesuits in China were first advised to adopt the Buddhist monks' dress, a strategy that had also proved successful in the Jesuits' mission to Japan.[26] Michele Ruggieri was the first to dress like a Buddhist monk, when living in Zhaoqing from 1582 to 1588, and he never questioned the adequacy of his Buddhist persona.[27] From 1584 onward, he lived in a church called the Temple of the

Holy Flower (Shenghua Si), a name actually identifying the church as a Buddhist temple (*si*).[28]

Other Jesuits, however, soon noted a major difference between the prestige of European Catholic churches and Chinese Buddhist temples. The elite of scholarly officials, according to Alessandro Valignano, did not hold Buddhist temples and monasteries in high esteem. They used them, indeed, in a most mundane fashion, something leading, in Valignano's view, to their desecration:

> The [mandarins] customarily see themselves as the masters of the houses and temples of the Chinese bonzes and priests. They use [these buildings] at their will for their recreation. They go there to eat, and they hold their banquets and invitations there. . . . Not only do the bonzes and fathers of these temples not have any means to prevent them from doing so, but they also have to keep everything ready in order to receive them. And all this happens although, as I have pointed out, the mandarins do not maintain any friendly relations with [the Buddhist monks]. In everything they have to serve them as though they were their servants, and our house in Zhaoqing was also subjected to this hassle.[29]

Although Valignano overstated the general uninterest and even hostility of Chinese scholar-officials toward Buddhism, his analysis of their relationship to Buddhist temples and monasteries highlighted something very relevant for the Jesuits: officials' propensity to visit Buddhist sites for recreation and amusement. On such occasions they expected to be entertained by the monks as their guests.[30] Although Buddhist temples were not part of the public (*gong*) realm in a strict sense, they were social spaces open to the gentry for public sociability.[31] Matteo Ricci complained about this tiresome Chinese custom, writing to his superiors about how the Jesuits' temple in Zhaoqing was "very much frequented and disturbed by the Mandarins."[32] This quotidian atmosphere of Buddhist monasteries was reinforced by how, unlike post-Tridentine monasteries, they were not equipped with cloisters, places where Buddhist monks and nuns could have shielded themselves from the worries that beset secular life. The Chinese literati's lack of esteem for Buddhist monks, so different from the clerics' prestige that the Jesuits had encountered in Japan, proved decisive for the missionaries' change of attitude toward Buddhism. Their writings started to adopt the position that "the laws of [the Buddhas] Shakyamuni and Amithaba are only good for deceiving and entertaining vulgar and ignorant people."[33]

They did not acknowledge the existence of the Tripitaka, the vast and sophisticated corpus of Buddhist texts, and appeared interested in Buddhist doctrine "only in proportion to the degree of antagonism they perceived" in it.[34] From Matteo Ricci onward, they repeatedly referred to Buddhist monks' humble social origins and lack of education.[35] They criticized them, furthermore, for the lack of seclusion in their monasteries. In the eyes of the Jesuits, who had witnessed the efforts of the post-Tridentine Catholic Church to enforce the cloistering of women's convents in Europe, the insouciance with which Buddhist nuns wandered about the streets in China was unmistakable proof of the Buddhist community's moral weakness.[36]

The Buddhist clerics' moral weakness was, according to Jesuit authors, especially evident when it came to their disregard for gender proprieties. Their writings repeatedly accused Buddhist monks of sexual immodesty and of making idolatrous women lapse into vice after associating with monks. These accusations were sometimes formulated in highly general terms, referring to how "although [the bonzes] do not have wives, there are those who do not even keep chastity" and insinuating that the bonzes "know how to associate with the young widows when making their devilries during the funeral of husbands, and on various other occasions."[37] Other authors referred to specific events that missionaries had heard of. Adrien Greslon, for instance, recounted how a soldier had discovered a group of bonzes amusing themselves with a woman in a Guangzhou temple, a crime that the bonzes subsequently, and unsuccessfully, tried to hide by murdering the person who had discovered them.[38] Originating with the Jesuits, this trope of the lecherous Buddhist monk became, over the course of the seventeenth century, relatively widespread in European proto-ethnographic writing about China. It also emerged in Protestant publications, such as Jürgen Andersen and Volquard Jversen's "Oriental Travelogue" (Orientalische Reise-Beschreibung, 1669), which was published by the German diplomat and scholar Adam Olearius and included a picture of the "Cloth Sack" (Budai) Buddha, labeled as the Chinese "God of Voluptuousness" (Deus Voluptatis; figure 2.1).

It is, of course, impossible to determine the extent to which every Jesuit accusation against Buddhist monks corresponded to historical fact. What is clear, however, is that Jesuit claims about the sexual immodesty of late Ming Buddhist monks did not match those monks' self-perceptions. Specialists in Ming Buddhism, it is true, have observed 64that the discipline (*vinaya*) of the late Ming Buddhist community was

FIG. 2.1. "Minusio, the God of Voluptuousness," depicted together with a "Priest of Amida Buddha," Confucius, and a literatus paying obeisance to the latter (*clockwise from left*). The "God of Voluptuousness" is probably inspired by the "Cloth Sack" (Budai) Buddha that is usually depicted with a big, naked belly. Copperplate engraving printed in "Oriental Travelogue" (1669) by Jürgen Andersen and Volquard Jversen. Courtesy of Universitätsbibliothek Bern, MUE Gross Xb 17:7.

relatively lax.[39] Indeed, contemporary Buddhist masters such as the famous Chan master Zhuhong (1535–1615) of the Yunqi monastery criticized their fellow monks for their worldliness and for their "pursuit of non-Buddhist interests and avocations, their greed for donations, and their love of material comforts."[40] Sexual transgression, however, was not a centerpiece of late Ming Buddhism's internal critique. Late Ming Buddhist monks' lack of attention to *vinaya* might well have provided a fertile ground for sexual transgression. The most important masters of reform in late Ming Buddhism did not, however, judge it a problem that needed to be addressed.[41] The legal record for the period largely confirms this picture, for actual legal cases of promiscuity in temples are relatively few.[42] This suggests that Jesuit accusations against Buddhist monks were likely based on unconfirmed rumor, not eyewitness testimony.

This reading of the missionaries' accusations against Buddhist monks is supported by the remarkably widespread deployment, in writings inspired by Confucian morality, of the topos of Buddhist monks' promiscuity. It was present in a wide variety of places, including "official reports, didactic materials, biographical writings, and literary sources."[43] Famous vernacular novels such as *The Plum in the Golden Vase* (Jinpingmei, 1618) and *The Water Margin* (Shuihuzhuan; fourteenth century) reminded their readers that "in this world Buddhist monks of such high virtue and attainments that they can remain impervious to the temptations of the flesh are few" and ridiculed them as "sex-starved hungry ghosts."[44] In the 1620s, the collection of anecdotes *Monks and Nuns in the Sea of Sin* (Sengni niehai) was dedicated to the topic of promiscuous monks.[45] This conspicuous presence of the trope of promiscuous monks in seventeenth-century fiction can be understood as the result of the conflict between the Buddhist monastic lifestyle and Confucian morality discussed in the first part of this chapter.

By representing the Buddhist temple as a site of immorality, where Chinese women were in danger of losing their chastity, the missionaries adopted part of the literati's mental map. They saw writing about the sexual impropriety of Chinese Buddhist monks as a means of adopting Confucian discourse, which, as literati Jesuits, they now regarded as authoritative for themselves. By speaking about the threats Buddhist monks posed to women's modesty, they signaled their adherence to the Confucian elite.[46] It also complemented their hostile attitude toward "vicious" and "idolatrous" Buddhist clerics, with whom the missionaries were often in direct competition as providers of religious services.[47] Although a Confucian trope, the representation of the "immoral idolater" was also easily understood by European readerships. Idolatry and immorality were often represented as closely connected in early modern Catholic missionary discourse.[48] The depictions found in Jesuit accounts of the immoral idolatrous priest and the sexually active idolatrous woman could therefore be easily integrated into an early modern European Catholic worldview.

In the Jesuit writings, however, the idolatrous temple as a site of sexual indecorum represented only one aspect of China's moral topography. The morally pure realm of women's inner quarters figured as the temple's antipode. These were an exclusively female space—a site usually beyond the missionaries' reach in everyday life thanks to their acceptance of the Confucian ideal of gender segregation.

FEMALE SECLUSION AND MODESTY

The Jesuits' proto-ethnographic writings provide rich testimony of the missionaries' interest in Chinese women's seclusion and its consequences for female virtuousness and chastity. Seventeenth-century Europeans were, of course, familiar with the idea that women's proper place was in the home, an idea repeated in European prescriptive literature throughout the early modern period. The construction of domesticity as women's only legitimate sphere of influence had not yet, however, become the dominant gender ideology that it would be in eighteenth- and (especially) nineteenth-century Europe.[49] The Chinese preoccupation with gender segregation was, therefore, perceived by the missionaries as a noteworthy phenomenon. The missionaries wrote detailed accounts of the delicately differentiated social space in Chinese residential houses and the close attention paid to the taboos associated with female quarters. Alvaro Semedo thus explained to his readership: "[Chinese literati families] have rooms especially designed for receiving guests. The first is indifferently accessible to everyone. You can enter it and sit down without asking anyone, even if there is no doorkeeper for guiding you inside. There is another, more interior room that they call the 'secret room' [*yinshi*] for [receiving] relatives and close friends. [Guests] stop there without going any further, because adjacent [to this room] are the *gui*, or women's quarters, where even domestics do not dare enter, except if they are very young."[50]

In the same vein, Giulio Aleni—who had been able to sightsee at the Catholic official Ma Chengxiu's residential palace when accompanying Ma to Shangzhou, where he had been appointed as an official—provided a lengthy account of the innumerable courtyards and gates that separated women's apartments from the outer world.[51] Aleni described the gentry women's quarters as calm and serene, far from the disturbances of public life: "[In the women's quarters, there] are a variety of rooms, cabinets, studios, halls, gardens, fishponds and other things of great commodity and recreation, which are very helpful for passing the time in this great solitude, and for entertaining happily those who live there."[52]

While Aleni depicted Chinese gentry women's boudoirs as blissfully tranquil, not all missionaries shared such views of female seclusion. Philippe Couplet imagined women's life in the inner chambers as a sort of "imprisonment."[53] In Alvaro Semedo's opinion, moreover, the inconvenience of seclusion was only softened by the fact that it had become a habit for those subjected to it.[54] However, although divided over whether Chinese women found the secluded lifestyle agreeable or displeasing, Jesuits commonly agreed that seclusion was commendable for augmenting women's modesty and families' peace and good fortune. Only a few authors, including the German polyglot Athanasius Kircher (who had never been to China himself), disapproved, seeing it as an expression of excessive male jealousy.[55] Female seclusion, in the eyes of most Jesuits, was the main reason for Chinese women's admirable chastity, a quality that, according to the Portuguese Jesuit Gabriel de Magalhães, they cultivated so thoroughly it appeared to be innate.[56]

Some Jesuit representations of the inner quarters conspicuously resembled those of the boudoir by Chinese literati. The latter's poems typically referred to women's quarters as a place of longing, where men could retreat from the everyday troubles of the world.[57] Alvaro Semedo drew on this literary theme in his suggestive description of the inner quarters as a space "venerated [by the Chinese] like a sacred place": "If someone wants to enter them without thinking, a word suffices for arresting him immediately."[58] Semedo also described the inner chambers as a place of refuge for husbands, where even their fathers could not follow them: "If a father wants to chastise his son (for the fathers never give up their authority over their children and retain their power to chastise them even if they are married), the son only has to quickly get as far as the apartment of his wife; this is a haven of refuge, where the father does not dare enter."[59]

Rather than representing the women's quarters from the perspective of their female inhabitants—describing them as sites of women's work and of busy everyday life—Semedo adopted the male literati's perspective, perceiving it as a "Gegenwelt" to the lives of men outside their homes. The two boudoir pictures printed in Athanasius Kircher's *China Illustrated* (China Illustrata, 1667) also draw on this imagery (figure 2.2). These pictures, modeled on Chinese images that Kircher had received from his confreres from the China mission, offer a close-up view of the realm of the inner quarters. They show two elegantly adorned palace women standing in beautifully furnished rooms decorated with two Chinese characters, together forming the word *yaotiao*, an idiomatic expression used by men to praise female modesty, reclusiveness, and attractiveness.[60]

Whereas some missionaries adopted the Chinese literati's perspective, describing the women's boudoir as a site of moral purity and tranquility, others discussed it from the vantage point of proto-ethnographic observers, contrasting China's customs with the customs back home in Europe. From this perspective, the Jesuits were usually full of praise for

FIG. 2.2. Two Chinese palace ladies in their boudoir. Taken together, the two characters in the calligraphies above the ladies' heads read *yaotiao*, expressing female modesty and grace. Copperplate engraving printed in Athanasius Kircher's *China Illustrated* (1667). Courtesy of Universitätsbibliothek Bern, MUE Gross Xb 7:1.

Chinese women's modesty, a quality that, in their view, was especially manifest in women's bodily attire. Like the walls and doors around the inner quarters, Chinese women's dress shielded the female body from prying eyes, covering women "from their heads to their feet, so that one cannot even see their fingertips."[61] It was obvious for many clerical observers that this modest attire, which left only the women's faces visible, was superior to that of European women. "If only certain European women followed them in this!" exclaimed Athanasius Kircher in his *China Illustrated*. "Certainly this would lead many of them to a more modest behavior."[62]

Another feature of Chinese women's bodily appearance, in addition to their dress, was perceived by the missionaries as an integral part of women's chaste and retired lifestyle—their bound feet. Although the

Jesuits knew that tiny feet were regarded by the Chinese as a feature of female beauty, they commonly interpreted footbinding as a result of Chinese men's efforts to enforce women's seclusion.[63] The missionaries observed that women's tiny feet made walking painful and their gait unsteady.[64] This lent plausibility to Matteo Ricci's hypothesis that the custom of tightly bandaging girls' feet to prevent them from growing was "the invention of a wise man, serving the goal not to let [the women] walk the streets and making them stay at home, as is most appropriate for women."[65] Not all missionaries approved of it as unequivocally as Matteo Ricci.[66] Some of them even roundly rejected it as a "folly" (*folie*) or "stupidity" (*stultitia*), which deformed women's natural and God-given body shape and was thus an abject custom unworthy of so cultivated a nation as the Chinese.[67] Despite these critical voices, however, the Jesuits generally accepted that footbinding had the positive effect of confining women to domesticity.

The imperial cult of female chastity, and especially widow chastity—promoted by both late Ming and early Qing emperors—fitted well with Jesuit perceptions of Chinese women's reclusiveness and modesty.[68] Alvaro Semedo praised the "commendable custom" (*loüable coustume*) of building triumphal arches for young widows who practiced chastity for the remainder of their lives.[69] Gabriel de Magalhães also approvingly mentioned how a conspicuous number of such exemplary women were "celebrated in books and poems, and honored by the Chinese with titles, inscriptions, temples, and triumphal arches."[70] However, while the Jesuits approved of the Chinese veneration of female chastity, and especially widow chastity, they were alienated by the practice of female suicide that many people in seventeenth-century China saw as a legitimate act of marital fidelity and chastity.[71] The fact that "especially Chinese women kill themselves for the slightest reason," as noted by the Portuguese Jesuit André Ferram in 1656, was incompatible with the Christian condemnation of suicide and thus was not accepted as an expression of female chastity.[72]

The above analysis of the Jesuits' representations of the inner quarters and of female modesty points toward a remarkable uniformity in their representations of Chinese women, whom they consistently depicted as chaste, secluded beings. It seems, indeed, that the Jesuits' close association with the Chinese scholar-gentry made them narrow the focus of their proto-ethnographic descriptions to women from literati families. The missionaries' writings acknowledged that female seclusion, at least as described in their accounts, was generally an elite phenomenon and was not implemented so strictly by every social and ethnic group in the diverse population of the empire.[73] No Jesuit, however, ever ventured into a detailed description of the life circumstances of any group of Chinese women other than those of the gentry elite. Jesuit authors only made, moreover, short references to female spheres that were not inner chambers. The existence of a market in women, in which poor girls were sold to wealthy households as concubines or maidservants, was mentioned in passing by a few authors.[74] However, almost no mention was made of late Ming China's rich courtesan culture.[75] The Jesuits also failed to acknowledge the different lifestyles of Manchu women, who, especially in the early years after the conquest, did not practice seclusion in the strict manner of Chinese gentry women.[76]

Some Jesuit authors even went so far as to deny altogether that some lifestyles did not include the seclusion practiced by Chinese elite women. In an account published in 1607, for instance, Diego Pantoja explained that the missionaries could learn nothing about Chinese women's lives, character, or customs, "for women stay within the home all their life and only go

FIG. 2.3. Two lower-class Chinese women, one bearing a child on her back and the other carrying water with a yoke. Ink drawing in Adriano de las Cortes's manuscript "Relation of His Voyage, Shipwreck, and Captivity" (Relación del viage, naufragio y captiverio). Made by an unknown artist in Manila, 1626–29. © The British Library Board (Sloane 1005, fol. 154v).

outside for visiting their mother, sisters, or close relatives—and even this they do very rarely."[77] This image of universally secluded Chinese women was perpetuated by the Jesuits' writings throughout the seventeenth century. Philippe Couplet was still taking the same line when writing about Candida Xu in the 1680s, explaining that he knew very little about the early life of his female patron, for "Chinese girls and women have so little contact with the outer world that you see them very rarely."[78]

There is one Jesuit account where the tenor differs sharply from that commonly found in the Jesuits' proto-ethnographic writings. This is the unpublished account written by the Aragonese Jesuit Adriano de las Cortes (1578–1629). Las Cortes's prolonged stay in China was the result of a mishap. He traveled the kingdom's southern coast for several months after a shipwreck in 1625.[79] An astute observer, Las Cortes filled his account with details of South China's bustling social life, vividly conveyed. He described crowds of Chinese women assembling in public temples to pay homage to their deities. He wrote about women who worked outside their homes, rowed boats, and tended to domestic animals (figure 2.3). In passing, he also expressed his surprise about seeing so many women in public. Before coming to China, he had heard from his confreres that women were very retired and discreet—a picture that did not match the social reality he encountered in southern coastal China.[80] Interestingly, Las Cortes's description of China did not meet with his superiors' approval. Its publication never saw the light of day.

Did Las Cortes's relation remain unpublished because its author had failed to inscribe his work in the tradition established by the Jesuits—that of idealized, homogeneous representations of a thoroughly "Confucianized" China?[81] What can be asserted with certainty is that the Jesuits' descriptions of female seclusion took on a remarkably uniform quality, focusing exclusively on the Confucian ideal, rather than taking into account the broad variety of lifestyles simultaneously present in every society. By drastically reducing the complexity of the experienced social world, the Jesuits' written accounts shaped strongly idealized representations of China and sustained their reading of China as an ancient civilization worthy of respect on account of its people's natural wisdom and virtue. The missionaries also, simultaneously, paved the way for their defense, against European critics, of some of their accommodatory practices, notably those regarding the administration of sacraments to women, which I address in the next chapter.

3 A SOURCE OF CREATIVE TENSION

Literati Jesuits and Priestly Duties

THE JESUITS' LITERATI IDENTITY GENERALLY COMBINED WELL with the humanist one adopted by many Jesuits in Europe, despite the many innovations and alterations it entailed for missionaries' social identity. But did it also combine well with their evangelical work? Was the literati identity compatible with the missionary vocation to convert infidels and tend to the religious needs of the converted, irrespective of their gender and social standing? And, more specifically, was it possible for literati missionaries to evangelize non-Catholic women, and tend to Catholic women's religious needs, without transgressing the taboos of "curtains and screens"?

Recent research on the roles assumed by religious specialists in Chinese religious life suggests that it was in fact difficult to steer a middle course between literati lifestyle and missionary vocation. Ritual specialists in China, indeed, did not enjoy the high social prestige of priests in Catholic Europe. While European priests assumed leading roles in local communities, ritual specialists were rather marginal figures held in low esteem by Chinese society.[1] Lay devotees rarely felt especially attached to one single monk or priest, preferring, rather, to use the paid services of various specialists with different religious affiliations, according to their religious needs and the efficacy attributed to them.[2] Ritual specialists were especially despised by members of the literati class, many of whom were inclined to anticlericalism.[3] Religious specialists' social inferiority was, in the eyes of the literati, confirmed by their tendency to disregard gender boundaries, increasing suspicions that they interacted with women in an indecent way.[4]

According to one of the most eminent scholars of Chinese Catholicism, Erik Zürcher, this image of ritual specialists in China posed a major obstacle to the China mission, and it may even have "contributed to its final breakdown in the early eighteenth century."[5] Zürcher maintains that "the Jesuits had to play two very different roles that typologically belonged to two different spheres": that of the priest (*sacerdos/duode*) and that of the literatus (*xiansheng*). In his view, the Jesuits "performed admirably [on both scores], but it created an inner tension that never was dissolved."[6] Zürcher's view implies that Catholicism's growth in China was impeded by the divergent behaviors toward women expected from the ideal-typical priest and literatus. This tension, however, was not necessarily purely obstructive for the Jesuits' China mission. On the contrary, the incompatibility between the two roles produced creative solutions in priests' daily performance. The Jesuits, in response to antagonisms between their literati identities and their catechetical and ritual duties, developed inventive strategies, integrating practices of gender segregation into their priestly performance and thus easing the tension between priest and literatus.

GENDER DISTINCTIONS AND EVANGELIZATION

The Jesuits' change of attire prompted them to make several modifications to their strategy for evangelizing women during the first three decades of the mission. Matteo Ricci, who initiated the Jesuits' adoption of the literati identity, had converted a first group of Chinese women, among them "some respected ladies." That was in the spring of 1589, during his last year in Zhaoqing, and when he was still wearing the Buddhist monk's garb.[7] After his change of attire in 1595, however, Ricci entirely abandoned women's evangelization. According to Ricci's close associate, João da Rocha, the "many difficulties in baptizing and dealing with [women]" had prompted Ricci to "concentrate on the conversion of men and to conceal for a moment the [conversion] of women."[8] In order to fully live up to his new social role of Western literatus, Ricci preferred to strictly maintain the ideal of the separation of the sexes. By the time da Rocha wrote his statement in 1602, however, the situation had already started to change again. After a short interlude of six years, Niccolò Longobardo—a young Sicilian who had arrived in China in the end of 1597 and had quickly become famous for adopting more popular evangelization strategies—started to baptize women, beginning in the southern residence of Shaozhou in 1601.[9] This change of strategy was seen as a major innovation by the missionaries in China. Several of them, including the famous procurator Nicolas Trigault, praised Longobardo's move as an important turning point in the history of the China mission, opening the door to a great number of potential converts previously beyond the missionaries' reach due to the seclusion of Chinese women.[10]

One of Longobardo's admirers, Fernão Guerreiro, described how the Sicilian had begun his experiments with the evangelization and baptism of women.[11] According to Guerreiro, Longobardo did not instruct the women but contented himself with instructing their male relatives, who then, in turn, took it upon themselves to catechize their female family members. Longobardo only met the female catechumens on the occasion of baptism. This ceremony usually took place in the women's homes. An altar with an image of the Lord was temporarily erected for the occasion in the main hall of the residence. Longobardo then examined the female catechumens' knowledge of the catechism in the presence of male relatives. Guerreiro noted that "each [woman answered] from the place where she was" (*cada huma do lugar onde esta*) during this examination. It is possible that this meant that the women were not even in the same room as the missionary, but were shielded from the latter's gaze by a curtain or door, as suggested by missionary reports describing the contacts with women "through curtains and screens" on other occasions.[12] If the women proved to be proficient in the catechism, Longobardo would eventually administer baptism. Guerreiro was at particular pains to highlight the women's readiness to interact with the missionary, an outsider to the family and a man. That "they were courageous and confident and did not refrain from being seen and examined by foreign men" was, for him, "a very new and strange thing" and a sign of divine intervention.[13]

Although Guerreiro praised the women for their courage during baptism, their male relatives were actually the key actors in Longobardo's new evangelization strategy. The Italian had understood that access to women was most safely gained by attaining the male relatives' confidence.[14] He nurtured this confidence by fully submitting to the men's authority over their families, making their consent a precondition for a woman's conversion.[15] This also meant that Longobardo did not refrain from rejecting women who presented themselves for baptism in the absence of male relatives. On such occasions, he asked the women to first obtain their fathers', husbands', brothers', or sons' consent and then return in their company.[16] This approach enabled Longobardo to reconcile the evangelization of women with the Confucian taboo of curtains and screens. This sharply distinguished the Jesuits from Buddhist monks, who visited women in their private quarters without male relatives' consent. It also meant, however, that the Jesuits did not accord to women the right to actively decide their religious identity. The missionaries accepted that it was the men who actually determined whether a woman was allowed to convert to the teaching of the Lord of Heaven. Even if women found ways to circumvent missionaries' and male relatives' authority, as I show later in the book, the Jesuits had clearly not originally envisaged an active role for women in China's evangelization.

Longobardo's evangelization of women was part of a new strategy that aimed at converting the broader population, including the poor, the uneducated, and women. However, unlike the Jesuits' other experiments with popular preaching, which were mainly attempted in the countryside, women's evangelization soon gained momentum in urban centers.[17] That it was carried out with the consent of male relatives made it acceptable even to upper-class families. As a consequence, a growing number of influential converts and sympathizers granted the missionaries access to their homes and allowed them to evangelize their female family members. Missionaries spent prolonged periods, for instance, in the homes of scholar-officials such as Xu Guangqi, Yang Tingyun, and Li Zhizao. Extended contacts with these gentry families facilitated the missionaries' access to women, and it is hardly surprising that women from these families became leading figures in Chinese Catholicism during the seventeenth century.[18] Less influential converts, however, also provided the missionaries with hospitality. The Catholics of Nanjing, for instance, showed solidarity with the missionaries during the anti-Christian repressions of 1616 and 1617. They permitted them to hide in their homes, something that, according to Nicolas Trigault, allowed them to evangelize the women of many of these families.[19]

When women's evangelization became, once again, an established practice in the China mission, it forged a distinct pattern of communication between missionaries and women during the evangelization process. The missionaries started to rely on different groups of intermediaries and media to establish channels of indirect communication. If personal contact between missionaries and women was inevitable, meanwhile, arrangements for controlled communication were made, sometimes literally involving conversation "through curtains and screens." These practices allowed the Jesuits to convert a growing number of women without transgressing the gender boundaries to which they were bound by their role as Western literati.[20]

Among the intermediaries the Jesuits relied upon for women's evangelization, four groups stand out. Male relatives were preferred as women's catechists because of their great social authority. However, this group was soon joined by another, which enjoyed the distinct advantage of having direct and frequent contact with women: children. Children were especially helpful intermediaries because they were not expected to respect the boundaries of gender segregation. They were praised, furthermore, for their quick perception, which made it easy for them to learn Latin prayers—whose incomprehensible syllables were difficult to remember for Chinese neophytes.[21] While missionaries were pleased that children often acted as catechists without being asked to do so, others experimented with deliberately employing children for their missions. Gaspare Ferreira, for instance, is reported to have taken small children with him on a rural mission near Beijing for the special purpose of teaching young women the basics of Catholic doctrine.[22]

The servants of rich households formed a third group of women's catechists. This is well illustrated by the conversion of the widow of a Nanchang literati family, who heard the teaching of the Lord of Heaven from her personal servant.[23] Nicolas Trigault reported that the lady became interested in the foreign doctrine during her conversations with the servant, asking him "to bring her an image of the Savior from the fathers in order to revere it, and a summary of the doctrine to learn [the teaching], and a rosary to recite [prayers]."[24] In 1610, after a short period of instruction, the lady was baptized in a splendid ceremony—an event seen as a major success for the fathers at the Nanchang residence.

A fourth group of intermediaries were eunuchs. This group was highly valued by the Jesuits, especially for the conversion of imperial palace ladies during the last years of the Ming dynasty. The Jesuits had probably converted the first palace eunuchs in Beijing during the early 1630s. In 1638 the Catholic eunuch Joseph started to convert palace women within the Forbidden City. Until the fall of the dynasty in 1644, female Catholics thus converted numbered around fifty. As Nicolas Standaert has pointed out, this group of Catholic imperial women remained "marginal and ceased to exist after the fall of the Ming."[25] This example provides, nonetheless, a vivid illustration of how effectively the Jesuits were able to reach women through intermediaries, at least in the setting of the court at Beijing.[26]

Although these groups of intermediaries all played an important role in the evangelization of women, the most important catechizers of women were, however, Catholic women, a group that does not fit neatly into the concept of "intermediary." In a society that encouraged homosocial bonding, Catholic women had many occasions to interact with non-Catholic women. They aroused non-Catholic women's interest in their religion by interspersing light conversation with commentary about the new doctrine (typically when interacting with non-Catholic female relatives or servants living under the same roof) or, alternatively, by providing neighboring women whose families were afflicted by illness or misfortune with salutary Christian objects, such as medals, branches, or holy water.[27] Women's role as catechists was accentuated by special papal dispensations granted to the China mission, allowing "mixed marriages" between Catholic and non-Catholic spouses.[28] Women who converted to Catholicism after marriage could, therefore, act as missionaries to their mothers, unmarried sisters, and sisters-in-law when visiting their families at home. And Catholic women marrying into non-Catholic families frequently tried to introduce their husbands' families to Catholic devotions. This predominant role for women in catechizing other women led to the emergence of a specifically female version of Catholic religiosity, which developed its own organizational forms and distinct expressions of piety.

Women's catechists usually relied on texts, images, and objects for their instruction of female neophytes. These media were important tools, serving as mnemonic devices for catechists and helping them to correctly instruct neophytes. Because missionaries were often (but not always) involved in their production and distribution, furthermore, they also granted missionaries a certain degree of control over the evangelization process.[29]

If religious instruction involved a literate person, it usually relied on Chinese catechetical books, referred to in Western sources as *Doctrina Christiana* and praised by missionaries as "domestic missionaries."[30] The first Chinese catechism was published by Matteo Ricci under the title *Outline of the Teaching of the Lord of Heaven* (Tianzhu jiaoyao) in 1605.[31] This work was inspired by the catechisms published in the 1590s by Robert Bellarmin, the famous Italian Jesuit and promoter of post-Tridentine religiosity. It included a collection of the basic Catholic prayers, such as the Our Father, Hail Mary, and Apostles' Creed, as well as an outline of the most important foundations of doctrine, such as the Decalogue and the seven sacraments.[32] It thus provided neophytes with the same basic knowledge of doctrine that Catholic reformers hoped to make a prerequisite for every European Catholic admitted to the sacraments.[33] Ricci's catechism was reprinted in a great number of modified and expanded editions, including Alfonso Vagnone's *Short Explanation of the Doctrine* (Jiaoyao jielüe, 1615), João Soeiro's *Abridged Record of the Holy Scriptures of the Lord of Heaven* (Tianzhu shengjiao yueyan, 1606), and many others, whose authors are not clearly identified. Unlike the mathematical and humanist texts published by the Jesuits, whose elegant prose was intended to capture the interest of a scholarly readership, the catechisms were written in plain, simple language.

This made them accessible to people with only basic levels of literacy—among them women from wealthier families who had mastered some basic reading skills.[34]

The Jesuits regarded the "apostolate through books" as an especially convenient means of reaching upper-class women, who, unlike commoner women, often had a remarkably high degree of literacy, especially in the urbanized Jiangnan region.[35] Among these women, there were some whose interest in the foreign doctrine was awakened by Catholic literature. Others, by contrast, are reported to have relied on it for their daily devotions. Some of them, including the famous Catholic lady Candida Xu, were even able to correspond with missionaries by letter about religious matters, using this as another channel of indirect communication.[36] Despite these exceptions, however, the missionaries knew that most Chinese women were not able to read Catholic texts by themselves. Illiterate women could only benefit from the Jesuits' written catechesis indirectly, either by attending religious congregations where texts were read or by receiving text-based oral instruction from the literate on other occasions.[37]

It is highly probable that images and devotional objects played a key role in the evangelization of those unable to read Catholic catechetical literature. Unfortunately, only little is known of the cheap printed Christian images and devotional devices that were readily available to large groups of people.[38] As indicated by the conversion story of the Nanchang widow recounted above, rosaries and printed images of Jesus were popular devotional objects gifted to neophytes. Other devotional objects circulating in Catholic networks included *veronicae* (pendants imprinted with an image of Christ's face), *nomina* (medals bearing the name of Jesus or Mary), *coronae* (a variant of the rosary made out of thirty-three beads), and, of course, the highly popular rosary.[39] The presence of these objects reminded neophytes of doctrine and sustained them in their daily devotions.

Although the Jesuits preferred to delegate women's evangelization to intermediaries and to communicate with women through written and visual media, they nevertheless encountered situations where personal instruction by a missionary or Chinese lay brother was inevitable. In such situations, teachers were ordered to pay painstaking attention to maintaining decorum. Most importantly, the Jesuits were admonished to only speak with women in the presence of husbands, fathers, "or a person comparable in trustworthiness."[40] The missionaries tried to impose this rule even in situations where women were of humble social background. Nicolas Trigault reported that Jesuit lay brothers were instructed never to enter a female neophyte's home if her husband was not there, even if the woman should insist on their so doing.[41] On some occasions, especially in upper-class households, the Jesuits communicated with women through "curtains and screens," shielding them from the missionaries' gaze. Matteo Ricci thus reported how in 1605 the Chinese lay brother Pascal Mendez instructed the mother of Joseph, a member of the royal family, in his Nanchang palace—doing so separated from the lady by a curtain hung in a doorway.[42] A curtain was also hung between the missionaries and female devotees on the occasion of confession, this at a time when the confessional had only just started to spread in European churches.[43]

Personally instructing small groups of women in their homes was a tiresome task for missionaries and claimed much of their precious time. It had, however, the benefit of providing the Jesuits with opportunities to expand the geographic reach of their mission. Missionaries often associated with members of the literati class in urban centers and were subsequently invited by these new supporters to visit their homes to instruct female family members. As the literati's hometowns were frequently situated in more peripheral regions, the Jesuits were thus able to travel to regions that had not previously been part of their missionary circuits.[44] On such occasions the Jesuits sometimes baptized large extended families.[45]

Once a family had converted to Catholicism, access to women for religious instruction ceased to be a pressing problem. Catholic instruction was now passed on among family members. Daughters of the family as well as young wives entering the household were instructed by their female relatives—typically by mothers and mothers-in-law. In this context, the question of how to instruct women was replaced by questions of how to organize their religious practice within the gendered spatial arrangements of Chinese households and of how to administer to Catholic women's religious needs.

FROM ORATORIES TO WOMEN'S CHURCHES (1600–1640)

Due to the Jesuits' concern for the separation of the sexes, new arrangements for spaces of Catholic worship that differed sharply from those in Europe emerged in China. In contrast to European Catholic communities, where men and women usually performed religious devotions together in the church's public space, separated only by an aisle, Chinese Catholic communities strictly separated men's and women's worship spaces.[46] Men and women, moreover, preferred different worship spaces. While missionaries soon started convoking their male converts in churches, they encouraged women to worship at home. House oratories, as a consequence, became primary sites of female Catholic worship. In the period from around 1600 to 1630 they were, indeed, the only worship spaces available to women, before later being complemented by women's churches.[47]

Although even before their change of attire the missionaries were already following a strategy of not encouraging Catholic women to visit churches, they seem to have started actively encouraging the construction of house oratories at the turn of the seventeenth century.[48] One of the first oratories recorded in the sources was established in 1601 by Anna and Maria Zhong, Longobardo's first female converts in Shaozhou.[49] Only slightly later, the Qin family in Nanjing established an oratory within the confines of their home, which also comprised a house next to the chapel "for the father," where he stayed when he came "to say Mass."[50] A house oratory was built in the capital, in the home of the Beijing literatus Li Yingshi (1559–1620), most probably in 1602. The rich convert amply embellished the chapel at his own expense, adorning it with beautiful images and other ornaments.[51] The role of house oratories as the primary female religious spaces was formally approved by the visitor and the superiors of the China mission in 1621. In the vice-province's foundational statement, they urged the missionaries to encourage the establishment of house oratories "where they could baptize the women, say Mass to them, and make them exercise their devotions."[52]

The domestic female piety that resulted from the missionaries' promotion of house oratories not only differed considerably from the Catholic female piety common in seventeenth-century Europe, but it also sharply contrasted with Buddhist popular piety, which was often attached to temples outside the home.[53] By strictly confining women's Catholic devotion to their homes, the missionaries prevented Catholic women's visits to churches from becoming the scorn of literati moralists. Indeed, they modeled Catholic female piety on Confucian female piety, something that, according to Confucian moralist authors, should ideally be focused exclusively on domestic ancestral rites.[54]

Like Chinese houses, which ranged from sumptuous manorial estates to simple peasants' cottages, house oratories could take various forms. Annual letters record that poor commoner families usually established a simple niche in the main room of their houses, where they worshipped in front of printed images of the Savior or characters written on paper pasted on the wall. Such simple oratories were probably combined with altars dedicated to the ancestors, which were also situated in the main halls of Chinese houses and were tolerated by seventeenth-century Jesuits.[55] These simple oratories contrasted with the house oratories of wealthier families, who often erected spacious separate chapels on their family estates. An outstanding example of such a Catholic gentry oratory was the large women's church built within the Xu residence around 1640, which subsequently became the most important religious center for Catholic women in Shanghai.[56] Spacious oratories in the houses of rich Catholic families were not only used by family members but were also used for religious gatherings, where women from the neighborhood or visiting female relatives from other households would be invited (see chapter 6). Other oratories were destined for individual women's worship only. Annual letters mention "tiny oratories" (*oratoriozinhos*), where Catholic women conducted worship in non-Catholic households.[57] In some cases, separate Catholic oratories seem also to have been installed on the "dew platform" (*lutai*), an upper-story room in the inner quarters where Chinese gentry women customarily had their Buddhist altars.[58] This indicates that Catholic devotion sometimes directly replaced Buddhist devotion for gentry women.[59]

Women's oratories, as religious spaces situated in the inner realm, corresponded well with the Confucian norms that the Jesuits upheld. Missionaries soon discovered, however, that administering to growing numbers of women in small, family-based house oratories had one major drawback: it was time-consuming. As Catholicism entered into its first period of substantial growth on the eve of the Manchu invasion—when the numbers of Catholics increased from about thirteen thousand in 1627 to about sixty thousand in 1640[60]—the time had come to find alternative organizational forms for female piety. And in the 1630s, as a consequence, the missionaries started to build separate churches for women.[61] The lessening of social control due to the political turmoil of the late Ming period seems to have facilitated this endeavor.[62] In 1633 the first women's church was opened in the prefecture-level city of Jianchang, Jiangxi, followed by churches in Jiangzhou, Shanxi (1634); Nanjing (1635); and Xi'an (1639).[63] By the end of the 1630s the establishment of women's churches, which Catholics usually referred to as "Holy Mother's churches" (*Shengmu tang*), had become an established practice for the China mission.[64] Where no Holy Mother's church existed, moreover, missionaries began inviting women to visit men's churches. In these cases, they usually said Mass twice, once for males and once, at another time, for females.[65] As Giandomenico Gabiani recorded in his 1667 history of the mission, therefore, "Under Tartar rule [women] for the first time were enabled to leave their homes in order to frequent the holy temples—although in different places and at different hours than men."[66]

It is difficult to specify the exact numbers and sizes of the women's churches that were established from the 1630s onward. An overview of ecclesiastical architecture dating from 1680 shows that women's churches were established not only in Catholicism's urban strongholds, such as Shanghai, Songjiang, and Hangzhou, but also in remote places, such as the small city of Yanping (Fujian). Most Catholic communities possessed only one women's church. The well-situated Catholic community of Beijing, however, boasted two women's churches toward the end of the century.[67] The churches were established in buildings either bought or constructed for this purpose by the missionaries.[68] According to the French Jesuit Jean de Fontaney, women's churches were sometimes extremely small, resembling more "a little chapel in the form of a salon or hall" than a European church.[69] They had, nevertheless, become a distinctive feature of early modern Chinese Catholicism.

The Holy Mother's churches were a significant innovation in the domain of Chinese Catholic women's piety. Their establishment marked the transition of Catholic women's piety from domestic to at least partly public settings and thus a deviation from the Confucian ideal, which confined female religiosity to the inner realm. As a consequence, the churches occasionally attracted the attention of Confucian magistrates, who suspected that these worship spaces were used as places for the indecent mingling of the sexes. The Jiangzhou church, for instance, was demolished upon the order of a hostile magistrate in the mid-seventeenth century, because "he had the impression that it did not befit female modesty."[70] A magistrate in Huguang, in the same vein, addressed a long memorial to his superior in the late 1680s, demanding the shutdown of the Holy Mother's churches in the area.[71] The missionaries, in turn, exercised great caution with regard to the women's churches. They canceled gatherings in women's churches whenever bad rumors about Catholicism started to spread. Inácio da Costa, who was stationed in Xi'an in 1647, even canceled the women's Christmas congregation because, as he explained, "the neighbors have accused us in front of the mandarins." In such cases, the female Catholics had to perform their devotions at home and did not receive the sacraments from the priest.[72]

The vulnerability of women's churches might have been one reason why they never fully replaced house oratories. As Chinese Catholic women continued to use established house oratories, Chinese Catholic families built new ones throughout the seventeenth century. The example of

Hangzhou vividly illustrates this fact. A wave of women's conversions in the 1630s did not instantly lead to the foundation of a women's church, but resulted instead in a considerable increase of oratories.[73] By the early 1630s four house oratories were already serving as gathering places for women's congregations; a fifth was established in 1634, and, by 1638, there were six oratories housing women's congregations.[74] These congregations were formed by women from the same city neighborhoods, so that they did not have to travel far to join their devotional groups—a practice that might have given rise to suspicion. This practice of grouping together women's congregations in oratories placed in different city neighborhoods was also established in other big cities, such as Beijing.[75]

Although house oratories remained focal points of female worship after the establishment of women's churches, their function shifted after the 1630s. During the early years of the mission, they had performed a double function as spaces where women could practice lay devotions and as spaces where they could hear Mass and receive the sacraments. When a priest visited the house oratory, the whole family assembled, sometimes also with people from the neighborhood, and a son of the family sometimes served as an acolyte during Mass.[76] After the establishment of women's churches, missionaries were advised to avoid, as far as possible, reading Mass in private houses.[77] The sacraments were now to be administered to women in the churches, where the women gathered "especially on major feast days."[78] House oratories consequently became spaces to be used mainly for lay devotions, where no priest was required. These independent devotions included everyday devotional practices, for which the family assembled, as well as periodic women's congregational meetings.

Neither house oratories in the period before 1630, however, nor churches in the later period, provided women with a frequent occasion for receiving the sacraments. On the contrary, Catholic women, and especially those living in rural areas, were fortunate if a missionary passed by once a year to administer the sacraments. From the 1620s onward there was a constant dearth of missionary personnel.[79] In the 1680s Juan Antonio Arnedo reported that one missionary could easily spend four months a year just visiting all the rural missions around Shanghai.[80] Catholic men living in the countryside were free to travel to town to see missionaries or catechists at their residence. Gender propriety, however, did not usually allow such trips for women.[81] Mass, furthermore, was only celebrated occasionally for women, not only in rural areas, but also in towns and cities. In mid-seventeenth-century Hangzhou, for instance, women only met three times a year to hear Mass in oratories.[82] It is therefore probable, in fact, that most Chinese Catholic women's religious practice consisted of lay devotions, without priestly presence. This is noteworthy in the light of contemporary developments in seventeenth-century European Catholicism, where the importance and frequency of administering the sacraments had dramatically increased in the wake of Tridentine reforms.[83] It does, however, appear less surprising once the nature of Chinese religiosity has been taken into account. This was characterized by strong tendencies toward lay religiosity, practices unguided by ritual specialists.

CONTESTED CONTACTS: SACRAMENTS AND THE RITES CONTROVERSY (1640–1690)

Although the Jesuits' dearth of manpower meant that Chinese Catholics received the sacraments relatively rarely, these rituals became, nonetheless, a major point of contention in the early modern China mission.[84] They became, indeed, the only issue that ever caused the Roman Curia to focus their attention on the life circumstances of Chinese women. This controversy originated in a Jesuit decision to adapt their performance of some sacraments—Catholicism's core rituals—to Chinese gender arrangements.[85] Anxious not to damage their reputation as Western literati, the missionaries sought to avoid physical contact between priests and female devotees by omitting certain ceremonies accompanying the sacraments of baptism and extreme unction.[86] More specifically, the ceremonies of the salt, saliva, and oil (discussed in more detail below) were omitted from the baptism of catechumens, as was the ceremony of anointing the feet (and sometimes the loins) with oil during extreme unction.[87] Although these ceremonies were prescribed by the *Rituale Romanum*, the binding liturgical work the Roman authorities published in 1614, the Jesuits maintained that they possessed the necessary papal privileges for these adaptations, accorded them by Popes Gregory XIII (r. 1572–85) and Urban VIII (r. 1623–44).[88] Their sacramental practice became a target for criticism, however, immediately after the arrival of the first mendicants in China in 1635.[89] When the Dominican Juan Bautista Morales (1597?–1664) and the Franciscan Antonio Caballero de Santa María (1602–1669) landed at the coast of the southern province of Fujian, they found that the religious practices of the local Catholics were, as they saw it, infested by idolatry and superstition. The Jesuits' adapted performance of the sacraments was, in their eyes, as little in accordance with Roman orthodoxy as their permissive attitude toward "pagan" ceremonies—such as those dedicated to Confucius, the ancestors, and the gods of walls and moats (*chenghuang*), which would later become the central issue in the Chinese rites controversy.[90]

What, however, was the actual nature of the ceremonies accompanying the sacraments that the Jesuits altered or omitted? The relevant liturgical texts indicate that they were regarded as an important part of the sacraments promulgated by the Council of Trent. Indeed, although the Council stated that the ceremonies did not affect the actual validity of the sacraments, it nonetheless prohibited any disregard, omission, or alteration of them.[91] It held that they had powerful salutary effects on the faithful and were therefore important elements of the baptismal ritual.[92] These salutary effects were closely intertwined with the body of the faithful and their physical contact with the priest. A closer look at the ceremonies accompanying baptism illustrates this point well. Initiation into the catechumenate included an exorcism. This consisted of the priest breathing three times upon the face of the candidate and saying blessings when he made the sign of the cross on the candidate's forehead and heart, placing some salt into the candidate's mouth. The ceremonies accompanying actual baptism included an exorcism where the ears and nose were anointed with spittle and the chest and back with oil. After the actual christening with water the candidate was finally anointed with chrism, symbolizing "the sacred quality of the newly-baptized Christian."[93] The importance attributed to physical contact between the priest and the candidate of baptism reflected the Catholic belief that priests could, as Christ's representatives, mediate divine grace. Priests' bodies were sanctified through the sacrament of ordination, and physical contact with their sanctified bodies ensured the transmission of the salutary effects of baptism to the body of the baptismal candidate.[94]

In China, however, the Council's guidelines confronted the sensitivities of a society whose elite generally despised physical contact, greatly valued the separation of the sexes and the inaccessibility of female bodies, and was especially suspicious of male-female physical contact during rituals.[95] The Jesuits' administering of baptism to women was, indeed, a primary criticism of the anti-Christian pamphlets collected and published by Shen Que, the magistrate who suppressed missionary activity in the city of Nanjing in 1616.[96] Shen's *Memorial to the Throne [Petitioning for] the Deportation of the Foreign Barbarians* (Faqian yuanyi huizou shu) criticized the missionaries for "anointing [people] with oil and sprinkling water over them, even if they are women"—a practice that, in his view, was proof of the Jesuits' "bad customs."[97] Xu Congzhi, another anti-Christian official involved in the Nanjing incident, also criticized the missionaries' suspect practice of publicly sprinkling women with water, an obscure ritual that was accompanied by "barbarian incantations" (*yizhou*).[98] Xu Dashou, a lay buddhist who was the author of a detailed refutation of Catholicism written in 1623, was very explicit about the impurity that he suspected as a result of the Jesuits' sacramental practices:

> [The foreigners] have established a prohibition which runs: "Thou shalt not look at thy neighbor's wife." As for the wives and daughters of their followers, however, they let them mingle with the crowd in order to receive the secret teaching of the barbarians. They pour holy water on them, drip holy oil on them, hand them the holy casket (*Agnus Dei*), let them sip the holy salt, light holy candles, share holy bread with them, wave the holy fan, cover themselves with a purple strip (stole) and wear strange vestments, and all this in the dark night and [men and women] intermingling. What more [do I have to tell]? The *Book of Rites* says: "If no distinction between males and females were observed, disorder would arise and grow," and I would not know on what their disorder is based?[99]

In Xu's eyes, that the Catholic priests (allegedly) committed "the crime of secretly lusting after [women] by placing their hands on five places of their bodies" was a clear sign of their doctrine's heretical character.[100] Other authors shared this view, comparing the "teaching of the Lord of Heaven" to Chinese sectarian groups such as the White Lotus Movement (Bailian Jiao) and the Non-Action Movement (Wuwei Jiao), which Confucian magistrates constantly accused of transgressing the boundaries of sexual decency under cover of darkness.[101] We do not know for sure when, exactly, the Jesuits started to adapt the performance of the sacraments to Chinese gender sensitivities.[102] It seems reasonable to assume, however, that the Nanjing hostilities, together with other accusations of sexual harassment raised against the missionaries, precipitated the Jesuits' decision. The impeachment by Shen Que caused a severe setback to the missionaries' evangelization project in the southern capital and was thus probably a lesson for the Jesuits.

To return to the two mendicants, Juan Bautista Morales and Antonio Caballero de Santa Maria, both took the view that the Jesuits' adaptations of sacramental ceremonies in China needed closer examination by the Roman authorities and soon started to take appropriate measures. In the late 1630s it was decided that Caballero should travel to Manila to report this discovery to his superiors, and Morales was dispatched to Rome. Morales arrived in the Eternal City in February 1643 and handed a catalog of questions (*quaesita*) over to the Roman Curia, demanding that the Roman authorities take a closer look at the issue. Morales's *quaesita* marked the beginning of the Chinese rites controversy as a major ecclesiastical debate, taking place simultaneously in Asia and Europe.[103] It also made the Jesuits' adaptation of sacramental practice—not previously a major subject of internal discussion among missionaries in China—an endlessly discussed problem, leaving behind an extensive record in the archives of the Propaganda Fide and the Holy Office.[104]

The Propaganda Fide answered Morales's *quaesita* in a decree issued on 12 September 1645. It not only rejected the Jesuits' permissive attitude toward Confucian rituals but also forthrightly condemned the Jesuits' adaptation of sacramental practices: "[The experts (*qualificatores*) of the Holy Office] are of the opinion that the sacramentals [i.e., the ceremonies accompanying the sacraments—N.A.] have to be given to the women during baptism, and that the last unction has to be administered to women." The theologians declared that the Jesuits' justification for their adaptations—gender segregation in China—was illegitimate. Instead of adapting ceremonies to Chinese customs, they stated, the missionaries should take care "that these salutary rites and ceremonies are introduced and observed, and that the missionaries administer them with circumspection." To make the rites acceptable to the Chinese, the missionaries were to instruct them about the meaning of the rituals. According to the *qualificatores*, that should suffice to dispel any suspicion.[105]

The decree from the Propaganda came as a blow to the Jesuits in China. Due to their papal privileges, they thought themselves in the right and, consequently, launched a counterattack. They sent a procurator to Rome to renegotiate the issue. The envoy was Martino Martini, who arrived in the Catholic capital in late 1654.[106] In a memorial presented to the theologians of the Holy Office, he asked the Propaganda Fide to reconsider. He emphasized how the missionaries' social intercourse with women scandalized the Chinese and seriously endangered their mission in China, because women there "surpassed all other nations of the world in honesty and modesty."[107] To strengthen his position, Martini drew on the Jesuits' proto-ethnographic representations of China, which showed Chinese women not walking the streets freely and withdrawing to their private quarters whenever their husbands received friends. Martini also pointed to how they avoided physical contact with men whenever possible, a fact especially relevant for his request: "They believe it to be a vice to take anything from the hands of a man. If anything is offered to them, it is put on a table or bench, where the woman takes it, not with the naked hand, but covered with the sleeve of her dress." According to Martini, that was why the Jesuits "did not administer [the ceremonies] to all women, but only to those who asked for them and in case there is no danger of insulting the infidels."[108] Martini's insistence on the particularity of Chinese women's situation induced a change of mind in the Roman Curia. Eight of the ten *qualificatores* in charge of the assessment of Martini's memorial responded positively to his request. The Holy Office then issued a new decree on 23 March 1656, which stated that some ceremonies prescribed for baptism and extreme unction could be omitted "in case of serious necessity" (*grave necessitate*).[109] With this decision, the Jesuits had officially regained the freedom to administer the sacraments to women in the way they found most suitable for Chinese conditions.

The new decision did not, however, put an end to the controversy. The Jesuits' adaptation of sacramental practice was discussed once more in 1667–68. That followed an involuntary gathering in Canton of the missionaries in China—twenty Jesuits, four Dominicans, and a Franciscan—in the wake of the Calendar Case (1664–69). This anti-Christian incident provoked by magistrates at the imperial court resulted in Johann Adam Schall von Bell's arrest and the expulsion of all Catholic missionaries to Canton.[110] The latter then took this opportunity to hold a "conference" aiming at unifying their evangelical practices, including baptismal ones.[111] The resolutions drafted at the end of the gathering regulated the ceremonies accompanying baptism to a level of unprecedented detail. They proposed that the oil of catechumens was to be administered only to little girls, and not to adult women, while missionaries were to completely desist from the administration of the saliva. They also suggested that adult women should be anointed with chrism, but that a silver pencil should be used in order not to anoint them "directly with the hand of the priest." While they did not object to the practice of pouring water over adult women's heads, they recommended that the women should not be forced to loosen their hair for this ceremony. Instead, the missionaries should pour the water over the uncovered parts of the face.[112]

The resolutions of the Canton gathering caused the conflict to flare up again. Not only the mendicants, who had been in the minority in Canton, voiced their discontent with the resolutions as soon as exile had ended, but a new protagonist entered on the stage in the 1660s.[113] This was François Pallu, whom the Propaganda Fide appointed vicar apostolic to Tonkin and the southern Chinese provinces in 1658, and he was soon to become a convinced opponent of the Jesuits.[114] Although Pallu was unable to enter China before 1684, he spent several years in Southeast Asia between 1662 and 1677 and was informed about the resolutions by a Dominican, Domingo Navarrete (1610–1689), during an accidental meeting in Madagascar in 1679.[115] After this Pallu appealed to the Propaganda Fide against them. In documents handed over to the Propaganda in April 1678, he expressed his doubts about the lawfulness of the Canton "conference" (since it was held in his absence) and the resolutions it issued (since they contradicted the decrees issued by the Holy Office in 1645 and 1654, which allowed the missionaries to omit these ceremonies only in cases of "grave necessity").[116] According to Pallu, the resolutions resulted from the machinations of the Jesuits, who alone maintained their erroneous ways of administering the sacraments in China: "The Dominicans have never omitted [the ceremonies] in the two Provinces of their mission, . . . and the Franciscans only occasionally desisted from administering them."[117] The Holy Office theologians reacted to Pallu's accusations in April 1678. They declared that the missionaries "were in no way allowed" (*nullatenus posse*) to hold a conference in the absence of the Vicar Apostolic and that they were obliged to observe the papal decrees of 1645 and 1656.[118] Two decrees, furthermore, were issued in 1677 and 1678, to prevent any further acts of disobedience by the China Jesuits. These commanded that all missionaries in China were to pledge their loyalty to the Propaganda Fide in a formal vow, the *giuramento*.[119]

While the *giuramento* led to new conflicts between the Propaganda Fide and the Jesuits, it did not lead them to alter their sacramental practices in the Middle Kingdom. For when François Pallu finally reached China in 1684, he noticed that they were continuing to administer sacraments to women in the adapted way, regardless of the papal decrees—Rome was proving too far away to effectively enforce its decisions in China. This time, however, Pallu desisted from accusing the Jesuits in front of the Curia. Toward the end of the seventeenth century, he seems, instead, to have switched course to that of the Jesuits. That is, at least, the impression conveyed by a letter Pallu wrote to the Propaganda Fide in 1684. There the Vicar Apostolic explained that physical contact between men and women was, after all, a delicate matter in China and that "more than once it has happened that the missionaries were accused of fornication with women even without administering the sacramental ceremonies of baptism." Although they never did receive Rome's full approval for their practices, the Jesuits were thus, finally, the informal victors in the debate surrounding the adaptation of sacraments in China.[120]

While only a small part of the larger debate of the rites controversy, the debate on the adaptation of sacraments is of particular interest for how it brought the Jesuits' accommodation to Chinese gender arrangements into the view of the Roman authorities. If the Curia was to make a reasonable decision, it faced the difficult task of obtaining reliable information about Chinese gender relations. Because of its geographic and cultural distance, it needed local knowledge acquired by missionaries in order to rule on the questions they raised.[121] Jesuit authors advocating the adaptation of sacraments were aware of this paradoxical situation, and they repeatedly referred to their local knowledge in their memorials.

An especially extensive contribution to the debate, the *Apology of [Our] Way of Proceeding* (Apologia Modi Procedendi) written by the Visitor to Japan and China Antonio Rubino (1578–1643), aptly illustrates this point.[122] According to Rubino, the Jesuits' local experience was the strongest argument for siding with them in the controversy. Rubino pointed out that the Jesuits' local expertise sharply contrasted with the mendicants' limited understanding of Chinese culture. While the Jesuits "had stayed in China for more than sixty years, being present in thirteen provinces of this vast empire, having baptized more than sixty thousand souls, and having friendly relations with literati and mandarins," the mendicants only had six or eight missionaries in China, and these were "youngsters without experience" (*moços sem experiencia*), who only evangelized commoners in the southern provinces.[123]

According to Rubino it was hardly astonishing that the rustic female populations of these areas happily grasped any opportunity that presented itself to escape the seclusion imposed on them by their fathers and husbands, and nor was it surprising that the mendicants encountered few difficulties in administering the sacramental ceremonies to women. Rubino's reasoning was, implicitly, that the Jesuits' intimate knowledge of China's educated urban elite had familiarized them with "true" Chinese civilization, something that the mendicants only knew perverted rural variants of. The Jesuits, for their part, had already learned these lessons long ago. Rubino traced their adaptations back to Feliciano da Silva, who was in China from 1605 to 1614 and had experienced extremely hostile reactions to his attempts at administering baptism to women using the ceremonies prescribed by the Council of Trent.

Although not approved by the Roman authorities—the *Apology* was placed on the *Index of Prohibited Books* (Index Librorum Prohibitorum) fifteen years after the publication of an Italian translation in 1680[124]—Rubino's strong emphasis on the Jesuits' experience in China nonetheless gave expression to the Roman Church's changing attitude toward knowledge in the late seventeenth century. Unlike scholasticism, this new understanding of knowledge conceded that empirical experience was pertinent to the assessment of theological questions and acknowledged that "the reference to the norm" had to be "tested against the particular case."[125] This new assessment of empirical knowledge made the Jesuits' proto-ethnographic representations of Chinese women a powerful instrument in their hands. They could draw on their "curious" and "edifying" writings to strengthen their position in the ecclesiastical controversies over the administration of sacraments to women.

* * *

The tension caused by the conflicting role models of the Catholic priest and the Confucian literatus made the Jesuits find creative ways to communicate with women. They developed means of indirect evangelization, created separate devotional spaces, and adapted sacramental ceremonies in order to reconcile their missionary vocation with Chinese expectations regarding scholars' attitudes toward gender propriety. The Jesuits' accommodation to Chinese gender sensitivities was not always uncontested by Chinese observers and ecclesiastical critics. It produced, nonetheless, workable solutions. Rather than being a mere obstacle for the Jesuits' mission in China, it was also a source of creative tension, giving rise to specifically Chinese forms of women's religiosity.

The next chapter turns to yet another issue straddling European Catholic and Chinese Confucian norms—the question of matrimony, which, although it touched less upon the question of the Jesuits' literati identity, led ecclesiastical critics and Chinese Catholics to focus their attention on some of the fundamental tensions inherent in the Confucianized Catholicism that the Jesuits promulgated in China.

4 STRENGTHENING THE MARITAL BOND

The Christianization of Chinese Marriage

IN HIS DIARY, MATTEO RICCI REMEMBERED A "NICE INVENTION" by Luca, a rich Catholic servant working in the household of Ricci's scholar-official friend Li Zhizao. Luca "said that he wanted to leave to his descendants a sign of Christianity, which he and his parents had started to follow."[1] He had a large commemorative picture made portraying all members of his descent group. It was fashioned in the manner of the multigenerational ancestor portraits that Chinese families displayed during ancestor worship at home on New Year's Day and other special occasions, a very popular genre. The portrait commissioned by Luca seems to have fulfilled all the conventions of this pictorial tradition, with one important difference. While a shared ancestor usually occupied a seat of honor in the center of traditional ancestor portraits, Luca assigned this place to Jesus. True-to-nature portraits of his relatives, placed around Jesus, were depicted with *coronae*—a sort of rosary—in their hands and small crucifixes and reliquaries around their necks.[2] Luca thus underlined the Catholic identity of his family. The picture, Ricci explained, led those relatives not yet converted to become Christians, for "if they had not, they could not have been painted."[3] It is likely that Luca intended to use the picture during domestic ancestor worship, when the descent group "receive[d] offerings and the kowtows of the family members."[4] That explains why his relatives were eager to be included in the painting. Not figuring in it would have been tantamount to exclusion from the lineage, a dreadful fate for anyone imbued with Confucian family values.

Luca's enhancing of this picture with Catholic elements provides remarkable testimony of one family's Catholic identity. Yet it simultaneously illustrates the persistence of Confucian views of the family within Chinese Catholic communities. Such views attached enormous value to the perpetuation of the patriline. They regarded relationships among members of the same patriline as the strongest bonds among family members and venerated agnatic antecedents in an almost religious manner.[5]

Confucian concern for the patriline also influenced the meanings attributed to marriage. As stated by *The Book of Rites*, marriage served primarily to strengthen the patriline: "Looking toward the past, [marriages] provide for service to the ancestral temple; looking toward the future, they provide for the continuation of descendants."[6] According to Confucian thinking, wives were part of their husbands' patriline from the moment they entered the household during wedding festivities. After their wedding, they owed filial behavior (*xiao*) to their parents-in-law, not their own parents. They were obliged to participate in the ancestral rituals of their husbands' families, and they were expected to accept that their husbands took concubines in order to ensure the continuity of the patriline. Although a wife's status was privileged in comparison with the markedly inferior social status of concubines, her legal status was insecure nevertheless. Confucian scriptures listed seven conditions (*qichu*) under which a husband was allowed to divorce his wife, while a wife was never allowed to divorce her husband.[7]

European Catholics were of course familiar with the fourth commandment, "Honor thy father and thy mother," and European social norms held the patriline in high esteem.[8] Agnatic progenitors did not, however, play particularly important roles in European Catholic doctrinal writing about marriage.[9] The Council of Trent stressed the sacred nature of the marital bond between man and woman and the importance of conjugal consensus as a primary prerequisite for valid matrimony, emphasizing the horizontal relationship between the spouses. Although the Council stated that spouses were joined for the sake of raising children, that was not the only goal of marriage, the other being the spouses' mutual aid and support.[10] Since the Middle Ages Christian doctrine had conceptualized marriage as a monogamous, indissoluble bond, sanctified and sanctioned by God. The Tridentine reformers tried to impose this view more effectively on all Catholics by making the sacrament of matrimony obligatory and a prerequisite for legal marriage.[11]

The differences between Chinese and Catholic notions of marriage were noticed by the Jesuits, who offered detailed analyses of these divergences in their writings. They noted how the Chinese married at a very young age and how "everything is settled between the parents, without asking the consent of the children."[12] They also observed how wives were regarded as members of their husbands' patriline. According to Gabriel de Magalhães, this was expressed by the Chinese characters related to marriage: "The character *qu* [娶], which means that a man gets married or takes a wife, is composed of the characters *qu* [取], 'to fetch,' and *nü* [女], 'woman.' The character *jia* [嫁], which signifies that a woman gets married, is composed of the characters *jia* [家], 'house,' and *nü* [女], 'woman.' This means that the woman is in her house or family [after being married], for the Chinese hold that women belong to the house of their husbands, not to that of their parents."[13]

The Jesuits did not have any objections to the idea of a wife being integrated into the lineage of her husband upon her marriage. Some consequences of the Confucian valuation of the patriline were, however, incompatible with the Catholic view of marriage and thus posed problems for the missionaries. As in other extra-European Catholic missions, the Jesuits had to tackle practices such as polygyny and divorce—practices that, while widespread among Asian and Native American peoples, were in contradiction to the very core of Catholic marriage.[14] The Jesuits had to find ways of resolving these contradictions, either by persuading the Roman authorities to grant them dispensations or by persuading their prospective Chinese converts to change their habits and marriage customs.

The Jesuits were uninterested in radically changing Confucian views of the family, but they saw a need to regulate (especially male) sexuality to make it compatible with post-Tridentine Catholic marriage norms. Their tolerant attitude toward Chinese customs is obvious in view of Chinese Catholic wedding ceremonies, which had an exclusively domestic and thus largely non-Catholic character. The ways in which the Jesuits tried to alter Chinese marriage become tangible by dint of a close reading of *The Government of the Family in the West* (Qijia xixue), a household manual published by Alfonso Vagnone in the late 1620s. It shows that there were primarily two aspects of Chinese marriage that needed to be adapted to Catholic doctrine: namely, divorce and polygyny.[15]

CHINESE, BUT NOT PAGAN: JESUIT VIEWS ON WEDDING CELEBRATIONS

Like the sacraments of extreme unction and baptism, the sacrament of matrimony confronted the Jesuits with a problem. Its performance required the priest to have close contact with women, thus endangering the missionaries' self-fashioned image as "Western scholars." While the Jesuits adapted the performance of extreme unction and baptism to the gender sensitivities of the Chinese elite, they found a different solution for matrimony: dispensing with it altogether. The Jesuits did not require their converts to validate their marriages through the Catholic sacrament, but allowed them to celebrate their marriages according to Chinese custom.[16] According to several Jesuit authors, this was necessary because of how explosive the issue of public marriage ceremonies was in the Chinese context.[17] To expose a young bride to the gaze of foreign missionaries and Catholic communities was a delicate matter in a culture where brides were usually led to their grooms' houses with the greatest discretion. As the missionaries emphasized, no one but the groom could see the bride during Chinese marriage ceremonies: "The bride is sent to the house of the groom in a sedan chair. . . . Then a servant hands the key of the sedan chair over to the groom, and he is the only one who is allowed to open it in order to receive the bride."[18] Marriage ceremonies were, in a sense, a condensed expression of how greatly valued female seclusion was in China's Confucian culture. Interfering with them therefore appeared unwise to the Jesuits.

The Jesuits could justify their omission of the sacrament of matrimony to Roman authorities by saying that the canons of the Council of Trent, which had declared the sacrament to be a necessary prerequisite for the validation of marriage, had not been published in China.[19] The administration of the sacrament was therefore optional in China by dint of this omission, as had already been declared in 1621, in an instruction issued by the superiors and visitors of the China mission.[20] The resolutions resulting from the Canton conference in 1667 repeated this view, instructing the missionaries to "carefully explain to their Christians the indissolubility of the marital bond, and teach them the necessary dispositions for that sacrament and for receiving its grace," while refraining from actually administering the sacrament.[21]

Because Chinese Catholic marriages were not celebrated in church and sanctioned by the sacrament of matrimony, the Jesuits increasingly turned their attention to Chinese wedding customs, some of which served as a substitute to Chinese Catholics for Catholic ceremonies.[22] According to a description written by Alvaro Semedo around 1640, these non-Catholic wedding celebrations traditionally lasted for a considerable period. They began with "compliments and civilities," exchanged as soon as the parents of the future spouses had agreed on the dowry: "First, the fiancé sends a present of meat, wine, and fruit to his fiancée. Second, the exact date is chosen with the help of astrologers and ceremonies. Third, the family of the fiancé asks the girl's name. Fourth, the husband has to send rings, earrings, and jewels to his future wife."[23] The day before the actual marriage took place, the future wife's furniture was carried over to her new home in a public procession. Another procession was held on the wedding day, when the groom and his close relatives went to fetch the bride, who was carried to her new home in a sedan chair closed by key. Upon arrival, the sedan chair was ceremoniously opened, and the spouses, who usually had never seen each other before, "retire[d] to an oratory of the idols," where the images of their ancestors were displayed. As Semedo described: "After four genuflections, which people usually do on such occasions, they go to a great hall in order to pay the same honor to their parents seated on chairs. Thereafter, the wife retires to the women's apartments together with her mother-in-law, her female attendants, and the marriage broker."[24] The bride's genuflections before her husband's ancestors and her parents-in-law marked the climax and the end of a Chinese non-Catholic wedding ceremony. Various festivities continued during the month that followed. These, however, were not described in detail by Semedo.

Did the Jesuits allow their converts to perform all the Chinese ceremonies described by Semedo? Only minor alterations, in fact, were imposed on Chinese Catholic marriages, aimed at purging them of superstition and idolatry. The Jesuits forbade Catholics from consulting astrologers to determine an auspicious wedding date, a practice they deemed superstitious.[25] They prohibited them, furthermore, from bowing before the "idolatrous" images that were sometimes displayed on the domestic altars next to the ancestral tablets.[26] The Jesuit practice of not attending Catholic marriage celebrations in person did, however, have a drawback: they could not exercise tight control over the rituals performed on these occasions. It is not surprising, then, that the mendicants accused them of neglecting strict enforcement of the prohibitions during the rites controversy.[27]

Preventing Catholics from performing superstitious or idolatrous marriage ceremonies proved especially difficult in cases of mixed marriages—marriages, that is, between Catholic and non-Catholic partners. Because of the difficulties arising from these unions, the Catholic Church had prohibited them by pronouncing that disparity of cult (*disparitas cultus*) was an impediment to marriage. Chinese Catholics were, however, allowed to contract such mixed marriages due to papal privileges obtained by the Jesuits that permitted them to dispense their flock from this impediment. Wedding ceremonies performed on the occasion of marriage between Catholic brides and non-Catholic husbands were an especially thorny issue because they took place in the grooms' home. Non-Catholic families often required Catholic brides to bow in front of images of Chinese deities. Although the missionaries proudly reported that several Catholic brides had heroically resisted the demands of their pagan in-laws, the fact that marriage celebrations lay beyond the missionaries' control made it difficult for them to find a durable solution to this problem. The Jesuits proposed that Catholic wives marrying non-Catholic husbands should pray in front of a cross while their husbands carried out their "idolatrous" devotions.[28] However, because this solution depended on the non-Catholic husband's consent, it was likely only partially implemented.

While Chinese ceremonies prevailed during Catholic marriages, the Jesuits nevertheless encouraged their followers to introduce additional Catholic elements into the celebrations. They reported that some Catholics, among them Xu Guangqi's nephew, Fulgence, prepared themselves for matrimony by way of a general confession.[29] Other Catholics asked the missionaries to read a Mass for the special occasion of their wedding.[30] Only in a few cases, and only when a Catholic couple expressly wished it, was the sacrament of matrimony administered in the form prescribed by the Council of Trent.[31]

"LIKE *YIN* AND *YANG*": ALFONSO VAGNONE'S ADVICE FOR HUSBANDS (CA. 1630)

The Jesuits' strategy of minimal intervention in Chinese weddings meant that their treatment of the issue in their Chinese catechetical writings was limited to brief references.[32] Nevertheless, they published one noteworthy treatise expounding their view of the marital bond to the Chinese in greater detail: *The Government of the Family in the West* (Qijia xixue).[33] This advice manual for male family heads was informed by Western ethics, and the first of the book's five scrolls (*juan*) contained a detailed chapter on the government of spouses (*qi fufu*). It offered practical advice about the selection of marriage partners, the organization of the conjugal relationship, and the virtues to be cultivated by husbands and wives. It addressed aspects of Chinese marriage, furthermore, that contradicted Catholic marriage custom, namely, polygyny, divorce, and remarriage. It is thus a valuable source for gleaning at least a general impression of how Chinese and European ideas about marriage converged and diverged and the way they were perceived by the treatise's author, Alfonso Vagnone.

Vagnone was an Italian Jesuit based in Jiangzhou, in southern Shanxi, from 1625 to 1640.[34] He was well versed in Chinese classical scriptures and a prolific writer of Chinese Catholic publications. With the help of a group of eminent Catholic literati from Jiangzhou—the Han and the Duan brothers—he authored a great many publications. These included books aimed at a Catholic readership and books addressed at educated, but not necessarily Catholic, audiences.[35] His *Government of the Family in the West* belonged to the second category. It was part of a tripartite series of writings introducing European ethics to a scholarly Chinese audience. Borrowing from formulations found in *The Great Learning* (Daxue), the three parts were dedicated to the "cultivation of the person in the West," the "government of the family in the West," and the "government of the country."[36]

The Government of the Family in the West was a curious graft of a European literary genre onto Chinese textual tradition. Its title resonated with the vast Chinese genre of household instructions (*jiaxun*), where male authors provided a male readership with advice about the management of domestic affairs.[37] It was modeled, simultaneously, on the European genre of *oeconomica* literature, treating classical *oeconomica* topics such as advice for married couples, children's education, and the government of servants.[38] The treatise presented the advice in the form of metaphors, proverbs, and short exemplary stories (*sententiae*). These rhetorical forms were readily understood by a Chinese audience, since one of China's most revered classical texts, Confucius's *Analects* (Lunyu), presented its contents in a similar way.[39]

The content of *The Government of the Family in the West*, and more specifically its chapter on the government of spouses, also oscillated between the European and Chinese literary traditions. On the one hand, it was strongly informed by contemporary European advice literature on marriage.[40] It made use of analogies recurrent in popular European moral tracts, comparing the process of selecting a spouse with that of catching a fish and comparing the collaboration between husband and wife with that between a pair of oxen joining forces to pull a vehicle under the same yoke.[41] Famous conjugal couples from the European literary tradition were deployed to illustrate some of the treatise's arguments. The stories of Socrates and Xanthippe exemplified how even wise men could fall prey to a quarrelsome wife, and the story of Samson and Delilah demonstrated the dangers loquacious wives posed to husbands.[42] Like other Jesuit authors of Chinese moral books, Vagnone also drew on a great number of Greek and Roman authors, including Plato, Plutarch, Diogenes Laertius, and Cato.[43] Reference to these authors showed Chinese readers, who had much appreciation for history, that Europe had its own tradition of wisdom that had been preserved since antiquity.[44]

In addition to these topoi, Vagnone integrated a conspicuous number of references to Chinese classical sources into the chapter on the government of spouses. He promoted the ideal of monogamy by referring to the correlative relation between the principles of *yin* and *yang*, a key metaphor for male-female relations in Chinese culture. He referenced a phrase from the "Xici" commentary of *The Book of Changes* (Yijing)—"Once *yin*, once *yang*, this constitutes what is called the Way."[45] And Vagnone explained how "the principle of 'one *yin*, one *yang*'" should reign in every household: "If there is too much *yin*, the time sequences are necessarily perverted, and the ten thousand things thrown into chaos. How should it work if many women are joined with one man in every house?"[46] Vagnone also found other concepts in *The Book of Changes* supporting favorable evaluations of monogamy. Referring to a passage from the "Tuanzhuan" commentary—"The man has his correct place in the outer, and the wife has her correct place in the inner"—Vagnone contended that inner and outer should be equally valued and a balance should be created by matching one woman with one man.[47] Vagnone also used Chinese classical texts to highlight principles accepted by both European Catholic and Chinese Confucian marriage ethics. Alluding to the *Balanced Inquiries* (Lunheng), and to the Confucian norm of the "Thrice Following" (*sancong*), he claimed that "the woman is *yin*, the man is *yang*; therefore the wife is obliged to follow the husband."[48] Vagnone reinforced this with a corresponding European metaphor that equated husband and wife with sun and moon, one radiating and the other reflecting the light.[49]

The Government of the Family in the West was written for a male readership and, as a consequence, was forthright with misogynist views on women. Misogynist authors in early modern Europe's dispute over the nature of women, the *querelle des femmes*, had bequeathed a vast reservoir of metaphors for Vagnone to tap into.[50] It is therefore not surprising that he was at pains to warn his readers about quarrelsome, jealous, and idle wives.[51] These statements were probably meant in part to satisfy the expectations of a Chinese male audience, which was acquainted with the misogynist views presented in Chinese "household instruction" literature, where women were often seen as the source of domestic chaos and evil.[52] They also, however, aided Vagnone in advocating celibacy, monogamy, and marital chastity. "If one [woman] is already difficult to govern, how much more difficult is it to govern many?" he asked, rhetorically, in his argument for monogamy.[53] And, in a paragraph promoting abstinence from remarriage, he explained that a spouse's death was less a misfortune than a chance for spiritual growth. "If a fish was lucky and escaped the basket trap, if a bird was lucky and escaped the cage, they know [about the danger] and take guard against it afterwards," he explained; "if men, although being much cleverer than wild beasts, do not act accordingly, they will surely hurt themselves."[54] Marriage was a necessary evil in Vagnone's eyes, from which most men could not escape and which, due to the indissolubility of the marital bond, had to be endured until death.[55] However, if men had to taste the bitterness of marriage, they could at least alleviate their situation by choosing a modest and virtuous wife, by refraining from taking concubines, and by living a chaste widower's life after their wife's death.

Despite its misogynist impetus, Vagnone's chapter on the government of spouses sought nevertheless to strengthen the marital bond—the foundation of Catholic marriage. Vagnone therefore attached great importance to collaboration between the spouses, which was, in accordance with Catholic views on marriage, represented as a key factor for the prosperity of the family.[56] He explained that husbands should not rule over their wives just as princes ruled over their subjects. "For the husband should regard his wife as a companion, not as a servant. Their relationship is not only a connection of things otherwise separate, but resembles the connection of bones and flesh. If a husband knows this, he will share his authority with his wife."[57] Vagnone encouraged men to choose a wife of equal age, social standing, and mental capacities in order to ensure conjugal harmony and further collaboration.[58] This envisioning of the conjugal relationship as a relationship between equals had a familiar ring for a Chinese audience. It corresponded with ancient Chinese conceptions of the wife as the "inner helpmate" of her husband, conceptions invigorated during the seventeenth century by an emerging "cult of emotion" (*qing*) praising the ideal of companionate marriage.[59] Vagnone, however, went even further in his efforts to strengthen the marital bond. He envisioned it as the most vital relationship within the family. It was, in his eyes, even more important than the relationship between father and son. The married couple, Vagnone reminded the reader at the chapter's outset, was the foundation of the family (*jia*): "First there are husband and wife, then there are sons and daughters. If there are husband, wife, sons, and daughters, then there are servants within and tenants without [the house]. A wide array of household chores result from this [order]. Therefore husband and wife are the root of the family."[60]

The idea that the marital couple was the principal unit of every family, and that the marital bond should, as a consequence, be held in particular esteem, was novel in China. The Confucian view of the family insisted on the primacy of the relationship between father and son over the conjugal relationship—a view upheld even by Chinese Catholic authors.[61] The implications of Vagnone's vision, namely, the impossibility of divorce and polygyny, were consequently hard for a Chinese audience to accept. The Jesuits tried to tackle these incompatible notions of marriage in various ways.

AN INDISSOLUBLE BOND?

Soon after arriving in the Middle Kingdom, the Jesuits remarked that divorce was a common practice in China. Manuel Dias the Elder addressed this fact in his "Information . . . about Marriage" (Informatione . . . circa il matrimonio; written in the early 1610s). There he stated that "the laws entitle the Chinese to repudiate their wives in six or seven cases" and that "commoners repudiate their women even more easily, either because they are not satisfied with them, or because they have no sons, or because the mandarins . . . order them to sell [their wives] in order to pay off debts."[62] Dias therefore suggested that the Pauline Privilege, which allowed divorced husbands to stay with their second wives if the latter agreed to become Christian, should be accorded to the Chinese, a request that was granted to the China mission during Nicolas Trigault's stay in Rome in 1615–16.[63] With this dispensation, the issue of divorce largely disappeared from the Jesuits' agenda. The Jesuits' correspondence only rarely referred to controversies arising from it. We do not know whether that was because they were able to resolve most problems with the help of the Pauline Privilege or because they passed over the issue in silence. However, while Chinese divorce played only a minor role in the Jesuits' field reports, it did later become the focus of an erudite theological debate in the second half of the seventeenth century. This focused on whether or not Chinese marriages were valid and erupted after a clash between the Jesuits and a Dominican, Domingo Navarrete, during the missionary gathering in Canton in 1667.

In canon law the question of the validity of marriages to infidels was a classical one. From Thomas Aquinas onward, the church generally answered it in the affirmative.[64] Aquinas had defined matrimony as an institution of natural, human, and divine law and thus declared marriages concluded prior to conversion as valid—provided that they had been concluded within the scope of natural and human law.[65] That made it necessary for the missionaries to pay close attention to indigenous marriage customs to clarify whether the previous unions of newly converted Christians were valid marriages. The latter were defined by being an indissoluble union between a man and a woman concluded for the goal of procreation.

Although marriage had to be monogamous in principle, polygamy was only a divine interdiction of secondary importance because it did not contradict procreation, the principal goal of marriage. Polygamous marriages were therefore essentially valid. However, because they went against the second goal of marriage—the union and collaboration of the spouses—they had to be transformed into monogamous marriages before conversion.[66]

Since polygyny did not present an obstacle to the validity of Chinese marriages, discussion focused around their indissolubility. Answers to this question determined the church's attitude toward the marriages of newly converted Catholics. If the unions concluded between infidels were deemed valid, they had to be respected by the church, and converts were obliged to stay with the wives whom they had married before converting. If they were considered invalid, newly converted Catholics were free to choose their marriage partners, regardless of their unions concluded prior to conversion. This also made the Pauline Privilege superfluous, because a spouse was not legally obliged to any spouse married before baptism. The Jesuits in China generally held the view that the marriages concluded between Chinese infidels were indissoluble and therefore valid.[67] As a case in point, Alvaro Semedo explained that ancient Chinese books clearly stated that "marriages are made in China by way of an indissoluble contract."[68] In their proto-ethnographic writing, Jesuit authors only rarely referred to the existence of the seven reasons for repudiating a wife, mentioning only the dissolubility of the unions with concubines.[69]

There was a specific reason why the Jesuits regarded the affirmation of the indissolubility of Chinese marriages to be of primary importance. The actual stakes were, in fact, not only the dissolubility of the marriages of Chinese converts but also the moral integrity and civility of the Chinese. According to a treatise written by Prospero Intorcetta in 1669, titled "On Chinese Marriages" (De Matrimonio Sinensium), the idea that Chinese marriages were invalid "would insult the whole Chinese nation. [It would mean that] the Europeans slandered the Chinese, without reason and bare of a firm fundament, . . . [by saying] that all those who had married according to the customs of the country were the parents of illegitimate children, and that all wives were concubines, and all men adulterers and fornicators."[70] Intorcetta's defense of the validity of Chinese marriages shows that this was a symbolically and highly charged question for the missionaries.[71] It is therefore not surprising that the Jesuits used their proto-ethnographic writings to ensure that the indissolubility of Chinese marriages was accepted by a European readership.

While the question of the validity of Chinese marriages had not led to major discussions during the first decades of the mission, the situation changed radically in the late 1660s. The resolutions formulated during the Canton conference in 1667 then triggered a major debate about the validity of Chinese marriages. In Canton, the Jesuits had stated that Chinese marriages were "true and legitimate, regardless of some abuses [that could be found in China]."[72] This opinion was not shared by the Dominican friar Domingo Navarrete. Indeed, Navarrete had the impression that Chinese men repudiated their wives with "great facility." During the discussions in Canton, furthermore, he had learned that the validity of Chinese marriages had been contested by no less than the famous Roman College (Collegio Romano) of the Society of Jesus, whose theologians had opined that Chinese marriages were invalid in 1616.[73] That the Jesuits in China had chosen to ignore the Roman College's unfavorable judgment of Chinese marriages prompted Navarrete to ask the Propaganda Fide for a fresh consideration of the issue.[74] After his detention in Canton, he immediately set out for Rome, where he arrived in December 1672 and lobbied against the Jesuits in China during a sixteen-month stay.[75] In a long catalog of doubts presented to the Propaganda Fide in 1674, he explained that there was "rather serious dissent among missionaries on the question whether marriages of those countries are valid or not." He pointed out that Confucius had "ordered his followers to observe five impediments that allowed the separation of a marriage." Did those impediments not run counter to the indissolubility of marriage?[76]

Navarrete's attack on the Jesuits' attitude toward Chinese marriage provoked a response from Prospero Intorcetta. This procurator was dispatched by the Jesuits in China and stayed in Rome at the same time as his Dominican opponent, trying to refute Navarrete's accusations in the (abovementioned) treatise "On Chinese Marriages." Intorcetta tried to substantiate the position maintained by the Jesuits during the Canton conference: that Chinese marriages were valid and that the instances of divorce occurring in China had to be regarded as exceptions to the rule. According to Intorcetta, the notion that Chinese marriages were invalid and could therefore be dissolved at will posed a great danger to the mission in China. He warned the Roman authorities that if missionaries started to dissolve Chinese marriages that would give rise to much scandal and could seriously damage the mission's reputation.[77] Although Intorcetta conceded that there were "seven conditions" mentioned in Chinese law and in the Confucian classics, he held that they had only marginal influence over educated Chinese discourse on marriage.[78] According to the Jesuit, Chinese literati unequivocally advocated the indissolubility of marriage. To substantiate his claim, Intorcetta quoted extensively from Chinese classics and documented his sources by rendering the Chinese wording in the margins of the manuscript.

Most prominently, Intorcetta referred to a sentence in *The Book of Rites* that declared: "If [a woman] is joined with her husband, she should stay with him until death. . . . Even if their husband should die, [women] do not marry again."[79] Although this was actually intended to illustrate the Confucian virtue of wifely faithfulness, Intorcetta pointed out that the Chinese interpreters (*interpretes*) of *The Book of Rites* had expounded the meaning of the passage in a more encompassing manner. The Han dynasty scholar Zheng Xuan, for instance, had stated that "'To join' [*qi*] means that [husband and wife] persevere in sharing their meals, and that they stay together, regardless of their social standing."[80] Intorcetta translated this with an additional emphasis on the indissolubility of marriage: "'To join' [*qi*] means that the conjugal bond should be such that [the spouses] shall be always united, firmly and with perseverance, also with regard to their sustenance, whether they are honorable or mean people, and whether they enjoy honors or have an adverse fortune."[81]

Intorcetta found additional evidence for the idea of an indissoluble marital bond in Chinese moral literature aimed at a female readership, a literary genre that was otherwise not frequently cited by the missionaries. Reading *Obligatory Readings for the Inner Quarter* (Guimen bidu)—a compilation better known under the title *Four Books for Women* (Nü sishu)—he found that it contained considerable evidence for the indissolubility of Chinese marriages.[82] In *The Classic of Filial Piety for Women* (Nü xiaojing), for instance, he found a statement that "the wife is earth, the husband is heaven; neither can be dispensed with." This was because, in the words of the "classic" once again, "heaven and earth are interconnected and pervasive, with no space between them," clear evidence for Intorcetta of the indissolubility of the Chinese conjugal bond.[83] Further evidence was provided by a sentence in Ban Zhao's *Lessons for Women* (Nüjie), which, in Intorcetta's translation, declared that "the affection and union between husband and wife should not separate or dissolve for all their lives." This was, however, an enhanced translation of the Chinese original, which actually did not contain the words *union* and *dissolve*, but merely stated that "the affection between husband and wife should not cease for all their lives."[84]

In seeking to prove the existence of the idea of an indissoluble marriage bond in China by referring to textual evidence of the Chinese literary tradition, Intorcetta used a strategy that he and his collaborators also employed in one of the China Jesuits' most famous publications, *Confucius, the Chinese Philosopher*. Just as his translation of the Confucian Four Books attempted to prove the existence of a natural religion in ancient China, the Chinese texts used in the treatise "On Chinese Marriages" were cited to convince the Roman authorities of the indissolubility of Chinese marriages. And, just as with the translation of the Four Books, which was also closely intertwined with the Jesuits' admiring view of Chinese civilization, such positive assessments influenced Intorcetta's translation of passages from Chinese classics.[85]

Nothing, unfortunately, is known about the reception of Intorcetta's treatise by the Roman authorities. What is known, however, is that the final settlement of the issue by the Holy Office was comparably favorable to the Jesuits. Instead of making a clear decision, the theologians contented themselves with stating that the reasons for divorce listed in Confucian scriptures were "not impediments that [allow for] a dissolution of marriage"[86]—which was to merely say that they disapproved of the Confucian "seven conditions." Rome remained silent about the consequences of this statement for the validity of Chinese marriages. This strategy was consistent with a statement on the validity of Japanese marriages made in 1669, when the Holy Office had declared that "this matter should not be defined."[87]

THE JESUIT STRIVE AGAINST POLYGYNY

Divorce was the focus of the missionaries' discussions about the validity of Chinese marriages. It was not, however, a major issue in the mission field, since it did not represent an obstacle to conversion. That was contrasted with another set of Chinese marriage customs: polygyny. Since polygynous men could under no circumstances be admitted to baptism, the Jesuits were confronted with the difficult task of persuading their prospective converts to follow the Christian principle of "one husband, one wife" (*yi fu yi fu*). This was a delicate undertaking. The most ancient Chinese texts had already referred to the practice of polygyny, stating that even the sage kings, Yao and Shun, had been married to several women.[88] As a consequence, the Jesuits generally regarded polygyny as one of the greatest obstacles to the spread of Catholicism in China.[89]

What made the problem of polygyny especially acute for the Jesuits was its preponderance among the Chinese scholarly elite, for whom it was an important symbol of social status.[90] Only a few male members of the scholar-gentry considered baptism worth the dismissal of their concubines. Matteo Ricci therefore wrote, in 1605, that "if their polygamy, which is rather common among the important people of this country, had not prevented them [from converting], we would already have gained some rather illustrious people."[91] Indeed, annual letters dating from the first half of the seventeenth century often reported that scholars, and even imperial officials, became interested in Catholicism, but then delayed baptism out of concern for their concubines and their reputation, which would have been damaged if they had sent the women away.[92]

Many literati sympathizers of Catholicism who chose to retain their concubines, instead of receiving baptism, contented themselves with supporting the conversion of their wives—who, unlike polygynous men and their concubines, were usually admitted to baptism. A famous example was the Nanjing viceroy Tong Guoqi (d. 1685), whose wife was baptized Agatha and then became one of the seventeenth century's most important female supporters of Catholicism.[93] In a society whose members did not emphasize religious affiliation, but rather made use of the services of religious specialists according to changing spiritual needs, these men probably felt relaxed about sharing in Catholicism's spiritual benefits by way of loose association with the missionaries and via their wives' pious devotion.[94] It was, in fact, uncommon that a religious specialist claimed the right to interfere with his devotees' personal lives—requiring them, as missionaries did, to change their sexual habits.[95] That Chinese literati struggled to comply with this requirement is illustrated by the biography of the famous Catholic official Yang Tingyun. It reported how, when talking with a Catholic friend, Li Zhizao, Yang complained about the Jesuits' inflexibility: "The Western Fathers are really strange. I, with [my power] as censor, am serving them, so, why is it not possible [to receive baptism]? Can they not just allow me to have one concubine? It would not have been the case with Buddhist followers!"[96]

Those literati who decided to send their concubines away seem to have been few in number. Some literati agreed to renounce polygyny during the last years of their lives.[97] This practice corresponded with a traditional Chinese cultural pattern, according to which concubines were likely to be "evicted from home if a sudden upsurge of morality overwhelmed an aging clansman."[98] Those Chinese officials who were at the height of a prolific career, however, and whose conversion would have substantially increased Catholicism's public visibility and political influence, were only rarely ready to risk loss of social prestige through public conversion. Younger literati who, like Yang Tingyun, eventually decided to send their concubines away were likely to experience backlash in their milieu, especially if a concubine had borne them sons.[99] Along with social pressure, emotional ties further complicated the matter for prospective converts. Annual letters reported cases where men hesitated to send a concubine away because they loved her or where they took their repudiated concubine back as soon as their legitimate wife died.[100] Some of them changed their minds after having sent the women away and took them back after baptism. This was only accepted by the missionaries if there was a pressing reason. Such was the case with a Shanxi Catholic who took back his deathly ill concubine in order to nurse her in 1632.[101]

Besides hindering the conversion of influential sympathizers of Catholicism, the prohibition of polygyny posed problems for Catholic literati whose legal wives did not bear them children. Edifying stories recorded in annual letters show that childless Catholic literati were often exposed to considerable pressure by their family and friends if they refused to take a concubine. Many of them struggled for a long time with the "temptation" of polygyny, as the Jesuits usually called it.[102] Some, among them the famous Catholic literatus Wang Zheng (1571–1644), eventually bowed to the pressure and took a concubine.[103] In a moving autobiographical document, Wang recounted how he had been persuaded by his family to take a concubine after his sons had died of smallpox: "My wife and my daughters knelt down and entreated me, the brothers and nephews wept." After that, Wang could no more resist the "heterodox thought" (*xienian*) of taking a concubine, which led to his excommunication.[104]

The Jesuits' perception of polygyny as a major obstacle for their mission stimulated their collection of proto-ethnographic knowledge about it. They were especially interested in the difference between legal wives (*qi*) and concubines (*qie*), which was important for their evaluation of their prospective converts' marriages. Matteo Ricci and Diego de Pantoja had already noted how the social status of concubines was much lowlier than that of legal wives, and how it was more accurate to speak of buying a concubine than of marrying her.[105] After Ricci and Pantoja, it was, again, Alvaro Semedo who wrote an especially detailed account of the differences between the two. He explained that legitimate marriages were concluded by contract and celebrated with ceremonies. Concubine marriages, by contrast, "entailed neither the form nor the duties of a marriage" and were therefore "strictly speaking not a marriage."[106] It was easy for a man to dissolve such a union, and society tolerated repudiated concubines entering unions with different men. Semedo also noted that concubines were often sold by brokers, who had taught these girls to sing and play music to get higher prices for them. After they entered the household, they were treated differently than legitimate wives: "They eat in a separate apartment. They are under the authority of the legal wives and have to serve them like servants. Their children do not pay respect to them like they do to legal wives; neither do they call them 'mother.'"[107] Although concubines' children were obliged to observe mourning upon the death of the legal wife, they were not required to do so when their biological mother died. While Chinese law permitted concubine marriage only in the case of childlessness, Semedo admitted that this law was not respected by most rich people, who took "concubines and mistresses without any difficulty even if they [already] had children."[108]

The Jesuits developed different strategies for refuting polygyny in their Chinese publications, especially in their catechetical and moral writings. These publications usually advanced two arguments in favor of monogamy. They maintained, first, that monogamy was a godly ordained principle and held, second, that monogamous unions were more likely to produce heirs and were thus more in accordance with the Confucian precept of filiality.

The argument for monogamy as a godly ordained principle was first made in Diego Pantoja's moral treatise on the seven deadly sins, *The Seven Victories [over Sin]* (Qike), published in the early 1610s.[109] In this Christian moral book, Pantoja explained that monogamy was a principle universally followed in Western countries, with no exceptions made, not even for princes. Men were allowed to marry a legitimate wife, but not to marry concubines. This principle, Pantoja explained, was as old as the world itself. Pantoja admitted that the patriarchs of the Old Testament had practiced polygamy.[110] But, he explained, this did not diminish the importance of the principle of monogamy: "In the beginning, the multiplication of people was the most urgent matter, and therefore men joined themselves with several wives, so that life was created more quickly. Afterward, however, the Lord of Heaven expressly made the principle of one husband joining one wife the only orthodox rite of marriage."[111]

The Jesuits both made such arguments from Christian tradition and tried to meet Chinese objections against them. One of these objections was that polygyny was a remedy against heirlessness. Giulio Aleni claimed that this was not the case. In his *Questions and Answers about the West* (Xifang dawen, 1637), he explained: "Many children are born and bred in my native country by the grace and favor of God, the Creator. On the other hand, in countries where marriage takes place early and concubines are allowed, people are often without heirs."[112] Concubines were not, in the missionaries' view, a good solution for those desiring to beget an heir, as they cost considerable sums of money and caused domestic chaos and sexual depletion.[113] The pointlessness of taking concubines was even more evident because, as Francesco Brancati explained in a catechetical text published in the 1670s, childbirth depended on God's will, which could not be altered. This also meant that polygyny could never be excused as an act of filiality. Rather, it was an unfilial act toward one's most authoritative father, the Christian God.[114]

Persuading prospective converts of the lawfulness of monogamy was thus one challenge facing the Jesuits. Organizing those prospective converts' transition from polygyny to monogamy was another. In this regard, two questions were especially pressing. Missionaries had to decide, first, with which woman the monogamous union was to be concluded and then, second, what should happen with the women repudiated by their converts.

As an answer to the first question, the laws of the church required polygynous prospective converts to stay with their legal wives.[115] Because this solution was not always workable in practice, an extension of the Pauline Privilege made it possible for the missionaries to accept unions with a concubine if the latter agreed to conversion. However, the Jesuits soon noted that this was insufficient for solving the problem. The missionaries of Nanjing reported in 1602, for example, that a literatus aspiring for baptism, despite being widowed, turned down their offer of making his concubine his legal wife—probably due to her humble social background.[116] They remarked that "it is a dishonor in China to make a woman who had previously been a concubine a legal wife," something that prevented many literati from converting.[117] During the early 1610s, Manuel Dias the Elder addressed this problem in his "Information." He requested a dispensation from the Holy See allowing Catholic literati to treat their concubines according to the rites specific to them, instead of paying them the honors due to a legitimate wife. According to Dias, this was an acceptable solution: "The divine law does not prescribe that the women have to be treated with such or such exterior courtesy, but only that a man should only have one wife and keep her forever."[118] Of course, his compromise contradicted the Christian idea of conjugal equality upheld by the Catholic Church. The Holy Office granted the Jesuits in China an appropriate dispensation, nonetheless, during Nicolas Trigault's stay in Rome in 1615–16.[119]

As to what should happen with repudiated concubines, the missionaries quietly accepted various solutions found by their converts: to marry their concubines to someone else (probably often tantamount to selling the women), "to give them separate dwellings," or to send them back to their native families.[120] The Jesuits recognized, however, that all these practices were considered dishonorable by the literati class.[121] As a consequence, they started to consider solutions less offensive to the latter's sensitivities. Specifically, they pondered whether their converts could be granted permission to retain a concubine in their home when they took solemn vows of sexual abstinence. In 1613 Niccolò Longobardo wrote a detailed justification of this practice. He maintained that there was reason to believe that polygyny would gradually disappear with increasing numbers of converted literati if this concession were made to Chinese Catholics. If, however, the Roman authorities were not prepared to make the concession, Longobardo feared that there was no hope for the conversion of the Chinese scholarly elite.[122]

Longobardo's request did not lead to a formal solution of the problem. The superior handed over his commentary to the procurator of the China mission, Nicolas Trigault, who was ordered to obtain a corresponding dispensation from the Roman authorities.[123] As far as we know, however, the latter did not respond positively or negatively to the request. The Roman silence may have encouraged the Jesuits to occasionally allow their converts to retain their old concubines after formally vowing sexual abstinence. That, at least, is suggested by some accusations made by the mendicants in the late 1660s.[124]

The Jesuits' discussions of Chinese polygyny are multifaceted. It is striking, however, that they focused almost exclusively on how to regulate polygynous men's sexuality to make them conform to Catholic notions of marriage and, as a consequence, fulfill the preconditions for conversion.[125] Women's fate, indeed, was only of secondary importance for the Jesuits. If it was taken into account—as, for instance, during debates about whether repudiated concubines should be allowed to stay in their master's household—it merely figured as a factor that might, potentially, affect a male convert's social prestige. The Jesuits' lack of interest in the fate of concubines points, once again, to how they concentrated their evangelical efforts on the much-honored and politically influential male literati elite. That meant that not only were the missionaries not especially interested in evangelizing women. It also meant that they would accept a Confucian scholar's conversion even when it implied that a concubine would face an uncertain future.

* * *

The Jesuits' imposition of Catholic marriage norms on their Chinese converts affected women's lives in various ways. The Jesuits' attempt to strengthen the conjugal bond by purging Chinese marriage customs from the practices of divorce and polygyny strengthened legal wives' position within the family and affected the lives of concubines in a less predictable way. Their toleration of mixed marriages confronted Catholic wives of non-Catholic husbands with the sometimes difficult task of continuing Catholic devotion in non-Catholic environments and of resisting participation in "pagan" devotions. The Jesuits' envisioning of Chinese Catholic marriage had these effects without women being their primary focus. The Jesuits aimed at regulating male literati's sexuality in order to facilitate their conversion, rather than to make female converts.

None of that, however, meant that women were insignificant opponents or advocates of Chinese Catholicism or that they were merely passive recipients of Jesuit evangelization. On the contrary, Catholic women used the freedom granted them by the Jesuits' restraint toward the female sex for their own ends, as I show in the next chapters. They created their own social networks and forms of sociability, they lent material support to the Catholic enterprise in their own ways, and they established their own forms of piety and devotion.

5 PRAYING FOR PROGENY

Women and Catholic Spiritual Remedies

THE JESUITS' ABHORRENCE OF THE CHINESE PRACTICE OF KILLING or abandoning unwanted infants after birth has received considerable attention from historians, but it was not the only Chinese practice connected to maternity that was of relevance to Catholic missionary work.[1] Another area of contact amply documented by the Jesuits was women's devotions aiming at reproductive success. These devotions are of particular interest to researchers because they were practiced by Chinese women across religious boundaries.

To give birth to and to raise (preferably male) offspring in order to ensure the continuity of the patriline was considered the most important duty of wives in late imperial China.[2] Women were accepted as full members of their husband's families only after having produced or adopted a male heir. So important was the birthing of children that it was usual in non-Catholic families to address women as "so-and-so's mother" instead of using a personal name.[3] Yet biological reproduction in Ming and Qing China, just as in other premodern societies, was a potentially dangerous and largely uncontrollable process threatened by sterility, complications during delivery, and infant mortality.[4] Hence, it is not surprising that spiritual support for reproductive success figured prominently among Chinese women's religious needs.

Historians of China, and especially historians of gender, have unearthed a vast range of spiritual remedies against reproductive disorders to which women of the late imperial period resorted.[5] Young married women hoping to become pregnant (and sometimes also their mothers-in-law) worshipped child-granting deities, whose altars were exclusively frequented by female devotees and could be found in virtually any large Chinese temple of the late imperial period.[6] Pregnant women tried to avoid inauspicious influences of ghosts and planets by consulting household almanacs for the "positions and directions" by which these could be evaded.[7] Furthermore, rituals and religious specialists played an important role during childbirth.[8] Practices belonging to "ritual obstetrics," which had been an integral part of erudite gynecology (*fuke*) during the Song dynasty, were probably still used by various sorts of medical practitioners and healers even after they had dropped out of erudite medical discourse during the Ming era.[9] Also, deities and religious specialists were asked for help during difficult deliveries. As a case in point, the late Ming scholar Zhang Dai recorded that his mother, facing a particularly difficult delivery, sought the protection of the Buddhist bodhisattva Guanyin, chanting the "White-Robed Guanyin Sutra" throughout her strenuous labor.[10] In the same vein, literati of eighteenth-century Hangzhou reported that parturient women of the city sought the help of Buddhist monks from the Bamboo Grove Monastery (Zhulin Si), who were famous for their miraculously effective birth medicine.[11]

Although it is unclear how far the Jesuits observed the richness of Chinese devotions aiming at reproductive success, it is clear that they soon understood that, if Catholicism was to appeal to women, it had to prove efficacious as a "fertility religion." Building on their general medical expertise, often sought after by the Chinese population, they developed a specialization in reproductive disorders.[12] Testifying to this development is the large Portuguese-Chinese dictionary compiled by Michele Ruggieri and Matteo Ricci between 1583 and 1598, which contained a wide range of vocabulary relating to the reproductive cycle, including entries for *sterility* (*busheng erzi*), *conception* and *pregnancy* (*youyun*, *huaiyun*, *youtai*), and *midwife* (*shengpo*), as well as a dozen entries for terms connected to infancy and lactation.[13] Annual letters, furthermore, show that the missionaries provided Chinese women with different "spiritual remedies" against reproductive disorders—sacred images and blessed medals, but also prayers and invocations.

Chinese women used Catholic "spiritual remedies" in the hope of receiving immediate spiritual support (*lingying*) and deliverance from reproductive disorders.[14] What made this adoption of Catholic devotions possible in the Chinese context was the conspicuous convergence of Catholic and Chinese views on divine intervention.[15] Both Chinese and Catholic devotees commonly shared the opinion that efficacy was a defining feature of a meaningful religious practice and that deities, saints or religious specialists had to be able to respond to the requests of their devotees in an immediate, practical way. In particular, there was a striking likeness between the Chinese idea that rituals and objects could mediate the process of "beseeching" (*qiu*) divine powers for help and the Catholic idea that holy objects and practices (*sacramentalia*) had the power to immediately affect the course of a devotee's life.[16]

Furthermore, the acceptance of Christian remedies for reproductive disorders by Chinese protagonists was also facilitated by the prevailing medico-religious pluralism of late imperial China. Chinese people usually did not hesitate to combine medical and spiritual remedies of different traditions. Equally, it was not unusual to simultaneously invite several different ritual specialists in the event of a serious illness—a behavior that has been aptly described as "ritual polytropy."[17] As a case in point, in a passage of the seventeenth-century novel *The Plum in the Golden Vase*, Buddhists, Taoists, and shamans were simultaneously called to perform their rituals at a woman's sickbed, where they prayed together in a "democracy of extremity."[18] According to the logic of such efficacy-based religiosity, what mattered was whether a spiritual remedy helped—not whether it was part of one particular religious tradition.

The Chinese inclination toward "ritual polytropy" was a double-edged sword for the Jesuits. On the one hand, the missionaries often took advantage of it, trying to proselytize those who had merely wanted to use their spiritual services. The conversion story of a husband previously opposed to his wife's Christian faith, in Beijing in 1687, shows that this strategy was sometimes successful, not least due to the immense psychological stress that desperate husbands underwent, fearing for their wives' lives:

> [The man] had a Christian wife, and when she was in the pain of childbirth in November of 1687, a [Jesuit] Father was called in order to take her confession. When this was done, the Father sent for the husband and started to exhort him: "If your wife cannot give birth to this creature, it is because she would have to teach him the cult of the Demon, which is a greater infelicity than not to have been born. Therefore if you believe in the one God, the creator of heaven and earth, and if you have the firm determination to embrace his holy law, I assure you that the childbirth will go well."[19]

In this particular case, the missionary succeeded in converting the husband by saving the lives of his wife and unborn child during the difficult delivery. Other stories, however, show that the dangers of childbirth also caused Catholics to seek aid from non-Catholic religious experts. The Annual Letter of 1618, for instance, reports the story of a Catholic woman from a rich family in Nanxiong who gave birth to her son with the help of a Buddhist midwife. After the delivery, the woman requested baptism for her newborn while giving thanks to the Buddha. As might be expected from a narrative included in an annual letter, this story ended with divine punishment for the syncretic mother, her baby dying only some days after baptism.[20] However, it is reasonable to assume that there were just as many cases in which similar relapses into "idolatry" went without the divine punishment expected by the Jesuits. That these cases were not mentioned in the annual letters, which aimed at documenting the mission's success and God's active presence in the world, is not surprising.

Missionaries are, however, not the main protagonists of the following two case studies. These focus instead on Catholic saints and the sacred objects used for women's fertility devotions, asking how these saints were addressed and how sacred objects were used by Chinese women struggling with reproductive disorders.[21] Although a great variety of Catholic devotional objects were used for all kinds of disorders, I concentrate on two Catholic intercessors and their respective powerful objects that proved especially effective in two distinctive realms: the Virgin Mary, as a sought-after mediator of conception, and St. Ignatius, as the protector of women facing difficult births.

THE SON-GRANTING HOLY MOTHER

While staying in Zhaoqing in 1586, Matteo Ricci was surprised to note that the Virgin Mary appealed to Chinese women for an unexpected reason. He reported: "Many sterile women went to the house of a Christian to whom we had given an image of the Madonna. They worshipped her and asked her for sons, and they wanted to give her money."[22] This happened after the rumor had spread that the city prefect's wife had given birth to a son thanks to the help of the "Western monks."[23] It eventually prompted Ricci to replace the image of the Holy Virgin with an image of Jesus to prevent visitors from thinking that "the God worshipped by the Europeans was a woman."[24]

Ricci's was not the only record of women praying for sons before images of the Virgin Mary. Such stories are in fact a recurrent theme in the Jesuits' writings. As a case in point, Pedro Canevari reported during the 1640s that Catholic women in Fujian advised their non-Catholic friends to worship the Holy Virgin in order to conceive a child.[25] In the same vein, the Annual Letter of 1639 mentioned a female catechist of Hangzhou who promoted the worship of the Holy Virgin among childless women by turning their attention to the Infant Jesus placed in Mary's arms.[26] Chinese women's worship of the Virgin Mary was probably facilitated by the fact that her picture circulated widely in China. Jesuits displayed European paintings and statues in churches and residences, and Chinese Catholics painted and printed reproductions. These were passed on within local Catholic networks, sold at temple fairs and book markets, and, in one case, even reprinted in a wholly nonreligious book for art connoisseurs edited by a Beijing literatus, Cheng Dayue (figure 5.1).[27]

Several factors contributed to Chinese devotees' acceptance of the Holy Virgin's son-granting power. The main reason was probably the iconography used in the majority of her images, which showed her with the Infant Jesus in her arms and thus conspicuously resembling images of the "Son-Granting Guanyin" (Songzi Guanyin). This Buddhist bodhisattva was,

FIG. 5.1. Virgin Mary with Child. The Chinese woodblock print is a copy of a European copperplate engraving that reproduced a painting hanging in the cathedral of Seville. Printed in *Master Cheng's Ink Garden* (Chengshi moyuan) by Cheng Dayue, 1606. Courtesy of American Museum of Natural History Library, Image 100214595_1.

from the sixteenth century onward, frequently depicted as a lady clad in long garments holding an infant in her arms and was commonly worshipped by women thanks to her power of granting children to those who offered "obeisance and alms" (figure 5.2).[28]

By analogy to the child held by the Son-Granting Guanyin, Chinese devotees interpreted the infant held by the Holy Virgin as a sign of her son-granting power.[29] What facilitated this interpretation was the fact that Guanyin was merely one of a whole range of Chinese goddesses who were worshipped as child-granting deities, many of whom were, just like the Virgin Mary, addressed by their devotees with the honorary title "Holy Mother" (Shengmu).[30] Although source evidence does not suggest that Chinese women mistook the Virgin Mary for any particular Chinese goddess, it is reasonable to assume that some of them perceived her as one of the numerous child-granting deities populating the large Chinese pantheon. That the boundaries the Chinese devotees drew between the Christian Virgin and Chinese deities were less clear than those of the missionaries is also suggested by an episode recorded by Niccolò Longobardo in 1598. He

FIG. 5.2. Statuette of the Son-Granting Guanyin (Songzi Guanyin). Unpainted porcelain, Dehua, second half of the seventeenth century. © Porzellansammlung, Staatliche Kunstsammlungen Dresden. Photograph: Werner Lieberknecht, Dresden, 2008.

narrated how the inhabitants of Shaozhou conferred the honorary title "Our Lady, the Holy Mother" (Shengmu Niangniang) on the Holy Mother, a common honorary title for many Chinese female deities, but one not usually used by missionaries to name the Christian Mother of God.[31]

The foregoing account suggests that the Holy Virgin was appropriated as a son-granting deity by Chinese women through a spontaneous process of cultural hybridization, rather than through a deliberate transfer by the Jesuits. There is some evidence, however, that the latter, despite their general rejection of popular Buddhism, actively supported Mary's metamorphosis into some form of Christian Guanyin. Alfonso Vagnone's *Biography of the Holy Mother* (Shengmu xingshi, 1631), in particular, contained a ten-page-long subchapter titled "The Holy Mother Helps Those Who Give Birth" (Shengmu hu shengchanzhe).[32] The main aim of the subchapter was to prove the Holy Mother's "efficacy" (*ling*) and "tremendous power" (*dali*) of granting sons in cases of infertility. Four of its six miracle tales were dedicated to this subject, the other two relating to an intercession during a difficult delivery and the resurrection of a stillborn infant.[33] Vagnone's insistence on the Virgin Mary's child-granting power is particularly surprising in view of how this facet of Marian devotion, even if it was present in medieval European miracle tales, was of no particular importance in seventeenth-century European Marian devotion. This suggests that, by emphasizing it, Vagnone was responding to a Chinese religious demand, rather than transporting European devotional practices to China.[34]

Despite adapting the Virgin Mary to the Chinese religious landscape, Vagnone nevertheless ensured that she remained recognizably part of the Christian tradition. He did so by linking Mary's child-granting quality with her own maternity, a fact intrinsically connected with a key element of the Christian doctrine: the incarnation and birth of Jesus Christ. According to Vagnone, "The grace by which the Lord of Heaven descended to Earth is now entrusted to the Holy Mother, who bestows it to women who are pregnant."[35] Furthermore, Vagnone mentioned that relics of the Nativity, such as the Infant Jesus's swaddling clothes in Milan, could be used by "whoever met with difficulties during childbearing."[36] By linking Mary's son-granting power to her own miraculous pregnancy and delivery, Vagnone made sure that the Christian doctrine was made known to son-seeking women who sought her divine intercession. Simultaneously, he also opened up possibilities for an alternative reading of João da Rocha's *Rules for Reciting the Rosary* (Song nianzhu guicheng, 1619), which prominently displayed pictures of the Annunciation, Visitation, and Nativity.

These pictures, which were modeled upon the engravings published in Jerónimo Nadal's *Images of the Story of the Gospel* (Evangelicae Historiae Imagines, 1593), were strongly adapted to Chinese visual conventions, with the Annunciation showing a fully Sinified Mary praying in a Chinese studio when conceiving her son by mediation of the Holy Spirit (figure 5.3).[37] This picture forcefully invoked Mary's motherhood for the minds of Chinese female devotees, and it probably also reminded them of the Holy Virgin's child-granting powers, on which they could rely.

Vagnone's *Biography of the Holy Mother* thus points to the Jesuits' active participation in the transformation of the Holy Mother into a Chinese son-granting deity. But it also tells about the devotions that Jesuits recommended to Chinese son-seeking women. Vagnone advised them to address the Holy Mother in regular prayer. He explained that people had their wishes for heirs granted after they "piously revered the Holy Mother at regular times" or after they "prayed to the Lord of Heaven and the Holy Mother every day and asked them to compassionately grant them [a son]."

FIG. 5.3. Annunciation scene showing Mary praying in a Chinese elite woman's studio. A sewing basket is placed behind her and to her left. Woodblock print from João da Rocha's *Rules for Reciting the Rosary* (1619). Digital image courtesy of Getty's Open Content Program.

Furthermore, Vagnone promoted the taking of vows as an effective means for obtaining the Holy Mother's help (a concept known equally to European Tridentine and Chinese religious cultures).[38] All these suggestions fitted well with traditional Chinese fertility devotions, where different forms of invocation and the taking of vows played a predominant role.[39]

Although it is probable that the Virgin Mary's female gender contributed to her acceptance as a child-granting deity, acting as the divine protector of reproducing women was not the prerogative of female "deities."[40] Indeed, the Jesuits' annual letters portray divine protection of parturient women as the domain of a male saint, St. Ignatius of Loyola. In what follows I investigate the ascent of St. Ignatius as a protector of birthing women in China and compare Ignatian devotions connected with childbirth to Marian devotions connected with conception.

POWERFUL IMAGES ON LABORING BODIES

St. Ignatius's help for parturient women was usually mediated through powerful objects (*sacramentalia*), especially names (*nomina*) and images (*imagines*).[41] These were mostly strips of paper printed with the saint's name or picture and consecrated by a priest.[42] Medals made of more lasting materials, such as metal or wood, are also mentioned by the sources, and, in some rare cases involving court Jesuits, precious relics of St. Ignatius were also used.[43] The sacramentals and relics were usually fixed on a string and hung around the neck of parturient women, who were encouraged to pray wholeheartedly to the saint and trust in his power. Intercessions of St. Ignatius during difficult delivery were recorded in numerous annual letters.[44] Furthermore, single annual letters sometimes recorded a great number of cases of successful interventions by St. Ignatius. The Annual Letter of 1633 alone, for instance, reports three such successful intercessions during three cases of difficult childbirth in Shanxi, in addition to an unspecified number of successful intercessions in Fujian.[45] In view of this, it is reasonable to suggest that, while other powerful objects of the Catholic tradition (consecrated candles, branches, holy water, Agnus Dei, and the image of the Savior) were also occasionally used during difficult childbirths, the Ignatian sacramentals were by far the most popular objects for this purpose.[46]

In contrast to the worship of the Virgin Mary as a fertility deity, the use of Ignatian sacramentals as birth amulets was not a singular development in Chinese Catholicism, but had its origin in Europe. From the early years of the seventeenth century, European Jesuits had started to propagate their patron saint as a powerful intermediary in the event of difficult deliveries.[47] Just like the missionaries in China, the European Jesuits advised parturient women to wear an amulet of the saint around their neck and to address the saint in fervent prayer. A highly developed Ignatian devotion practiced by pregnant women evolved in many regions of seventeenth-century Europe. Parturient women made use of a variety of sacramentals such as Ignatian signatures, girdles, and images, and pregnant women drank "water of St. Ignatius" previously blessed by a priest.[48] By propagating their founding father as a protector of parturient women, the Jesuits in China therefore were not reacting to a preexisting Chinese cult but rather were expanding the geographical scope of an originally European Catholic devotion.

That the latter found broad acceptance among Chinese women was apparently connected with the way Catholic sacramentals worked. Just like many powerful objects used by devotees of Chinese popular religion, sacramentals were freely accessible to believers and could be used without priestly assistance.[49] They could be easily integrated into late imperial folk medical culture, in which people customarily had recourse to relics and other powerful objects that provided spiritual assistance against illness, misfortune, or natural hazards.[50] In particular, the *nomina* and *imagines* distributed by the Jesuits to parturient women conspicuously resembled indigenous written charms (*fu*), which were esoteric characters inscribed on paper and pasted on a wall of the birth chamber or swallowed by the birthing mother.[51] It is probable that the Jesuits aimed at replacing such "idolatrous" practices when introducing Ignatian sacramentals in China, just as their brethren tried to replace non-Christian, "magical" birth amulets with Catholic sacramentals in contemporary Europe.[52] They not only testify to the dissemination of post-Tridentine religious culture on a global scale but also demonstrate the high capacity of Chinese popular religion to integrate novel practices into its "tool kit."[53]

How did the practice of using Ignatian sacramentals during difficult deliveries spread across Chinese Catholic networks? Unlike the Virgin Mary, St. Ignatius was not particularly vigorously promoted as a protector of reproducing women by the Jesuits' writings. In the *Biography of St. Ignatius* (Sheng Yinajue zhuan, 1629) Alfonso Vagnone made only brief reference to the saint's efficacy in helping "women who meet with difficult delivery" (*nü zao chan nan*) and did not use miracle stories to help illustrate this power.[54] This suggests that, rather than the written record, oral transmission played a major role in the spread of Ignatian sacramentals.

Furthermore, since childbirth was virtually an exclusively female domain in late imperial China, it is reasonable to suggest that word of St. Ignatius's protecting power spread mainly through female networks.[55]

The way in which the use of Ignatian sacramentals spread within female networks by word of mouth is aptly illustrated by a story reported in the Annual Letter of 1619. It recounts how a Catholic woman in Hangzhou helped her non-Catholic neighbor during a dangerous delivery. When she learned that her neighbor had been in heavy labor for several days and her life was in danger, she carried the image of St. Ignatius to this neighbor's home. The Catholic woman had herself previously experienced the power of the image during childbirth, and she therefore knew how to put it to use. After entering the birth chamber, she first readjusted the room's furnishings, removing the pictures of non-Christian deities. She then helped her neighbor to affix the image on her laboring body. When everything was in place, the Catholic woman started to invoke the names of Jesus, Mary, and St. Ignatius. After a short while, her neighbor suddenly delivered her baby. Thanks to the Ignatian sacramental, the story concludes, "the same person who had previously been cruelly tormented and had seen her death approaching rose from her bed after three days and took up her work."[56] The story of the Hangzhou birth miracle shows how women, both relatives and neighbors, shared their best practices with one another during childbirth, without paying much attention to religious affiliation. That it was included in an annual letter suggests that the Jesuits approved of this practice—because, certainly, they hoped that the use of Catholic objects by non-Catholics might lead them to convert.[57]

* * *

A focus on reproducing women's appropriation of efficacy-based Catholic religiosity shows that Chinese female devotees, far from perceiving Catholicism as an unchangeable, monolithic block, adopted isolated Catholic practices according to their specific individual needs. By adapting these practices to the Chinese cultural context, they divested them of their confessional character and transformed them so that they functioned according to the logics of Chinese efficacy-based religiosity.

Catholic sacramentals responded well to the needs of Chinese female devotees, for several reasons. They could be revered individually, without the assistance of a religious specialist, either in a church or at home, and they circulated freely beyond the threshold of the inner quarters. They could attain multiple meanings in the course of this circulation and therefore could be adapted well to different needs and into different belief contexts. The sacramentals used by son-seeking and pregnant women were linked to the Chinese religious landscape and to post-Tridentine Catholic religiosity in highly variable ways. While the worship of the Virgin Mary by son-seeking women was a development specific to the Sino-Western cultural encounter, the use of Ignatian sacramentals during delivery was tightly connected with a post-Tridentine cult promoted by the Jesuits in Europe. The promotion of the respective cults relied, furthermore, on different media. While the Jesuits actively supported the transformation of the Virgin Mary into a child-granting deity in their *Biography of the Holy Mother*, written text apparently played a less important role in the spread of Ignatian sacramentals.

Individually practiced, efficacy-based religiosity was, of course, not the only modality by which Chinese devotees made use of Catholic religious practices. To the contrary, many women also clearly identified themselves as Christians and had higher spiritual aspirations than occasional recourse to the Catholic spiritual remedies that were on offer in the vast Chinese religious market. For these women's devotional lives, Catholic congregations—groups with a certain degree of institutionalization and a comparably clear definition of confessional boundaries—were usually the focal point.

6 DOMESTIC COMMUNITIES

Women's Congregations and Communal Piety

CHINESE CATHOLIC COMMUNITIES WERE CONCEPTUALIZED BY missionaries and Chinese Catholics in different ways. While missionaries generally used the term *christianitas* to designate the totality of Catholics living in a certain place (a notion inspired by the concept of the post-Tridentine parish), Chinese Catholics usually perceived of the religious congregation (*hui*) as their ritual community.[1] Congregations aimed at organizing and nurturing people's communal lay piety, especially in the missionaries' absence. They were usually subjected to statutes (*huigui*), in which their spiritual father determined terms of admission, internal organization, and devotional routine.[2] Many of them were modeled upon the Jesuits' Marian congregations in Europe.[3] Although congregations could vary considerably in scale—some resembled European sodalities, whereas others seem to have been rather open devotional groups that were used by the missionaries "to organize and administer the larger group of people in the area"[4]—congregations were, generally speaking, highly localized bodies. Several congregations could be found in larger cities, where the Catholics of different neighborhoods organized their own devotional groups. This "fragmented system of church organization" had the advantage of diminishing the visibility of Catholic communal worship while granting all Catholics frequent access to communal devotion.[5] Given the congregations' preeminence as "communities of effective rituals," the totality of Catholics living in a certain place hardly ever assembled as a group.[6] Although well-instructed Chinese Catholics were probably aware that their congregation was part of a larger religious institution, their community of worship was usually a strictly local, and often rather small, religious congregation.

Introducing a gender perspective into research on Chinese Catholic communities leads us to the important insight that, as well as being heavily localized organizations, these communities were also strictly homosocial.

Although connections between men's and women's congregations existed—missionaries reported that men and women closely watched each other's pious activities and often entered into "holy competition" with each other[7]—Catholic men and women only rarely met jointly for religious worship, but they engaged in separate communal pious activities.

Which Chinese models influenced the organization of Catholic women's congregations? Which devotions did these groups practice, and who were the women responsible for their organization? And, finally, what role did church-based, priestly rituals play for their devotional lives?

AN UNCANNY LIKENESS: BUDDHIST AND CATHOLIC WOMEN'S CONGREGATIONS

Chinese models were important for the great success of the Jesuits' introduction of congregations in China, as they were embedded into a rich landscape of Chinese common-interest groups ranging from erudite societies attached to semiprivate academies (*shuyuan*) to different kinds of "cultural groups" (*wenshe*) dedicated to the arts and from "societies for sharing pleasure" (*tonglehui*) to "benevolent societies" (*tongshanhui*) created for the purpose of helping the poor.[8] However, it is noteworthy that all these associations, with the exception of a few poetry clubs frequented or formed by gentry women, were a predominantly male domain.[9] Therefore, unlike Chinese Catholic men's congregations, which were often inspired by the model of non-Catholic charitable societies, women's congregations probably did not draw inspiration from these common-interest groups.[10] Rather, they likely used non-Catholic religious associations, the only associations commonly created and frequented by women, as models for their congregations.

Lay Buddhist congregations for women emerged in particularly great numbers during the Buddhist renewal in the late Ming period.[11] Women gathered in Buddhist "societies for reciting the Buddha's name" (*nianfo hui*), organized "sutra chanting societies" (*songjing hui*), and established groups for the purpose of receiving the teachings of local nuns and monks. Still highly popular among middle-aged women in China today, these groups were not usually characterized by a strict confessional identity, but were organizations that provided the especially devout with opportunities for communal worship and spiritual sustenance.[12] Simultaneously, these groups often organized temple visits and pilgrimages, granting women an exceptional degree of extra-domestic autonomy and opportunities for social amusement.[13]

Chinese women's penchant for lay Buddhist practices was noticed by the Jesuits, who perceived of Buddhism as a powerful rival in the Chinese market of religion.[14] They repeatedly mentioned in their writings that women converting to Catholicism had previously been Buddhist followers. As a case in point, Manuel Dias the Younger remarked in 1628 that a woman who had received baptism in the city of Ningbo had previously been a devotee "of the idol that they call Guanyin pusa," and João Monteiro mentioned the conversion of a woman who had previously worshipped the Amida Buddha.[15] The missionaries' writings also contain numerous references to Chinese women's penchant for lay Buddhist practices. Missionaries complained about women's inclination toward vegetarian fasts (a practice often inspired by the Buddhist precept of non-killing), and they commented on Chinese women's love for reciting the Buddha's name (*nianfo*).[16] They explained that many Chinese women made close contact with monks and were so heavily involved with "paganism" (*grandes pagodentas*) that it was difficult to win them to Christianity even if their husbands and sons had already converted.[17] They commented disapprovingly, furthermore, on women's membership in lay Buddhist associations.[18] Unfortunately, they do not describe the latter's organization in detail, but merely mention their regular meetings and the vegetarian diet observed by their members.

Although the Jesuits harbored resentment toward Chinese women's involvement with Buddhism, they nevertheless profited from it in curious ways. This is shown by the fact that women's "congregations of idols" occasionally converted to Catholicism as groups. Several examples of this noteworthy phenomenon are recorded in annual letters. The Annual Letter of 1642, for instance, narrates how a Buddhist congregation in Huai'an converted to Catholicism.[19] It had started with the conversion of a noble lady of the city, who had been the founder and head of the "pagan" women's congregation, which was dedicated to the worship of one certain "idol." The woman, who was christened Monica, wished to "turn away from the idols and to direct toward Christ those spirits whom she herself had induced to join the impious congregation."[20]

When the congregation assembled in a temple to offer sacrifices to their deity, Monica joined the group and tried to persuade them to become Christians. When they did not listen to her, she wholeheartedly asked God to reveal to them the diabolic nature of their cult. Her prayers were heard, for "they had an oven full of ember in which they threw incense and slips of paper with superstitious vows and prayers written on them. . . . However, [the slips] did not catch fire, and [the incense] did not emit any fragrance. Rather, everything remained uncorrupted by the fire. In the view of this miracle, the women stood in great stupefaction." When Monica took advantage of the situation and again enjoined them to abdicate the "cult of the demons," the women were finally convinced and wanted to embrace Catholicism. Monica thereupon "acted as their catechist, instructed them in the mysteries of the faith, and imbued them with the notice of the divine matters."[21] The women were baptized during the Italian Jesuit Francesco Sambiasi's next stay in Huai'an, and Monica became the spiritual leader of the group, which was formalized using a Catholic congregational rule and put under the protection of the Holy Virgin. Similar events were recorded by missionaries in Hangzhou (1645) and Xi'an (1647).[22] In the latter case, the newly converted women redirected their alms, which were previously collected for the purpose of sustaining a monk, toward poor Catholics and the church.[23]

Although the transformation from Buddhist to Catholic women's congregations remained a rather marginal phenomenon that gained momentum only during the crisis-ridden years preceding and following the fall of the Ming dynasty, it nevertheless points to curious "elective affinities" between Buddhist and Catholic congregations.[24] Indeed, a comparison of the two types of organizations shows that some conspicuous similarities existed between them. They were both led by female lay leaders, and their activities consisted mainly of regular meetings during which the group engaged in common prayer, pious discussion, and simple ritual acts.[25] Unlike the domestic meetings of Catholic women, Buddhist women's congregational meetings were not necessarily held in private houses, but could also take place in temples.[26] The similarities, however, probably prompted Chinese women to regard the difference between Catholic and Buddhist congregations as a "difference of degree rather than kind."[27] That the Jesuits agreed on transforming congregations from Buddhist into Catholic organizations without altering their internal structure suggests that they found these similarities useful rather than troubling.

LAY DEVOTIONS AND FEMALE RELIGIOUS LEADERSHIP

Unlike for men, no statutes of women's congregations have come down to us. We therefore have to resort to the Jesuits' annual letters to reconstruct these congregations' organizational and devotional patterns. These sources reveal that women's congregations were generally of a domestic nature.

They usually assembled in "particular" (i.e., residential) houses for regular gatherings, often in the absence of a priest.[28] Yet annual letters show that most women's congregations were not purely "domestic congregations" in the sense of consisting only of the members of one single household. Rather, although a single congregational group usually had a fixed meeting place in one particular house oratory, most of them were frequented by women of several different households, thus forming what might be called an "extended domestic congregation."

First mentioned by the Jesuits in the 1600s, extended domestic congregations seem to have gained special momentum during the 1630s, when conversions to Catholicism increased considerably.[29] The Annual Letter of 1692 testifies to how they remained important throughout the seventeenth century, explaining that the Catholic women of Beijing were still organized in congregations led by "women who invite[d] their female relatives and neighbors" for joint worship in their homes.[30] Women's extended domestic congregations were probably a predominantly urban phenomenon, gender segregation being somewhat less insisted upon in rural China, where Catholic men and women sometimes also assembled in one large mixed congregation.[31]

Extended domestic congregations were usually headed by the senior lady of the hosting family.[32] These congregational leaders were referred to in the missionaries' writings in Latin as *superiorae* and in Portuguese as *majordomos*; their Chinese form of address was probably *huizhang* ("heads of the group," a term used for male congregational leaders).[33] According to the Annual Letter of 1607, they were in charge of organizing the congregation's meetings, convoking its members for sermons and religious instruction. Furthermore, they oversaw the admission of new members, collecting and destroying the latter's "idols"—that is, non-Catholic images, statues, and devotional objects—upon their entry into the group.[34] They were also responsible for the maintenance of the oratory, "just like sacristans," as Matteo Ricci noted in his diary.[35] Finally, later annual letters contain evidence that congregational leaders figured as a link between the missionary and the female Christian flock, arranging meetings with the priests where women received the sacraments.[36]

Annual letters contended that the heads of women's congregations—preferably middle-aged and elderly women, whose religious activities were broadly accepted in late imperial China—were usually of noble origin.[37] This claim is supported by the fact that their house oratories had to be spacious enough to host comparably large groups of women and that congregational leaders were often singled out for their generous charity toward poor Catholics.[38] Source evidence shows, however, that the female leaders of extended domestic congregations were usually not members of the upper echelon of the literati elite. Such women preferred to gather in strictly domestic congregations, rather than in general congregations that admitted women of other families to meetings (see chapter 7). It is therefore probable that most female leaders of women's extended domestic congregations were members of literati families who had never entered the ranks of the office-holding gentry because their male members had failed to earn a degree in imperial examinations. This assumption is supported by the fact that the milieu of local intellectual and community leaders was a group that responded especially well to the Jesuits' evangelization.[39]

While congregational leaders were generally members of wealthy families, the social composition of congregations seems to have varied. Some female congregational leaders—especially, it is likely, those of comparably high social standing—attached great importance to the social homogeneity of their groups of devotees and invited only women of the same social standing to their meetings.[40] In other cases, however, female congregational leaders also invited Catholic women of lesser social standing to join their congregation, some even admitting women from the surrounding villages to their gatherings.[41] These congregations were usually referred to in annual letters as "universal congregations."[42]

Although women's congregations also involved pious activities such as penance and charity to the sick, the dying, and the poor, congregational meetings were organized mainly for the purpose of joint prayer. During regular prayer sessions, women joined in chanting the litanies and other prayers recorded in the Chinese prayer books of the Jesuits, a preferred prayer of many women's congregations being the Rosary.[43] The missionaries often praised women for the great zeal with which they attended these meetings. They suggested that women were in many places more fervent participants in congregations than men were.[44] Although statistical data supporting this statement are lacking, it fits well with the "division of religious labor" in late imperial Chinese society, which saw women as responsible for most religious activities, with men primarily responsible only for infrequent, larger community rituals.[45]

The Annual Letter of 1634 includes a description of the weekly celebration of the "Day of the Lord" by a women's congregation in Xi'an, vividly recording the solemnity with which women's congregations usually conducted their prayer meetings. As recounted in the letter: "[The women] meet every Sunday in a beautiful hall and erect an altar, on which they place the images of the Lord and the Virgin [adorned] with many candles and incense, and they rival each other with their donations with which they pay the expenses."[46] Images, candles, and incense assimilated the sensory religious experience of these meetings to rituals held in Catholic churches and Chinese temples, which both had similar appeal.[47]

The meetings allowed the devout to worship together, but they also provided opportunities for non-Catholics to become acquainted with the "teachings of the Lord of Heaven." Several sources mention that non-Catholic relatives and friends were actively invited to attend the congregations to incite their interest in Catholicism. This strategy seems to have been rather successful. Annual letters reported that many women sought baptism after obtaining religious instruction in a congregation, without ever having met a priest prior to conversion.[48] In addition to non-Catholic friends, small children were also brought along to congregational meetings by their mothers, aunts, or grandmothers. Since this presence ensured the intergenerational transmission of Catholic knowledge, missionaries generally approved of this practice.[49]

While attendance at congregational meetings constituted the main obligation for members of a Chinese Catholic women's congregation, missionaries also tried to encourage fervor in everyday life. For this purpose, they created a second group of lay leaders: female catechists (probably *jiaozhang* in Chinese).[50] Unlike the sedentary congregational leaders, catechists were usually itinerant. They saw the congregation's members for religious instruction during visits to their homes, where they propagated the "teachings of the Lord of Heaven" among Catholic and non-Catholic women.[51] Some of them became highly influential local religious leaders. Martino Martini mentioned in the Annual Letter of 1644 that the women of Changzhou were instructed by a certain catechist named Agatha: "[She] may rightly be called the apostle of this place, because all women are instructed by her and obey her orders. They continually invite her to visit their houses in order to talk about God and to perform their devotions."[52] In the absence of any source references, it is unclear whether (and rather improbable that) female catechists were, like their male counterparts, organized in special congregations for catechists.[53] We know, however, that at least some of them received remuneration for their work—either from the missionaries or from influential local Catholics, such as the eminent gentry lady Candida

Xu.[54] Furthermore, source evidence suggests that an increasingly dense network of catechists evolved during the seventeenth century. The Annual Letter of 1697 thus reported that the missionaries in Beijing assigned a catechist to each women's congregation, entrusting them with the religious instruction of both Catholics and non-Catholics and expecting them to report back about their work.[55]

Despite increasingly close links between catechists and missionaries, female catechists did not always correspond to the image of European Catholic lay catechists such as the semireligious *dévotes*, who dominated women's religious instruction in contemporary France. While the latter were usually characterized by an elevated social standing and a strong interiorization of Tridentine religiosity, the itinerant nature of Chinese catechists' work entailed that most of them were of comparably humble social background.[56] Some of them even seem to have been influenced by indigenous religious role models such as shamanesses (*wu*) or spirit mediums (*tongji*).[57] This is illustrated by the story of Martha, a woman who worked as a catechist in the surroundings of Xi'an during the late 1630s. According to the Annual Letter of 1638, Martha had been cruelly tormented by "demons" for a long time before her husband summoned the Jesuits in 1638. The demons had been taking possession of the woman with great frequency, speaking through her and making her lose her mental faculties. After a two-week exorcism administered by the Jesuits, Martha was freed from thirty-two demons and became a fervent Christian. As a catechist, she converted some dozen people from her village. Her success was probably connected to the fact that her ties to the spiritual world were not severed after conversion. According to the annual letters, several miracles happened in Martha's proximity, such as holy signs appearing on her garments and idolatrous statues spontaneously shattering into pieces in her presence.[58]

We know that in eighteenth-century Fujian a great number of different offices were held by lay people from Catholic communities administered by Spanish Dominican friars. Lay people acted not only as congregational leaders and catechists but also as sacristans (*tangzhu*), heads of sacristans (*zongtang[zhu]*), and prayer leaders (*niantou*).[59] In view of the differentiated organizational structure of the Fujian communities, it is reasonable to assume that the two lay offices described above were only a part of a more intricate lay hierarchy whose complete structure the missionaries do not describe in detail. Nevertheless, the Jesuits' reports point to the preeminent importance of female lay leaders for the functioning of women's congregations' devotional activities.

PRIESTLY RITUALS AS INSTANCES OF INTENSE RELIGIOUS EXPERIENCE

What was the place of church-based, priestly rituals in the devotional routine of women's congregations? In view of the importance of lay leadership and lay devotions for the congregations, it is not surprising that church visits and the reception of sacraments they involved were not part of congregations' day-to-day activities. The frequency with which church visits were organized varied, however, from place to place. While some urban women's congregations (such as those of Canton during the 1690s) received the sacraments every other week, congregations in small towns or cities without a resident missionary met priests only every few months or even less frequently.[60] Whenever possible, missionaries invited women's congregations to major church festivals. As a consequence, these occasions attracted the greatest number of women to churches. Francesco Brancati explained in 1658 that virtually all Catholic women, even villagers, visited the women's church of Shanghai during Advent and Lent, and Inácio da Costa noted in 1647 that some hundred Catholic women usually visited the church in Xi'an on Christmas to hear Mass and adore the Infant Jesus.[61] To prevent crowds of women from assembling in church, missionaries invited different congregations on different days before and after the feast day. Special days for church visits were also assigned to village women coming from the surrounding countryside.[62] Women occasionally also celebrated Chinese feast days in church. These festivals, "on which the heathen use[d] to go to their temples," probably included the Lantern Festival (Yuanxiao Jie), celebrated fifteen days after the Chinese New Year, and the Tomb Sweeping Festival (Qingming Jie), which took place fifteen days after the spring equinox.[63] At least in the later years of the seventeenth century, the organization of church visits usually fell to the female lay leaders of the congregation, who functioned as links between the congregation and the missionary. This is illustrated by an annual letter dating from the early 1690s. It related how the women's congregations of Beijing usually gathered in private houses for lay-led prayer and visited the women's church for the administration of sacraments on a few days throughout the year, the exact dates communicated to their *majordomo*.[64]

That Catholic women were eager to receive the sacraments at least on major feast days shows that these church-based rituals, although only rarely administered, helped define their Catholic identity nevertheless. Edifying stories recorded by the Jesuits support this assumption. The Annual Letter of 1694, for instance, contains the story of a Catholic commoner woman who was married to a non-Catholic husband and who went to great lengths to receive the sacraments despite her husband's prohibitions.[65] Philippe Couplet also noted that Candida Xu, the eminent granddaughter of the Catholic scholar-official Xu Guangqi, never missed an occasion to receive the sacraments. Not even the harshest weather conditions would persuade her to stay at home.[66] Although such stories tended to be strongly idealized, they nevertheless suggest that church-based priestly rituals might be best understood as comparably rare but highly meaningful moments of intense religious experience, moments cherished by devout Catholic women.

For most Catholic women, their congregation's communal church visits were the only occasions on which they would meet a missionary. However, we should not think of these gatherings as occasions for intimate contact between priests and female devotees. Missionaries were advised to pay careful attention to the maintenance of decorum. In some places, they kept their faces constantly turned toward the altar, even during the sermon.[67] During confession, meanwhile, a curtain or folding screen would separate the priest from the female penitent.[68] This practice anticipated the use of the confessional, still in its initial phase in many places in seventeenth-century Europe.[69]

While the administration of sacraments was an important object of theological debate between the Jesuits and the Roman Curia (see chapter 3), not much is known about Chinese Catholic women's attitudes toward the sacraments. What can be said, however, is that of all those sacraments administered to Catholics on a regular basis, confession played an outstanding role.[70] The Jesuits repeatedly referred to the great numbers of women's confessions, easily outnumbering men's confessions.[71] The French Jesuit Louis Le Comte, who stayed in China from 1688 to 1691, held that Chinese Catholic women "would have been happy to confess every day if they had had the liberty to do so." According to Le Comte, Chinese women often confessed their sins in painstaking detail. He added that he did not know "whether this [was] because of their tender conscience, their esteem for the sacrament, or for another reason."[72] There is evidence that Catholic women perceived confession as the ritual distinguishing their ritual communities from other, non-Catholic ones. In 1662, for example, Prospero Intorcetta reported that a Catholic woman in Jianchang joined a Buddhist congregation when her husband prohibited her from receiving confession in church. The woman returned to the Catholic community only when her husband died, enabling her to once again receive the sacrament of confession on a regular basis.[73]

In Chinese Catholicism, attachment to confession was not a specifically female phenomenon. As pointed out by the authors of a recent volume on Chinese Catholic confessions, the sacrament of penance can be regarded as the most important ritual of Chinese Catholicism as a whole.[74] Liturgical as well as doctrinal reasons account for this fact. From a liturgical viewpoint, confession was, in contrast to the more exclusive sacrament of the Eucharist, accessible to all baptized Catholics.[75] It was, indeed, a precondition for admission to it, further enhancing its importance. From a doctrinal viewpoint, the special attention that Chinese Catholics paid to the concept of divine retribution accounts for the central importance they attached to confession. Chinese Catholic writings point to the centrality of the idea of an omnipotent Lord of Heaven who rewards and punishes all souls. In combination with a strong awareness of sin, this monotheistic belief resulted in a special position for the ritual of "confession-and-absolution" (*gaojie*).[76] This was further enhanced by a cultural context in which self-examination played an outstanding role and in which people were deeply aware of men's inclination to evil.[77]

What were the reasons for women's extraordinarily strong inclination toward confession, surpassing, according to the missionaries, even men's love for this ritual? It is probable that their traditionally strong engagement with individual piety, and more specifically their special penchant for practices of spiritual purification, accounts for this preference.[78] Since Chinese women were traditionally more deeply involved in Buddhist pious practices than men were, they were also more concerned with the Buddhist concept of karmic retribution. This held that evil deeds (*zuiye*) invariably affected a person's rebirth in a negative way, while meritorious deeds had positive effects on rebirth.[79] Chinese women were also keen practitioners of Taoist "inner alchemy" (*neidan*), which aimed at spiritual purification in order to attain immortality.[80] Female adepts of Buddhist and Taoist practices were especially concerned about cleansing themselves from the polluting effects of childbearing, which, according to popular Buddhist belief, could result in a woman's rebirth in an abominable blood-pond hell.[81]

That many women converting to Catholicism had previously incorporated non-Catholic concepts of pollution and divine retribution into their personal beliefs is made clear by numerous sources written by the Jesuits. The innumerable cases of women practicing vegetarianism, either as part of a quest for Taoist immortality or for Buddhist moral perfection, have already been mentioned above. The missionaries also described women who felt utterly relieved when hearing that Catholics rejected karmic retribution. The Annual Letter of 1642, for instance, noted that a woman converted as soon as she heard that Catholics did not believe in transmigration.[82] In 1614, in the same vein, Francesco Sambiasi narrated the conversion of a woman who was happy to hear that Catholic women did not risk rebirth in the Buddhist blood-pond hell.[83]

Since spiritual purification was traditionally a concern reserved for middle-aged and elderly women, it is not surprising that Catholic penitential practices were especially appealing to older Chinese women. An annual letter covering the early 1640s, for example, mentions one particular penitential group (*kuhui*) for elderly women who wanted to prepare themselves for death and who engaged, accordingly, in harsh penitential practices, including fasts and the wearing of cilices.[84]

While many Chinese Catholic women were probably interested in the benefits of confession as a ritual of spiritual purification, it is unlikely that women always perceived of confession as a tool for moral perfection. On the one hand, there seem to have been many women who, through daily examinations of conscience and harsh penitential practices, succeeded in embodying the model penitent moved to "sorrowful repentance" (*tonghui*) that the Jesuits evoked in their prescriptive texts.[85] On the other hand, others were probably interested more in receiving the priest's absolution for their sins than in pursuing a quest for spiritual progress.[86] Regardless of their inner disposition, however, Catholic women generally seem to have perceived the ritual of confession, and the church visits during which it was performed, as opportunities for individual as well as communal redemption. This was because confession fostered, albeit via highly individualized ritual, a strong sense of community.[87]

* * *

Liam M. Brockey, in his book on the Jesuits' seventeenth-century mission to China, maintains that mission stations and churches were the actual centers of gravity in Chinese Catholic communities. Taking the Hangzhou church as an example, he shows that churches were places where whole communities as well as small devotional groups—penitential, Marian, and charitable—gathered for worship.[88] If we look at Chinese Catholicism from a gender perspective, it becomes evident that the bustling religious life of Catholic churches principally reflects the male aspect of

Chinese Catholic communal religiosity. Rather than being oriented toward churches, women's communal religiosity was predominantly domestic, with the house oratory as its center of gravity. Due to their domestic nature, Chinese Catholic women's communities differed from men's communities in two ways.

First, with regard to their internal organization, women's congregations were more tightly connected with particular Catholic families than men's congregations were. While the latter chose their congregational head in an annual election, women's groups were generally headed by the senior lady of the hosting family over a long period.[89] These women were endowed with considerable power, deciding, for instance, about who was admitted to the group. Since they were often reported to have invited neighbors and relatives, it is probable that family and neighborhood networks played a more important role in women's congregations than in men's.

The second difference between men's and women's congregations concerns the religious purposes for which they were founded. Men's congregations were formed for two different purposes. General congregations were established for the simple purpose of Catholics' regular communal worship, while more exclusive devotional confraternities were established for specific religious purposes, such as penitence, charity, or prayer.[90] The situation was different for women. Devotional sororities, which would have required close supervision by the priest, were only rarely formed (the Xi'an penitential group for elderly women mentioned above was a noteworthy exception). In some rare cases, women were admitted to devotional congregations formed for men, but only under the condition that they practice their devotions at home rather than with the group.[91] Most women, however, organized the totality of their devotions within the ambit of their general congregations, rather than form particular groups for this purpose. The effects of this less differentiated organization of women's collective piety were twofold. On the one hand, it resulted in a situation in which women's opportunities to participate in community-based Catholic activities supervised by a priest were much less frequent than men's. On the other hand, it conferred considerable power on female lay leaders. Due to the Jesuits' reservations about close supervision of women's devotional groups, lay leaders were responsible for most female communal piety. As a consequence, although occasional priestly rituals were crucial for Catholic women's identities, congregational organization nevertheless strongly resembled the devotional autonomy of indigenous Buddhist groups.

Sources on Chinese Catholic gentry women—whose religious activities are far better documented than the activities of Catholic women of lower social strata—also support the hypothesis that the absence of a strong priestly presence provided women with considerable agency and religious autonomy. Such facets of these women's Catholic religiosity are examined in the following chapter, which focuses on the women of a particularly well-documented family: the Xus of Shanghai.

7 SHARING GENTEEL SPIRITUALITY

The Female Networks of the Xus of Shanghai

IN LATE IMPERIAL JIANGNAN, "TALENTED WOMEN" (*CAINÜ*)—highly educated women whose literary talent and beauty were seen as a badge of honor for their families[1]—not only became enthusiastic readers of novels and prolific writers of poems, but they also formed dense domestic and inter-domestic networks where letters, poems, and other pieces of writing circulated. As a consequence, the inner chambers of elite households saw the emergence of a distinctive female culture characterized by specific forms of entertainment, attitudes toward manual work, and codes of spirituality.[2]

Late imperial Jiangnan was also a major center of gravity of seventeenth-century Chinese Catholicism. Several eminent Catholic gentry families lived in this region, among them the Xus of Shanghai, the Lis and the Yangs of Hangzhou, and the Suns of Jiading.[3] Only a few women from these families followed a literary vocation, their domestic culture being centered on the Catholic religion rather than scholarly pursuits.[4] Nevertheless, Catholic gentry women's domestic culture is comparable to the domestic culture of "talented women" in several ways. Just as literature and poetry provided "talented women" with opportunities for personal fulfillment, Catholic piety gave devout elite women's leisurely lives a meaningful focus. Although a genuinely individual pursuit, it provided women with opportunities for homosocial conviviality and helped foster strong homosocial bonds by way of a common language of religion.

The Xus of Shanghai were a particularly well-documented Catholic gentry family. Their involvement with Catholicism started in 1603, when the famous scholar-official Xu Guangqi (1562–1633; *jinshi* 1604) received baptism.[5] Xu Guangqi became the ancestor to an impressive Catholic genealogy. His son, Xu Ji (1582–1646), and his five grandsons, four granddaughters, and innumerable great-grandchildren were Catholics. Some branches of his family also remained Catholic into the twenty-first century, and descendants of Xu Guangqi played an eminent role in the reestablishment of the Jesuit presence in nineteenth-century Shanghai.[6]

The generation of women in this family from the second generation after Xu Guangqi, most of whom actively participated in and shaped Catholic religiosity from circa 1630 to 1660, are an especially apt focus for a case study on Catholic elite women's domestic religiosity because of the rich information about them contained in the Jesuits' annual letters. Although previous research has focused almost exclusively on Xu Guangqi's most famous granddaughter—Candida (1607–1680), portrayed in Philippe Couplet's *The Story of a Christian Lady of China*—a close examination of archival data on the Shanghai mission shows that this eminent Christian lady was in fact embedded in a tightly knit network of devout kinswomen. This network included Xu Guangqi's descendants' wives along with their young daughters, who were the organizers and primary participants in the rich religious life of the Xu family's Shanghai ancestral home. It also included his four granddaughters, who, after marrying into other families, maintained contact with their natal family and continued their religious devotion even outside their Catholic family environments.[7]

The religious biographies of all these women must be analyzed against the background of more general biographical patterns in late imperial Chinese women's lives, which, in turn, were intricately connected to the patriarchal family system of the period. Due to patrilocal and patrilineal marriage patterns, women only rarely remained members of the same household for their entire lives. Instead, most young ladies faced the fate of being "married out" (*chujia*). This was often a rather traumatic experience for a young bride, as it was usually on the wedding day that she first encountered her husband and his family—the family she was to live with for the rest of her life.[8] The transition into the new family was further hampered by the fact that a young bride, especially until the birth of her first child, occupied a lowly position in her husband's family. She had to abide by her mother-in-law's regime, usually had little freedom, and was subjected to hard work.[9] However, gentry women's freedom of action began to increase after they bore children and even more so when they became the household's matriarch upon the death of their mother-in-law.[10] When their children grew older, they could rely on their support, thus harvesting the fruits of their efforts as their children's teachers.[11] When their sons married, they could leave the hard household work to their young daughters-in-law and could spend their newly won hours of leisure in pious devotion.[12] If their husband died and left them enough property, they even enjoyed the social prestige and exceptional freedom of chaste widows (*jiefu*), who, as personifications of the Confucian ideal of marital fidelity, were bestowed special honors by the government and enjoyed extraordinary legal protection during the Ming-Qing period.[13]

The biographies of the women in the Xu family network were affected by these general patterns that shaped gentry women's lives. What made their lives special, however, was their connection with a Catholic "women's culture" that emerged in several households integrated into the Xu family network.[14] This culture fostered homosocial bonds among the women that persisted even beyond the ruptures caused by patrilocal marriage.

A GENTRY FAMILY'S DOMESTIC CONGREGATION

The Xujiahui area, located some four kilometers southeast of Shanghai's ancient city center, has been an important *lieu de mémoire* for Chinese Catholics for almost two centuries. Acquired by the Jesuits in 1849, it became the home of Jesuit-run Catholic schools, a seminary, an orphanage, and the famous Xujiahui library.[15] The library is still accessible to the public today, together with the Xujiahui Catholic Church (Xujiahui Tianzhujiao Tang), dating from the early twentieth century, and the Xu Guangqi Memorial Hall (Xu Guangqi Jinian Guan), built on Xu Guangqi's grave site in 2003.[16] This current conspicuousness of Catholicism in the Xujiahui area contrasts with its much lower visibility in the seventeenth century, when its most noteworthy Catholic building was probably the Holy Mother's Church (Shengmu Tang), a woman's church built "in a big hall of the [Xu] palace."[17] After opening its doors in the 1640s, it served as the meeting place of the Xu women's domestic congregation.[18]

In contrast to the extended domestic congregations described in the previous chapter, admission to domestic congregations of eminent Catholic scholar-official families such as the Xus of Shanghai was usually reserved for female members of the household. Headed by the household's senior lady, these domestic congregations were frequented by female members of the family (including daughters, daughters-in-law, and sometimes nieces and granddaughters) as well as its female servants. Source evidence shows that these congregations usually gathered daily. The women of the famous Catholic scholar-official Sun Yuanhua's household in Jiading, for instance, gathered every morning for communal morning prayers led by Sun Yuanhua's mother, Mary, during the 1630s.[19] In Songjiang, Candida Xu organized communal evening devotions, which were frequented by all her female relatives and servants during the 1670s.[20] The female leaders of these pieties, many of them highly literate, relied on liturgical calendars and prayer books, such as the *Daily Exercises of the Holy Teaching* (Shengjiao rike), to ensure correct worship. Annual letters indicate that women consulted these texts on a regular basis and sometimes even knew large portions of the *Daily Exercises* by heart.[21] Gentry women's domestic congregations also organized special devotions on major religious feast days, such as Christmas, Easter, and the Assumption.[22]

In the 1640s and 1650s the congregation at Xujiahui was led by Flavia Yu, the wife of Xu Guangqi's firstborn grandson, Peter Xu Erjiao. Flavia was praised by the Jesuits as an especially fervent Catholic. She was a donor to the above-mentioned Holy Mother's Church, and she had the esteem of everyone due to her qualities as "preacher, catechist, and good example for all other Christians."[23] In the early 1640s, Flavia was, strictly speaking, not the senior lady of the Xu household. Although her mother-in-law, Lady Gu, had died in 1622, her grandmother-in-law, Lady Wu, was still alive, until 1646, when she died at age eighty-one. Since Lady Wu was only rarely mentioned in the annual letters, it is reasonable to assume that the elderly lady had already withdrawn from active leadership at an earlier stage and had delegated the responsibilities of the female family head to her successor. Under Flavia's aegis, the congregation counted about thirty women.[24] Besides the Xu clan's wives and their daughters, this number also included female servants of the Xu household.[25]

Besides Flavia, the main protagonists of the Xu women's domestic congregation were her sisters-in-law: the wives of her husband's four brothers. With the exception of Lady Wang, the wife of Xu Guangqi's third son, Xu Erdou, and niece of Sun Yuanhua, they were all descendants of non-Catholic families.[26] Nevertheless, most of them seem to have willingly engaged in the practice of the new religion, which they were probably introduced to by their husbands or female family members. If, however, a woman marrying into the Xu household was unwilling to assimilate Catholic family practices, she would have been placed under considerable pressure, it seems. The Annual Letter of 1638 narrated, as a case in point, the story of a bride recently wed to one of the Xu brothers. This lady's family had been "gentiles, and very devout to the idols [*pagodes*]." When the woman wanted to maintain the religiosity of her native family, and refused to attend the domestic congregation's gatherings, warnings in her dreams prompted her to repent irreverence toward Catholicism in a general confession and, eventually, to join the congregation's daily devotions.[27]

While this sister-in-law of Flavia's only reluctantly integrated into the female Catholic network at Xujiahui, other women saw the congregation as an opportunity for living a religious life outside conventional female roles. That was the case of a daughter and a daughter-in-law of Flavia's, who lived as religiously vowed virgins on the Xujiahui estate. According to Francesco Brancati, they had apartments close to the Holy Mother's Church, where they lived a secluded life fully dedicated to the service of the Holy Mother. Despite the general suspicion that the Chinese elite harbored against religiously vowed virginity, incompatible as it was with the Confucian valuation of marriage (see chapter 8), these women enjoyed their family's respect.[28] That the virgins at Xujiahui were accepted by the Xu family was, however, also facilitated by their life histories. While Flavia's daughter, who was sickly, was prevented from marrying because of her poor health and eventually died at a young age, the wife of Flavia's first son was widowed before her wedding and, by keeping her virginity, embraced the Confucian ideal of the "chaste maiden" who maintained lifelong fidelity to her late fiancé even though the marriage had not been consummated.[29]

It is noteworthy that the women's congregation at Xujiahui, in the period under consideration, was frequented by Xu Guangqi's granddaughters-in-law but not by his granddaughters. Felicitas, Candida, Monica, and Martina Xu, who had been fervent participants in female pious activities at Xujiahui during the 1610s and 1620s, were probably all married by 1630, so that none of them were living with their native family at Xujiahui at that time.[30] That a Catholic women's culture existed at the Xujiahui estate during the 1640s and 1650s was, as a consequence, not the result of the Xu family's successful matrilineal transmission of Catholicism, but the result of its successful integration of previously non-Catholic brides into a Catholic family culture. This raises the question of how Xu Guangqi's granddaughters' Catholic religiosity was affected by their marriages into other families. Did their integration into non-Catholic families prompt their apostasy, or did these women maintain their Catholic religiosity in spite of marrying non-Catholic husbands?

MAINTAINING MATRILINEAL TIES

Just like many other Chinese brides, Xu Guangqi's four granddaughters seem to have experienced their wedding as a painful rupture in their lives. For these ladies, their marriage was tantamount not only to irrevocable separation from their native families but also to separation from their religious community. For, although their father, Xu Ji, had chosen descendants of Catholic converts to be their husbands, none of them were actually Catholic at the time of his daughters' marriages.[31] As a consequence, the Xu ladies faced many kinds of adversity in their efforts to maintain their Catholic practice after marriage. Some of them were handicapped in their devotions by their husbands' opposition to what they perceived as overzealous dedication to foreign superstition.[32] Furthermore, the husbands also endangered the Xu women's salvation by taking concubines and thus plunging their wives into the sin of polygamy, as in the case of Candida Xu.[33] Unlike the husbands, however, the mothers-in-law were apparently quite tolerant toward the Catholic practice of their daughters-in-law. Although some, like Felicitas Xu's mother-in-law, were zealously devoted to lay Buddhist practice, they were not reported to have opposed the Catholic presence in their households.[34]

Tolerance toward the plurality of religious practice within gentry households' inner chamber partly accounts for how none of the Xu sisters abdicated Catholicism, despite their husbands' intermittent anti-Catholic outbursts. The strong bonds of friendship maintained among the sisters seem, however, to have been equally important for their persevering with their native family's religion during their first years of marriage. After being physically separated from one another, the Xu sisters stayed in contact through letter writing and mutual visits.[35] They encouraged steadfastness in their religious practice and provided emotional sustenance. If possible, they even actively intervened on another's behalf. Thus, for example, one of the Xu ladies visited a sister in the late 1630s to assist her in an ongoing conflict with her non-Catholic husband over her and her children's Catholic religiosity.[36]

The Xu ladies also, conversely, used the language of religion to strengthen their emotional bonds after their separation. A letter, allegedly penned by one of the Xu women's most prolific writers, Candida Xu, during the first years of her marriage, demonstrates this bond.[37] In it, she expressed feelings of painful loss and tender love toward one of her sisters: "My sister, since I have parted from you, the hours and moments were rare in which I have not thought back to you and the peace and tranquility in which we had cultivated the matters of salvation in Shanghai. Now I live here among gentiles, where no one cultivates these matters and what is worse, my husband not only incessantly fails on this account, but also prevents me from my holy exercises; therefore I appeal to you to truly recommend me to Our Lord."[38] In her letter, Candida expressed her hope that a priest would come to Songjiang, and she pressed her sister to speak with the missionaries to this end. However, although Candida's wish was probably forwarded to the missionaries, it was fifteen years after her wedding, and only after her husband had converted to Catholicism, that the Jesuits finally agreed to establish a permanent residence in Songjiang.[39]

The Xu sisters also expressed their close emotional ties in their occasional reports of shared pious experiences. The 1659 Annual Letter of the Songjiang residence reported, for instance, how Candida Xu was afflicted with a severe illness that brought her near to death. She spent her time in deep meditation, envisioning herself praying at the feet of the Holy Mother. Simultaneously, her sister Monica was hearing Mass in the Holy Mother's Church in Shanghai, when she suddenly had a vision of her elder sister praying at the feet of the Holy Mother's image that was placed on the altar. When Candida had recovered from her illness, she visited her sister in Shanghai, where Monica shared her vision with her. The two ladies thus found out about Candida's meditation and praised God for this special grace.[40]

While matrilineal ties helped the Xu ladies to maintain their Catholic identity during their first years of marriage, as the years passed their situation in their husbands' families also started to provide them with opportunities to effect change. These opportunities usually derived from their responsibility for the religious education of their children. For, just like any other Chinese women, the Xu women personally saw to the religious instruction of their offspring, overseeing their religious practice and exhorting them if they became neglectful.[41] According to the Jesuits' writings, the Xu women made their children receive baptism even if their husbands were not Catholic or did not much care about the Catholic religion.[42] Candida's sons, for example, were reported to be well instructed in the faith even though her husband was known to be "not very devout."[43] In 1640, meanwhile, João Monteiro noted with admiration that Candida's firstborn son, Basil Xu Zuanzeng, at thirteen years of age, not only was well instructed in the faith, but also took great interest in matters of religion, even asking the missionary tricky questions about the Eucharist.[44] While non-Catholic husbands did not, apparently, interfere with their children's Catholic education so long as it remained in private, the Xu women occasionally met with opposition if their sons' Catholic education threatened to interfere with their designated public role. The non-Catholic husband of one Lady Xu, for example, became extremely angry when he learned that his young son had decorated his Confucian study books with Christian prayers. He turned his fury toward his wife, who struggled to prevent him from demolishing her oratory and burning the Savior's picture.[45]

While this story shows that the position of Catholic women living in non-Catholic families remained fragile even after they had become mothers, the example of Candida Xu also demonstrates how power relations within the family shifted in their favor when their children were grown up. As the years went by, Candida's husband, who had previously strongly opposed her Catholic practice, became more tolerant of his wife's religiosity and, in keeping with a cultural pattern common in China, he even started to take interest in religious practice himself when he reached advanced age, receiving baptism in 1638.[46] Candida's social prestige was, furthermore, greatly enhanced when her eldest son, Basil, attained the *jinshi* degree upon successful completion of the imperial examinations in 1649, making Candida the respected mother of an imperial official serving in various provinces.[47] Within the family, her power increased considerably upon Basil's marriage, allowing her to advance her position from a mother responsible for the education of her children to a mother-in-law responsible for the education of her daughter-in-law. Candida used the power granted her by this position to further strengthen her family's Catholic identity. She took it upon herself to evangelize her daughter-in-law, who, as a devout lay Buddhist, agreed to baptism only after a lengthy process of persuasion.[48] After conversion, the young woman, who had received the Christian name Philippa, became a fervent supporter of her mother-in-law's pious activities. She not only converted two of her brothers to Catholicism, but she also assisted Candida in organizing a domestic women's congregation, becoming its head after Candida's death in 1680.[49]

Widowhood, to an even greater extent than the upbringing of sons, provided the Xu ladies with opportunities to reshape the religious culture of their non-Catholic husbands' families according to their own vision. As "chaste widows," three Xu ladies—Felicitas, Candida, and Martina—succeeded in transforming their husbands' families into Catholic households, despite having entered them as young wives committed to widely scorned and outlandish devotions.[50] Felicitas, who had married into the Shanghai gentry family Ai, managed to establish Catholicism as the Ai family's religion for the next two and a half centuries, and the Ai house oratory constructed under her aegis was still in use at the turn to the twentieth century.[51] Martina, who had married into the gentry family Pan, became the leader of the Pan women's domestic congregation and was a donor to a church established by Francesco Brancati in 1638 outside Shanghai's

West Gate.[52] And Candida, most famously, who was widowed in the early 1650s, became one of the leading Catholics in the China mission.[53] She not only transformed her husband's family, but she also transformed the whole city of Songjiang—previously described by missionaries as a "city off the travel routes" (*cidade desviada*)—into a major center of Chinese Catholicism, equipped with a residence, twenty-five churches, and six oratories (see also chapter 9).[54]

Does the Xu ladies' successful establishment of Catholicism in their non-Catholic husband's families point to a general phenomenon, one allowing us to assume that matrilineal ties actually played an important role in the transmission of Catholicism from one generation to the next? Or, alternatively, were they rather striking exceptions to a rule, that Catholic women marrying non-Catholic husbands were usually forced to give up their religion? The sources do not provide definitive answers on this point. On the one hand, missionaries certainly saw mixed marriages as dangerous. Experience had taught them that Catholic daughters were sometimes married as concubines and, at other times, were legally married but had to accept a concubine at their side. Some Catholic wives were forced by their non-Catholic husbands to give up their religious practice, and others, most probably, simply forgot it after living for a long time in a non-Catholic environment.[55] It is not surprising, then, that a rule established for a "Congregation of Angels" (Tianshen Hui), which instructed young children in the Christian faith, stated that girls who entered the congregation should be taught only basic prayers. This was out of fear that they would neglect their souls after being married to a gentile.[56] The Xu ladies' example indicates, on the other hand, that there was some basis to Philippe Couplet's claim that marriages between Catholic women and non-Catholic husbands were "a means for gaining many people for [the] Religion."[57] It also shows how matrilineal transmission of Catholicism was actually possible in seventeenth-century Chinese Catholic communities.

Although the Xu ladies' success in converting their husbands' families to Catholicism was probably facilitated by the fact that their husbands came from families who had previously sympathized with Catholicism, this chapter has shown that it was also intrinsically connected with the Xu ladies' deep commitment to Christianity, nurtured through their close contact with their natal family.[58] That these matrilineal contacts were usually much stronger than the prevailing Confucian "rhetoric of patrilineality" might suggest has been highlighted by recent historical and anthropological research.[59] The Xu women's role as missionaries of their husbands' families was also facilitated by the proselytizing character of Catholicism, which presented a stark contrast to the only weakly confessionalized Buddhist or Taoist devotions of non-Catholic gentry women, who were usually rather tolerant toward religious practices diverging from their own devotion. That probably also accounts for how the Xu family's daughters-in-law (discussed above) all converted to Catholicism, while all of the Xu sisters maintained their Catholic identity.

In view of the role played by matrilineal and affinal relations in the intergenerational transmission of Catholicism in seventeenth-century Chinese families, we might have to expand our notion of Chinese Catholicism as a family religion. When speaking of Catholicism as a family religion, previous research has pointed, mainly, to the powerful connection between Catholicism and Chinese ancestral cults, a connection making descendants of Catholic ancestors decide to remain Catholics out of filial obligation.[60] This view has turned the attention of historians to the important role played by the patriline in the intergenerational transmission of Catholicism. However, the example of the Xu ladies teaches us that, despite the overwhelmingly strong presence of Confucian values in Chinese elite families, this was not the only possible pattern of transmission. Women's prominent role in almost all forms of domestic religiosity makes it probable that the number of women who played an active part in the shaping of the religious culture of their husbands' families was not limited to a few rare exceptions and that religious beliefs and practices were also transmitted through relationships established by marriage.[61]

PRAYERS AND VISIONS

What was the nature of these women's individual spirituality? In what sort of practices did they engage, and how did these practices shape their Catholic identities? Far from conveying a complete picture of the Xu women's religiosity, the Jesuits' writings only allow for some rare glimpses into these women's spiritual lives. They show, however, that gentry women usually fostered a strongly interiorized spirituality that corresponded well with the "personal-cultivational modality of religion," which was the modality of doing religion preferred by the Chinese elite.[62] They also suggest that gentry women's religiosity was closely interconnected with Catholic devotional books and images, which were usually strongly present in Chinese Catholic gentry households.[63]

Candida Xu's veneration of the Rosary neatly illustrates this interiorized spirituality. Candida was taught to pray the Rosary by her mother, Lady Gu, when she was still a child. At the age of ten, she took a vow that obliged her to pray the Rosary daily, which she took very seriously, spending an hour every day in meditation.[64] Candida was deeply convinced of the efficacy of the prayer. She asked poor Catholics who received her financial support to recite the Rosary to alleviate the suffering of souls in purgatory.[65] Her own practice of the prayer, however, was probably aimed not at efficacy but at personal spiritual cultivation. This is indicated by the diligence with which she undertook these "pious exercises" (*exercices de pieté*), which she did not want to dispense with even when gravely ill.[66] It is thus probably not a mere coincidence that the portrait of Candida Xu rendered in the Flemish version of Couplet's biography shows her holding a rosary (figure 7.1).

The prayer's objectives of interiorized piety and visualization corresponded well with the personal-cultivational religious practices popular in

FIG. 7.1. Ancestral portrait of Candida Xu, depicted with a rosary. Copperplate engraving printed in the Flemish version of Couplet's *The Story of a Christian Lady of China* (Historie van eene groote, christene mevrouwe van China, 1694). Courtesy of Maurits Sabbe Library, Faculty of Theology, KU Leuven.

the late imperial gentry milieu.[67] In particular, its combination of repetitive recitation and focused meditation would have struck a familiar chord with anyone acquainted with the Buddhist spiritual practices of Chinese gentry women.[68] Simultaneously, the prayer's focus on the female figure of Mary—who, in her role as the Virgin Mother of Jesus, symbolized positive and powerful aspects of femininity—was a major incentive for women to recite it.[69] It is probable that Candida relied for her exercise on the *Rules for Reciting the Rosary* (Song nianzhu guicheng, 1619) written by João da Rocha, who had been a close friend of the Xu family.[70] The very first pictures in this devotional book showed Mary in a Chinese gentry boudoir setting, certainly facilitating gentry women's identification with her (see figure 5.3).[71]

Another example of a gentry woman's interiorized spirituality—focusing again, notably, on a female saint—was Monica Xu's devotion to St. Catherine of Siena. The Annual Letter of 1659 reports that Monica had developed a special veneration for St. Catherine and for her mystical relation with Jesus.[72] Next to her bedstead she kept a painting of the Sacred Heart of Jesus, probably reminding her of Catherine's mystical exchange of hearts with the Savior.[73] Monica was especially fond of this picture, to which she ascribed special powers. She once reported to the missionaries that she had observed how the painting had started to mysteriously radiate its divine light, illuminating the whole house. Although the sources do not contain information about the textual basis for Monica's devotion, it is probable that she knew of St. Catherine's mysticism thanks to the *Biographies of the Saints of the Holy Teaching of the Lord of Heaven* (Tianzhu shengjiao shengren xingshi), published by Alfonso Vagnone in 1629. This devotional work contained an account of St. Catherine's life, with a strong focus on the saint's intimate relation with Jesus and her painful inner struggles with evil. Vagnone described how Catherine was finally accepted by Jesus after harsh penance—including abstinence from food, rest, and speech—and was then praised for her steadfastness before subsequently having her heart taken to heaven to "please it with indescribable joy and consolation."[74] It is possible that such exemplary stories are what motivated the Xu women to engage in harsh penitential practices themselves, including fasts, the use of scourges and cilices, kneeling, and nocturnal prayer.[75]

Gentry women's personal spirituality was not necessarily a strictly individual practice. Some personal devotions were practiced by all female members of the household and thus contributed to the emergence of Catholic group identity within the inner chambers. As cases in point, Mary Sun made all female members of the household celebrate their patron saint's day with special devotions, and Candida Xu made the members of her congregation participate in selecting "saints of the month," a practice that required people to "draw slips of paper from a bowl, each bearing the name of a saint" who would serve as a personal patron during the following month.[76] Even more than by these shared devotions, however, the Xu women's group identity seems to have been strengthened by shared religious experiences—especially holy dreams and visions.

The Jesuit sources report over a dozen dream visions experienced by especially virtuosic dreamers among the women of the Xu clan. Namely, Lady Wang (the wife of Xu Guangqi's third grandson and niece of Sun Yuanhua) as well as Felicitas, Monica, and Candida Xu experienced and discussed religious dreams with high frequency.[77] Candida's dream visions were so frequent that Philippe Couplet saw himself forced to question their visionary nature in *The Story of a Christian Lady of China*. Certainly writing with a critical European readership in mind, he stated that Candida was so dedicated to God that dreams in general were for her like visions and that it would therefore "be difficult to determine whether they were true visions or mere effects of her mind's efforts."[78]

Most of the Xu women's pious dreams involved communication with the spiritual world—with saints, the Holy Mother, and dead or absent relatives. Thomas-Ignatius Dunyn-Szpot's *History of China* contains an account on how Felicitas, exhausted by her daily chores, addressed a prayer to the Holy Mother before going to sleep. In her dream, she saw the Virgin Mary holding the Infant Jesus in her arms and consoling her with the words "Felicitas, I am ready to suffer for your love." This dream was followed by two subsequent dreams in which the Virgin encouraged her to deepen her piety.[79] In the Annual Letter of 1648, Felicitas's sister Monica was reported to have had a vision during prayer that brought her into contact with the world of the dead. She saw her pagan brother-in-law's soul suffering in hell—a frightening prospect that prompted her to renew her pious fervor.[80] The Xu ladies also claimed to receive spiritual messages via their dreams. A relation dedicated to Candida's journey to Huguang in 1662 thus reported how the Lady Xu was told in her dream to buy land from a certain family named Yuan in order to build a new church. Underlining her claims about spiritual communication, Candida even recalled the precise wording of this vision, duly recorded by the accompanying missionary, Jacques Motel, in his notes and included in a travelogue by the vice-provincial Jacques le Faure.[81]

Dreams and visions were not a female prerogative in Chinese Catholicism.[82] Like everyone in late imperial China, Chinese Catholic men and women saw dreams as a real and common way of communicating with the spiritual world.[83] Dream interpretation was practiced in every segment of seventeenth-century Chinese society, and members of the literati class relied on dream manuals to understand the meaning of their dreams.[84] However, while dreams were highly valued throughout late imperial Chinese society, they played a particularly important role in women's domestic spiritual culture, with women spending hours discussing and interpreting their dreams together.[85] The many dreams reported by the Xu family women suggest that the practice of dream interpretation was also common in the female networks of Catholic gentry families. These women's acceptance of dreams as natural encounters with the spiritual world was rooted in Chinese culture. It contrasted sharply with the Jesuits' understanding of dreams, which held that dreams of divine origin were reserved only for a chosen few. The Jesuits warned against a naive belief in the divine origin of one's dreams. Giulio Aleni, in his *Expositions of the Sciences of the Psyche* (Xingxue cushu, 1646), asked his readers: "How can we expect the average person to have [holy dreams]?"[86] But that seems not to have affected the Xu women's enthusiasm for dreams. They continued to haunt the female quarters—a place where priestly control was difficult to enforce and religious demand great.[87]

The sources do not inform us about the impact of the Xu women's Catholic spirituality on their understanding of femininity. Their dreams and visions, however, alongside their other religious activities, do nonetheless provide us with a vivid demonstration of their self-consciously lived-out Catholic spirituality. These expressions of pious experience were largely independent from male Catholic hierarchies and the male world in general. Of course, women took advantage of opportunities to discuss their dreams with the Jesuit priests visiting their homes. However, it was not these encounters that provided them with their central religious experiences. These took place in the female world of the inner chambers, where gentry women shared both their daily chores and religious devotions and their dreams and visions.

* * *

The Xu family of Shanghai was only one of several eminent gentry families of the Jiangnan region whose members openly practiced the Catholic religion during the seventeenth century. Their example shows that the "teachings of the Lord of Heaven" were, at least to some of them, an integral part of their lives. Albeit largely restricted to the domestic realm, these women nevertheless diligently practiced Catholic devotion within the homosocial setting of the inner quarters. The women of the Xu family network were, as a consequence, crucial in the process of establishing and maintaining Catholicism as a family religion. Although Chinese marriage patterns and the Jesuits' toleration of mixed marriages hampered the intergenerational transmission of Catholicism, some branches of the Xu family network remained Catholic over many generations. It is clear that women contributed to this continuity and that they were, indeed, the supporting pillars of the Xu family's Catholic identity.

8 A WIDOW AND HER VIRGINS

The Domestic Convents of Hangzhou and Nanjing

UNLIKE IN CONTEMPORARY CATHOLIC EUROPE, WHERE RELIgious women's nunneries thrived, Chinese communities administered by the Jesuits were not characterized by the emergence of institutions for women who had taken a religious vow of chastity.[1] This absence of religiously vowed chaste women distinguished the situation of Catholic communities administered by the Jesuits during the seventeenth century from the very different situation of communities administered by Dominican friars in Fujian during the eighteenth century, which saw the emergence of a thriving "third order" for women, numbering between two and three hundred women.[2] A noteworthy exception to the earlier pattern was the establishment, around 1630, of two Catholic "convents" for virgins and chaste widows in Nanjing and Hangzhou, on the initiative of Agnes Yang, a daughter of Yang Tingyun.[3]

A CULTURE-STRADDLING VIRTUE?

Christian notions of virginity were largely incompatible with Confucian notions of chastity.[4] Because emphasis on the continuation of the patrilineal descent line made Confucian thinkers perceive of marriage as an obligatory institution for every woman, the ideal of religiously motivated female virginity, which acquired enormous influence in European post-Tridentine Catholicism, was utterly incompatible with Confucian values.[5] Unlike the Confucian ideal of widow chastity, the ideal of religiously vowed virginity—traditionally embodied in China by Buddhist nuns, held in low esteem—was not an expression of the Confucian virtue of marital fidelity. It was, therefore, perceived by Confucian literati as belonging to the obscure, potentially heterodox, realm of popular religion, an antipode, in their minds, to Confucian orthodoxy.[6]

Despite these reservations, the Jesuits introduced the Christian concept of religiously vowed virginity to a Chinese audience in one of their Chinese books: the *Biographies of the Saints of the Holy Teaching of the Lord of Heaven* (Tianzhu shengjiao shengren xingshi; in the following shortened to *Biographies of the Saints*) published by Alfonso Vagnone in 1629 (figure 8.1).[7] This book contained hagiographic accounts of the lives of twenty-four women, twelve of them "chaste women" (*jiefu*), the other twelve virgins (*shou tongshen*, literally "those who keep a child's body").[8] A short explanation was provided to illuminate the meaning of this latter category. According to Vagnone, it referred to "women with high religious aspirations [*gaozhi*] who neither marry nor sully themselves through sexual contacts for their whole lives." Vagnone explained that such women had existed from the earliest times of Christianity and that they "diligently cultivated purity of body and

天主聖教聖人行實
凡有七卷
聖人
宗徒第一
司教第二
致命第三
顯修第四
隱修第五
聖女
童身第六
守節第七
武林超性堂
崇禎二年刻
耶穌會士高一志述

FIG. 8.1. Frontispiece of Alfonso Vagnone's *Biographies of the Saints* (1629). At the center of the frontispiece is a table of contents in the form of a cross, indicating that five *juan* are dedicated to male saints (*shengren*) and two to female saints (*shengnü*). Courtesy of Archivum Romanum Societatis Iesu, Jap. Sin. 65 I.

mind in order to attain heaven at the end of their lives."[9] By identifying spiritual purity rather than marital fidelity as the ultimate goal, this explanation clearly distinguished Christian female virginity from Chinese concepts of chastity. This difference was further underlined by how nine of the twelve virgins portrayed in the *Biographies of the Saints* were virgin martyrs, most of whom suffered martyrdom because of marriage resistance.[10] The Jesuits thus clearly made themselves vulnerable to anti-Christian accusations of heterodoxy, praising as "holy people" (*shengren*) young women who had committed so grave a crime of unfiliality as resistance to marriage.

A close reading of the virgins' biographies suggests, however, that Vagnone and his collaborators were well aware of the disruptive potential of these stories and that, wherever possible, they tried to prevent people from interpreting the virgins' marriage resistance as a lack of filiality. This is especially aptly illustrated in the biography of St. Agnes, where Vagnone made a number of subtle, but significant, alterations in order to dispel any suspicions of a lack of filiality. Christian tradition held that Agnes, who had lived in late antiquity, was the daughter of a wealthy Roman noble family. Agnes took a vow of chastity at a young age and suffered martyrdom after she refused to marry the Roman city prefect's son. The young girl's marriage refusal was described by *The Golden Legend* (Legenda Aurea)—tentatively identified by Li Sher-shiueh as the source for the *Biographies of the Saints*—as follows: "When [Agnes] returned from school, the prefect's son fell in love with her. He promised her jewels and abounding wealth if she consented to marriage. Agnes answered him: Begone from me, tinder of sin, nourishment of malefaction, fodder of death! For I have already been chosen by another lover."[11]

According to *The Golden Legend*, it was Agnes, therefore, who deliberately chose to reject her admirer's proposal. In Vagnone's biography of Agnes, this passage was slightly altered. In this version the parents decided not to give their daughter in marriage to the city prefect's son:

> When [Agnes] was twelve years old, the son of an official of the city heard of the holy woman's virtue and her attractive looks and he therefore proposed marriage. Her parents refused the young man's proposal. However, he did not give up. He waited until the woman left the house in company of her mother. He greeted her and proposed to her in person, forcing her to take the betrothal gifts. The holy woman was panic-stricken. She refused his gifts and shouted at him, saying: Stupid,

> shameless fellow! Now you have seen in person that I am a chaste woman. Alas! Alas! I have had for a long time a master whom I love and who I follow. . . . [The Lord of Heaven] is my beloved one whom I follow. . . . How could I abandon him in order to marry you?[12]

By letting Agnes's parents decide about their daughter's marriage, Vagnone made clear that the refusal of marriage by the virgin saint amounted to a fulfillment of her filial duty toward her parents, who had consented to her spiritual marriage with Jesus and, therefore, wished that their daughter become a "chaste woman." Vagnone, indeed, even opened up the possibility of reading Agnes's biography as the story of a "chaste martyr"—one of those Chinese women who suffered death (usually by suicide) when defending their honor against an unlawful suitor.[13] Agnes's filial and chaste nature was also underscored, furthermore, by how she met her suitor when she left home in the company of her mother, behavior becoming of an honorable young lady, and not when walking the streets alone.

Not all hagiographies offered themselves for adaptation to Confucian norms as Agnes's biography did. The biography of Catherine of Siena, for instance, recounted the lengthy process by which the saintly woman convinced her parents that she was destined to serve the Lord of Heaven as a virgin. St. Catherine's parents, determined to betroth her, were infuriated when they learned about their daughter's resistance. When Catherine shaved her head and disfigured her face as a sign of her refusal of marriage, they ordered her to perform lowly household tasks as though she was a servant, hoping that this would break her will. Only when they found Catherine praying in her room with a white pigeon hovering above her head did they understand that their daughter enjoyed the special favor of God, and they allowed her to remain a virgin.[14] In St. Catherine's case, the struggle with her parents was an important stage of her journey toward sainthood, one that could not simply be dispensed with. As a consequence, Vagnone could not resolve the tension between the virgin's loyalty to the Lord of Heaven and the Confucian precept of filiality, as he had for St. Agnes's biography.

Vagnone's biographies of St. Agnes and St. Catherine illustrate both the Jesuits' attempts to resolve conflicts between these Christian and Confucian concepts and the impossibility of doing so completely. They point to yet another aspect of the tension inherent in the persona of the literati Jesuits, who deployed practical strategies in an attempt to mitigate this on a daily basis.

THE JESUITS' STRATEGIES ON ASPIRING VIRGINS

Throughout the seventeenth century, consecrated virgins remained a marginal phenomenon in the Catholic communities administered by the Jesuits. Although there is evidence that a fairly small number of virgins lived among some of Jiangnan's most eminent Catholic gentry families (such as the Xus, discussed in the previous chapter, and the Yangs, discussed later in this chapter), the total number of recorded cases is not more than a dozen.

The few recorded cases nevertheless illustrate a resemblance between the phenomenon of consecrated virgins living under the Jesuits' supervision and the contemporary phenomenon of *beatas* (consecrated virgins who do not live in a convent) that emerged under Dominican supervision in Fujian. Both the Fujianese *beatas* and the virgins supervised by the Jesuits usually lived with their natal families, who provided for their subsistence. As a consequence, both were overwhelmingly daughters of wealthy Catholic families, who were able to support an unmarried daughter and who seem to have perceived of a religiously vowed virgin as a source of social prestige within the local Catholic network.[15] Parallels in size and development also existed between the two groups. Both groups of virgins remained comparably small during the seventeenth century. The number of *beatas* in Fujian only started to grow considerably during the eighteenth century.[16] Although the role of virgins in the Jesuits' eighteenth-century mission has yet to be studied in detail, it is likely that this group also grew considerably in number during this time. This is the only way we can explain the situation encountered by the Jesuits in mid-nineteenth-century Jiangnan, where virgins played a prominent role in Catholic communities.[17]

Despite these similarities, there was one major difference between the Jesuits' and the Dominicans' promotion of virginity. In Fujian, the decision of Catholic women to embrace virginity sometimes resulted in considerable social tensions with the local community. This is shown by the case of Maria Miao, who was brought before the local magistrate by her fiancé's family during the last years of the Ming dynasty. The plaintiffs accused Maria of turning down her parents' long-formulated marriage plans because she desired to become a consecrated virgin.[18] Another conflict erupted in Fu'an in the mid- to late 1640s, when the consecrated virgin Petronilla Chen, after being forced into marriage by her parents, stubbornly refused to consummate her marriage. Petronilla finally escaped from her groom's home and found shelter at the Dominicans' mission station.[19] That

Maria Miao and Petronilla Chen were willing to go to great lengths to save their virginity is remarkable. It bespeaks not only the women's deep religious vocation but also how their spiritual directors, the Dominican friars, supported them to the point of engendering conflicts with the local community over the women's desire to embrace virginity. The situation was different in the Catholic communities administered by the Jesuits. Indeed, the Jesuits' writings do not contain any mention of social tensions caused by a woman's decision to embrace virginity. Evidence suggests that this was due to the different strategy adopted by the Jesuits. Unlike the Dominicans, who unconditionally supported women's decisions to embrace virginity, the Jesuits supported aspirant virgins only if it was obvious that no social unrest would result. If a woman desired to maintain her virginity despite her family's opposition, the Jesuits did not actively support her, but instead advised her to adopt a conciliatory attitude and to agree to marriage.

Two stories rendered in the Jesuits' annual letters of the 1630s aptly illustrate this strategy. The first is about a fifteen-year-old maidservant named Paula, who was admitted by the Jesuits to the state of virginity in 1638. Paula was the personal servant of Cecilia, the senior lady of a Catholic literati household in a small town near Xi'an. On the occasion of a missionary's stay with the family in 1633, Paula had converted to Catholicism. During her religious instruction, she had learned of the Christian ideal of virginity and thereafter expressed the wish to become a consecrated virgin. Paula's wish was backed by Cecilia, who, according to the 1633 Annual Letter, loved her like a daughter and "promised to look after her for all her life, and to leave her property to her after her own death."[20] On All Saints' Day in 1638, Paula took the vow of virginity in a solemn ceremony held after Mass, with Cecilia assisting as her godmother. The missionaries allowed Paula to take the vows of virginity only because her mistress's ideological and financial support ensured that the girl's virginal state would remain uncontested.

The protagonist of the second story is another girl named Paula, this time from the city of Fuzhou. According to the Annual Letter of 1637, Paula of Fuzhou had made "the firm decision not to marry, and not to have for her whole life another spouse than Jesus."[21] She had, however, already been betrothed to a gentile during her childhood. When she reached marriageable age, this man claimed his bride, and the girl's parents decided to marry off their daughter. When Paula heard that an auspicious day had already been chosen for the wedding celebrations, she was panic-stricken. She immediately informed her spiritual father about her imminent marriage and asked him for advice. The missionary, however, did not encourage active resistance. Rather, he counseled her to pray to the Holy Virgin Mary and to her guardian angel for help. Heeding the advice, the virgin spent eight days fasting and praying. When the wedding day approached, she confessed and received the Holy Communion. Then, during the night before the wedding celebrations, her fiancé unexpectedly died. The virgin and the Catholics rejoiced. They "understood that this was [because] of the protection granted by the Lord to his brides."[22] Although it is unclear how Paula's story would have turned out had her fiancé not died, the episode nevertheless illustrates that the Jesuits were not willing to risk confrontation by actively supporting the desire of young betrothed girls to remain virgins. Rather than risking open conflict, they hoped for divine intervention.

It seems reasonable to suggest that the Jesuits' adoption of Confucian norms was an important explanation for their cautious approach toward the promotion of virginity in China. As shown in the previous analysis of Vagnone's biographies of virgins, the Jesuits knew that virginity was, unlike widow chastity, not deemed honorable by Confucian literati and that their active promotion of virginity would have damaged their image as "Western literati." However, this might not have been the only reason for the Jesuits' reluctance to encourage the formation of a female third order in China. What probably increased their restraint was the Society of Jesus's general attitude toward women. Imbued with Tridentine values, the Jesuits were extremely alert to the possible moral dangers that attended the task of supervising groups of virgins, perceived by the early modern Catholic Church as highly gendered and sexualized beings.[23] From an early stage, the Society had tried to prevent its members from having close contact with women, and it had thwarted various attempts by religious communities to be accepted as female branches of the Society.[24] This cautious approach toward religiously vowed virgins set the Jesuits apart from the Dominicans, who had a long tradition of ministry to women and of supervision of female congregations both in Europe and in the Spanish colonies.[25]

AGNES YANG'S DOMESTIC CONVENTS (CA. 1630–1650)

Despite the missionaries' reservations about the active promotion of female virginity, a group of virgins and chaste widows started to live as tertiaries—women living in semi-cloistered religious communities in accordance to a religious rule—in the city of Hangzhou around 1630. Their spiritual leader was Agnes Yang, a widowed daughter of the Catholic *jinshi* degree holder

Yang Tingyun. Agnes's non-Catholic husband had died around 1627. He had been a wealthy man who had entertained several concubines, and he left his wife a considerable amount of property. Thanks to this property, Agnes was able to lead an economically secure life as a chaste widow and the matriarch of her late husband's household.[26] The position of relative power and self-determination that this status granted her, furthermore, allowed her to transform her household into a domestic convent of a sort, something resembling more "a nunnery than a house of a Mandarin," and allowed virgins and chaste widows to live together in a life dedicated to pious practice.[27]

The sources are rather vague about the exact composition of the group of chaste women living in Agnes's household. Among them figured her husband's concubines and one of her daughters, as well as "one noble lady invited by [Agnes]."[28] The group may also have included some of Agnes's female servants who embraced chastity. It is unclear how many chaste women actually lived in Agnes's home. One relation written by Francisco Furtado referred to "quite a big number" of women, some of them virgins, others chaste widows.[29] Not all of the women had formally taken vows of chastity, although some of them had.[30]

The women lived in a separate part of Agnes's residence. There they maintained a sumptuously decorated oratory, where they invited the missionaries on festive occasions to celebrate Mass and administer the sacraments. According to the Annual Letter of 1633, the women spent their days with "different pious works and devotions."[31] These devotions included stern penitential practices such as prolonged fasts. The women also engaged in textile work, embroidering, in particular, precious pieces of cloth destined for religious use.[32] The Annual Letter of 1645, furthermore, testifies to how they were engaged in the production of raw silk. It reported that Agnes Yang asked Martino Martini to bless their silkworms in the fourth lunar month of 1645, an act that may have substituted for the traditional sacrifice to the Silkworm Deity (Canshen) usually made during this period of the year.[33]

Although the domestic convent in Hangzhou owed its existence to coincidence, Agnes apparently thought of it as a possible model for other, similar institutions. Alongside her own institution in Hangzhou, she also sponsored the establishment of a domestic convent in Nanjing, which, according to Furtado, allowed "many young women to embrace the state of consecrated virginity—an unheard thing in this kingdom."[34] Like Agnes's group of chaste women in Hangzhou, the virgins of Nanjing were subjected to the authority of a chaste widow.[35] Rodrigo de Figueredo, with whose help the Nanjing domestic convent was established, gave the chaste women statutes inspired by the model of European female tertiaries.[36] The Nanjing community of virgins existed for at least two decades. During the 1640s, it was administered by Francesco Sambiasi, who acted as the virgins' spiritual adviser.[37]

The annual letters suggest that the special religious status of the group of women living in the domestic convents of Hangzhou and Nanjing was widely acknowledged by their neighbors. They report that the chaste women's saintly reputation was accepted by both "Christians and gentiles" and that people of all sorts wished to be included in the women's prayers.[38] Furthermore, they mention that some virgins became the focus of special veneration because of their saintliness. The Catholics of Nanjing, for instance, cherished the memory of one vowed virgin whose body was found without signs of decomposition in 1652, fourteen years after her death—a clear sign of a person's sanctity in both seventeenth-century China and Europe.[39]

Given the important role attributed to virgin saints in Catholic religious culture, and to virgin deities in Chinese popular religious culture, the veneration of the chaste women of Nanjing and Hangzhou by both Catholics and non-Catholics is not surprising.[40] What is noteworthy, however, is that this utterly un-Confucian religious phenomenon was made possible by Agnes Yang's realization of the Confucian ideal of widow chastity. As a chaste widow, Agnes Yang was the legitimate caretaker of her late husband's property, providing her with substantial financial means. She was "the authority in her dead husband's household," which gave her great freedom of decision in domestic matters.[41] This freedom enabled her to lead a life similar to that of those European pious widows who played a crucial role in the semireligious organizations thriving in contemporary Catholic Europe.[42] Thanks to Agnes Yang's intertwining of Chinese and European ideals of widowhood, the domestic convents of Nanjing and Hangzhou assumed a striking double identity. On the one hand, they were Chinese elite households led by a widowed matriarch. On the other hand, they strongly resembled European communities of tertiaries. The one minor, but important, difference was that they, in accordance with the Chinese elite's ideal of female seclusion, probably exemplified Tridentine notions of cloistered communities to a greater extent than many European semireligious institutions. Yet, despite these remarkable similarities, the dependence of the domestic convents on the support of individual "chaste widows" prevented them from becoming institutions that survived intergenerational transitions. It is therefore not surprising that the record of the Hangzhou and Nanjing domestic convents stops in the second half of the seventeenth century. It seems that these communities ended abruptly after the death of Agnes Yang, probably during the 1650s.[43]

Although unique in the history of the Jesuit China mission, Agnes Yang's use of a Confucian female role model for the pursuit of a personal religious vocation was not without precedent in late imperial China. In fact it bears some resemblance to the case of the famous religious virtuosa Tanyangzi (1558–1580), a daughter of a *jinshi* degree holder living in a village near Suzhou. Like Agnes Yang, Tanyangzi was the member of a highly respected family, and she did not set out primarily to challenge Confucian norms. Indeed, as a teenage girl she embraced the status of chaste maidenhood when her fiancé died prior to their wedding. However, like Agnes Yang, Tanyangzi also used the freedom provided by this Confucian ideal for her own purposes. She started to live an extremely secluded life dedicated to pious devotion to a Taoist goddess, the Queen Mother of the West (Xiwangmu). She thus became a religious virtuosa, one whose spiritual insights found many followers and whose alleged physical ascent to heaven at the point of her death in 1580 became an occasion for major religious fervor.[44] Taken together, the stories of Agnes Yang and Tanyangzi point toward the flexibility of Confucian cultural norms in late imperial China. They show that Chinese elite women could pursue their utterly non-Confucian religious quests under the guise of Confucian womanly ideals and that such activities did not necessarily provoke repressive action by the government. They also show that the same Confucian norms that exercised considerable constraints upon the lives of some women could be used as cultural resources by others—depending on the social and financial circumstances of their lives.[45]

9 FABRICS OF DEVOTION

Catholic Women's Pious Patronage

CATHOLIC WOMEN DEVELOPED THEIR OWN FORMS OF INDIVIDUAL piety, separate places for collective devotion, and distinctive modes of social organization over the course of the seventeenth century. Although the forms of piety practiced by women of different social backgrounds varied, they were all characterized by their close association with domesticity, so that one might speak of a multifaceted "domestic Catholicism" practiced by Chinese women.[1] However, although Chinese Catholic women's religiosity possessed distinctive features, their "domestic Catholicism" was not a phenomenon sui generis, wholly isolated from Catholic men's religious activities. It was, rather, closely intertwined with the Chinese Catholic Church as a broader whole. Nothing illuminates this point more lucidly than women's material contributions to Chinese Catholic networks.

Women played an important role as patronesses of Chinese Catholicism, despite the fact that female patronage was virtually absent from other Chinese religions. Their sponsorship of the China mission is revealing of their religious identities, showing that noble Chinese Catholic benefactresses imagined themselves as members of a multilayered religious community, embracing both the small, local congregation and the globe-spanning Universal Catholic Church.

FEMALE PATRONESSES OF THE CHINESE CATHOLIC CHURCH

To any contemporary observer, women's contributions to the Chinese Church were probably most visible in the form of embroidered textiles. European reports suggest that precious fabrics, usually donated by local women, were an important decorative element of church interiors during the seventeenth century. As a case in point, on a stop in Nanjing in 1670 Manuel de Saldanha, a Portuguese ambassador to the Chinese emperor, was impressed by the local church's sumptuous decorations of damask and silk tissues. He noted that these tissues were the gift of a local Catholic benefactress, Agatha Tong.[2] Similarly, the missionaries of Hangzhou reported that their church was embellished with a beautifully embroidered altar frontal, presented to them by the Yang women in 1620, and also by embroidered draperies and a baldachin, made by the women of the same family in 1638.[3] Since women preferred to offer textiles to those churches that they themselves frequented, missionaries repeatedly reported that women's churches generally surpassed men's churches with regard to their ornaments and beauty.[4]

There were several reasons for the popularity of textiles as gifts presented to churches by Chinese Catholic women. First, precious textiles were an indispensable ingredient of the Catholic liturgy. In Europe, churches used sumptuously decorated liturgical garments, chalice covers, and altar hangings (which were often crafted by religious women) to underline the sanctity of Catholic rituals.[5] The missionaries therefore warmly welcomed Chinese women's gifts of textiles, which otherwise had to be bought or imported from faraway places. Furthermore, textiles were also an inherent part of Chinese women's indigenous religious culture. Devout Buddhist lay women often perceived of embroidery—"the cleanest, purest, and most refined of the womanly arts"—as a devotional act, choosing religious motifs for their needlework and combining the work with prayer or pious recitation.[6] Simultaneously, special symbolic value was attributed to textiles by Confucian moralists, who praised textile-producing women as the cornerstones of a well-ordered society and as symbols of female virtuousness, thus enhancing the symbolic dimension of textiles and making them a source of pride for the women who produced them. Finally, textile production was, moreover, a genuinely female domain, closely connected with most women's lives.[7] The Annual Letter of 1626 reports, for example, that the Catholic women of a village near Jianchang, Jiangxi, used the traditional weaving and spinning gatherings at dusk for communal prayers, probably substituting traditional songs with Christian texts.[8]

Catholic women's embroideries were decorated with various motifs, ranging from floral patterns to complicated biblical scenes.[9] What these embroideries might have looked like is illustrated by two surviving eighteenth-century liturgical textiles made of embroidered Chinese silk.[10] They are apt illustrations of how European Christian and Chinese symbolism was blended together in Chinese Catholic liturgical embroideries, resulting in a unique testimony of the Sino-European cultural encounter.

The first example is a chasuble that was probably commissioned by a member of the Geelhands, a Catholic family in Amsterdam, and brought to Europe by the Dutch East India Company in the eighteenth century (figure 9.1).[11] The chasuble is, at first sight, dominated by Catholic motifs: a medallion showing the Virgin Mary with child is framed by a large cross that stretches over the whole garment. A second look, however, reveals the Chinese origin of the embroidery. Not only the Chinese-looking faces of the Madonna and the baby Jesus, the distinctive shape of their bodies, and the Chinese auspicious clouds that surround them hint at this fact, but the ornamental birds and flowers that decorate the whole chasuble do as well. The phoenixes (*fenghuang*) and peonies were, in China, auspicious symbols of fertility and abundance. The butterflies, furthermore, symbolized joy—in this case, the joy of the Nativity.[12]

The second example is an antependium that was possessed by the Austrian Jesuit Gottfried-Xaver von Laimbeckhoven. While the Geelhand family chasuble was never used in a Chinese Catholic community but brought directly to Europe, this antependium was used in China (figure 9.2). Laimbeckhoven, who lived in China from 1739 until his death in 1787 and was consecrated bishop of Nanjing in 1755, had commissioned

FIG. 9.1. Embroidered silk chasuble decorated with a medallion showing the Madonna with child. As the family crest suggests, the chasuble was commissioned by the Geelhand family of Amsterdam in the mid-eighteenth century. Courtesy of Museum Catharijneconvent, Utrecht.

FIG. 9.2. Embroidered silk antependium showing a pelican feeding its young with its own blood. The antependium was commissioned by Gottfried-Xaver von Laimbeckhoven, Jesuit missionary and bishop of Nanjing, in a Nanjing embroidery workshop in the mid-eighteenth century. Courtesy of Museum Catharijneconvent, Utrecht.

the antependium in a Nanjing embroidery workshop. Its signs of wear show that it was used frequently—be it by Laimbeckhoven or by his successors (the textile was brought to Europe and given to the Episcopal Museum in Haarlem around 1880).[13] Like the Geelhand chasuble, the Laimbeckhoven antependium displays Christian and Chinese symbolism. At its center is a representation of a pelican feeding its young with its own blood, an ancient symbol of Christ's suffering for mankind.[14] This Christian symbol is combined with decorative elements that are dominated by Chinese auspicious symbolism—peonies and pomegranates—that probably ought to remind the faithful of resurrection and eternal life.

As early photographs of Catholic churches in China suggest, such products of the inner chambers were exhibited and used in the visible and symbolically highly charged environment of the sanctuary (figure 9.3). It is reasonable to contend, therefore, that Chinese women contributed considerably to the creation of a genuinely Chinese Catholic religious material culture during the seventeenth century and beyond.

Women's financial contributions to the China mission were somewhat less visible than their textile gifts, but they were no less important. Although incomplete records do not allow for an exact quantification of these donations, source evidence nevertheless suggests that they were immensely significant. In particular, two different groups of women

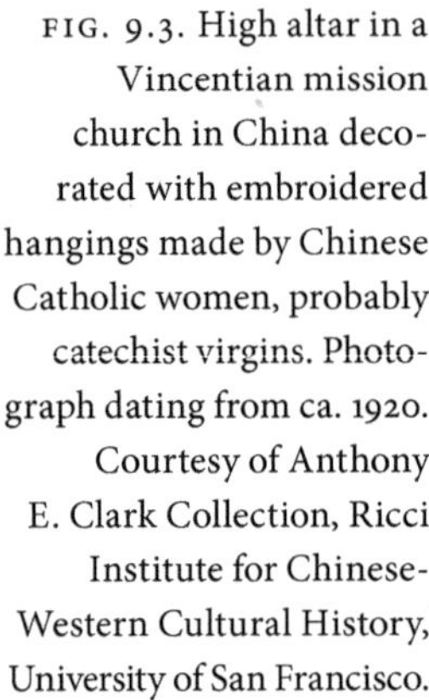
FIG. 9.3. High altar in a Vincentian mission church in China decorated with embroidered hangings made by Chinese Catholic women, probably catechist virgins. Photograph dating from ca. 1920. Courtesy of Anthony E. Clark Collection, Ricci Institute for Chinese-Western Cultural History, University of San Francisco.

emerge as donors: moderately wealthy women supporting missionaries with rather modest, but frequent, alms and rich gentry women who pledged large sums of money to the China mission.

The main source on moderately rich women's patronage of the mission is an account book kept by the Changzhou-based Jesuit François de Rougemont during the 1670s, according to which local Catholic communities, and especially Catholic women, played a central role in de Rougemont's funding.[15] Of the fourteen donations given to de Rougemont over a period of seven months between November 1674 and March 1676, eleven were made by women. Most of the donations, viewed in isolation, were rather modest, ranging from 0.3 to 4.0 taels.[16] Taken together, however, they amounted to an estimated sum of up to 80 taels per year, covering about one-third of de Rougemont's annual expenditures of around 230 taels.[17] This was a respectable sum, especially when compared with European pensions. If these made their way through conflict-ridden South China, they would have amounted to only 50–60 taels per year.[18] In the absence of other comparable sources, it is impossible to know whether the predominant role of moderately rich Chinese Catholic women's donations, as revealed by de Rougemont's account book, corresponded to a general pattern for the China mission. The account book does, however, suggest that these women contributed substantially to the mission's finances in the Jiangnan region during the second half of the seventeenth century.

Gentry women also played a crucial role in the funding of the China mission. A catalog of China's church buildings compiled by Philippe Couplet around 1680, among other sources, points to this fact. Of the seventeen recorded church buildings funded by Chinese Catholics, twelve were funded by gentry women, and another two were sponsored by gentry men who were close relatives of these noble patronesses. The catalog shows that gentry women's patronage was especially important during the second half of the seventeenth century. Eleven of the twelve donations made by gentry women date from this period, while the churches sponsored by gentry men all date from the earlier years of the mission.[19] The catalog suggests, furthermore, that the Jesuits relied upon a small number of patronesses who supported the mission over a comparably long time span. The twelve donations made during the second half of the seventeenth century were contributed by only three gentry women, all of whom had funded at least two church buildings. Agatha Tong was the patron of a new church established in Fuzhou around 1670, and she induced her husband to establish another church in Ganzhou in 1679. Justa Zhao, the wife of a Manchu nobleman, provided funds for the establishment of the East Church (Dongtang) in Beijing as well as for a church in Yangzhou during the 1650s and the 1660s.[20] Candida Xu's donations, finally, allowed for the establishment of no fewer than eight churches in four provinces during the 1660s and 1670s.[21] These few gentry women were exceedingly generous toward the missionaries. They not only provided funds for the establishment of churches, but they also donated large sums to cover the Jesuits' daily expenditures.[22]

Of the Jesuits' female supporters in China, Candida Xu was clearly the most generous patroness. Several substantial donations by her, made during the period of her widowhood between circa 1650 and 1680, are recorded by the Jesuits. At some point before 1664, when the missionaries were in an especially constrained financial situation, Candida supported each of the twenty-five Jesuits living in China with a onetime payment of 200 taels, which provided for their subsistence for a whole year.[23] When the missionaries were exiled in Canton between 1664 and 1669, Candida provided them with an amount of 12,000 taels, a sum that, according to Adrien Greslon, was key to alleviating the missionaries' acute penury during their exile.[24]

From 1671 until her death in 1680, she provided an annual stipend of 1,000 taels to Philippe Couplet, which was probably distributed among several missionaries. In total, the donations made by Candida over about a thirty-year period amounted to, according to Couplet's estimate, no less than 50,000 taels (church donations probably excluded)—a sum that would have sufficed to cover the daily expenditures of all Jesuits in China for almost a decade.[25]

MOTIVATIONS AND RESOURCES

That gentry women played an important role as patronesses of Chinese Catholicism is especially noteworthy in view of their conspicuous absence from traditional Chinese networks of religious patronage. As historian Timothy Brook points out in his study of the Chinese gentry's patronage of Buddhist monasteries, Chinese religious patronage "tended to be a male activity, and tended even more so to be represented as such."[26] With the exception of court ladies, who occasionally acted as patrons of imperially sponsored temples, women were virtually absent from donor lists of Chinese religious institutions.[27] Why was it, then, that women played such an important role in the patronage of Chinese Catholicism?

To examine this question, it is helpful to turn our gaze to Europe and to the Jesuits' attitudes toward religious patronage. A look into the history of the Society of Jesus shows that the missionaries' openly acknowledged reliance on funding from Chinese gentry women formed part of a longer tradition. Since its beginnings, the Society had sought the support of wealthy ladies. Noblewomen like the Marchesa della Tolfa (the original patron of the Roman College) and Giovanna d'Aragona (the founder of the Society's first Roman novitiate) had played an important role in the founding years of the Society in Rome. Similarly, when the Jesuits established themselves in Bologna and Florence, their enterprise was financially supported by local noblewomen.[28] Although the tremendous influence of female patrons decreased after the founding era, noblewomen remained important supporters of the Jesuits throughout the early modern period.[29] It is probable that the Jesuits' European experience with female religious patronage made them look for a similar support system in China. The missionaries' focus on female benefactors may also have been stimulated, during the second half of the seventeenth century, by the wealthy literati's lack of inclination to publicly subsidize the "foreigners" from the far West. The financial basis of the mission was also, generally speaking, highly vulnerable in the decades after the

Manchu conquest, which may have provided additional impetus.[30] Although the sources do not contain information about the ways Chinese benefactresses were recruited, it is reasonable to assume that the Jesuits actively encouraged Catholic gentry women in China to financially support them.

Gentry women's important role as benefactresses of Chinese Catholicism shows that the absence of women as patrons of Chinese religious institutions cannot be explained, as previous research has assumed, by the restrictive property laws imposed on Chinese women.[31] Gentry women's donations show that Chinese women, although not formally entitled to inheritance, had access to financial resources and were able to use them for religious patronage.[32] As the example of Candida Xu suggests, widowhood facilitated women's activities as benefactresses. It was, however, no precondition. Agatha Tong, for example, was an active benefactress of the mission during the years of her marriage to Tong Guoqi, while François de Rougemont's account book also mentions several married women who financially supported the mission (among them the wife [*niangniang*] of a certain Yuen Xicheu, the wife of a one Hoam Ye Kim, and the wife of an official called Yang).[33]

On which financial resources did women draw for their donations? One might expect that the most obvious financial source for Catholic gentry women to exploit was their dowry, late imperial women's only private property.[34] Dowries, and especially nuptial jewelry, do indeed seem to have played a role in donations to the mission. For instance, the daughter of Stephan Han Yun, a Catholic *juren* degree holder from Jiangzhou, was reported to have donated necklaces, earrings, and "other nuptial jewelry" for the building of a women's church in her father's house in 1629.[35] It is probable, similarly, that the "hairpins, rings, and bracelets" contributed by the Catholic women of Songjiang for the funding of a gold chalice in late 1670 also came from women's dowries, as did the "gold and silver jewelry such as rings, earrings, and golden buttons of their dress" contributed by the Catholic women of Beijing to fund the decoration of the newly established women's church in 1693.[36]

Dowries were, however, neither the only nor, it seems, the most important resource on which Catholic benefactresses drew. Widows, especially, also donated money that they had earned with their manual work.[37] This is aptly illustrated by Candida Xu, who became the most important benefactress of the Jesuits' mission despite the fact that her family was not exceedingly rich.[38] Philippe Couplet explained that Candida donated money that she had earned with her textile work to the missionaries and that she never touched the property and income of her son. Couplet claimed that it was Candida's proficiency in silk embroidery and weaving that enabled her to earn considerable sums of money. He informs us that Candida and her daughters and maidservants produced textile products that they sold in the local market. Candida then invested her earnings in an unspecified business run by two of her servants. Since these business activities went well, she became rich "thanks to their clever investments, and to God's blessing."[39]

While no specific information about Candida's business activities is available, it is possible to shed some light on the nature of her involvement with textile production. As usual in seventeenth-century Jiangnan, Candida's household was engaged in various stages of textile production. The first step was probably the production of raw silk. As pointed out by Xu Guangqi's family letters, the Xu women in Shanghai had great skill in raising silkworms, and it is probable that Candida also made use of these skills after she married into her husband's family in Songjiang.[40] It is unlikely that Candida and her maidservants spun silk yarn themselves (a task that was often performed by peasant women). Rather, it was a common custom for genteel households to sell their raw silk and buy ready-made yarn.[41] As a consequence, weaving, not spinning, was the second step of textile production in which Candida's household was involved.[42] According to Couplet, the production of "silk weaves" (*tissus de soye*) was Candida's main source of income.[43] Embroidery, the third stage of production that Candida was involved in, was, as shown above, a very popular activity among gentry women in late imperial China.

In view of previous research, the finding that textile production was the basis of Candida Xu's lavish patronage of the China mission is noteworthy. Proto-industrialization, by the seventeenth century, had prompted significant shifts in the gendered division of labor in textile production, not least in Candida's hometown, Songjiang, which was a major center of proto-industrialized textile production. According to Francesca Bray, women, who had domestically produced all types of textiles at the beginning of the Ming dynasty, were by the seventeenth century divested of their role as independent producers by urban "loom households," which were dominated by male family heads and manufacturers hiring male weavers. These relegated women to the performance of single stages of textile production, such as the raising of silkworms or the spinning of yarn, generally resulting in their marginalization.[44] Candida's example shows how the new gendered division of labor prevalent in China's seventeenth-century textile production did not necessarily result in a devaluation of women's work. Rather, women's active participation in various steps of textile production could still be a source of wealth for a family, and it could even provide women with financial resources for individual use.

CHARITY AND WOMEN'S CATHOLIC IDENTITY

What do women's donations tell us about their relationship to Chinese Catholicism? For which purposes did they pledge money, and how did this relate to their perception of the Jesuits' mission? A study of Chinese gentry women's donations is especially rewarding for these questions. While moderately rich women usually supported only local missionaries, gentry women also directed their alms toward other goals. This reveals gentry women's identification with the Catholic community at different levels: the local, the imperial, and the global.

Direct donations to the local community were the dominant pattern in Chinese Catholic women's almsgiving. Numerous sources testify to that. While François de Rougemont's account book reveals that missionaries relied heavily on their local Catholic communities for subsistence, numerous references in annual letters illustrate how major pious projects, such as the establishment of new house oratories, were usually funded by women from the locality.[45] Furthermore, Couplet's biography of Candida Xu provides ample evidence of her activity as benefactress of the local church in Songjiang.

Couplet's book is particularly instructive about the different directions that women's patronage of the local Catholic communities could take. The Jesuit mentions the wide array of charitable activities his spiritual daughter pursued. First, Candida directly supported a large number of people with direct monetary contributions. She gave alms to poor Catholics of Songjiang and covered their funeral costs, provided for the livelihood of catechists and Catholic women caring for the sick, and supported the evangelizing work of Catholic midwives and blind storytellers.[46] Second, Candida supported the manufacturing of various pious commodities for the local church, including the printing of devotional books and the fabrication of devotional objects and images distributed among the Catholics of Songjiang.[47] Third, she provided funds for the establishment of around thirty smaller churches established in the surroundings of Songjiang, which thus became one of the most important centers of gravity of early modern Chinese Catholicism.[48] Fourth, and finally, she supported projects in which Catholic charity converged with non-Catholic Chinese charity. As a case in point, she indirectly supported an orphanage established as a joint effort between her son, Basil Xu Zuanzeng, and other, non-Catholic officials.[49] The nature of Candida Xu's various charitable activities, from which the Songjiang Catholics benefited, clearly indicates how she aimed to play an active part in the Jesuits' missionary projects in her husband's home city. Rather than see herself relegated to the purely receptive role of a newly converted Catholic, Candida perceived of herself as a missionary. She not only actively engaged in the business of conversion by financing missionary personnel but also strengthened new Catholics' loyalties to their religion through financial support.

The Songjiang area was not, however, the only beneficiary of Candida's patronage. Candida, along with other Catholic gentry women, also entertained a more abstract project: the building of a "Chinese Church," which would ideally embrace all people living under the aegis of the Chinese emperor. These women's awareness of the existence of an empire-wide Catholic network is especially well illustrated by the data concerning their sponsorship of church buildings, which spans an astonishing geographical range. Justa Zhao patronized churches in Beijing and in Yangzhou and Hangzhou, more than a thousand kilometers south of the capital. The Nanjing-based Agatha Tong and her husband provided funds for churches in Ganzhou and Fuzhou. Candida Xu's patronage spanned the greatest distances. Based in Songjiang, she sponsored the establishment of churches in four provinces: Jiangnan (former South Zhili), Jiangxi, Huguang, and Sichuan, the fourth located two thousand kilometers from her hometown.[50] How did this female sponsorship of Catholicism in the remote corners of the Chinese empire come about?

The biographies of the women under consideration show that their patronage of church buildings in far-flung regions of the Chinese empire was closely intertwined with the mobility of their male family members. Justa Zhao, in particular, like Candida Xu, traveled in the retinue of her son, who, as an imperial official, held office far from his hometown. This behavior was not unusual for gentry women in contemporary China. Wives and mothers of officials often traveled with their husbands and sons when they took office in a different province. Dorothy Ko has pointed out that gentry women perceived of these journeys as duties resulting from the Confucian imperative of "Thrice Following" (*sancong*). Simultaneously, these women welcomed them as sightseeing experiences that made for an exciting change from their otherwise sedentary life.[51] The opportunities they provided to actively participate in the Jesuits' attempts to construct a Chinese Church lent them yet another dimension.

The record of Candida Xu offers an especially apt illustration of how Catholic women used their journeys for their own evangelizing purposes. Traveling in the retinue of her son, Basil, Candida covered a distance of more than four thousand kilometers over a comparably short period, between 1660 and 1662. She traveled from Songjiang westward to Nanchang, the capital of Jiangxi; from Nanchang northwestward to Wuchang, in Huguang; and then all the way back to Songjiang. Both in Nanchang and Wuchang, Candida spent much of her energy revitalizing or creating a local church. During her stay in Nanchang, she supervised the restoration of the missionary station, which had been destroyed during the Manchu invasion, and she provided the funds for establishing a new church. The local Catholics reportedly loved her for her piety and largesse. When Candida left the city, they gathered in large groups to accompany her to her ship and bid her farewell.[52] During her stay in Wuchang, Candida also oversaw the establishment of a new church. This time, she was in the company of a Jesuit, Jacques Motel, who assisted her in her religious endeavors and served as the church's priest.[53]

Just like Candida, Justa Zhao traveled in the retinue of her son. A native of Liaodong in the far north, she converted to Catholicism together with her son, Simon, during her stay in Beijing. There, in 1653, she sponsored the East Church for the missionaries Ludovico Buglio and Gabriel de Magalhães. When Simon took office in Yangzhou, she accompanied him south to his new place of residence, where she patronized the renovation of the local church in 1662. She also traveled with her son when he was appointed to a post in Fujian. Her plan to establish a church in Fujian, however, was thwarted by a pirate attack. That forced Justa and Simon to prematurely retire to Yangzhou.[54]

Candida Xu and Justa Zhao apparently saw it as their religious vocation to personally oversee mission work during their stays in different cities of the Chinese empire. Candida, for instance, was reported to have compared her journey to the itineraries of the European missionaries, who "traveled so many miles [*li*] for the salvation of the Chinese and for the glory of the true God." According to information collected for an annual letter, the Jesuits' devotion to the mission made her want to make some similar sacrifice: "Am I to fear [a journey of] nine thousand miles in honor of God and for the eternal salvation of my people?"[55] Candida's self-perception as a missionary was also emphasized in a vision experienced by one of her maid-servants, who allegedly dreamed that the Holy Mother wished her mistress "to work in the uncultivated fields" of China's western provinces.[56]

Poor travel conditions probably reinforced Candida's perception of her journey as a spiritual exercise. Jacques Motel, who accompanied the lady on the boat trip from Nanchang to Wuchang, stressed how incommodious travel was with the Xus, as compared, at least, with life onshore. That was despite the party's consisting of a veritable small fleet, with separate boats for Basil; his wife, Philippa; his mother, Candida; and Motel himself. The travelers were troubled by bad weather when winter approached and as the party moved eastward into more mountainous areas. They also lived in constant fear of banditry, and they were thrown into a veritable panic when they mistook approaching boats for a pirate's fleet.[57] These challenges assimilated Candida's experience to the experiences of European missionaries, who had to endure all sorts of hardship and privation for their missionary vocation.

Although gentry women probably found the role of the female missionary to the Chinese provinces a fulfilling one, their personal presence was not compulsory for the financial support of Catholic communities living in remote places. Instead, it was possible to entrust the realization of projects for church patronage to a close male relative who traveled the empire. Basil Xu Zuanzeng's initiative to establish a residence in Chengdu and Chongqing (both in Sichuan), and in Kaifeng (Henan), probably resulted from this gendered division of labor, just like Tong Guoqi's initiatives for church buildings in Ganzhou (Jiangxi) and Fuzhou (Fujian).[58] This gendered division of labor resembled that of lay Buddhist women patrons, who are known to have frequently moved their sons or husbands in order to make a contribution to a monastery.[59]

Catholic gentry women's sponsorship of churches in different corners of the Chinese empire indicates that they strongly identified with the Jesuits' aim of building a Chinese Church.[60] This suggests that women of literati families perceived of the Chinese empire as a meaningful point of reference for their personal identities and were far from exclusively interested in domestic matters or the welfare of their local community. In this regard, they resembled their male relatives, who strongly identified themselves as Chinese thanks to their close ties to government, forged by imperial examinations and the distribution of offices.[61]

While most Catholic gentry women's patronage stopped at the borders of the Chinese empire, some Chinese Catholic women's donations extended even farther. As a case in point, Candida Xu and other Catholic women of Songjiang furnished their spiritual father, Philippe Couplet, with lavish gifts—a gold chalice, many embroidered pieces, and other ornaments—when he traveled to Europe as a procurator in 1680. Some of these gifts were destined for different places crucial to the Jesuits' global mission: the sepulchers of St. Francis Xavier in Goa or St. Ignatius in Rome. Others, furthermore, were given to some of the Society's smaller European institutions, such as the church in Couplet's hometown, Mechelen, and the novitiate in Paris. The Songjiang women's gifts were—with only one exception—destined for institutions of the Society of Jesus, which shows the strong loyalty that Candida Xu and other Catholic women felt toward the Jesuits.[62] But they also testify, at least to some extent, to their donors' awareness of their local religious community's embeddedness into a globe-spanning enterprise.[63] They suggest that the missionaries' attempts to convey the idea of the "Universal Catholic Church" to their Chinese flock were, to some extent, successful and that the Jesuit presence in China prompted a small group of Catholic women to take an active interest in previously unknown regions at the other end of the Eurasian continent.[64]

CONCLUSION

Women and Gender in Global Catholicism

IN A 1994 ARTICLE ON THE ROLE OF WOMEN IN THE CATHOLIC mission to China, Jean-Pierre Duteil speculated about the state of Chinese women. According to Duteil, the latter were condemned to seclusion and mutilation, which was probably "one of the main obstacles to the general conversion of the Middle Kingdom that the Catholic missionaries aimed for."[1] These assertions were strongly influenced by what historians of women in China have criticized as a distorted "victimized 'feudal' women" viewpoint.[2] In light of the preceding chapters, they must be revised in two ways. First, the Jesuits' difficulties in gaining access to women was not merely the result of Chinese women's great seclusion but was also an effect of the missionaries' deliberate decision to adapt their lifestyle to that of the literati elite. Second, the missionaries' limited contact with women did by no means result in the latter's passivity. Rather, it prompted women to organize their piety independently and to rely on predominantly female religious networks to do so. Although the Confucian ideal of the separation of the sexes structured Chinese Catholic devotional life in crucial ways, it did not preclude women's agency within the domestic realm and their determining role in seventeenth-century Chinese Catholicism. These two hypotheses—the crucial importance of missionary masculinities and of Chinese Catholic domestic piety for the understanding of women's role in Chinese Christianity—encapsulate the main findings of this study.

How did Chinese Catholic women and their unique religious culture fit into the larger whole of the Catholic Church that was becoming, during the early modern era, a global institution?[3] Is it possible to integrate their religiosity into a more complete picture, encompassing female Catholic religiosity around the globe?

CONNECTIONS

If we believe Philippe Couplet, Candida Xu was not satisfied with the idea of sending gifts to Europe. She would have wished "to cross the seas and come to Europe [herself] in order to find new missionaries who were ready to join the small number of missionaries" working in Asia.[4] Although this wish was not fulfilled during Candida's lifetime, it was posthumously realized by Couplet. With his biography of Candida Xu, he brought the Jesuits' Chinese patroness into the studies and reading rooms of pious European Catholics, hoping that it would transform his late spiritual daughter into a forceful promoter of the Jesuits' China mission in Europe by inciting the pious fervor of devout Catholic noblewomen and encouraging them to direct alms toward the China mission.[5]

Couplet's hopes were not baseless. When he wrote Candida's biography, a small, but potent, network of rich European ladies supporting the Jesuits' China mission already existed.[6] In Madrid, the Jesuits could rely on the support of the Portuguese noblewoman Maria de Guadalupe of Lencastre y Cárdenas Manrique, Duchess of Aveiro (1630–1715).[7] In Genoa, they received alms from a woman of the Lomellini clan, a Genoese elite family heavily involved with their city's maritime trade.[8] In Antwerp, Elisabeth, Maria Anna, and Clara Johanna de Prince—three sisters involved in selling the famous religious prints of the city—were fervent supporters of the Jesuits in China.[9] Finally, the Jesuits were also in contact with ladies of the French upper nobility based in Paris, including Marie d'Orléans-Longueville, Duchess of Nemours (1625–1707), and Marie Anne Mancini, Duchess of Bouillon (1649–1714).[10] These women's support for the China mission was not only part of the long tradition of close Jesuit ties to pious elite women but was also embedded within a general trend of female elite religiosity in late seventeenth-century Catholic Europe. At the time, many influential Catholic women, prodded by their Jesuit confessors, became fervent supporters of the overseas missions of the Society of Jesus.[11]

Despite the importance of the mission's female noble supporters in seventeenth-century Europe, Couplet's *The Story of a Christian Lady of China* apparently failed to trigger a wave of enthusiasm among female patrons. Although the mission found new female supporters during the eighteenth century, these women do not seem to have taken special interest in the life of Candida Xu, and it is not even clear whether they knew of Couplet's book.[12] We do know, however, of at least one case in which Couplet's stay in Europe prompted European women to financially support the mission. A donation deed stored in the Roman Archives of the Society of Jesus proves that Couplet's stay in Antwerp in 1684 motivated the three de Prince sisters to offer "to the Revered Father Couplet, the procurator of the Chinese province, a sum of six hundred florins . . . for the building of a chapel in the mission of the Chinese province." According to the deed, the chapel should be dedicated to Jesus, Mary, and Joseph and decorated with a picture that the three ladies ordered from the painter Jacob de Nijs of Mantua.[13] Unfortunately, Couplet died on his return to China, and as a consequence we do not know whether the de Prince sisters' plan ever came to fruition. Although they had started to become connected thanks to some fine threads spun by the Jesuits, the worlds of Chinese and European women remained largely separate at the end of the seventeenth century.

COMPARISONS

How did Chinese women's position within the Catholic Church differ from the position of Catholic women elsewhere in the world, and what does that tell us about women's place within Catholicism on a global scale? When we look at the issue from a comparative perspective, one element of Chinese Catholic women's religiosity stands out: its tendency to be domestic in nature. The crucial role of domesticity for Chinese Catholic women's piety distinguished the latter not only from Chinese Christian men's piety, which was closely tied to the (semi)public space of the church, but also from European post-Tridentine religious cultures. These have been aptly described as essentially clerical, public, and community-based—as opposed to the strong emphasis of domestic religion in Reformed and Lutheran communities.[14] Although community-based devotion also mattered in China, Christianity's special status as a minority religion on the fringes of heresy prevented it from becoming the public religion characterized by pilgrimages and processions that it had become in Catholic Europe. Like Catholic minorities in Protestant countries such as England and the Dutch Republic, Chinese Christians, and especially Chinese Christian women's congregations, often sought shelter in the domestic realm for the unhindered practice of their religion.[15] The household thus became the focal point of female Catholic religiosity. Thanks to Chinese women, Catholicism became a domestic religion in seventeenth-century China.

The ways Chinese Catholic women's religiosity deviated from the standard religiosity propagated by Tridentine reformers in Europe fits well into the larger picture of early modern Asian Catholic communities. As research carried out over the past two decades has shown, these often defy the traditional picture of the post-Tridentine period as an era of religious standardization and homogenization (a picture that, incidentally, is also increasingly challenged by specialists of European religious history).[16] While the Catholic religious culture of coastal South India has been described as a "tropical Catholicism," created by various "process[es] of appropriation," the Christians of the Middle East have been characterized as a people with multifaceted religious identities who moved between cultures.[17] As for early modern Chinese Catholicism, several historians have pointed to its great degree of indigenization, showing how local actors interwove different cultural strands, and have suggested that we understand Chinese Catholic communities as "local Christianities" that were, at one and the same time, part of the Universal Catholic Church and genuinely Chinese religious communities.[18]

A focus on gender relations has the potential to add a new perspective to the research on the plurality of early modern Catholicism. It can show that local forms of Catholicism were shaped not only by cultural and social patterns of local societies but also—and crucially—by the ways societies imagined and practiced differences between the sexes. It can help shed new light on how missionaries' masculine identities shaped their options for action and how gender relations influenced the social organization of the church. Last but not least, it brings into focus a group of people largely neglected in studies on early modern Catholicism: non-European, female Catholics, who were frequently less visible in the dominant, European discourse but nevertheless active participants in early modern Catholicism.

That gender is a fruitful perspective not only for the study of the early modern China mission but also for research on Catholic communities in other regions of the world has been demonstrated by pioneering studies focusing on Catholic women in the Americas, India, and Japan.[19] All of them are successful efforts to salvage information on female religious lives from predominantly male source records. They point to how Catholic women's experiences varied in colonial and non- or semicolonial settings: while women in colonial South America were frequently integrated into religious institutions under close European surveillance, Asian women often enjoyed a remarkable degree of freedom within the Catholic Church. In the future, historians might be able to assemble these single pieces to form a more complete picture comparing and contrasting the gender arrangements of different early modern Catholic communities across the globe.[20] This will doubtlessly further complicate our picture of the post-Tridentine Church and will help to unearth additional evidence of historical realities that diverged from, or ran counter to, the European, male discourse that has for so long dominated the history of early modern Catholicism.

GLOSSARY

Ai 艾
Amituofo 阿彌陀佛

Bailian Jiao 白蓮教
Baladuo 罷辣多
Ban Zhao 班昭
Bianxue shugao 辯學疏稿
bie 別
Bixia Yuanjun 碧霞元君
Budai 布袋
Buluda[ge] 布路大[各]
busheng erzi 不生兒子
buzi 補子

cainü 才女
caizi 才子
Canshen 蠶神
Chan 禪
Chen 陳
Chen Houguang 陳侯光
Cheng Dayue 程大約
chenghuang 城隍
Chengshi moyuan 程氏墨苑
chujia 出嫁

Da Ming huidian 大明會典
Da Ming lü 大明律
dali 大力
Daxue 大學
daying 大答
Diarinuo 第阿日搦
Dizui zhenggui lüe 滌罪正規略
Dongtang 東堂

Duan 段
duode 鐸德
Duoshu 鐸書

fanbai 梵唄
Faqian yuanyi hui zoushu 發遣遠夷回奏疏
fashi 法師
fei 妃
fen 分
fenghuang 鳳凰
fu 符
fuke 婦科

gaojie 告誡
gaozhi 高志
gong 公
Gu 顧
Guanyin 觀音
gui 閨
gui zong 歸宗
guige 閨閣
guimen 閨門
Guimen bidu 閨門必讀
guiren 貴人
guixiu 閨秀

Han 漢 (dynasty)
Han 韓 (surname)
Han Lin 韓霖
Han Yun 韓雲
Hongloumeng 紅樓夢
huaiyun 懷孕
huanyuan 還願
hui 會
huigui 會規
huizhang 會長

jia 家
Jiaduo 加多
Jiang Shaoshu 姜紹書
jiaren 家人
Jiaoyao jielüe 教要解略
Jiaoyou lun 交友論
jiaozhang 教掌
jiaxun 家訓

jiefu 節婦
jijin 祭巾
Jinpingmei 金瓶梅
Jinsheng 敬慎
jinshi 進士
juan 卷
junzi 君子
juren 舉人

kuhui 苦會

li 里 (mile)
li 禮 (ritual)
Li Can 李璨
Li Madou 利瑪竇
Li Yingshi 李應試
Li Zhi 李贄
Li Zhizao 李之藻
liang 兩
lifu 禮服
Liji 禮記
ling 靈
lingying 靈應
luan 亂
Lunheng 論衡
Lunyu 論語
lutai 露臺

Ma Chengxiu 馬呈秀
Mai Yuan jia difang [geng?] hao 買袁家地方[更?]好
Miao 繆
Ming 明

nan nü you bie 男女有別
Nangong shudu 南宮署牘
nannü zhi bie 男女之別
nanse zhi yin 男色之淫
nei 内
neidan 內丹
nianfo 念佛
nianfo hui 念佛會
niangniang 娘娘
niantou 念頭
Nü sishu 女四書
Nü xiaojing 女孝經

nü zao chan nan 女遭產難
Nüjie 女誡
nüren guo 女人國

Pan 潘
Po xie ji 破邪集
pusa 菩薩

qi 齊 (to govern; to join)
qi 妻 (wife)
qi fufu 齊夫婦
qichu 七出
qie 妾
Qijia xixue 齊家西學
Qike 七克
Qin 秦
qing 情 (emotion)
Qing 清 (dynasty)
qing qing 請請
Qingming jie 清明节
qiu 求
Qiu you pian 逑友篇
Qu Rukui 瞿汝夔

ru 儒

sancong 三從
Sengni niehai 僧尼孽海
shanshu 善書
Shen Que 沈漼
Sheng Yinajue zhuan 聖意納爵傳
Shenghua Si 聖花寺
Shengjiao rike 聖教日課
Shengmu 聖母
"Shengmu hu shengchanzhe" 聖母護生產者
Shengmu Niangniang 聖母娘娘
Shengmu tang 聖母堂
Shengmu xingshi 聖母行實
shengnü 聖女
shengpo 生婆
shengren 聖人
Shi Bangyao 施邦曜
shou tongshen 守童身
Shuihuzhuan 水滸傳
Shun 舜

shuyuan 書院
si 寺
Sima Guang 司马光
Sishu 四書
Song nianzhu guicheng 誦念珠規程
songjing hui 誦經會
Songzi Guanyin 送子觀音
sui 歲
Sun Yuanhua 孙元化

tangzhu 堂主
Tanyangzi 曇陽子
Tianshen Hui 天神會
Tianshen huike 天神會課
Tianzhu jiaoyao 天主教要
Tianzhu shengjiao yueyuan 天主聖教約言
Tianzhu shengren xingshi 天主聖人行實
Tianzhu shijie quanlun shengji 天主十誡勸論聖迹
Tianzhu shiyi 天主實義
Tianzhujiao 天主教
Tong 佟
Tong Guoqi 佟國器
tonghui 痛悔
tongji 童乩
tonglehui 同樂會
tongshanhui 同善會
Tuanzhuan 彖傳

wai 外
Wang 王
Wang Pan 王泮
Wang Zheng 王徵
weibu 帷簿
wen 文
Wen Zhenheng 文震亨
wenshe 文社
Wu 吳 (family name)
wu 武 (military)
wu 巫 (shaman, shamaness)
wuchang 五常
Wusheng shishi 無聲詩史
Wuwei Jiao 無為教

xiansheng 先生
xiao 孝

Xiaoluan bu bingming shuo 鴞鸞不並鳴說
Xici 繫辭
xie 邪
xienian 邪念
Xifang dawen 西方答問
Xingxue cushu 性學觕述
xiru 西儒
xiseng 西僧
xishi 西士
xiucai 秀才
Xiwangmu 西王母
Xu 徐 (Candida's family name)
Xu 許 (Candida's husband's family name)
Xu Caibai 許采白
Xu Changzhi 徐昌治
Xu Congzhi 徐從治
Xu Dashou 許大受
Xu Erdou 徐爾斗
Xu Erjiao 徐爾覺
Xu Guangqi 徐光啟
Xu Guangqi Jinian Guan 徐光啟紀念館
Xu Ji 徐驥
Xu Yuandu 許遠度
Xu Yunxi 徐允希
Xu Zongze 徐宗澤
Xu Zuanzeng 許缵曾
Xujiahui 徐家汇
Xujiahui Tianzhujiao Tang 徐家汇天主教堂
xuyuan 許願

yang 陽
Yang 杨 (Agnes's surname)
Yang Tingyun 杨廷筠
Yao 堯
yaoren 妖人
yaotiao 窈窕
Ye Mengzhu 葉夢珠
yi fu yi fu 一夫一婦
Yi yin yi yang zhi wei dao 一陰一陽之謂道
Yi yu zhi qi, zhongshen bu gai. Gufu si bu jia. 壹與之齊， 終身不改。故夫死不嫁。
yiduan 異端
yiguan 衣冠
Yijing 易經
yin 陰
yinshi 陰室

yizhou 夷咒
Yongzheng 雍正
You Wenhui 游文輝
youtai 有胎
youyun 有孕
Yu 俞
yuanshi 院試
Yuanxiao Jie 元宵节
Yueshi bian 閱世編
Yunqi 雲棲

Zengzi 曾子
Zhang Dai 張岱
Zhao 趙
zhen 貞
zheng 正
Zheng Xuan 鄭玄
zhi 智
Zhong Mingren 鐘鳴仁
Zhuhong 袾宏
Zhulin Si 竹林寺
zongtang[zhu] 總堂[主]
zuiren 罪人
zuiye 罪業
zuoyi 作揖

NOTES

Introduction

1. King, "Couplet's Biography," 43. On Couplet's trip to Europe, see Foss, "The European Sojourn."
2. After the French version, which I will mainly use, enhanced translations into Spanish, Flemish, and Italian of *The Story of a Christian Lady of China* appeared, making it a comparably well-known book. For an overview of the events of the rites controversy, see HCC, 680–88. On "Confucius, the Chinese philosopher," see Meynard, *Confucius Sinarum Philosophus*.
3. Indeed, *The Story of a Christian Lady of China* corresponds to the highly popular literary genre of women's religious life-narratives written by their confessors (see Amsler, "Fromm, aber unfrei?").
4. On the proto-ethnographic style in the Jesuits' writings, see Mungello, *Curious Land*, 13–14, and Rubiés, "Travel Writing."
5. It was translated into Chinese by a Chinese nineteenth-century scholar, the Jesuit Xu Caibai (see Xu, *Xu taifuren zhuanlüe*), and served as a primary source on women for several studies of seventeenth-century Catholicism. See the bibliography in HCC, 393–98.
6. Couplet, *Histoire*, 7. All English translations are mine if not indicated otherwise.
7. See Couplet, *Histoire*, 107, passim.
8. See Sangren, "Female Gender," 21. On the worship of household deities, see McLaren, "Women's Work," 177. On life-cycle and seasonal rituals, see Mann, *Precious Records*, 55–75, 175–79. On domestic ancestor worship, see Freedman, "Ritual Aspects," 283.
9. The practices that were part of Chinese Catholic women's domestic religion were characterized by a striking diversity that is probably best understood with the help of recent research on the nature of Chinese religion. This has highlighted the socially fragmented, dynamic, and practice-orientated nature of Chinese religiosity. Adam Yuet Chau distinguishes five overlapping modalities of doing religion in China and proposes that we understand the Chinese religious landscape as "competitions between different modalities . . . as well as competitions within each modality" rather than competitions between the textual religious

traditions (Chau, "Modalities of Doing Religion," 548). On the flexibility of Chinese devotees, see Thoraval, "The Western Misconception."

10. On urbanization and monetization, see Brook, *The Confusions of Pleasure*, 153–237. On printing culture, see Chow, *Publishing, Culture, and Power.*
11. On late Ming culture of luxury and consumption, see Clunas, *Superfluous Things*. For a portrait of the living circumstances of the late Ming elite, see Spence, *Return*, 13–136.
12. See Berling, *The Syncretic Religion*, and de Bary, "Individualism."
13. On the Manchu conquest, see Wakeman, *The Great Enterprise*. On the installation of the new elite, see Crossley, "The Conquest Elite." On Ming loyalists' retrospection on the late Ming era, see Huang, *Negotiating Masculinities*, chapter 4.
14. See Ko, *Teachers*, 9, 12.
15. See Sheieh, *Concubines*; Gates, "The Commoditization"; and, on wife-selling, Sommer, *Polyandry.*
16. See T'ien, *Male Anxiety*, and Lu, *True to Her Word*. For an eighteenth-century perspective, see Theiss, *Disgraceful Matters.*
17. See Goossaert, "Irrepressible Female Piety," and Zhou, "The Hearth."
18. See Ko, *Teachers*; Widmer and Chang, *Writing Women*; and Idema and Grant, *The Red Brush*.
19. See Wang, "Ming Foreign Relations."
20. See Wills, *China and Maritime Europe.*
21. See Boxer, *South China.*
22. On the history of the Society of Jesus during the first decades after its founding, see O'Malley, *The First Jesuits*. On Francis Xavier, see Schurhammer, *Francis Xavier.*
23. For an overview on the place of the Society of Jesus within the post-Tridentine church and the Catholic world, see O'Malley, Bailey, Harris, and Kennedy, *The Jesuits*. On the Council of Trent and the Tridentine reform's implementation, see Bamji, Janssen, and Laven, *The Ashgate Research Companion to the Counter-Reformation*.
24. See Moran, *The Japanese.*
25. On Ruggieri's and Ricci's years in Macao and Zhaoqing, see Hsia, *A Jesuit*, 51–96.
26. On the Portuguese Padroado in the Chinese missions, see HCC, 286–87.
27. The monopoly of the Jesuit mission under the Portuguese Padroado ended in the 1690s, when French Jesuits started their own mission in China (see Brockey, *Journey*, 182–83; Hsia, *Sojourners*, chapters 5–8). The Propaganda Fide was a curial congregation founded in 1622 to strengthen the Pope's control over the overseas missions. On its difficulties to do so in the China mission, see Margiotti, "La Cina."
28. On the difficulties of government and information management over long distances, see Brendecke, *Imperium und Empirie*. On the duration of travel between Europe and China in the early modern era, see Golvers, "Distance."
29. On the Nanjing incident, see Kelly, *The Anti-Christian Persecution*, and Dudink, "*Nangong shudu* (1620)." On the Calendar Case, see Menegon, "Yang Guangxian's Opposition," and Chu, "Scientific Dispute." For an overview and contextualization of seventeenth- and eighteenth-century anti-Christian movements, see HCC, 503–33.

30. See HCC, 382–83. The numbers of Jesuits also increased over the course of the seventeenth century, albeit less significantly, from a handful in the 1610s to twenty or thirty later in the seventeenth century (see HCC, 307).
31. For comments on this change, see Rule, "From Missionary Hagiography." For an overview on the state of research, see HCC.
32. On lay people and lay institutions, see Brockey, *Journey*, chapters 9–10, and Yan and Vanhaelemeersch, *Silent Force*. On Chinese peoples' views on Catholicism, see Sachsenmaier, *Die Aufnahme*, and Standaert, *Yang Tingyun*. On Chinese Catholic literati's identities, see Huang, *Liangtoushe*, and Xu, "Seeking Redemption and Sanctity." For an exemplary study of a Jesuit's embeddedness in Chinese social networks, see Hsia, *A Jesuit*. For studies of several of the Jesuits' Chinese publications, see Li, *Yishu*; Meynard, *Confucius Sinarum Philosophus*; and Li and Meynard, *Jesuit Chreia*.
33. See Standaert, *The Interweaving of Rituals*, esp. 220–21.
34. For a comment on the lack of research on Chinese Catholic women, and a review of existing literature, see HCC, 393–98.
35. See Menegon, *Ancestors*, chapter 8; Zhang, *Guanfu*, 271–91; Entenmann, "Christian Virgins"; and Li, *God's Little Daughters*. See also the contributions to Lutz, *Pioneer Chinese Christian Women*, and Bays, *Christianity in China*, part 3.
36. For a case study on women's piety in post-Tridentine Catholicism, see Laqua-O'Donnell, *Women and the Counter-Reformation*. For overviews, see Fairchilds, *Women in Early Modern Europe*, chapters 4, 9–11, and Wiesner-Hanks, "Women and Religious Change."
37. On clerical masculinities, see Thibodeaux, *The Manly Priest*, and Le Gall, "La virilité des clercs." On the Jesuits' masculinity, see Strasser, "'The First Form and Grace.'" On their relationship to women, see Mostaccio, *Early Modern Jesuits*, chapter 4; Molina, *To Overcome Oneself*, chapters 2 and 7; and Bilinkoff, *Confessors and Their Female Penitents*. See also the contributions to Laven, "The Jesuits and Gender," which contains two articles on the early Jesuits' close ties to elite women. Other important studies on this topic are Valone, "Piety and Patronage"; Hufton, "Altruism and Reciprocity"; and Kirkham, "Laura Battiferra."
38. For an insightful synthesis, see Brownell and Wasserstrom, *Chinese Femininities*. On elite women, see Ko, *Teachers*; Mann, *Precious Records*; and Bray, *Technology and Gender*. See also, on female authors, Widmer and Chang, *Writing Women*, and Idema and Grant, *The Red Brush*. On discourses and practices of female chastity in China, see Theiss, *Disgraceful Matters*, and T'ien, *Male Anxiety*. On the status of women from the perspective of legal history, see Sommer, *Sex, Law, and Society*.
39. For overviews on late imperial women's religiosity, see Grant, "Women, Gender, and Religion"; Huang, Valussi, and Palmer, "Gender and Sexuality"; and Jia, Kang, and Ping, *Gendering Chinese Religion*.
40. On early modern European concepts of gender, see Wunder, *He Is the Sun*. On late imperial Chinese views, see Brownell and Wasserstrom, "Introduction: Theorizing Femininities and Masculinities," esp. 34, and Rowe, "Women and the Family," 2–7.

41. On the "legitimizing function" of gender, see Scott, "Gender: A Useful Category," 1070. For case studies on intercultural situations, see Montrose, "The Work of Gender," and Vigarello, "Le viril et le sauvage."
42. On masculinity as an "inherently relational" concept, see Connell, *Masculinities*, 76–86.
43. Although seventeenth-century Chinese gentry women had a high degree of literacy, no seventeenth-century sources on Catholicism written by women are known today. For an overview on sources about Chinese Catholicism, see HCC, 113–237.
44. On the Jesuits' journey to China, see Hsia, *A Jesuit*, chapter 2. On their curriculum in Europe as well as their subsequent studies of Chinese in the Middle Kingdom, see Brockey, *Journey*, chapter 6.
45. See HCC, 309–10.
46. For an exemplary study of the Society's administrative and organizational work in Europe, see Friedrich, *Der lange Arm.*
47. See Brockey, *Journey*, 73–77.
48. For a list of the China mission's vice-provincials, visitors, and procurators, see Dehergne, *Répertoire*, 314–23. For a study of André Palmeiro, visitor to China in the late 1620s, see Brockey, *The Visitor.*
49. On the exchange of written documents of the Jesuits in China and Europe, see Golvers, *Building Humanistic Libraries.*
50. See Friedrich, "Government and Information-Management," and idem, "Circulating and Compiling."
51. Already in 1907, Bernhard Duhr pointed to the problematic nature of the annual letters circulating in the German provinces (Duhr, *Geschichte der Jesuiten*, vol. 1, 674–78). For a recent work that rejects the annual letters as sources on local realities, see Paschoud, *Le monde amérindien*, 11.
52. More than 65 percent of all Catholics lived in Jiangnan toward the end of the seventeenth century (see HCC, 560). On the economic importance and cultural centrality of the Jiangnan region during the late imperial period, see Naquin and Rawski, *Chinese Society*, 147–57. For studies focusing on Jiangnan elite women, see Ko, *Teachers*, and Mann, *Precious Records*. On Jiangnan Catholicism, with one chapter dedicated to women (211–60), see Zhou, *Shiqi, shiba shiji.*
53. There will be no separate discussion of the small community of converted Ming palace women that existed from circa 1630 to 1644, because this was a rather marginal phenomenon in seventeenth-century Chinese Catholicism (see HCC, 439). On the conversion of one empress of the Southern Ming dynasty, which received some attention in contemporary Europe, see Boym, "Briefve relation de la Chine," and Struve, *Voices*, 235–38.
54. On Jesuit missionaries' preference for cities over rural areas, see HCC, 538–40. On rural circuits, usually conducted for several months every year, see Brockey, *Journey*, 94–98, passim.
55. On Chinese women's non-Christian domestic religious cultures, see Mann, *Precious Records*, chapter 7, and McLaren, "Women's Work."

56. Information on these two groups of people is unequally distributed. While much biographical data is available on missionaries, many of the Chinese women whose activities are discussed remain nameless or are only known by their Christian names.

1. Clothes Make the Man

1. The entry-level exam (*yuanshi*) did not yet qualify a candidate for office, but was merely a qualification for taking the provincial exam. See Miyazaki, *China's Examination Hell*, 26–32. See also Elman, *A Cultural History of Civil Examinations.*
2. *Fonti Ricciane*, vol. 1, 336.
3. See *Fonti Ricciane*, vol. 1, 336.
4. See Heijdra, "The Socio-Economic Development," 552–54.
5. On temple renovation, see Brook, *Praying for Power*, esp. parts 2 and 3. On irrigation projects, see Heijdra, "The Socio-Economic Development," 564–67. On charitable institutions, see Smith, *The Art of Doing Good.*
6. See Spence, *Return*, esp. 13–46.
7. Since the indispensable missiological work of Johannes Bettray (Bettray, *Die Akkommodationsmethode*, esp. 1–10), the Jesuits' change of dress has been interpreted by historians as the starting point of Jesuit accommodation. See Hsia, "From Buddhist Garb," and Peterson, "What to Wear?"
8. *Fonti Ricciane*, vol. 1, 338.
9. Sociologists have pointed out that this view of attire is true not only for the early modern period but also for more recent times. See Barthes, "Histoire et sociologie du vêtement," 440, and Simmel, "Die Mode."
10. See Dinges, "Von der 'Lesbarkeit der Welt.'"
11. On European regulation of clothing, see Iseli, *Gute Policey*, 39–43. On China, see Yuan, *Dressing the State*, 50–51.
12. Yuan, *Dressing the State*, 51.
13. See Rowe, "Women and the Family."
14. See Dinges, "Von der 'Lesbarkeit der Welt,'" 94–98.
15. See Rublack, *Dressing Up*, 7, 15.
16. See Brook, *The Confusions of Pleasure*, and Clunas, *Superfluous Things.*
17. See Pantoja, "[Letter to] Ludovicus Guzmanus," 72. On the regulations of the *Collected Statutes of the Ming Dynasty*, see Dauncey, "Illusions of Grandeur," 47.
18. Ye Mengzhu, *Yueshi bian* (Notes on crossing an era), 1700, cited in Yuan, *Dressing the State*, 167. The blurring of social boundaries coincided with a significant rise of the number of holders of bachelor's degrees during the Ming, from around thirty thousand in the fourteenth century to about five hundred thousand in the sixteenth century. See Heijdra, "The Socio-Economic Development," 561.
19. See Li, *Fen shu*, 35.
20. On standardized religious garments, see Rublack, *Dressing Up*, 81.
21. See von Severus, "Habit."
22. Levy, "Jesuit Identity," 140.

23. See "The Constitutions of the Society of Jesus" (1558), part VI, chapter 2, article 15, in Padberg, *The Constitutions of the Society of Jesus*.
24. See Hsia, "From Buddhist Garb," 144.
25. The Society's high degree of interiorization of religious norms has also been highlighted in Molina, *To Overcome Oneself*, and Reinhard, "Gegenreformation als Modernisierung?," esp. 240.
26. See Levy, "Jesuit Identity."
27. Roberto de Nobili, famous for his accommodation to the Indian Brahmanic culture, was most explicit in separating religious from civil customs. See Županov, *Disputed Mission*, chapter 1.
28. See *Fonti Ricciane*, vol. 1, 338.
29. This preference was remarked on by Peter Paul Rubens, who painted Nicolas Trigault in his literati attire when he passed through the Southern Netherlands in 1617. See Logan and Brockey, "Nicolas Trigault, SJ," 157.
30. On the great variety of literati clothing styles, see Hsia, *A Jesuit*, 179, and Huang, *Negotiating Masculinities*, 81.
31. On the dress worn by the Jesuits in Rome, see O'Malley, *The First Jesuits*, 341–42.
32. Trigault, "Lettera Annua della Cina del 1610," 50.
33. See Prospero Intorcetta to the Propaganda Fide, Rome, 10 December 1671, APF, SOCG, vol. 432, 19r–20r. On the China Jesuits' preference for selecting mature men as candidates for priesthood, see HCC, 462. On the establishment of Chinese indigenous priests—a project especially promoted by the Propaganda Fide—see Bornet, "L'apostolat laïque." Also in Europe, lay brothers were not allowed to wear the same dress as ordained priests. See Menegon, "The Habit."
34. While the Dominicans wore Chinese robes from the beginning of their mission, Franciscans continued to wear their cassocks and European attire during their first years in China. This, however, led to conflicts that prompted them to cede this practice. See Menegon, *Ancestors*, 83.
35. A local leader from the city of Fu'an, Fujian, thus denounced the mendicants as sorcerers (*yaoren*) and criminals (*zuiren*), while all the while respecting the Jesuits as literati (*xiansheng*). See Juan Bautista Morales to the Propaganda Fide, Philippines, 4 April 1649, APF, SOCG, vol. 193, 222r. For an analysis of the events that led to this letter, see Menegon, *Ancestors*, 99–102.
36. See *Fonti Ricciane*, vol. 1, 337. On the differences between informal and ceremonial dress, see Menegon, "The Habit." In fact, there was an internal debate among the Jesuits about whether silk should be worn on a daily basis. See Brockey, *The Visitor*, 305.
37. See Brockey, *Journey*, 95, and Hsia, "From Buddhist Garb," 149–50.
38. On the *jijin*, see anon., "Une pratique liturgique."
39. See Brook, *The Confusions of Pleasure*, 153–73, and Spence, *Return*.
40. During the first decade of the seventeenth century, no fewer than ten servants attended to the missionaries' needs in the Beijing residence. See Ricci, *Lettere*, 392.
41. On Ricci starting to use sedan chairs, see Hsia, *A Jesuit*, 136.
42. Couplet, *Histoire*, 16–17.

43. See Brockey, *Journey*, 32, 46, and Menegon, "Amicitia Palatina."
44. See Clunas, *Superfluous Things*.
45. See Mungello, *The Forgotten Christians*, 11–12.
46. See the anonymous, undated letter filed in BNCR 1383, 385r.
47. See Brockey, *Journey*, 46.
48. See Golvers, *François de Rougemont*, 629–30.
49. Le Comte, *Nouveaux mémoires*, vol. 1, 103.
50. On the Jesuits' translation of *ru*, see Standaert, "The Jesuits Did NOT Manufacture 'Confucianism,'" 118–19.
51. See Brockey, *Journey*, 243–86 (chapter 7).
52. See Brockey, *Journey*, 257.
53. See Meynard, introduction to *Confucius Sinarum Philosophus*, 10.
54. On prior translations of the Four Books into European languages, see Meynard, introduction to *Confucius Sinarum Philosophus*, 4–10.
55. On the concept of *lumen naturale* in the China mission, see Amsler, "'Sie meinen,'" 95. On its role in early modern mission on a global scale, see Milhou, "Die neue Welt," 283.
56. See Brockey, *Journey*, 212, 264, and O'Malley, *The First Jesuits*, 216. On the influence of Latin and Greek authors on the Jesuits' spirituality, see Maryks, *Saint Cicero*.
57. On the comparability of Chinese and European notions of antiquity during the early modern period, see the contributions in Miller and Louis, *Antiquarianism*.
58. See Rowe, "Women and the Family," 2–6.
59. *Fonti Ricciane*, vol. 1, 338.
60. See Hsia, *A Jesuit*, 212–14.
61. Although the text claimed to describe courtesies in use throughout Chinese society (cf. *Fonti Ricciane*, vol. 1, 71), Ricci focuses in fact exclusively on those of the literati.
62. *Fonti Ricciane*, vol. 1, 72.
63. Sabatino de Ursis, "Rellaçam [*sic*] da morte do P[adr]e Matheos Ricio da Companhia de JESUS, que entrára no Reino da China, com algumas couzas de sua vida," Beijing, 20 April 1611, BA-JA 49-V-5, 103r–116r, 108v.
64. Trigault, "Lettera Annua della Cina del 1610," 16.
65. One way to manage this tension was to establish different institutions for different social strata. Some religious congregations the Jesuits founded were reserved for members of the literati class, while others were open to "more humble people" (see Trigault, "Lettera Annua della Cina del 1610," 16).
66. See Laven, *Mission to China*, 181. Mary Laven's chapter "Jesuits and Eunuchs" (161–93) is the only current attempt to analyze Jesuits in China within the framework provided by the concept of masculinities. Laven gives much room to an analysis of Matteo Ricci's view of Chinese eunuchs and his apology for celibacy. She does not address, however, the Jesuits' adoption of literati masculinity.
67. On Chinese criticism of late Ming masculinities, see Huang, *Negotiating Masculinities*, 78–81. In contrast to Chinese effeminate masculinities, the Jesuits described Manchu masculinities as fierce and brave. See anon., "Relatione della Conversione alla nostra Sta fede della Regina, e Prencipe della China . . . l'anno

1648," s.l., s.d., ARSI, Jap. Sin. 125, 139r–153r, 149r. Later accounts also noted the Sinicization of Manchu masculinities in the second half of the seventeenth century. See Thomas-Ignatius Dunyn-Szpot, "Historia Sinarum Imperii, 1641–1687," ARSI, Jap. Sin. 103, 107r.

68. For a discussion of Aristotle's views of Asians, see Frank, *A Democracy*, 30–32. On the importance of European classical authors for early modern travel writing, see Osterhammel, *Die Entzauberung*, 152.
69. *Fonti Ricciane*, vol. 1, 72.
70. *Fonti Ricciane*, vol. 1, 98.
71. See Matteo Ricci to Girolamo Costa, Nanjing, 14 August 1599, in Ricci, *Lettere*, 362.
72. It seems unlikely, on this view, that the Jesuits' remarks about Chinese effeminacy served primarily to develop a sense of European masculine superiority, as was the case for those later authors—with their colonial and imperial mind-sets—studied by Hellman, "Using China at Home," and Sinha, *Colonial Masculinity.*
73. According to Song Geng, it was the "signifier of the official masculinity in traditional China" (Song, *The Fragile Scholar*, 97).
74. On cultured and martial masculinity, see Louie and Edwards, "Chinese Masculinity."
75. Song, *The Fragile Scholar*, 93.
76. See Song, *The Fragile Scholar*, 93.
77. As an ideal promoted by Confucius, sagehood was the goal pursued by a gentleman in Confucian moral discourse. "Disciple of the sage" was therefore synonymous with "gentleman." See Song, *The Fragile Scholar*, 89.
78. Translation by Kelly, *The Anti-Christian Persecution*, 295. A *jinshi* is a successful candidate in the highest imperial examination.
79. See Kelly, *The Anti-Christian Persecution*, 306–7.
80. Translation by Hsia, *A Jesuit*, 193.
81. See Höllmann, "Ein Zeichen." Beards were, however, not only positive symbols. According to a different line of interpretation, they were also attributes of barbarians. Nineteenth-century anti-Christian controversialists often drew on this interpretation. See Dikötter, *The Discourse of Race*, 45.
82. See Song, *The Fragile Scholar*, 89.
83. See *Fonti Ricciane*, vol. 1, 337.
84. The Annual Letter of 1621, for instance, mentioned that the missionary Johannes Ureman had started to grow his beard upon arrival in Macao, implying that he could enter China only after having attained the right look. Cf. Trigault, "Litterae Annuae 1621" (1625), 227.
85. "Treslado de hum itinerario, que o Padre Andre Palmeiro mandou ao Padre Geral, composto por elle," s.l., s.d. [1628], BA-JA 49-V-8, 507r–536r, 521v. On Palmeiro, see Brockey, *The Visitor*; on Palmeiro's beard, see esp. 252–53.
86. "Treslado de hum itinerario, que o Padre Andre Palmeiro mandou ao Padre Geral, composto por elle," s.l., s.d. [1628], BA-JA 49-V-8, 507r–536r, 522r.
87. See *Fonti Ricciane*, vol. 1, 104–7.
88. Mish, "Creating an Image," Chinese text 12, English translation 48–49.

89. See Huang, *Negotiating Masculinities*, 135. On the broad acceptance of homosexuality in Ming society, see Hinsch, *Passions*, chapter 6. In contrast to the Ming, the Qing were rather hostile against homosexuality. See Sommer, "The Penetrated Male."
90. The identification of the "talented scholar" as the masculine antitype in Jesuit writings somewhat differs from the reading proposed by Mary Laven, in which she suggests that eunuchs were regarded by the Jesuits as the primary embodiment of vicious Chinese masculinity (see Laven, *Mission to China*, 161–93). Laven is certainly right that the Jesuits sometimes borrowed Chinese stereotypes about eunuchs (179). However, the hypothesis that missionaries had a depreciative view of eunuchs in general is not convincing. In fact, the Jesuits heavily relied on eunuchs for converting palace ladies, and some of the most famous Catholics of the Ming court were eunuchs (see HCC, 438–43).
91. For references to homosexuality, see, for instance, Aleni, *Dizui zhenggui lüe*, 397, and Brancati, *Tianshen huike*, 111–13.
92. *Fonti Ricciane*, vol. 1, 98. Translation adapted from Spence, *The Memory Palace*, 220–21.
93. Ricci, *The True Meaning*, 349.
94. On the publication of *Master Cheng's Ink Garden* and Ricci's contribution, see Spence, *The Memory Palace*, esp. 11; Clarke, *The Virgin Mary*, 37; and Clunas, *Pictures and Visuality*, 173–74.
95. Translation by Spence, *The Memory Palace*, 203. Chinese wording in Duyvendak, Review of *Le origini dell'arte Cristiana Cinese*, 394.
96. Ricci was not the only missionary presenting the story of Sodom to a Chinese audience. It was also included in Brancati, *Tianzhu shijie quanlun shengji*, 52v.
97. See Vitiello, "Exemplary Sodomites."
98. On friendship in late Ming discourse, see Huang, "Male Friendship," 2. On the Jesuits' praise of friendship, see Xu, "The Concept of Friendship." On the importance of homosocial bonds in the Society of Jesus, see Strasser, "'The First Form and Grace,'" esp. 48–49.
99. Cited by Vitiello, "Exemplary Sodomites," 250.
100. Ricci, *On Friendship*, 119. For an interpretation of this warning as a criticism of homoeroticism, see Vitiello, "Exemplary Sodomites," 251.
101. Translation by Legge, *The Works of Mencius*, chapter 14.
102. See Laven, *Mission to China*, 184–90; Lin, *Wan Ming zhongxi xinglunli de xiangyu*, 77–89; and Menegon, "Child Bodies," 199–205. Only a few non-Catholic literati appreciated celibacy as a sign of self-cultivation, comparing the Jesuits with other religious specialists rather than with the literati class. One of them was Zhang Dai, who admiringly noted in his memoirs that in Europe "all those engaged in academic pursuits never marry" (cited in Spence, *Return*, 132).
103. Shi, *Fujian xunhai dao gaoshi*, 32a. A similar accusation was made by a literatus named Li Can. He claimed that Ricci should have brought his family with him to China, just as Zengzi, a student of Confucius, had, traveling together with his parents, wife, and children. See Li, *Pixie shuo*, 26b. Both accusations were published by the Nanjing magistrate Shen Que in a collection of pamphlets titled

Documents from the Southern Palace (Nangong shudu), which was reproduced with minor omissions by the lay Buddhist Xu Changzhi under the title *Collection Destroying Heresy* (Po xie ji) in 1639. In the following, I cite from *Collection Destroying Heresy*, which circulated more widely than *Documents from the Southern Palace*. For a detailed analysis of both editions, see Dudink, "*Nangong shudu* (1620)."

104. See Menegon, *Ancestors*, 312.
105. See *Fonti Ricciane*, vol. 2, 383–84. The case was mentioned in several Jesuit letters. For an earlier accusation against Michele Ruggieri, see Bartoli, *Dell'historia*, 212–15.
106. See Ricci, *The True Meaning*, 349–51. For detailed recapitulations and analyses of Ricci's argument, see Laven, *Mission to China*, 185–90, and Spence, *The Memory Palace*, 228.
107. Ricci, *The True Meaning*, 434–35.
108. Ricci's idea of filiality was directly attacked by Fujian literatus Chen Houguang. See Chen, *Bianxue chuyan*, 4a.
109. See Menegon, "Child Bodies," 205.
110. See Vagnone, *Qijia xixue*, 496.
111. Translation adapted from Menegon, "Child Bodies," 205.
112. Vagnone, *Qijia xixue*, 496.
113. See Bake, *Spiegel.*
114. For a similar reading of the misogynous passages in Pantoja's *Seven Victories*, see Menegon, "Child Bodies," 203.

2. A Kingdom of Virtuous Women

1. On the emergence of the practice of female seclusion in the Song dynasty, see Ebrey, *The Inner Quarters.*
2. Hinsch, "The Origins," 602.
3. See Mann, *Precious Records*, 50. On houses in early modern Europe, see Eibach, "Das offene Haus."
4. Cited by Ebrey, *The Inner Quarters*, 23–24.
5. See Ko, *Teachers*, 13. For how the categories inner and outer referred not only to physical spaces but also to a functional differentiation between the sexes, see Rosenlee, *Confucianism and Women*, chapter 4.
6. On people and goods transgressing the boudoir door, see Bray, *Technology and Gender*, 54.
7. In China, a newborn child was considered to be one *sui* of age. Age was calculated by adding one year at each Chinese New Year's Day.
8. See Bray, *Technology and Gender*, 130. Several events in seventeenth-century rural Shandong recounted in Spence, *The Death*, illustrate this practice (see 56, passim).
9. On Han literati's representations of gender relations among non-Han populations in southern China and Taiwan, see Teng, "An Island," and Miles, "Strange Encounters."
10. On the Kingdom of Women, see Teng, "The West," 101–2. On the late imperial cult of female chastity, see Carlitz, "Desire, Danger, and the Body"; T'ien, *Male Anxiety*; and, with a focus on the eighteenth century, Theiss, *Disgraceful Matters.*

11. *Zheng* is a key term in late imperial Confucian discourse on religious doctrines. There is a broad scholarly debate about its many meanings. A starting point was Yang Ching Kun's definition of *zheng* as politico-moral orthodoxy (Yang, *Religion*, 196). In response, other Sinologists have highlighted the importance of understanding *zheng* also as "orthopraxy" and have started to speak of an "orthopraxy-orthodoxy continuum" (see Watson, "Orthopraxy Revisited," 154). See also the contributions in Liu, *Orthodoxy*.
12. For this characterization of the Chinese idea of heterodoxy, see Cohen, *China and Christianity*, 5, 16–17. See also the contributions in Liu and Shek, *Heterodoxy*.
13. For a discussion of the Confucian elite's reactions to women's temple visits, see Goossaert, "Irrepressible Female Piety," and Zhou, "The Hearth." On the control imperial institutions imposed on Buddhism and Taoism, respectively, see Yü, "Ming Buddhism," 904–5, and Berling, "Taoism," 960–70. For reflections on the process of labeling movements as heterodox, see ter Haar, *The White Lotus Teachings*.
14. On the emergence of popular Buddhist movements in the late imperial era, see Overmyer, *Folk Buddhist Religion*.
15. On the tensions between the Buddhist *sangha* and the Confucian model of society, see Zürcher, "Buddhismus," 217–18.
16. See Mann, *Precious Records*, 191–93, and Grant, *Eminent Nuns*, 1–4.
17. See Zhou, "The Hearth," 120.
18. See Goossaert, "Irrepressible Female Piety," 222.
19. See Zhou, "The Hearth," 110.
20. See Taylor, "Official Religion," 886–88. On the topos of the promiscuous monk, see Durand-Dastès, "Désirés, raillés, corrigés."
21. Trigault, "Lettera Annua della Cina del 1610," 50.
22. Couplet, *Histoire*, 8.
23. The term *moral topography* is based on the idea that people rely on individual or socially shared "mental maps" when navigating in social space (see Gould and White, *Mental Maps*).
24. I am primarily interested in Sino-Western interactions taking place in China and, in the following, do not discuss the Jesuit writings' reception in Europe. For an insightful study on representations of Chinese gendered virtue in eighteenth-century England, see Yang, *Performing China*.
25. The term *bonze* was derived from the Japanese term *bozu* (Chinese *fashi*). It was mostly used to refer to Buddhist monks (see Dalgado, *Glossário*, vol. 1, 138–39). Although the Jesuits often distinguished Buddhist "bonzes" from Taoist "sorcerers," they often failed to draw clear distinctions between Buddhist and other religious specialists, and therefore it is not always clear which sort of ritual expert is denoted by the term.
26. The first missionaries in China had even maintained that Buddhist communities might have been perverted remnants of St. Thomas's ancient mission to China. See Gonzales de Mendoza, *Historia*, 37–39, and *Fonti Ricciane*, vol. 1, 123–24. On the Jesuits' accommodation in Japan, see Moran, *The Japanese*.
27. See Hsia, *A Jesuit*, 97.

28. See Michele Ruggieri to Claudio Acquaviva, Zhaoqing, 30 March 1584, ARSI, Jap. Sin. 9 II, 263r–264r, 264r. Ruggieri's rendering of this name as "Church and New Flower of the Saints" (Ecclesia e Fior Novello Degli Santi) is an incorrect translation.
29. Alessandro Valignano to Claudio Acquaviva, Macao, 10 November 1588, ARSI, Jap. Sin. 11 I, 1r–8r, 1v.
30. On the gentry's use of monastic space, see Brook, *Praying for Power*, 107–19.
31. See Brook, *Praying for Power*, 29–34.
32. Ricci, *Lettere*, 8.
33. Alessandro Valignano to Claudio Acquaviva, Macao, 10 November 1588, ARSI, Jap. Sin. 11 I, 1r–8r, 1v.
34. Brockey, *Journey*, 410. Lionel Jensen has argued that the Jesuits were uninterested in the corpus of Buddhist texts because of its lack of systematization, which made it difficult for them to navigate. See Jensen, *Manufacturing Confucianism*, 31–76.
35. See Matteo Ricci to Claudio Acquaviva, 4 November 1595, in Ricci, *Lettere*, 297–321, 309.
36. See Simão da Cunha, "Apontamento para annua de [1]648 da Christandade de Kien yam, Vui xan cum, Tin cheu, Kien nim hien, Tai nim hien," s.l., s.d., BNP, CÓD. 722, 365r–373r, 371r. On the Tridentine cloistering of Catholic nuns' convents, see Strasser, "Cloistering Women's Past."
37. *Fonti Ricciane*, vol. 1, 126; Diogo Motel, [Beijing?], 1675, ARSI, Jap. Sin. 125, 111r–111vvv [*sic*], 111v–111vv. A similarly general accusation about such associations was also brought forward by the visitor André Palmeiro during his stay in China in the 1620s. See Brockey, *The Visitor*, 227.
38. See Greslon, *Histoire*, 31–32. For other accounts criticizing the bonzes' immoral behavior, see Semedo, *Histoire*, 131–32; Le Comte, *Nouveaux mémoires*, vol. 2, 173–74; and various letters in the *Lettres édifiantes* (e.g., vol. 9, 339; vol. 29, 86–101).
39. See Yü, *The Renewal*, 4.
40. See Yü, *The Renewal*, chapter 7, quotation 182.
41. On masters of reform in Buddhism in late Ming China, see Yü, "Ming Buddhism."
42. See Zhou, "The Hearth," 113.
43. See Zhou, "The Hearth," 113.
44. See the translation in Roy, *The Plum in the Golden Vase*, vol. 1, 165–66. See also Roy, *The Plum in the Golden Vase*, vol. 3, chapter 51, and Shi, *The Water Margin*, 561–62.
45. See Durand-Dastès, "Désirés, raillés, corrigés," 98.
46. It is noteworthy that the Jesuits inscribed themselves into this Confucian discourse primarily in their writings aimed at a European readership. This suggests that it was not a strategical move aimed at persuading Chinese literati of their Confucian identity, but rather was the result of the Jesuits' strong identification with the Confucian viewpoint.
47. See Brockey, *Journey*, 287.
48. On the connection between immorality and idolatry in early modern Catholic discourse, see Županov, *Missionary Tropics*, 8, 26.

49. See Wunder, *He Is the Sun*, 96–117. On how eighteenth-century enlightened authors saw gender segregation in non-European societies as a sign of cultural inferiority, see Stollberg-Rilinger, *Europa*, 145–46.
50. Semedo, *Histoire*, 92–93.
51. On Aleni's accompanying Ma to Shanxi, see Margiotti, *Il cattolicismo*, 83. For the identification of Ma, see HCC, 421.
52. Trigault, "Litterae Annuae 1621" (1625), 237.
53. See Couplet, *Histoire*, 7.
54. See Semedo, *Histoire*, 48.
55. See Kircher, *China Illustrata*, 115.
56. See Magalhães, *Nouvelle relation*, 126.
57. See Mann, *Precious Records*, 49, and Li, *Women's Poetry*, 20–51.
58. Semedo, *Histoire*, 47.
59. Semedo, *Histoire*, 48. This trope is also found in late imperial Chinese literary sources, such as the eighteenth-century novel *Dream of the Red Chamber* (Honglou meng). See Cao, *The Story of the Stone*, vol. 2, 148–49.
60. The women's delicate body shape, their ways of hiding their hands within the sleeves of their robes, and their modestly bowed heads belong to a Chinese visual tradition of depicting *guixiu*—young, beautiful women of good family. See Wu, "Beyond Stereotypes," 350, passim. For the identification of European elements in the two pictures, see Staatliche Schlösser und Gärten Potsdam-Sanssouci, *China und Europa*, 157.
61. Couplet, *Histoire*, 110.
62. Kircher, *China Illustrata*, 115. Several other authors expressed a wish that Europeans would also adopt the Chinese abhorrence of nudity. See Couplet, *Histoire*, 110–11, and Magalhães, *Nouvelle relation*, 126–27. In their praise for Chinese women's modest dress, the Jesuits failed to acknowledge the great diversity of women's sartorial practices in the vast Chinese empire. As shown by a set of costume pictures, printed without commentary in Kircher's *China Illustrata* (figures Aa 2 and Aa 3), dresses worn by women in the southern provinces of Zhejiang and Fujian offered rather revealing views of the women's necks and hands, with the Fujian woman even depicted with naked feet.
63. In contrast to the eighteenth- and nineteenth-century ethnographic writings examined by Patricia Buckley Ebrey (Ebrey, "Gender and Sinology," 20–21), the Jesuits' accounts did not mention footbinding's sexual connotations. That women's feet were regarded by the Chinese as an intimate body part was discussed, however, in the context of the administration of extreme unction, when the Jesuits abstained from anointing them (see, for instance, Couplet, *Histoire*, 104). On the cultural meanings of footbinding in the late imperial period, see Ko, *Cinderella's Sisters*.
64. See Pantoja, *Relatione dell'entrata*, 78.
65. *Fonti Ricciane*, vol. 1, 89. Although the Jesuits' suggestion that footbinding prevented female mobility was too simple, they were right to assert a connection between seclusion and footbinding. Indeed, Susan Mann has maintained that "the desirability of footbinding and the spread of women's home handicrafts in peasant

households were systematically related." Mann, *Precious Records*, 168. This hypothesis has recently been confirmed by anthropological fieldwork. See Bossen and Gates, *Bound Feet*.

66. See, for instance, Pantoja, *Relatione dell'entrata*, 78.
67. See Semedo, *Histoire*, 47, and Martini, *Novus Atlas Sinensis*, vol. 1, 7. These critical voices qualify Ebrey's hypothesis that Western perceptions of footbinding were directly related to perceptions of Chinese civilization (see Ebrey, "Gender and Sinology"). Although it is true that "those who largely had good things to say about China, like Marco Polo and the Jesuits" tended to describe Chinese women in positive terms (Ebrey, "Gender and Sinology," 10), it was not the case that all Jesuits approved of footbinding.
68. On the cult of female chastity, see Theiss, *Disgraceful Matters*; Lu, *True to Her Word*; and Carlitz, "Desire, Danger, and the Body."
69. Semedo, *Histoire*, 41.
70. Magalhães, *Nouvelle relation*, 59–60.
71. See T'ien, *Male Anxiety*; Ropp, "Passionate Women"; and Lu, *True to Her Word*, chapter 5.
72. André Ferram, "Annua da Vice-Provincia da China [1656]," Macao, 29 January 1659, BA-JA 49-V-14, 62r–93r, 73r. On the conflict between Confucian and Christian understandings of suicide, see Huang, "'Liangtoushe zu' de suming," 468.
73. See, for instance, Semedo, *Histoire*, 48, and Pantoja, *Relatione dell'entrata*, 78.
74. See *Fonti Ricciane*, vol. 1, 98; Pantoja, *Relatione dell'entrata*, 53; and Semedo, *Histoire*, 104. For an analysis of women as objects of exchange in late imperial China, see Gates, "The Commoditization of Chinese Women."
75. For rare exceptions, see *Fonti Ricciane*, vol. 1, 98, and Martini, *Novus Atlas Sinensis*, vol. 1, 104.
76. Interestingly, Jesuit writings contain relatively few remarks about Manchu women in general. The most detailed seventeenth-century Western account of Manchu women was written, therefore, not by a Jesuit, but by a member of a Dutch embassy, Johan Nieuhof (see Nieuhof, *Die Gesandschaft*, 117, 122–23, 163–64, 394–95).
77. Pantoja, *Relatione dell'entrata*, 78.
78. Couplet, *Histoire*, 7.
79. Las Cortes had been working as a missionary in the Philippines for twenty years, when, early in 1625, he was sent on a diplomatic mission to Macao. The mission ended in a shipwreck some 350 kilometers east of Macao (see Girard, introduction to *Le voyage en Chine*, 21–26).
80. See Las Cortes, *Le voyage en Chine*. On women's temple visits, see 69, 291, 332.
81. See Girard, "Les descriptions," 174–77, 184.

3. A Source of Creative Tension

1. See Chau, "Modalities of Doing Religion," 558.
2. See Standaert, *The Interweaving of Rituals*, 222–28, and Thoraval, "The Western Misconception."
3. See Goossaert and Zuber, "Introduction: La Chine," 14.

4. See Rosner, "Frauen als Anführerinnen." The association of baptism with the rituals of Chinese secret societies was even clearer because of similar initiation ceremonies practiced by the latter. See Bays, "Christianity," 41.
5. Zürcher, "Confucian and Christian Religiosity," 650. See also idem, "A Complement."
6. Zürcher, "Confucian and Christian Religiosity," 632.
7. See *Fonti Ricciane*, vol. 2, 261.
8. João da Rocha to [?], Nanjing, 5 October 1602, BA-JA 49-V-5, 10r–16v, 13v. Da Rocha was Ricci's successor as superior of the Nanjing residence. For biographical data, see Dehergne, *Répertoire*, 223.
9. Longobardo initiated this change of strategy with the consent of his superiors (see Guerreiro, *Relaçam annal*, bk. 2, 20r). The first women baptized by Longobardo were the mother and grandmother of a Shaozhou literatus named Zhong (see *Fonti Ricciane*, vol. 2, 205). On Longobardo's evangelization strategy, see Brockey, *Journey*, 293–96. For biographical data, see Dehergne, *Répertoire*, 153–54.
10. See *Fonti Ricciane*, vol. 2, 202.
11. See Guerreiro, *Relaçam annal*, bk. 2, 20r–20v.
12. See *Fonti Ricciane*, vol. 2, 338.
13. Guerreiro, *Relaçam annal*, bk. 2, 20r.
14. The importance of Chinese men's confidence is especially highlighted by João da Rocha. See da Rocha to [?], Nanjing, 5 October 1602, BA-JA 49-V-5, 10r–16v, 13v.
15. This precondition did not mean that these men had to be Catholic themselves. In many cases, women were baptized earlier than their male relatives, who nevertheless consented to the women's conversion.
16. Guerreiro, *Relaçam annal*, bk. 2, 20v.
17. On Jesuits preaching in the countryside, see Brockey, *Journey*, 293–96.
18. On the Jesuits' stay in Yang Tingyun's residence in Hangzhou, see Trigault, "Litterae Annuae 1621" (1625), 270–71. On their residence in the Xu ancestral home in Shanghai, see Trigault, "Litterae Annuae 1621" (1627), 218.
19. See Trigault, "Litterae Annuae 1621" (1625), 345.
20. On strategies of indirect conversion, see also King, "Spaces for Belief."
21. In the Annual Letter of 1627, Manuel Dias the Younger (1574–1659) described a scene of children instructing country women in a village near Ningbo. Dias was delighted that the children, "who had learned more rapidly," shuttled between their mothers and fathers, instructing them in making the sign of the cross. See Manuel Dias Jr., "Litterae Annuae 1627," Shanghai, 9 May 1628, ARSI, Jap. Sin. 115 I, 119r–153v, 147v.
22. See Du Jarric, *Histoire*, vol. 3, 1064.
23. Cf. Trigault, "Lettera Annua della Cina del 1610," 49–52. It seems that some Chinese elite women, especially widows commanding over a household, also had close contact with male servants.
24. Trigault, "Lettera Annua della Cina del 1610," 49.
25. HCC, 439.
26. For an overview of this group of female court converts, see HCC, 438–43. For a detailed contemporary account, see Bernard, *Lettres et mémoires d'Adam Schall S.J.*, 46–65. Additional information on the community is provided by João

Monteiro, "Annua da Viceprov[inci]a da China do anno de 1637," s.l., 16 October 1638, ARSI, Jap. Sin. 115 II, 369r–435v, 382r–384r. This letter suggests that the converted palace ladies were in fact not imperial consorts (*fei*), as suggested by previous research cited by Standaert, but rather were low-ranking female officeholders; most of them were part of a group called "responders" (*daying*), who were "a low-status group of palace women, ranking below 'Worthy Ladies' (*guiren*)" (see Hucker, *A Dictionary of Official Titles*, 475). I would like to express my thanks to Dr. Ellen Soulliere, who shared her thoughts about Monteiro's letter with me in written correspondence.

27. For a Catholic woman converting non-Catholic women in her neighborhood, see João da Costa, "Annua da Christandade da China do anno de 1614," s.l., 10 August 1615, ARSI, Jap. Sin. 113, 372r–392r, 377v. For a woman demanding baptism after receiving efficacious devotional objects from a neighbor, see Dias Sr., "Litterae Annuae 1619," 52. According to Patricia Buckley Ebrey, transmission of religious teachings among women was also usual in Song-dynasty lay Buddhism. See Ebrey, *The Inner Quarters*, 128.
28. On mixed marriages, see von Collani, "Mission and Matrimony."
29. On Catholic communities producing devotional objects without involving missionaries, see Spence, *The Memory Palace*, 245–47.
30. Couplet, *Histoire*, 38.
31. See HCC, 609–12.
32. For the full table of contents of Ricci's catechism, see Dudink, "*Tianzhu jiaoyao*," 48.
33. On the mixed success of this strategy in Europe, see Hsia, *The World*, 52–53.
34. See King, "The Gospel for the Ordinary Reader."
35. See Couplet, *Histoire*, 38. The term *apostolate through books* (*Apostolat der Presse*) was coined by Johannes Bettray (see Bettray, *Die Akkommodationsmethode*, 191–213). For the English expression, see HCC, 600–631. On Chinese elite women's ability to read and write, see Ko, *Teachers*. On literacy in late imperial China in general, see Rawski, *Education*.
36. Letters written by Candida Xu to her confessor, Philippe Couplet, are mentioned in Couplet, *Histoire*, 27–28.
37. For lectures at women's congregations, see Pedro Marquez, "Missao da Ilha de haynão," Hainan, 13 August 1634, BA-JA 49-V-10, 348v–355r, 352r.
38. See HCC, 809–22, for an overview.
39. See Brockey, *Journey*, 400.
40. "Ordens que o P. André Palmeiro Visitator de Japao, e China deixou a Viceprovincia da China vizitandoa no anno de 1629," s.l., 15 August 1629, ARSI, Jap. Sin. 100, 20r–30v. On similar rules applied in certain localities in Catholic Europe, see Tippelskirch, "Der Kleriker," 262, 280.
41. See Trigault, "Lettera Annua della Cina del 1610," 50.
42. See *Fonti Ricciane*, vol. 2, 338.
43. See Couplet, *Histoire*, 106. On the spread of the confessional in Europe, see Hersche, *Muße und Verschwendung*, vol. 2, 685.
44. See Dias Sr., "Litterae Annuae 1625," 180, and HCC, 534–75.
45. See Menegon, "Popular or Local?," 260.

46. On Tridentine gender arrangements in European churches and the difficulties to enforce them, see Hersche, *Muße und Verschwendung*, vol. 2, 707–10.
47. See Niccolò Longobardo, "Litterae Annuae 1612," Nanxiong, 20 March 1613, ARSI, Jap. Sin. 113, 215r–263r, 228r. The HCC, interestingly, does not mention oratories in its essay on church buildings in China (see HCC, 580–91). Instead, it only mentions the multifunctional rooms where rural missions celebrated Mass (HCC, 580). Source evidence shows, however, that oratories established in the urban households of comparably rich Chinese converts differed from the multifunctional rooms used during rural missions.
48. See Michele Ruggieri, "Relatione del Successo della missione della Cina del mese di Novembre 1577 alli 1591 del P. Roggieri al nostro P. Generale," s.l., s.d., ARSI, Jap. Sin. 101, 8r–111r, 109r.
49. See *Fonti Ricciane*, vol. 2, 207–8.
50. *Fonti Ricciane*, vol. 2, 246.
51. *Fonti Ricciane*, vol. 2, 263.
52. Gabriel de Matos, "Ordens dos Vizitadores e Superiores universaes da Missao da China com algumas respostas de nosso R. P. Geral," s.l., 1621, BA-JA 49-V-7, 229r. Probably at the same time, the missionaries reaffirmed the rule that women should not visit churches. See anon., "Alguas Couzas que se cao de guardar na Igreja Missas, baptismos, e enterramentos, para em todas as cazas aver conformidade," s.l., s.d. [1621?], BA-JA 49-V-7, 315r–317r, 315v.
53. See Goossaert, "Irrepressible Female Piety," and Zhao, *Kuanghuan yu richang*, chapter 9.
54. See Zhou, "The Hearth."
55. The hypothesis that the Christian "oratory" might have been combined with the ancestral altar in poor households has been advanced by Erik Zürcher. See Zürcher, "Confucian and Christian Religiosity," 631–32. For supporting source evidence, see Bernardus Regius, "Annuae ex V[ice]provincia Sinarum An[no] 1629," s.l., s.d., BA-JA 49-V-8, 608v–627v, 611r. On the Jesuits' permissive attitude toward domestic ancestor worship, see Dehergne, "Les tablettes." Since Chinese women were responsible for domestic ancestor worship, the Jesuits' tolerance toward the latter was a crucial precondition for women's conversion to Catholicism. A study on Protestants in nineteenth-century Guangdong, conversely, has found that the Protestant missionaries' prohibition of ancestor worship prevented many women from conversion. See Klein, *Die Basler Mission*, 206.
56. See Francesco Brancati, "Annua da Residencia de Xam hai do anno de 1647 do Rey Xun Chi 4.° anno," s.l. [Shanghai], s.d., BA-JA 49-V-13, 458v–464v, 459v.
57. See João Froes, "Annua da V[ice]provincia da China do anno de 1633, China," s.l. [Hangzhou?], 20 September 1634, BA-JA 49-V-11, 1r–99v, 37r. It is probable that, in cases like the one described by Froes, the woman had converted to Catholicism together with her native family.
58. See de Gouvea, *Cartas Ânuas*, 411. On Buddhist altars on the dew platform, see Bray, *Technology and Gender*, 105, 133–35.
59. On gentry women's inclination to practice Buddhist devotions, see Mann, *Precious Records*, 187–98, passim.

60. See HCC, 382–84.
61. See Couplet, "Breve relatione dello stato e qualità delle missioni," ARSI, Jap. Sin. 125, 164r–199v, 189r.
62. See Brockey, *Journey*, 326–27.
63. On the Jianchang church, see João Froes, "Annua da V[ice]provincia da China do anno de 1633," s.l. [Hangzhou?], 20 September 1634, BA-JA 49-V-11, 1r–99v, 75v. For Jiangzhou, see João Froes, "Carta Annua da Missao da China do anno de 1634," Hangzhou, 8 September 1634, ARSI, Jap. Sin. 115 II, 266r–317r, 281v. For Nanjing, see Thomas-Ignatius Dunyn-Szpot, "Historia Sinarum Imperii, 1580–1649," ARSI, Jap. Sin. 102, 244r. For Xi'an, see Stephan Fabre, "Pontos da Annua da Residencia da Provincia de Xensi 1638," Xi'an, 20 January 1639, BA-JA 49-V-12, 263r–275r, 265r.
64. João Monteiro, "Annuae Sin[ae] 1639," s.l., 8 October 1640, ARSI, Jap. Sin. 121, 221r–313r, 222r.
65. See PQD, 136v–137r.
66. Giandomenico Gabiani, "Incrementa Sinicae Ecclesiae," 1667, ARSI, Jap. Sin. 108, 19r.
67. On Yanping, see Simão da Cunha, "Rol[o] das Igrejas e Christandades," Yanping, 25 January 1647, BNP, CÓD. 722, 50v–51v. On Hangzhou, Shanghai, Songjiang, and Beijing, see Couplet, "Litterae Annuae Vice-Provinciae Sinicae ab 1677 ad 1680," s.l., s.d., ARSI, Jap. Sin. 116, 214r–275r, 272r–275v. The use of some of these churches had to be given up or suspended. The Yanping church, for instance, seems to have been abandoned in the 1650s due to the turmoil of the Manchu conquest and pirate attacks. It was probably revived by Inácio da Costa in 1667 (see Pfister, *Notices biographiques*, 219).
68. For a women's church established in an existing building bought for this purpose, see Manuel Jorge, "Annua da V[ice]provincia da China 1657," Nanjing, 12 May 1658, BA-JA 49-V-14, 148r–169v, 167r.
69. "Extrait d'une lettre du P. Fontanay au P. la Beuille," Beijing, 28 October 1693, APF, SOCP, vol. 20, 471r–472r, 471r. Some women's churches were also sizable structures, especially when women's congregations were able to take over former men's churches. See Brockey, *Journey*, 364.
70. Couplet, "Breve relatione dello stato e qualità delle missioni," ARSI, Jap. Sin. 125, 164r–199v, 189r. The Hangzhou women's church also fell prey to anti-Catholic repression between 1688 and 1692, when it was permanently transformed into a non-Catholic temple. See Pfister, *Notices biographiques*, 324.
71. See Juan Antonio Arnedo, "Litterae Annuae Missionis Sinicae ab Anno 1685 ad An[num] 1690," Ganzhou, 30 September 1691, ARSI, Jap. Sin. 117, 203r–228v, 221v.
72. Inácio da Costa, "Annua da Viceprov[incia] do Norte na China do ano 1647," s.l., s.d., ARSI, Jap. Sin. 122, 282r–304r, 290v. The women's churches also remained closed for an extended period in many places after the calendar case of 1664. See Christian Herdtrich, "Annua Viceprovinciae Sinensis Societatis Jesu Anni 1662," Shanxi, 24 August 1663, BA-JA 49-V-16, 356r–381v, 361r.
73. See João Froes, "Annua da ViceProvincia da China do anno de 1632," Hangzhou, 1 August 1633, BA-JA 49-V-10, 76r–130r, 91v.

74. See João Froes, "Carta Annua da Missao da China do anno de 1634," Hangzhou, 8 September 1634, ARSI, Jap. Sin. 115 II, 266r–317r, 285r, and João Monteiro, "Annua da Viceprovincia da China de 1638," s.l., 20 September 1639, ARSI, Jap. Sin. 121, 142r–193r, 174r.
75. See Manuel Dias Jr., "Carta Annua da China de 1635," Nanchang, 1 September 1636, ARSI, Jap. Sin. 115 II, 321r–344r, 323r.
76. See *Fonti Ricciane*, vol. 2, 263, and Niccolò Longobardo, ["Littera Annua 1612"], Nanxiong, 20 March 1613, ARSI, Jap. Sin. 113, 215r–263r, 228r.
77. See PQD, 137r.
78. Matias da Mathos to [?], s.l., s.d. [between 1664 and 1667], ARSI, Jap. Sin. 124, 47r–54v.
79. See Brockey, *Journey*, 79.
80. See Juan Antonio Arnedo, "Litterae Annuae Missionis Sinicae ab Anno 1685 ad An[num] 1690," Ganzhou, 30 September 1691, ARSI, Jap. Sin. 117, 203r–228v, 213v. On rural circuits, see also Brockey, *Journey*, 93–98.
81. Nevertheless, annual letters occasionally report peasant women's trips to missionary residences. See, for instance, Christian Herdtrich, "Annua Viceprovinciae Sinensis Societatis Jesu Anni 1662," Shanxi, 24 August 1663, BA-JA 49-V-16, 356r–381v, 361v.
82. See João Froes, "Carta Annua da Missao da China do anno de 1634," Hangzhou, 8 September 1634, ARSI, Jap. Sin. 115 II, 266r–317r, 285r.
83. The situation in China thus resembled the situation in many parts of Europe before the Tridentine reforms had had their effect. How long it took the rituals of the reformed church to gain a foothold in the predominantly rural societies of early modern Catholic Europe has been shown by Forster, *The Counter-Reformation.*
84. Studies such as Standaert's *The Interweaving of Rituals* and Standaert and Dudink's *Forgive Us* have only recently started to turn our attention toward Chinese Catholic ritual practice. An overview of Chinese Catholic rituals, in general, and sacraments, in particular, is still lacking.
85. Some other authors have mentioned the adaptation of sacraments to Chinese gender norms, but none has yet discussed it in any greater depth. See HCC, 393–98; Touboul-Bouyeure, "Famille chrétienne," 964; and Margiotti, *Il cattolicismo*, 344–48. On similar debates among the Jesuits in Vietnam, see Brockey, *The Visitor*, 343–44.
86. Of the two sacraments analyzed in this chapter, baptism—which was indispensable for anyone who wished to become Catholic—was administered more frequently than extreme unction. Because of baptism's initiatory character, it was especially important that it did not deter women or their relatives from converting to Catholicism. This explains why baptism was discussed in greater detail than extreme unction, which was only occasionally administered.
87. They sometimes, moreover, deliberately refrained from administering the sacrament of extreme unction to women (see *Collectanea S. Congregationis*, 31–32).
88. The privileges are mentioned in Antonio Rubino and Diego Morales, "Resposta as calumnias que os Padres de S. Domingos, e de S. Francisco impoem aos Padres da Companhia de Iesus, que se occupao na conversao do Reino da China," 1641, ARSI, Jap. Sin. 155, 67r–74v, 67v. On the breve *Ex pastorali officio* issued by Gregory XIII

in 1585 and the constitution *Ex Debito Pastoralis Officii* issued by Urban VIII in 1633, see HCC, 296–97. These privileges had been granted to the missionary orders *ad perpetuum* and gave them great freedom with regard to circumstantial adaptations. The Propaganda Fide tried to adjust the faculties' scope in the seventeenth century. However, this attempt was only partially successful. Only Propaganda missionaries felt obliged by the new rules. See Pizzorusso, "I dubbi sui sacramenti," esp. 40–49. See also Broggio, Castelnau-L'Estoile, and Pizzorusso, "Le temps de doutes."

89. On Juan Bautista Morales's stay in Fujian and the beginning of the rites controversy, see Cummins, *A Question of Rites*, 58–62.
90. On the central issues of the rites controversy, see Rule, *K'ung-tzu or Confucius?* Adaptions of sacraments in the context of early modern missions in general triggered major debates in the Roman Curia. For recent research on the topic, see the contributions to Broggio, Castelnau-L'Estoile, and Pizzorusso, *Administrer les sacrements.*
91. See Canon XIII of the seventh session of the Council, in Perceval, *The Roman Schism*, 216–18. The doctrine that grace was conferred during the sacraments "by the actual performance of them" (*ex opere operato*) was recorded during the seventh session of the Council (1547) in Canon VIII.
92. See Dowdall, "A Study," 62.
93. Dowdall, "A Study," 77.
94. On physical contact as a means of transmitting spiritual goods, see Classen, *The Deepest Sense*, 31.
95. On the literati elite's aversion to physical contact, see Song, *A Fragile Scholar*, 83. On the Chinese notion that the female body was a pure realm, see Edwards, "Women in *Honglou meng*." On how the literati elite regarded the mingling of the sexes as a feature of heterodox sects, see Rosner, "Frauen als Anführerinnen," and Bays, "Christianity," 41.
96. On this collection of pamphlets, published under the title *Documents from the Southern Palace* (Nangong shudu), see Dudink, "*Nangong shudu* (1620)." On the Nanjing incident, see Kelly, *The Anti-Christian Persecution.*
97. Shen, *Faqian yuanyi huizou shu*, 3b.
98. See Xu, *Huishen Zhong Mingren Zhang Cai deng fan*, 16b–17a. On Zhong Mingren, a Jesuit lay brother known under the Christian name Sebastian Fernandes, see Hsia, *A Jesuit*, 129. On Xu Congzhi, see Dudink, "*Nangong shudu* (1620)," 260–61.
99. Xu, *Shengchao zuopi*, 18a. The translation is from Dudink, "The *Sheng-ch'ao tso-p'i*," 114–15.
100. Xu, *Shengchao zuopi*, 135a–135b. The translation is from Dudink, "The *Sheng-ch'ao tso-p'i*," 114–15.
101. See [Yu?], *Po Li yi jian tian wang shi*, 15b. On the stereotyped view of these sectarian movements by the literati class, see ter Haar, *The White Lotus Teachings*, esp. the introduction. On the history of these movements, see Liu and Shek, *Heterodoxy.*
102. Later sources mention how the Jesuits' adaptation of sacramentals was implemented by the Visitors Francesco Pasio (Visitor in 1611–12) and André Palmeiro (Visitor in 1626–35) (see Antonio Rubino and Diego Morales, "Resposta as

calumnias que os Padres de S. Domingos, e de S. Francisco impoem aos Padres da Companhia de Iesus, que se occupao na conversao do Reino da China," 1641, ARSI, Jap. Sin. 155, 67r–74v, 69v–70r). It was only possible to identify a part of the respective instructions in the archives. An anonymous and undated document, probably issued in 1621, instructed missionaries that if the salt of baptism was given to women, it should be done by a male relative. See anon., "Alguas Couzas que se cao de guardar na Igreja Missas, baptismos, e enterramentos, para em todas as cazas aver conformidade," s.l., s.d. [1621?], BA-JA 49-V-7, 315r–317r, 315v. An instruction issued by Visitor André Palmeiro in 1629, furthermore, told them to omit the administration of extreme unction to Chinese women except when they and their husbands or fathers both wished it expressly and were present during the ritual. See "Ordens que o P. André Palmeiro Visitator de Japao, e China deixou a Viceprovincia da China vizitandoa no anno de 1629," s.l., 15 August 1629, ARSI, Jap. Sin. 100, 20r–30v, 27r.

103. On earlier efforts by the Roman authorities to reach a decision on the controversy, see Margiotti, "I riti cinesi."
104. The discussion about sacramental adaptation took place in the context of the rites controversy, which extended, in a first stage, to a broad range of questions concerning positive church law. On the respective tasks of the Propaganda Fide and the Holy Office in the examination of missionaries' questions, see Metzler, "Orientation," 185–96, and Windler, "Uneindeutige Zugehörigkeiten," 334–39.
105. *Collectanea S. Congregationis*, 31–32. The *qualificatores* were outside experts assigned by the Holy Office to give their opinion on theological questions. See Schwedt, "Die römischen Kongregationen," 97–99.
106. See *Collectanea S. Congregationis*, 38.
107. Memorial presented by Martini and votes of the *qualificatores*, ACDF, S.O., St. St., OO 5 f, 275r–296v, 280r–280v, cited by Vareschi, "Martino Martini," 239–53, 242.
108. Vareschi, "Martino Martini," 239–53, 242.
109. For the statements of the *qualificatores*, see Vareschi, "Martino Martini," 242–44. For an overview of the genesis of the 1656 decree, see Vareschi, "The Holy Office's Decree." The decree has been reprinted in *Collectanea S. Congregationis*, 38.
110. On the Calendar Case, see Chu, "Scientific Dispute." The resolutions were published in 1678 in Rome. See *Constitutiones Apostolicae*.
111. The first seven of the forty-two resolutions all concerned the sacrament of baptism, and four of them were related to the baptism of adult women. For an overview of the content of the resolutions, see Metzler, *Die Synoden*, 22–35.
112. PQD, 136v.
113. See Navarrete, *Tratados historicos*, 470, 495–96. On the fact that the group of missionaries gathered in Canton was not as harmonious as the resolutions resulting from it suggest, see Cummins, *A Question of Rites*, 152.
114. On Pallu, see Baudiment, *François Pallu*. Prior to Pallu's arrival, the Holy Office had already taken notice of the Canton resolutions through the Jesuit procurator Prospero Intorcetta (see Intorcetta, "Informationes," BA-JA 49-IV-62, 331v–336r) and the Dominican Domingo Navarrete (see Cummins, *A Question of Rites*).
115. On Pallu's meeting with Navarrete, a participant in the Canton gathering, during his stay in Madagascar in 1671, see Cummins, *A Question of Rites*, 175–76.

116. "Scritture originali della Congregazione della China de 26. Aprile 1678, E: Estratto di molte lettere concernenti gli affari spirituali della China fatto dal Vescovo d'Eliopoli con alcune sue Petitioni," APF, Fondo di Vienna 21, 130r–135v, 133r–134v. The missionaries in Canton were, indeed, aware that their conference lacked legitimacy thanks to the absence of the Vicar Apostolic. They had therefore sought to obtain faculties from the Jesuit Visitor Luis de Gama and the Dominican Vicar provincial Francisco Varo, who both approved of the gathering. See Metzler, *Die Synoden*, 23.
117. "Observationes Episcopi Heliopolitani in Quosdam Articulos Coetus Missionariorum Cantoni in Sina Coacti An[no] 1669," APF, Fondo di Vienna 21, 130r–135v, 142r–146r, 143v.
118. See the answer of the Holy Office dating from July 1678, in APF, Fondo di Vienna 21, 160r–163v, 160r–160v. The same document is also filed in ACDF, S.O., St. St., L 5 d, 280r–283v.
119. See Margiotti, "La Cina," 615–25.
120. Launay, *Lettres*, 567–79, 572. For how the Dominicans in Fujian also changed their attitude toward the adaptation of sacraments in the late seventeenth century, see Menegon, *Ancestors*, 311.
121. On the difficulty of ruling over dominions situated at great geographic distance, and the role of information in the practice of ruling, see Brendecke, *Imperium und Empirie*. On the importance of information management within ecclesiastical structures, see Friedrich, *Der lange Arm*.
122. "Resposta as calumnias que os Padres de S. Domingos, e de S. Francisco impoem aos Padres da Companhia de Iesus, que se occupao na conversao do Reino da China," 1641, ARSI, Jap. Sin. 155. The Portuguese Diego Morales figures as coauthor of the treatise. According to Asami Masakazu, it is probable that the treatise was written by Morales, with Rubino responsible for its content (see Masakazu, "Solutions," 128). On Rubino, see Perera, *The Jesuits in Ceylon*, 163–64.
123. "Resposta as calumnias que os Padres de S. Domingos, e de S. Francisco impoem aos Padres da Companhia de Iesus, que se occupao na conversao do Reino da China," 1641, ARSI, Jap. Sin. 155, 69r.
124. See Lach and Van Kley, *Asia*, vol. 3, 382–83. The treatise seems to have widely circulated in manuscript form and can today be found in various European archives (see ARSI, Jap. Sin. 155, and BA-JA 49-V-12, 449r–476v. According to S. G. Perera, further versions can be found in the Biblioteca Vittorio Emanuele in Rome as well as in the Bibliothèque Nationale in Paris (see Perera, *The Jesuits in Ceylon*, 164).
125. Pizzorusso, "I dubbi sui sacramenti," 60. The Roman theologians' change of attitude toward empirical knowledge coincides with a comparable change of attitude in travelogues. See Osterhammel, *Die Entzauberung*, 152. On the limits of the change, see Menegon, "European and Chinese Controversies," esp. 221.

4. Strengthening the Marital Bond

1. *Fonti Ricciane*, vol. 2, 481.
2. *Coronae* were rosaries "with thirty-three beads commemorating the number of barbs in the crown of thorns as well as the years in Christ's life." Brockey, *Journey*, 398.

3. *Fonti Ricciane*, vol. 2, 481–82.
4. Stuart and Rawski, *Worshiping*, 47.
5. The question of whether ancestral rites were religious rituals was a key issue in the rites controversy (see HCC, 680–88). Recent research, however, has shown that the European concept of "religion"/"religious" is problematic in the Chinese context (see Chau, *Miraculous Response*, 74, passim). Nevertheless, it seems clear that ancestors occupied a far more central place in Chinese visions of the spiritual/transcendent world than they did in Europe.
6. Translation by Ebrey, *The Inner Quarters*, 45. See also Legge, *The Lî Kî*, part 2, 428.
7. See Bernhardt, "A Ming-Qing Transition," 53–54. For a discussion of social practices of divorce, see Ebrey, *The Inner Quarters*, 250–60.
8. See Holzem, "Familie und Familienideal," 254.
9. On contradictions between social and religious sets of norms in early modern Europe, see von Thiessen, "Das Sterbebett."
10. See Westphal, Schmidt-Voges, and Baumann, *Venus und Vulcanus*, 10.
11. See Fairchilds, *Women in Early Modern Europe*, 229–32.
12. *Fonti Ricciane*, vol. 1, 85.
13. Magalhães, *Nouvelle relation*, 86–87.
14. For case studies, see Leacock, "Montagnais Marriage," and Županov, *Missionary Tropics*, chapter 5.
15. In contrast to divorce and polygyny, mixed marriages and marriages going against the Catholic interdictions of affinity were less pressing problems. The Jesuits found workable solutions for them by way of papal dispensations. For privileges regarding the disparity of cult, see "Facultas ad Dispensandum in Impedimento Disparitatis Cultus, ad Decennium," 23 May 1616, BA-JA 49-V-5, 193r–193v, and "Japoniae, et Synarum Facultates," ACDF, S.O., St. St., OO 5 a, 71r–96r. See also Margiotti, *Il cattolicismo*, 361, note 129. On the dispensations regarding affinity, see "Petunt Patres Societatis Jesus, qui versantur in Missionibus Indiae Orientalis . . . ," ACDF, S.O., St. St., E 4 f, 244r–244v, and Castelnau-L'Estoile, "Le mariage," 102–3.
16. See Couplet, "Breve relatione dello stato e qualità delle missioni," ARSI, Jap. Sin. 125, 164r–199v, 190r, and PQD, 140r.
17. See André Palmeiro to the father general, Macao, 20 December 1629, ARSI, F.G. 730, cited by Margiotti, *Il cattolicismo*, 360, note 124. See also Couplet, *Histoire*, 15.
18. Martini, *Novus Atlas Sinensis*, vol. 1, 9.
19. See Touboul-Bouyeure, "Famille chrétienne," 968–69, as well as Margiotti, *Il cattolicismo*, 360, note 128.
20. See Gabriel de Matos, "Ordens dos Vizitadores e Superiores universaes da Missao da China com algumas respostas de nosso R. P. Geral," s.l., 1621, BA-JA 49-V-7, 217r–232r, 230v.
21. PQD, 140r.
22. Several Jesuit authors wrote accounts of the ceremonies observed during Chinese marriages (see, for instance, *Fonti Ricciane*, vol. 1, 85–87; Pantoja, *Relatione dell'entrata*, 54; and de Gouvea, *Asia Extrema*, vol. 1, 275–79). In the following, I refer to the account in Semedo, *Histoire* (106–7), which stands out for its great detail.

23. Semedo, *Histoire*, 106.
24. Semedo, *Histoire*, 106–7.
25. See *Fonti Ricciane*, vol. 1, 94–95.
26. See Couplet, *Histoire*, 12–13.
27. See "Pluria alia dubia, et quaesita circa idem a variis proposita in pluribus foliis pro Missione," ACDF, S.O., St. St., UV 47, 381r–381v. It seems that these accusations did not produce a response from the Roman Curia.
28. See Couplet, *Histoire*, 13. That this suggestion was sometimes followed is testified to by the Annual Letter of 1661. See Johann Adam Schall von Bell, "Annua Pequinensis Antiquae Ecclesiae Societatis Jesus Anni 1661," s.l. [Beijing?], s.d., BA-JA 49-V-15, 45r–54r, 48r–48v.
29. See Dias Sr., "Litterae Annuae 1625," 149–50.
30. See Luiz Pinheiro, "Carta annua da V[ice]provincia da China do anno de 1654, Macao," [Macao?], 3 December 1654, BA-JA 49-VI-61, 229r–326r, 314v.
31. For one such case, see Rodriguo Girolamo Joann[is?], "Annua da China do anno de 1613 [*sic*]," Macao, 20 February 1615, ARSI, Jap. Sin. 113, 310r–331v, 323r.
32. On the treatment of matrimony in Chinese catechetical literature, see HCC, 626. Matrimony also played a marginal role in European catechetical texts (see Holzem, "Familie und Familienideal," 248). One significant omission in Chinese catechetical texts was that they did not cover premarital sexuality, a major topic in their European equivalents (see Holzem, "Familie und Familienideal," 263–69). Because male premarital sexuality was widely accepted by the late Ming scholar-gentry (see Zurndorfer, "Prostitutes and Courtesans"), the Jesuits seem to have judged it premature to ask converts to change such habits.
33. See Vagnone, *Qijia xixue.*
34. On Vagnone's time in Jiangzhou, see Margiotti, *Il cattolicismo*, 89–105.
35. For an overview of Vagnone's publications, see Pfister, *Notices biographiques*, 91–95. On Vagnone's collaborative work with literati, see Meynard, "Aristotelian Ethics," 146–47.
36. These subjects allude to the three opening sentences of *The Great Learning*: "The ancients who wished to illustrate illustrious virtue throughout the kingdom, first governed well their own countries. Wishing to order well their countries, they first governed their families. Wishing to regulate their families, they first cultivated their persons." See Verhaeren, "Un livre inédit du P. Vagnoni," 39.
37. See Huang, *Negotiating Masculinities*, 185–91, and Furth, "The Patriarch's Legacy."
38. On European *oeconomica* texts, see Eibach and Schmidt-Voges, *Das Haus*, esp. 643–742.
39. See Meynard, "Illustrations," 112.
40. A possible inspiration may have been Juan Luis Vives's famous *Advice for Husbands* (see Vives, *De Officio Mariti*). For a broad analysis of the genre of marriage treatises, see Bake, *Spiegel.*
41. See Vagnone, *Qijia xixue*, 505, 530. On the prevalence of those two analogies in European advice literature, see Bake, *Spiegel*, 69, 93. The comparison with the oxen was especially evident in Latin, because the Latin term for *marriage* (*coniugium*) literally referred to the yoke (*iugium*).

42. See Vagnone, *Qijia xixue*, 496, 516. For the common use of these couples as negative examples in European treatises on marriage, see Bake, *Spiegel*, 224, 286.
43. The respective Chinese names are Baladuo, Buluda[ge], Diarinuo, and Jiaduo.
44. See Meynard, "Illustrations," 115–16.
45. *Yi yin yi yang zhi wei dao*. James Legge translates this phrase as "The successive movement of the inactive and active operations constitutes what is called the course (of things)." Legge, *The Yî King*, 355.
46. Vagnone, *Qijia xixue*, 494. Vagnone's interpretation of this formulation transformed *yin* and *yang* from alternating forces into clearly circumscribed entities that could be weighed against each other.
47. Vagnone, *Qijia xixue*, 494–95. The reference is to the "Tuanzhuan" commentary on the *jiaren* (household) hexagram, which says that in this hexagram "the wife has her correct place in the inner (trigram), and the man his correct place in the outer." Translation by Legge, *The Yî King*, 242.
48. Vagnone, *Qijia xixue*, 503. The passage probably refers to *Lunheng* (Balanced inquiries), chapter 46, which states that "the man is *yang* and the woman is *yin*." On the Thrice Following, see Ko, *Teachers*, 6.
49. See Vagnone, *Qijia xixue*, 503. On this metaphor in European marriage literature, see Wunder, *He Is the Sun*, 9–10.
50. On the debate, see Maihofer, "Die Querelle des femmes." For the topos of dangerously uncontrolled women in early modern European popular culture, see Zemon Davis, "Women on Top."
51. For an example of the manual's misogynist stories, see Vagnone, *Qijia xixue*, 510–11.
52. Many authors of household instructions saw women, who entered their husbands' families as strangers, as a threat to the patrilineal family and warned male family members against the "divisive influence of wives" (Furth, "The Patriarch's Legacy," 196–97). The misogynist stances within household regulations thus reflected women's problematic place within the Chinese family system. See Huang, *Negotiating Masculinity*, 187, and Bossler, "'A Daughter,'" 77.
53. Vagnone, *Qijia xixue*, 495.
54. Vagnone, *Qijia xixue*, 530.
55. Vagnone, *Qijia xixue*, 496–97, 500. The idea that marriage was a misfortune for a man was a classical topos of the *querelle des femmes*. See Roth, "*An uxor ducenda*."
56. On Catholic views on marriage, see Signori, *Von der Paradiesehe*, 55–56.
57. Vagnone, *Qijia xixue*, 504.
58. See Vagnone, *Qijia xixue*, 497–99.
59. On the concept of the inner helpmate, see Ebrey, *The Inner Quarters*, chapter 6. On the "cult of *qing*," see Ko, *Teachers*, 18, 69–111.
60. Vagnone, *Qijia xixue*, 494.
61. Even a close collaborator and admirer of Vagnone, the Jiangzhou Christian Han Lin, in his *Book of the Bell* (Duoshu, 1641), disapproved of families in which the spouses were closer to each other than the father was to the son. See Sun and Xiao, "*Duo shu*" *jiao zhu*, 65.
62. Manuel Dias Sr., "Informatione . . . circa il matrimonio," s.l., s.d., ACDF, S.O., St. St., D 4 a, 187r–189r, 187r. It is difficult to assess how frequently divorce was

actually practiced in Chinese society. It is, however, probable that it was more frequent in the lower strata of society because men of humble financial means were unable to buy concubines (see Ebrey, *The Inner Quarters*, 258). On the illegal, but apparently rather frequent, practice of wife-selling, see Sommer, *Sex, Law, and Society*, 57–64.

63. Manuel Dias Sr., "Informatione . . . circa il matrimonio," s.l., s.d., ACDF, S.O., St. St., D 4 a, 187r–189r, 189r. On the Pauline Privilege, see von Collani, "Mission and Matrimony," 17.
64. For an overview of how early modern Catholic missionaries tackled this question, see Castelnau-L'Estoile, "Le mariage."
65. See Castelnau-L'Estoile, "Le mariage," 96.
66. See Castelnau-L'Estoile, "Le mariage," 100–102.
67. The indissolubility of marriages had already been discussed in Japan during the sixteenth century, where no consensus was reached. See López Gay, *El matrimonio*, 19.
68. Semedo, *Histoire*, 99. This sentence was not included in the Spanish edition. See Semedo, *Imperio de la China*, 161–67.
69. See *Fonti Ricciane*, vol. 1, 85, and Pantoja, *Relatione dell'entrata*, 54.
70. Intorcetta, "De Matrimonio Sinensium," 24 July 1668, ARSI, Opp. NN. 147–48, 1r–15v, 14v.
71. In this regard, Intorcetta's defense of Chinese marriage resembled the position of missionaries in the New World who wanted to show that the Indians were ready for conversion. See Castelnau-L'Estoile, "Le mariage," 104.
72. See PQD, 140r.
73. See Navarrete, *Tratados historicos*, 72. Nicolas Trigault had, indeed, presented Manuel Dias's "Information . . . about Marriage" to the Roman College, whose theologians explained that the Chinese law's justification of divorce was "against the essence of marriage" and that Chinese marriages were therefore invalid. This response was transmitted in Nicolas Trigault to Francesco Pasio, Rome, 21 March 1614, BA-JA 49-V-5, 151v–152r.
74. See Navarrete, *Tratados historicos*, 72.
75. See Cummins, *A Question of Rites*, 179.
76. Navarrete, *Tratados historicos*, 497.
77. See Intorcetta, "De Matrimonio Sinensium," 24 July 1668, ARSI, Opp. NN. 147–48, 1r–15v, 14v.
78. See Intorcetta, "De Matrimonio Sinensium," 24 July 1668, ARSI, Opp. NN. 147–48, 1r–15v, 10v.
79. Intorcetta, "De Matrimonio Sinensium," 24 July 1668, ARSI, Opp. NN. 147–48, 1r–15v, 6v. Intorcetta provided a (fairly accurate) translation of the phrase "Yi yu zhi qi, zhongshen bu gai. Gu fu si bu jia." Zheng, *Liji*, vol. 3, *juan* 8, 10a. James Legge has translated this phrase as "Once mated [joined (*qi*)] with her husband, [the wife will] all her life not change (her feeling of duty to him), and hence, when the husband dies she will not marry (again)." Legge, *The Lî Kî*, part 1, 439.
80. See Zheng, *Liji*, vol. 3, *juan* 8, 10a.

81. Intorcetta, "De Matrimonio Sinensium," 24 July 1668, ARSI, Opp. NN. 147–48, 1r–15v, 6v.
82. On *Four Books for Women*, a Ming-period collection including four classical moral treatises written by women for women, see Kelleher, "Confucianism," 158.
83. See Intorcetta, "De Matrimonio Sinensium," 24 July 1668, ARSI, Opp. NN. 147–48, 1r–15v, 10r. The Chinese characters rendered by Intorcetta are identical with the wording in *The Complete Collection of Illustrations and Writings from Ancient and Modern Times*. See Chen and Jiang, *Gujin tushu jicheng*, "Guiyuan dian," *juan* 3, 3a. Translation adapted from Ebrey, "The *Book*," 59. For information on the *Nü xiaojing*, see Ebrey, "The *Book*," 47–49.
84. Intorcetta, "De Matrimonio Sinensium," 24 July 1668, ARSI, Opp. NN. 147–48, 1r–15v, 10r. The injunction is taken from the "Jinsheng" chapter. See Fan, *Houhan shu*, 2784–91. On Ban Zhao, see Raphals, *Sharing the Light*, 236–46. On Ban's legacy in the late imperial period, see Mann, *Precious Records*, 78–80.
85. See Meynard, *Confucius Sinarum Philosophus*.
86. Navarrete, *Tratados historicos*, 497.
87. López Gay, *El matrimonio*, 19. On the Holy Office's strategy of nondecision, see Windler, "Uneindeutige Zugehörigkeiten," 334–39.
88. The polygyny of China's sage kings was a thorny issue. To state that polygyny had made Yao and Shun endure hell insulted the Chinese (see, for instance, Xu, *Shengchao zuopi*, 17b–18a). Jesuits therefore chose their words prudently when speaking about the issue. See, for instance, Zürcher, *Kouduo richao*, vol. 1, 345–47.
89. Since the ceremonies with which a concubine was welcomed to her master's house were far less formal than those accompanying marriage to the legitimate wife, the term *polygyny* is preferable to *polygamy* (see McMahon, *Polygyny*, and Bray, *Technology and Gender*, 351–58). On the institution of polygyny in late imperial China, see Sheieh, *Concubines*. On Chinese polygyny and Catholicism, see Amsler, "'Ein *yin*, ein *yang*'?"; Touboul-Bouyeure, "Famille chrétienne," 958–61; HCC, 659–67; Kang, "Lun Ming Qing"; and Tian, "Mingmo tianzhujiao."
90. See Huang, "Rujiahua de tianzhujiaotu."
91. Matteo Ricci to Girolamo Costa, Beijing, 10 May 1605, in Ricci, *Lettere*, 395–400, 397. See also Francisco de Petris to Claudio Acquaviva, 15 November 1592, ARSI, Jap. Sin. 11 II, 341r–342r.
92. See Francisco Furtado, "Carta Annua da China," Hangzhou, 1622, BA-JA 49-V-5, 309r–325v, 320r–320v; João Froes, "Annua da V[ice]provincia da China do anno de 1633," s.l. [Hangzhou?], 20 September 1634, BA-JA 49-V-11, 1r–99v, 16v; Niccolò Longobardo, "Annua [1609?]," Shaozhou, 21 December 1609, ARSI, Jap. Sin. 113, 91r–104v, 91v.
93. See Couplet, *Histoire*, 122–23, and Francisco Pimentel, "Breve relação da jornada que fez a Corte de Pekim o Senhor Manoel de Saldanha Embaxador extraordinario del Rey de Portugal ao Emperador da China e Tartaria," s.l., s.d. [1670], BA-JA 49-VI-62, 715r–732r, 731v. On Tong Guoqi, see Crossley, *A Translucent Mirror*, 111–13. Unlike principal wives, concubines were usually only admitted to baptism if they made a vow of chastity. See Duteil, "L'évangélisation et les femmes," 250; and

anon., "Annua da Viceprovincia da China de 1629," s.l., s.d., ARSI, Jap. Sin. 115 I, 197r–207v, 203r. For a Catholic girl to be married as a concubine was, in the view of the missionaries, tantamount to apostasy. See Gabriel de Magalhães, "Annuas das Rezidencias do Norte da Viceprovincia da China do anno 1658," Beijing, 20 September 1659, BA-JA 49-V-14, 224r–265v, 259r.

94. Conversion to Christianity in China often "involved the addition of beliefs and practices, not their replacement." See Jordan, "The Glyphomancy Factor," 294.
95. See Standaert, *The Interweaving of Rituals*, 226–27.
96. Standaert, *Yang Tingyun*, 54.
97. For two such cases, see Couplet, "Litterae Annuae Vice-Provinciae Sinicae ab 1677 ad 1680," s.l., s.d., ARSI, Jap. Sin. 116, 214r–275v, 240v, and Lazzaro Cattaneo, "Annua da Vice-Provincia da China de 1629," s.l., 12 September 1631, BA-JA 49-V-8, 581r–593v, 598r.
98. Spence, *Return*, 103.
99. See, for instance, André Ferram, "Annua da Vice-Provincia da China [1656]," Macao, 29 January 1659, BA-JA 49-V-14, 62r–93r, 64r. For an opponent criticizing the Jesuits for encouraging people to repudiate their concubines, see Xu, *Shengchao zuopi*, 18a.
100. See Couplet, "Litterae Annuae Vice-Provinciae Sinicae ab 1677 ad 1680," s.l., s.d., ARSI, Jap. Sin. 116, 214r–275v, 254r, and Francesco Furtado, "Annua della Viceprovincia della Cina del 1643," Beijing, 24 December 1643, ARSI, Jap. Sin. 119, 1r–20v, 13r.
101. See João Froes, "Annua da Viceprovincia da China do anno de 1632," Hangzhou, 1 August 1633, BA-JA 49-V-10, 76r–130r, 87r–87v, quotation 87v.
102. See André Ferram, "Annua da Vice-Provincia da China [1656]," Macao, 29 January 1659, BA-JA 49-V-14, 62r–93r, 75r, 89r.
103. On Wang Zheng, see Huang, "Rujiahua de tianzhujiaotu," and Peterson, "Learning from Heaven," 124–26.
104. Wang, *Qiqing jiezui qigao*, 834. Situations such as that encountered by Wang Zheng could also occur in less affluent families. See anon., "Carta Annua do Collegio de Macao e Missao das Residencias de Cantao do anno de 1692," s.l., s.d., BA-JA 49-V-22, 97r–125r.
105. See *Fonti Ricciane*, vol. 1, 86–87, and Pantoja, *Relatione dell'entrata*, 54.
106. Semedo, *Histoire*, 104.
107. Semedo, *Histoire*, 104–5.
108. Semedo, *Histoire*, 104–5. Society, indeed, expected literati to take a concubine after examination success or career advancement, as is shown by Xu Guangqi's example. See *Fonti Ricciane*, vol. 2, 252–53. Literati were sometimes, furthermore, presented with concubines by friends. See João Monteiro, "Annua da Viceprov[inci]a da China do anno de 1637," s.l., 16 October 1638, ARSI, Jap. Sin. 115 II, 369r–435v, 401v.
109. For an analysis of *The Seven Victories* in the context of late Ming moral books (*shanshu*), see Waltner, "Demerits."
110. The Jesuits often compared the Chinese with the Hebrews, who also practiced polygyny due to extraordinary consideration for the continuation of the descent line. See, for instance, André Ferram, "Annua da Vice-Provincia da China [1656]," Macao, 29 January 1659, BA-JA 49-V-14, 62r–93r, 89r.

111. Pantoja, *Qike*, 1043.
112. Mish, "Creating an Image," Chinese text 16, English translation 58.
113. See Pantoja, *Qike*, 1044–48; *Fonti Ricciane*, vol. 1, 98.
114. See Brancati, *Tianshen huike*, 113. By labeling concubine marriage a breach of filiality toward the Christian God, Brancati promoted a Christian understanding of filiality that had already been proposed by Matteo Ricci (see chapter 1).
115. See Castelnau-L'Estoile, "Le mariage," 105.
116. See Ebrey, *The Inner Quarters*, 225, passim.
117. See Diogo Antunes, "Annua do Collegio da Madre de D[io]s da Comp[anhi]a de Jesu de Machao, e Residençias da China do anno de [1]602," s.l., 29 January 1603, ARSI, Jap. Sin. 46, 318r–322v, 321r.
118. Manuel Dias Sr., "Informatione . . . circa il matrimonio," s.l., s.d., ACDF, S.O., St. St., D 4 a, 187r–189r, 188v.
119. See Manuel Dias Sr., "Informatione . . . circa il matrimonio," s.l., s.d., ACDF, S.O., St. St., D 4 a, 187r–189r, 189r. For the Jesuits' criticism of the treatment of concubines as servants, see Pantoja, *Qike*, 1046.
120. See Thomas-Ignatius Dunyn-Szpot, "Historia Sinarum Imperii, 1580–1640," ARSI, Jap. Sin. 102, 174r–174v; Standaert, *Yang Tingyun*, 54; and Trigault, "Lettera Annua della Cina del 1611," 135.
121. Sending a woman back to her native family (*gui zong*) was especially dishonorable; the practice often served as penalty for adulterous women. See Sommer, *Sex, Law, and Society*, 174.
122. See Niccolò Longobardo, "Appontamentos a cerca da Ide do nosso P[adr]e Procurador a Roma," Nanxiong, 8 May 1613, ARSI, Jap. Sin. 113, 301r–309r, 304v–305r. Longobardo's proposal is interesting because it conceptualizes moral norms as personal, interiorized norms.
123. In 1612 Longobardo had already addressed the Society's visitor of Japan and China, Francesco Pasio, asking for the same dispensation. See Niccolò Longobardo, "Informação da Missao da China, pera o P[ad]re Fran[cisco] Pasio da Comp[anhia] de Jesu, Visitador de Japao e China," Nanxiong, 20 November 1612, ARSI, Jap. Sin. 113, 265r–281r, 269r.
124. See the protocol of the Congregatio Particularis held on 28 January 1669, Acta CP, 1A, 25r–34r, 31r, and Pierre Brindeau (Missions Étrangères de Paris, MEP), "Relatio Cuiusdam Missionarii . . . de Partibus, et Regnis Chinae Anno 1670," s.l., s.d., BAV, Borg. Lat., Ms. 93, 136r–194r, 193v–194r.
125. That women were of secondary importance has also been stated by Touboul-Bouyeure, "Famille chrétienne," 960.

5. Praying for Progeny

1. On the killing of female infants, see King, *Between Birth and Death*; Mungello, *Drowning Girls*; and Sachdev, "Contextualizing Female Infanticide."
2. See Bray, *Technology and Gender*, part 3.
3. On Chinese naming practices, see Watson, "The Named," 626–27. Margery Wolf has argued that motherhood was also an important way for a woman to create her

own network within the family (Wolf, *Women and the Family*, esp. chapter 3). For, while the bond between husbands and wives was usually weak, strong emotional bonds could be forged between mothers and sons.

4. See Ebrey, *The Inner Quarters*, chapter 9. The dangers and contingencies of childbirth made it a ritually polluting event. See Ahern, "The Power and Pollution."
5. On medical pluralism in late imperial China, see Wu, *Reproducing Women*, 18. On similar phenomena in premodern Europe, see Gentilcore, *Healers and Healing.*
6. See Wicks, "The Art of Deliverance." For an ethnographic case study, see Overmyer, *Local Religion*, 11, 14, 175–76. For a Catholic literatus's criticism of Buddhist rituals performed to ensure male offspring, see Zürcher, "Xu Guangqi," 161.
7. See Furth, *A Flourishing Yin*, 106–16.
8. See Wu, *Reproducing Women*, 18.
9. See Furth, *A Flourishing Yin*, 106–16; on the disappearance of ritual obstetrics during the Ming, see 174–75. On the important role played by various sorts of religious and nonreligious female healers who specialized in childbirth, see Wu, *Reproducing Women*, 18–19, 178–86.
10. See Spence, *Return*, 78. The bodhisattva Guanyin will be a recurrent theme in what follows. She was the Chinese transformation of the Indian bodhisattva Avalokiteśvara, whose gender changed from male to female in the process of Sinification. See Yü, *Kuan-yin.*
11. See Wu, *Reproducing Women*, 54–65.
12. On Jesuits in China as medical specialists, see Zhang, "The Metaphor of Illness." Interestingly, this study of French Jesuits' medical work in eighteenth-century Fujian shows that women and children made up the largest group of patients treated by the missionaries (591).
13. See Ruggieri and Ricci, *Dicionário Português-Chinês.*
14. *Spiritual remedy* (*remedio spiritual*) is a term used by the Jesuits to designate devotions and devotional objects that people turned to for solving a particular problem or illness (see, for instance, João Froes, "Annua da Provincia da China do anno de 1631," s.l., s.d., BA-JA 49-V-10, 1r–32v, 24v). They fit well into the devotions classified by Adam Yuet Chau as the "immediate-practical modality" of doing religion (see Chau, "Modalities of Doing Religion," 551–52).
15. This convergence was not readily acknowledged by the missionaries, who often ridiculed Chinese efficacy-based religiosity, pointing to the lack of respect paid by Chinese deities to their "false gods." See, for instance, Boxer, *South China*, 215.
16. On Chinese ideas of efficacious response (*ling*), see Chau, "Efficacy, Not Confessionality"; idem, "Modalities of Doing Religion"; and Sangren, *History and Magical Power.* On Catholic sacramentals (*sacramentalia*), that is, objects and rituals that were used as spiritual remedies against the adversities of everyday life, see von Thiessen, *Die Kapuziner*, 411–49; Hersche, *Muße und Verschwendung*, vol. 2, 873–79; and Kürzeder, *Als die Dinge.*
17. See Chau, "Modalities of Doing Religion," 549.
18. See Furth, *A Flourishing Yin*, 274–75. For a discussion of Buddhist medical specialists treating women in their homes, see Chen, "Buddhism," esp. 282–84.

19. Juan Antonio Arnedo, "Litterae Annuae Missionis Sinicae ab Anno 1685 ad An[num] 1690," Ganzhou, 30 September 1691, ARSI, Jap. Sin. 117, 203r–228v, 205v.
20. Manuel Dias the Elder reported this story, with minor differences, in two different annual letters. See Manuel Dias Sr., "Carta Annua da Missam da China do anno de 1618," Macao, 7 December 1618, BA-JA 49-V-5, 232v–264v, 263r, and idem, "Litterae Annuae 1619," 87–88.
21. The approach focusing on Chinese women's uses of Catholic sacred objects hinges on recent research on material culture. The latter proposes understanding objects as expressions of relations among people (see Findlen, "Early Modern Things," 5). It points to the social construction of religious objects' efficacy (see Bynum, *Christian Materiality*) and demonstrates that objects are gendered in various ways (see Kirkham and Attfield, introduction to *The Gendered Object*).
22. Matteo Ricci to Ludovico Maselli, Zhaoqing, 20 October 1586, in Ricci, *Lettere*, 123.
23. The city prefect was Wang Pan, a devout Buddhist who acted as a patron for the Jesuits during the early decades of the mission. See Hsia, *A Jesuit*, 79–112, passim, and esp. 88 (on the birth of a son to Wang).
24. Thomas-Ignatius Dunyn-Szpot, "Historia Sinarum Imperii, 1580–1640," ARSI, Jap. Sin. 102, 84v–85r. That Chinese observers sometimes indeed mistook the Holy Virgin for the Christian God is suggested by a passage in the *History of Poems without Words* (Wusheng shishi, ca. 1640) by Jiang Shaoshu, who wrote that "Li Madou [Matteo Ricci] brought from the Western Regions an image of the Lord of Heaven, being a woman holding a small boy." Translation by Clunas, *Pictures and Visuality*, 177.
25. See Pedro Canevari, "Pontos da Annua de Ciuen Cheu do anno de 1643," Quanzhou, 30 December 1643, BNP, CÓD. 722, 256r–265r, 262v.
26. See João Monteiro, "Annuae Sin[ae] 1639," s.l., 8 October 1640, ARSI, Jap. Sin. 121, 221r–313r, 282r.
27. On paintings of the Virgin brought to China by the first Jesuits, and the reproductions made by Chinese converts and others, see Spence, *The Memory Palace*, 245–47. For two Chinese paintings of the Christian Virgin, see Schüller, *Die Geschichte*, 19–21, and Clarke, *The Virgin Mary*, 212, note 98. On Chinese reprints of European devotional pictures and their circulation via temple fairs and book markets, see HCC, 811, and Clunas, *Pictures and Visuality*, 173.
28. Guanyin's son-granting power was praised in the twenty-fifth chapter of the Lotus Sutra. See Wicks, "The Art of Deliverance," 139, and Yü, *Kuan-yin*, 259. The resemblance between depictions of the Holy Virgin and Guanyin was also remarked upon by Catholic missionaries. See Las Cortes, *Le voyage en Chine*, 131, and Boxer, *South China*, 213.
29. On Guanyin's power to facilitate conception and childbearing, see Reed, "The Gender Symbolism," esp. 166–70. On iconographical similarities between Guanyin and the Virgin Mary, see Bailey, *Art on the Jesuit Missions*, 89; Laamann, "Von Bodhisattva Guanyin"; and Song, "Between Bodhisattva and Christian Deity." Specialists of Buddhist art assume that the iconography of the son-granting Guanyin developed under the influence of the European Marian iconography that had reached China by that time. See Yü, *Kuan-yin*, 258–59.

30. In particular, "Holy Mother" was also a common title of address for the famous son-granting "Lady of the Azure Cloud" (Bixia Yuanjun) revered on Mount Tai. See Sangren, "Female Gender," 9 (for titles of address), and Pomeranz, "Power, Gender, and Pluralism," 193 (for the deity's son-granting power). For an anthropological study of one single child-protecting goddess, see also Baptandier, *The Lady of Linshui*. On the multiplicity of Chinese local goddesses, see Watson, "Standardizing the Gods," 298–99.
31. Niccolò Longobardo to [?], Shaozhou, 18 October 1598, ARSI, Jap. Sin. 13 I, 174r–177v, 177r.
32. See Vagnone, *Shengmu xingshi*, 1497–1503. For an analysis of this chapter from the perspective of literary studies, see Li, "San mian Maliya," 185–91.
33. For the terms *dali* and *ling*, which were usually also applied to describe the power of non-Catholic deities, see Vagnone, *Shengmu xingshi*, 1502. On the phenomenon of the miraculous revival of stillborn children in Catholic Europe, see Gélis, *Les enfants des Limbes*.
34. As a case in point, the *Atlas Marianus* (1672, first edition 1655), a compendium of approximately twelve hundred Marian miracle tales published by the German Jesuit Wilhelm Gumppenberg, registers only two miracles connected with delivery (Gumppenberg, *Atlas Marianus*, 571, 894).
35. Vagnone, *Shengmu xingshi*, 1489–99. This passage is also cited in Li, "San mian Maliya," 185.
36. Vagnone, *Shengmu xingshi*, 1502. It is possible that this comment relates to a local cult of relics that Vagnone knew of from his years as a student of theology in Milan (see Pfister, *Notices biographiques*, 85). On the relics of the Infant Jesus, see Oosterwijk, "The Swaddling Clothes."
37. On the pictures displayed in *Rules for Reciting the Rosary* and their adaptation to Chinese visual conventions, see Qu, "*Song Nianzhu Guicheng*." For reflections on these pictures' relationship to Chinese elite women's religiosity, see Lin, "Seeing the Place."
38. On parallels between Catholic vows (*vota*) and the Chinese vows (*xuyuan*, *huanyuan*), see Li, "San mian Maliya," 187.
39. See Wicks, "The Art of Deliverance," 139 (on prayers), and Overmyer, *Local Religion*, 175 (on vows taken by son-seeking women).
40. On how Chinese female deities were worshipped predominantly by women, see Sangren, "Female Gender."
41. Alternative expressions for *nomen* and *imago* were *firma* ("signature") and *veronica*. See Alfonso Vagnone and Michel Trigault, "Annua da Caza Kiam cheu de 1639," s.l. [Jiangzhou], s.d., BA-JA 49-V-12, 431r–438r, 434r.
42. *Nomina* printed on paper are mentioned in Kirwitzer, "Litterae Annuae 1624," 99. These probably resembled prayer cards used in post-Tridentine Europe (see Kürzeder, *Als die Dinge*, 171–77).
43. A medal is mentioned in João Frois, "Carta Annua da Missao da China do anno de 1634," Hangzhou, 8 September 1634, ARSI, Jap. Sin. 115 II, 266r–317r, 304v. It was usual for Jesuits who were sent to China to carry relics in their baggage (see Spence, *The Memory Palace*, 238). Relics of St. Ignatius are referred to in the

writings of Johann Adam Schall von Bell. See Schall von Bell, *De Ortu et Progressu Fidei*, 269–71.

44. See Dias Sr., "Litterae Annuae 1619," 52–55; João Froes, "Annua da Provincia da China do anno de 1631," s.l., s.d., BA-JA 49-V-10, 1r–32v, 24v; Alfonso Vagnone and Michel Trigault, "Annua da Caza Kiam cheu de 1639," s.l. [Jiangzhou], s.d., BA-JA 49-V-12, 431r–438r, 434r; anon., "Annuas do Chan cheu Prov[incia] Kiamsi dos annos 1658, [16]59, e [16]60," s.l., s.d., BA-JA 49-V-14, 555r–555v, 648r–658v; Juan Antonio Arnedo, "Litterae Annuae Missionis Sinicae ab Anno 1685 ad An[num] 1690," Ganzhou, 30 September 1691, ARSI, Jap. Sin. 117, 203r–228v, 205v.

45. See João Froes, "Annua da V[ice]provincia da China do anno de 1633," s.l. [Hangzhou?], 20 September 1634, BA-JA 49-V-11, 1r–99v, 25r (Shanxi) and 91v (Fujian).

46. It is noteworthy that St. Francis-Xavier, the first Jesuit missionary to China, who was known for his efficacious intercession during childbirth in Europe (see Schreiber, "Heilige Wasser"), did not figure as a patron saint of parturient women in China.

47. The first recorded case of Ignatian intervention during childbirth dates back to the early 1600s, when the Roman noblewoman Vittoria Delfina Altieri, mother of the future pope Clemens X, was rescued from perilous bloodshed during delivery after she was provided with an image of Ignatius by her confessor. See Bartoli, *Della vita*, vol. 5, 580–81.

48. The Ignatian devotion of parturient women in German-speaking countries has been particularly well researched. See Schreiber, "Heilige Wasser," 203, and Sieber, *Jesuitische Missionierung*, 124, passim. However, Ignatian sacramentals were also used in Italy, Spain, and France as remedies during difficult childbirth. See Bartoli, *Della vita*, vol. 5, 582, passim.

49. See von Thiessen, *Die Kapuziner*, 428–29.

50. See Harrison, "Rethinking Missionaries and Medicine," 138–39.

51. See Furth, *A Flourishing Yin*, 117–18, 175. The swallowing of small images of saints was also practiced by early modern Catholics. See Kürzeder, *Als die Dinge*, 78, note 249; 129–30.

52. See von Thiessen, *Die Kapuziner*, 425, 439. On the ways European Jesuits used popular religious culture when introducing post-Tridentine sacramentals, see Johnson, "Blood, Tears, and Xavier-Water," 198.

53. Hagiographic writing on St. Ignatius supports the view that the use of Ignatian sacramentals in China can be understood as not merely the result of a transfer of European religious culture to China but rather the result of a single process of dissemination of post-Tridentine religious culture on a global scale. Vigilio Nolarci's *Compendio della vita di S. Ignatio*, dating from 1680, contained birth and pregnancy miracle stories worked by the saint from various European countries, but also from Tenerife (Canary Islands), Persia, and the Philippines, testifying to how devotion to Ignatius as an intercessor for birthing women had spread globally by the close of the seventeenth century.

54. Vagnone, *Tianzhu shengjiao shengren xingshi*, *juan* 4, 45a.

55. On the birth chamber as a strictly female space and how ritual knowledge and objects concerning childbirth were passed on in predominantly female networks,

see Furth, "The Patriarch's Legacy," 202. In this respect, social practices surrounding birth in seventeenth-century China closely resembled practices in contemporary Europe. See Rublack, "Pregnancy."

56. Dias Sr., "Litterae Annuae 1619," 52.
57. Such was, indeed, also the case with the Hangzhou woman, who became Catholic after being saved by the sacramental.

6. Domestic Communities

1. The first volume of the *Handbook of Christianity in China* uses the *christianitas* concept for the analysis of Christian communities, following Joseph Dehergne's definition of "Christian community." See HCC, 536–37. On the Chinese Catholic ritual community, see Standaert, *The Interweaving of Rituals*, 110–15.
2. For discussion of one such *huigui*, see Brockey, *Journey*, 388–92.
3. See Väth, "Die Marianischen Kongregationen," and, on Marian congregations in Europe, Châtellier, *L'Europe des dévots*.
4. Standaert, *The Interweaving of Rituals*, 111. See also Brockey, *Journey*, 328–401. This differentiation, however, did not apply to women's congregations.
5. See Brockey, *Journey*, 332–33.
6. The term *communities of effective rituals* is introduced in Standaert, *The Interweaving of Rituals*, 222–28.
7. See anon., "Pontos da annua do Singan fu Metropoli da Provincia Xen si anno de 1649," s.l., s.d., BA-JA 49-V-13, 493r–502r, 496v. See also Gabriel de Magalhães, "Annua das Residencias do Norte da Provincia da China anno de 1659," Beijing, 20 November 1661, BA-JA 49-V-14, 513v–551r, 547r–547v.
8. See Standaert, *Yang Tingyun*, 63–64.
9. See Smith, *The Art of Doing Good*, 5–6. On gentry women's participation in poetry clubs, see Ko, *Teachers*, 232–42.
10. For one case of especially close links between a Catholic men's congregation and a benevolent society, see Zürcher, "Christian Social Action."
11. This increase in women's lay Buddhist congregations is particularly true for the urbanized lower Yangzi. See Yü, *The Renewal*, 91.
12. See Dudbridge, "Women Pilgrims."
13. On women's lay Buddhist associations in twentieth-century China and Taiwan, see Sangren, "Female Gender," 8, passim. On extra-domestic autonomy, see Dudbridge, "Women Pilgrims"; Zhou, "The Hearth"; Zhao, *Kuanghuan yu richang*, 259–96; and Naquin, *Peking*, 278–80.
14. On the rivalry between Jesuits and indigenous religious specialists, see Brockey, *Journey*, 410.
15. Manuel Dias Jr., "Annua 1627," Shanghai, 9 May 1628, ARSI, Jap. Sin. 115 I, 119r–153v, 146r. *Pusa* is the Chinese term for bodhisattva. Amida (Sanskrit: Amithaba) is spelled by Monteiro "o mi to fe," which refers to the Chinese Amituofo. See João Monteiro, "Annua da Viceprov[inci]a da China do anno de 1637," s.l., 16 October 1638, ARSI, Jap. Sin. 115 II, 369r–435v, 379r.

16. On vegetarianism, see, inter alia, João da Costa, "Annua da Christandade da China do anno de 1614," s.l., 10 August 1615, ARSI, Jap. Sin. 113, 372r–392r, 377r; Dias Sr., "Litterae Annuae 1619," 74; and Bartolomeo da Costa, "Carta Anua do Collegio de Macao, e rezidencias a elle anexas . . . de [16]63, e [16]64," Macao, 21 November 1664, ARSI, Jap. Sin. 22, 183r–187r, 185v. Vegetarianism was also an aspect of Taoist "inner alchemy" (*neidan*; see Mann, *Precious Records*, 71), and it is therefore not always clear whether these examples refer to Buddhist practices. On Chinese women's recitation of the Buddha's name, see João Monteiro, "Annua da Viceprov[inci]a da China do anno de 1637," s.l., 16 October 1638, ARSI, Jap. Sin. 115 II, 369r–435v, 379r.
17. On women's contact with Buddhist monks, see Alfonso Vagnone, "Annua della China del 1618," Macao, 20 November 1618, ARSI, Jap. Sin. 114, 152r–163v, 160r–160v. The expression "pagodenta" is recurrent in the writings of the Jesuits. See, for instance, Manuel Dias Jr., "Annua 1627," Shanghai, 9 May 1628, ARSI, Jap. Sin. 115 I, 119r–159v, 127v. It is difficult to ascertain the nature of the Chinese group hidden behind this expression, but it is probable that it refers to some sort of women's lay Buddhist congregations, even more so because the sources sometimes mention that the members of these "diabolical confraternities" often maintained a strictly vegetarian diet.
18. See, for instance, João Monteiro, "Annua da Viceprov[inci]a da China do anno de 1637," s.l., 16 October 1638, ARSI, Jap. Sin. 115 II, 369r–435v, 415v.
19. See João Monteiro, "Annua della Viceprovincia della Cina dell'anno 1641," s.l., 7 September 1642, ARSI, Jap. Sin. 118, 5v.
20. Thomas-Ignatius Dunyn-Szpot, "Historia Sinarum Imperii, 1641–1687," ARSI, Jap. Sin. 103, 7v.
21. Thomas-Ignatius Dunyn-Szpot, "Historia Sinarum Imperii, 1641–1687," ARSI, Jap. Sin. 103, 8r.
22. See anon., "Annua da Caza de Ham cheu del 1645," s.l. [Hangzhou], s.d., BNP, CÓD. 722, 298r–304r, 302r.
23. See Inácio da Costa, "Annua da Viceprov[inci]a do Norte do ano 1647," s.l., s.d., ARSI, Jap. Sin. 122, 282r–304r, 288v. The transformation of congregations from non-Catholic to Catholic took place mainly among female organizations (for one exception, see anon., "Annua da Residencia de Han Chum na Provincia de Xen Si anno de 1644," s.l., s.d., BA-JA 49-V-13, 205r–213r, 212v). That was probably because men were often involved in the worship of territorial deities, whose close links with the political organization of the community precluded their replacement with a different cult (see Sangren, "Female Gender").
24. The annual letters of earlier periods report the conversion of single members of "idolatrous congregations" but not the conversion of whole congregations. See, for instance, Nicolas Trigault, ["Littera Annua 1612?"], Cochinchina, 1613, ARSI, Jap. Sin. 117, 2r–10v, 6v. On the mid-seventeenth-century crisis in China, see Struve, *Voices*, 2.
25. On Buddhist groups' activities, see Zhao, *Kuanghuan yu richang*, 259–96, and Mann, *Precious Records*, 188, passim.

26. See Sangren, "Female Gender," 17, and Naquin, *Peking*, 278–80, 555–58.
27. See Huang, "Christian Communities," 10.
28. See Lazzaro Cattaneo, "Annuae Sin[ae] 1630," s.l., 12 September 1631, ARSI, Jap. Sin. 121, 132r–141r, 136v.
29. For early references to women's congregations, see Ricci, "Litterae Annuae 1606–1607," 180–81, and Francisco Furtado, "Annuae Sinae et Cochinchina[e] 1618," Macao, 1 November 1620, ARSI, Jap. Sin. 114, 220r–233r, 228r. See also Margiotti, "Congregazioni mariane," 134 (on a 1611 foundation in Nanjing). On the multiplication of congregations during the 1630s, see Brockey, *Journey*, 275.
30. Anon., "Breve relação da Christandade da Corte de Pekim," s.l., s.d. [1692], BA-JA 49-V-22, 140r–145v, 141v.
31. See Inácio da Costa, "Annua da Viceprov[incia] do Norte na China do ano 1647," s.l., s.d., ARSI, Jap. Sin. 122, 282r–304r, 285v–286r. There are, however, references to separate congregations for women in rural areas. See, for instance, André Ferram, "Annua da Vice-Provincia da China [1656]," Macao, 29 January 1659, BA-JA 49-V-14, 62r–93r, 68v.
32. For an early reference, see Kirwitzer, "Litterae Annuae 1620," 138–39.
33. On male *huizhang*, see Brockey, *Journey*, 343. For the terms for female lay leaders in European languages, see Gaspare Ferreira, "Missione fatta a certi luoghi vicini [di Beijing]," in Ricci, *Lettere*, 431–54, 447.
34. See Gaspare Ferreira, "Missione fatta a certi luoghi vicini [di Beijing]," in Ricci, *Lettere*, 431–54, 447.
35. *Fonti Ricciane*, vol. 2, 249–50.
36. See Juan Antonio Arnedo, "Litterae Annuae Missionis Sinicae ab Anno 1685 ad An[num] 1690," Ganzhou, 30 September 1691, ARSI, Jap. Sin. 117, 205v.
37. P. Steven Sangren has argued that Chinese elderly women's religious activities should be seen as a form of "ritual postparenthood," which provided women's lives with a new center of gravity after their children had grown up. See Sangren, "Female Gender," 17. On the noble origin of leaders of women's congregations, see Gaspare Ferreira, "Missione fatta a certi luoghi vicini [di Beijing]," in Ricci, *Lettere*, 431–54, 447.
38. On female congregational leaders' charity, see Francisco Furtado, "Annua delle Provincie della Cina spettanti al Norte del 1643," Beijing, 10 August 1643, ARSI, Jap. Sin. 119, 21r–38r, 32r–32v.
39. See Zürcher, "The Jesuit Mission," 419.
40. See João Froes, "Annua da V[ice]provincia da China do anno de 1633," s.l. [Hangzhou?], 20 September 1634, BA-JA 49-V-11, 1r–99v, 13v. See also José Soares, "Annuae Litterae Collegii Pekinensis. Ab Exitu Julii Anni 1694 ad Finem Usque Julii Anni 1697," Beijing, 2 July 1697, ARSI, Jap. Sin. 116, 277r–301v, 279r.
41. See anon., "Annua da Viceprovincia do Norte dos annos 1643, 1644, 1645," s.l., s.d., BA-JA 49-V-13, 102v–122r, 116r; anon., "Pontos da Annua da Caza de Ham cheu de 1648," s.l. [Hangzhou], s.d., BA-JA 49-V-13, 609r–612v, 609r. See also Standaert, *The Interweaving of Rituals*, 112.
42. See Bernardus Regius, "Annuae ex V[ice]provincia Sinarum An[no] 1629," s.l., s.d., BA-JA 49-V-8, 608v–627v, 616v.

43. See anon., "Carta Annua da Collegio de Macao e Missao das Residencias de Cantao do anno de 1692," s.l., s.d., BA-JA 49-V-22, 97r–125r, 141v. On the Rosary, see Lazzaro Cattaneo, "Annua da Viceprovincia da China de 1629," s.l., 12 September 1631, BA-JA 49-V-8, 595r–608r, 605r. On Chinese Catholics' habit of chanting (rather than murmuring) prayers, see Manuel Dias [Jr.?], "Annua 1626," s.l., s.d., ARSI, Jap. Sin. 115 I, 93r–118v, 111r. This practice was inspired by sutra chanting (*fanbai*). See Chen, "The Chant of the Pure," 80–82.
44. See Francisco Furtado, "Annua delle Provincie della Cina spettanti al Norte del 1643," Beijing, 10 August 1643, ARSI, Jap. Sin. 119, 21r–38r, 31v; André Ferram, "Annua da Vice-Provincia da China [1656]," Macao, 29 January 1659, BA-JA 49-V-14, 62r–93r, 91v.
45. See McLaren, "Women's Work," and Sangren, "Female Gender," 21, passim.
46. See João Froes, "Annua da V[ice]provincia da China do anno de 1633," s.l. [Hangzhou?], 20 September 1634, BA-JA 49-V-11, 1r–99v, 13v.
47. See Zürcher, "Buddhist *Chanhui*," 109.
48. See, for instance, João Froes, "Annua da Viceprovincia da China do anno de 1632," Hangzhou, 1 August 1633, BA-JA 49-V-10, 76r–130r, 107v; Lazzaro Cattaneo, "Annuae Sin[ae] 1630," s.l., 12 September 1631, ARSI, Jap. Sin. 132r–141r, 136v.
49. See João Monteiro, "Annua da Viceprov[inci]a da China do anno de 1637," s.l., 16 October 1638, ARSI, Jap. Sin. 115 II, 369r–435v, 378r. In Europe, the presence of noisy toddlers in churches was a target of criticism by Tridentine reformers. See Hersche, *Muße und Verschwendung*, vol. 2, 705. On children's presence in late imperial women's lives and work, see Bray, *Technology and Gender*, 201.
50. *Jiaozhang* was the title of address for catechists as used by Catholics in eighteenth-century Fujian. See Menegon, *Ancestors*, 249. A letter dating from 1640 shows that men occasionally also acted as Catholic women's catechists. It mentions a certain Denho, "catechist and master of the women," See "Carta do Padre R[odrigo de] Figueredo para o P[adre] V[ice]provincial," s.l., s.d. [1640], BA-JA 49-V-12, 488v–492r, 490v–491r). This is, however, the only reference to a male catechist that I have found.
51. See anon., "Pontos da Annua do Singan fu Metropoli da Provincia Xen si anno de 1649," s.l., s.d., BA-JA 49-V-13, 493r–502r, 494v; anon., "Carta Annua da Collegio de Macao e Missao das Residencias de Cantao do anno de 1692," s.l., s.d., BA-JA 49-V-22, 97r–125r, 141v.
52. "Annua do Padre Martino Martini do anno 1644," Hangzhou, 6 July 1644, BA-JA 49-V-22, 328r–332r, 329v.
53. On male catechists' congregations, see Brockey, *Journey*, 352–53.
54. See Golvers, *François de Rougemont*, 137. On Candida Xu's sponsoring of female catechists in the Jiangnan region, see Thomas-Ignatius Dunyn-Szpot, "Historia Sinarum Imperii, 1641–1687," ARSI, Jap. Sin. 103, 206r.
55. See José Soares, "Annuae Litterae Collegii Pekinensis. Ab Exitu Julii Anni 1694 ad Finem Usque Julii Anni 1697," Beijing, 2 July 1697, ARSI, Jap. Sin. 116, 277r–301v, 279r.
56. On European semireligious women, see Rapley, *The Dévotes*, 54, and Conrad, *Zwischen Kloster und Welt*.

57. On Chinese shamans and spirit mediums, see Jordan, *Gods*. Spirit mediums in China were often female. As Margery Wolf points out, this was connected with the belief that women, as the weaker sex, were more easily possessed by spirits than men were (Wolf, *A Thrice-Told Tale*, 34).
58. See João Monteiro, "Annua 1638," s.l., 20 September 1639, BA-JA 49-V-12, 277r–344v, 293r–295r.
59. See Menegon, *Ancestors*, 249.
60. On Canton, see anon., "Carta Annua do Collegio de Macao e Missao das Residencias de Cantao do anno de 1692," s.l., s.d., BA-JA 49-V-22, 97r–125r, 112r. Toward the end of the seventeenth century, the women's congregation of Songjiang had access to the sacraments five times a year (see Couplet, *Histoire*, 27), while the women in the rural surroundings of Shanghai are reported to have received the sacraments only once a year (see José Soares, "Annuae Litterae Collegii Pekinensis. Ab Exitu Julii Anni 1694 ad Finem Usque Julii Anni 1697," Beijing, 2 July 1697, ARSI, Jap. Sin. 116, 277r–301v, 293v).
61. See Francesco Brancati, "Carta Annua da rezidencia de Xam hai do anno de 1658 Xun chi 15," s.l., s.d., BA-JA 49-V-14, 472r–479v, 473r, and Inácio da Costa, "Annua da Viceprov[incia] do Norte na China do ano 1647," s.l., s.d., ARSI, Jap. Sin. 122, 282r–304r, 290v.
62. See André Ferram, "Annua da Vice-Provincia da China [1656]," Macao, 29 January 1659, BA-JA 49-V-14, 62r–93r, 82v.
63. Francesco Furtado to [?], s.l., 8 February 1640, ARSI, F.G. 722-20, 1v. On the celebration of Chinese festivals in men's churches, see Gabriel de Magalhães, "Annua das Rezidencias do Norte, da V[ice]provincia da China no anno de 1660," Beijing, 20 July 1662, BA-JA 49-V-14, 674r–702v, 692r, 697r.
64. See Juan Antonio Arnedo, "Litterae Annuae Missionis Sinicae ab Anno 1685 ad An[num] 1690," Ganzhou, 30 September 1691, ARSI, Jap. Sin. 117, 205v. See also André Ferram, "Annua da Vice-Provincia da China [1656]," Macao, 29 January 1659, BA-JA 49-V-14, 62r–93r, 82v–83r; Francesco Brancati, "Carta Annua da rezidencia de Xam hai do anno de 1658 Xun chi 15," s.l., s.d., BA-JA 49-V-14, 472r–479v, 473r.
65. See José Soares, "Annuae Litterae Collegii Pekinensis. Ab Exitu Julii Anni 1694 ad Finem Usque Julii Anni 1697," Beijing, 2 July 1697, ARSI, Jap. Sin. 116, 277r–301v, 181r–181v.
66. See Couplet, *Histoire*, 112.
67. See Couplet, *Histoire*, 107.
68. See Couplet, *Histoire*, 106. See also Menegon, "Deliver Us," 38, 52–53.
69. According to Peter Hersche, only 28 percent of the churches in the German diocese of Cologne were equipped with confessionals in 1663 (Hersche, *Muße und Verschwendung*, vol. 2, 685).
70. On the connections between community gatherings and confessions in Chinese Catholicism in general, see Menegon, "Deliver Us," 48–52.
71. See André Ferram, "Annua da Vice-Provincia da China [1656]," Macao, 29 January 1659, BA-JA 49-V-14, 62r–93r, 91v; de Gouvea, *Asia Extrema*, vol. 1, 78–79, 217, 238. The situation seems to have been similar in the communities administered by the Dominicans. See Menegon, "Deliver Us," 40, note 107.

72. Le Comte, *Nouveaux mémoires*, vol. 2, 283–84.
73. See Prospero Intorcetta, "Annua de Kien cham do 1662," Jianchang, 31 December 1662, BA-JA 49-V-16, 391r–394r, 392v.
74. See the contributions in Standaert and Dudink, *Forgive Us*; see esp. Menegon, "Deliver Us," 47, and Zürcher, "Buddhist *Chanhui*," 105.
75. The Eucharist was accessible only to those devotees who had acquired adequate knowledge about it. See anon., "Annua da Caza de Ham cheu del 1645," [Hangzhou], s.d., BNP, CÓD. 722, 298r–304r, 298v.
76. See Zürcher, "Buddhist *Chanhui*," 105.
77. See Wu, "Self-Examination," 6. See also Brokaw, *Ledgers*, and Yü, *The Renewal*, chapter 5. On convergences between Christian and Chinese practices of self-examination, see Waltner, "Demerits," and Zürcher, "Confucian and Christian Religiosity," 634.
78. On how individual piety was a predominantly female sphere, see Sangren, "Female Gender," 21. On women's quest for "spiritual purification," see Mann, *Precious Records*, 69.
79. On the profound entrenchment of the concept of karmic retribution in seventeenth-century Chinese society, see Yü, "Ming Buddhism," 949.
80. See Mann, *Precious Records*, 69–75.
81. See Grant and Idema, *Escape from Blood Pond Hell*, and Ahern, "The Power and Pollution."
82. See Francesco Furtado, "Annua da Viceprovincia da China de 1642," Beijing, 10 August 1643, ARSI, Jap. Sin. 122, 124r–178v, 141v–142r.
83. See Francesco Sambiasi to the European Fathers [PP. Europaeis Nostris], Nanjing, 18 May 1614, ARSI, Jap. Sin. 116, 11r–28v, 25v. The idea of the Buddhist blood-pond hell was strongly rejected by Chinese Catholics. See, for instance, Zürcher, "Xu Guangqi," 159, 163.
84. See anon., "Annua da Viceprovincia do Norte dos annos 1643, 1644, 1645," s.l., s.d., BA-JA 49-V-13, 102v–122r, 116r. In contrast to this women's congregation, men's penitential congregations usually did not specifically aim at preparing for death and, therefore, were probably also frequented by young men. See Brockey, *Journey*, 395–99.
85. For examples of daily examinations of conscience, see João Monteiro, "Annua della Viceprovincia della Cina dell'anno 1641," s.l., 7 September 1642, ARSI, Jap. Sin. 118, 32r. On penitential practices, see João Froes, "Annua da V[ice]provincia da China do anno de 1633," s.l. [Hangzhou], 20 September 1634, BA-JA 49-V-11, 1r–99v, 14r. For an analysis of Chinese Catholic prescriptive texts on penitence, see Menegon, "Deliver Us," 9–46.
86. On missionaries' occasional complaints about Chinese penitents' lack of contrition, see Menegon, "Deliver Us," 51.
87. See Menegon, "Deliver Us," 40.
88. See Brockey, *Journey*, 367.
89. An election of a men's congregational head is prescribed in Augery, *Shengmu huigui*, 447.
90. See Brockey, *Journey*, 328–401.

91. See [Soares?], *Shengmu lingbao huigui*, 240. Other societies expressly excluded women. On this practice, see, for instance, Zürcher, "Christian Social Action," 279.

7. Sharing Genteel Spirituality

1. See Ko, *Teachers*, esp. chapter 5; Berg, *Women*; and Mann, *Precious Records*, esp. chapter 4. See also the contributions to Widmer and Chang, *Writing Women*, and Fong and Widmer, *The Inner Quarters*.
2. See Ko, *Teachers*, esp. part 3.
3. On the four principal converts of these families, namely, Xu Guangqi, Li Zhizao, Yang Tingyun, and Sun Yuanhua, see HCC, 404–21.
4. There is evidence that some "talented women" existed in Catholic gentry families (see Liu, "Xu Guangqi," 98). However, historians have so far not found any writings attributed to a Catholic woman.
5. On Xu Guangqi's family background, see Brook, "Xu Guangqi." For a synthesis considering Xu's different fields of activity, see the essays in Jami, Engelfriet, and Blue, *Statecraft*.
6. On Xu Guangqi's son and his five grandsons and four granddaughters, see Fang, *Zhongguo tianzhujiaoshi renwuzhuan*, vol. 2, 65–66. Outstanding nineteenth-century descendants of Xu Guangqi were Xu Yunxi, a ninth great-grandson, who was the director of the Jesuit library at Xujiahui from 1876 to 1922, and Xu Zongze, a tenth great-grandson, who entered the Society of Jesus and became the director of that library in 1923 (see Shi, "The Christian Scholar," 206). Xu Yunxi was the author of a partial translation of Couplet's *Histoire* into Chinese. See Xu, *Yi wei Zhongguo fengjiao taitai*.
7. With the notable exception of Candida Xu (see King, "Candida Xu"), the female members of the Xu family have received little attention from historians. For short discussions of Xu Guangqi's four granddaughters, see Shi, "The Christian Scholar," 200–201, and Liu, "Xu Guangqi," 99–100. Xu Guangqi's family—grandchildren included—lived with him in Beijing from circa 1605 to 1607. Then Xu was forced to retire temporarily from office and returned to Shanghai (see King, "The Family Letters," 5, 9). Although it is not entirely clear, it seems plausible that the grandchildren remained in Shanghai when Xu resumed office in 1610.
8. See Mann, *Precious Records*, 60.
9. See Ko, *Teachers*, 198, passim.
10. See Mann, *Precious Records*, 62–75.
11. Wolf describes this phenomenon in her influential study *Women and the Family*, in which she maintains that the "uterine family," consisting of a woman and her own children, was a woman's main source of power in traditional Chinese families.
12. On elderly Chinese women's religious devotions, see Mann, *Precious Records*, 68–75. On this phenomenon as a ritual "postparenthood," see Sangren, "Female Gender," 17.
13. Matthew Sommer has pointed out that chaste widows enjoyed "the strongest rights of any women with regard to property and independence" (Sommer, *Sex, Law, and Society*, 166). This contrasts with the situation in early modern Europe, where

unmarried widows were generally in a less privileged legal position than married women (see Wunder, *He Is the Sun*, 53).

14. On the concept of "women's culture," see Ko, *Teachers*, 179–218.
15. See King, "The Xujiahui (Zikawei) Library," 459.
16. See Clarke, *Catholic Shanghai*, 13–14.
17. Thomas-Ignatius Dunyn-Szpot, "Historia Sinarum Imperii, 1641–1687," ARSI, Jap. Sin. 103, 72v.
18. See Francesco Brancati, "Annua da Residencia de Xam hai do anno de 1647 do Rey Xun Chi 4.° anno," s.l., s.d., BA-JA 49-V-13, 458v–464v, 459v.
19. See João Froes, "Annua da Provincia da China do anno de 1631," s.l., s.d., BA-JA 49-V-10, 1r–32v, 23v.
20. See Couplet, *Histoire*, 112–13.
21. Catholic women's use of the "little book of Christian exercise" is mentioned in Dias Sr., "Litterae Annuae 1619," 36–37; idem, "Annua 1626," s.l., s.d., ARSI, Jap. Sin. 115 I, 93r–118v, 111r; and Gabriel de Magalhães, "Annua das Rezidencias do Norte, da V[ice]provincia da China no anno de 1660," Beijing, 20 July 1662, BA-JA 49-V-14, 674r–702v, 688r. On the content of the *Daily Exercises*, see Brunner, *L'euchologe de la Chine*, 184–86.
22. See João Froes, "Annua da Provincia da China do anno de 1631," s.l., s.d., BA-JA 49-V-10, 1r–32v, 23v.
23. Francesco Brancati, "Annua da Residencia de Xam hai do anno de 1659 Xun Chi ano 16,", s.l., s.d., BA-JA 49-V-14, 551r–565v, 560v.
24. See Francesco Brancati, "Annua do anno 1643 de Cum Chim da Residencia da Xam Hay," Shanghai, March 1644, BNP, CÓD. 722, 237r–252v, 237v.
25. See Thomas-Ignatius Dunyn-Szpot, "Historia Sinarum Imperii, 1641–1687," ARSI, Jap. Sin. 103, 5r. For female servants to be included in Chinese gentry women's social activities was common practice. See Mann, *Precious Records*, 61.
26. On Lady Wang, see Liu, "Xu Guangqi," 100.
27. See João Monteiro, "Annua da Viceprovincia da China de 1638," s.l., 20 September 1639, ARSI, Jap. Sin. 121, 142r–193r, 170r.
28. On the Confucian elite's difficulty with accepting Catholic virgins in eighteenth-century Fujian, see Menegon, *Ancestors*, 312–18.
29. On Flavia's sickly daughter, see Francesco Brancati, "Annua da Residencia de Xam hai do anno de 1659 Xun Chi ano 16," s.l., s.d., BA-JA 49-V-14, 551r–565v, 553r–554v. The story of Flavia's daughter-in-law is recorded in Francesco Brancati, "Annua da Rezidencia de Xam hai do anno de 1648," s.l., s.d., BA-JA 49-V-13, 473r–479v, 474r–475r. On faithful maidens in the Ming period, see Lu, *True to Her Word*.
30. Fang Hao and Auguste M. Colombel record the Christian names of only the first, second, and fourth granddaughters of Xu Guangqi—Felicitas, Candida, and Martina—claiming that the name of the third granddaughter is unknown (see Fang, *Zhongguo tianzhujiaoshi renwuzhuan*, vol. 2, 65, and Colombel, *Jiangnan chuanjiao shi*, 249–50). The annual letters suggest, however, that the third granddaughter's name was Monica. See Francesco Brancati, "Annua da Rezidencia de Xam hai do anno de 1648," s.l., s.d., BA-JA 49-V-13, 473r–479v, 474r, and idem, "Annua da Residencia de Xam hai do anno de 1659 Xun Chi ano 16," s.l., s.d.,

BA-JA 49-V-14, 551r–565v, 561v. Candida Xu's wedding is the only celebration that can be dated with some certainty. According to Couplet, it took place in 1623, when Candida was aged sixteen (see Couplet, *Histoire*, 11). Because Candida was the second of the four Xu daughters, it seems reasonable to assume that Xu Guangqi's four granddaughters' weddings were probably all celebrated during the second decade of the seventeenth century.

31. See Liu, "Xu Guangqi," 100. Felicitas's, Candida's, and Martina's husbands, in particular, were members of families sympathizing with Catholicism. These were the Ai, Xu, and Pan families, all eminent gentry families of the Shanghai area.
32. See João Monteiro, "Annua da Viceprovincia da China de 1638," s.l., 20 September 1639, ARSI, Jap. Sin. 121, 142r–193r, 171v, and idem, "Annuae Sin[ae] 1639," s.l., 8 October 1640, ARSI, Jap. Sin. 121, 221r–313r, 275r–275v.
33. According to Adrien Greslon, Candida's husband, Xu Yuandu, had several women, which had prompted her to live "like a widow" during the last years of her marriage (Greslon, *Histoire*, 64).
34. See Francesco Brancati, "Annua do anno 1643 de Cum Chim da Residencia da Xam Hay," Shanghai, March 1644, BNP, CÓD. 722, 237r–252v, 240r. According to Brancati, Felicitas was even able to convert her mother-in-law in the face of death.
35. On Chinese ladies' visits to their natal homes, see Lowe, *The Adventures of Wu*, vol. 1, 152–53.
36. See Francisco Furtado, "Novas da China," Nanchang, 10 July 1638, BA-JA 49-V-12, 199r–216r, 200v.
37. On the Xu women writers, see Couplet, *Histoire*, 26–28, 124.
38. João Monteiro, "Annua da Viceprovincia da China de 1638," s.l., 20 September 1639, ARSI, Jap. Sin. 121, 142r–193r, 171v. Monteiro only included a Portuguese translation of Candida's letter in his Annual Letter of 1638; the Chinese original is unavailable. However, as argued by Haruko Nawata Ward, who has studied similar sources for her analysis of Japanese Catholic women of the sixteenth and seventeenth centuries, it is reasonable to suppose that such letters cited and translated by Jesuits were not mere products of a missionary's imagination, despite the Jesuits' apologetic tendency (see Ward, *Women Religious Leaders*, 16).
39. See João Monteiro, "Annuae Sin[ae] 1639," s.l., 8 October 1640, ARSI, Jap. Sin. 121, 221r–313r, 275r–275v.
40. See Francesco Brancati, "Annua da Residencia de Xam hai do anno de 1659 Xun Chi an[n]o 16," s.l. [Shanghai?], s.d., BA-JA 49-V-14, 551r–565v, 561r.
41. On Candida Xu's role as religious teacher of her children, see anon., "Missao de Sum Kiam," [fragment of an annual letter], Songjiang, s.d. [ca. 1649], BA-JA 49-VI-61, 472r–475r, 474r. On mothers as teachers of their children in seventeenth-century China, see Ko, *Teachers*, 158–59; for a twentieth-century example, see Madsen, *China's Catholics*, 57. On mothers as their children's catechists in early modern Catholicism, see Chaix, "De la piété à la dévotion."
42. Such was the case with Candida Xu's children, who, according to Fang Hao, were all baptized (see Fang, *Zhongguo tianzhujiaoshi renwuzhuan*, vol. 2, 68).
43. See Francesco Brancati, "Annua da Rezidencia de Xam hai do anno de 1648," s.l. [Shanghai?], s.d., BA-JA 49-V-13, 473r–479v, 474r–474v.

44. See João Monteiro, "Annuae Sin[ae] 1639," s.l., 8 October 1640, ARSI, Jap. Sin. 121, 221r–313r, 275r.
45. See Francisco Furtado, "Novas da China," Nanchang, 10 July 1638, BA-JA 49-V-12, 199r–216r, 200v. On how Chinese officials separated their Confucian public role from domestically practiced religiosity, see Stein, "Les religions."
46. For Xu Yuandu's conversion, see João Monteiro, "Annua da Viceprovincia da China de 1638," s.l., 20 September 1639, ARSI, Jap. Sin. 121, 142r–193r, 171r. For aged Chinese men's religious practice see Spence, *Return*, 103.
47. See Liu, "Xu Guangqi," 104.
48. See Couplet, *Histoire*, 40.
49. See Couplet, *Histoire*, 40, 139.
50. The special freedom enjoyed by "chaste widows" was also remarked upon by the Jesuits. See Couplet, *Histoire*, 12.
51. See Colombel, *Jiangnan chuanjiao shi*, 249.
52. On Martina's role as congregational leader, see Francesco Brancati, "Annua do anno 1643 de Cum Chim da Residencia da Xam Hay," Shanghai, March 1644, BNP, CÓD. 722, 237r–252v, 240r. On her providing the financial means for a church, see Colombel, *Jiangnan chuanjiao shi*, 244.
53. There is some confusion about Xu Yuandu's year of conversion and his year of death. Philippe Couplet wrote that Candida married Yuandu at the age of sixteen (ca. 1623), that Yuandu died when they had been married for fourteen years (ca. 1637), and that he converted to Catholicism two years prior to his death (ca. 1635) (see Couplet, *Histoire*, 11, 13, 24). However, archival sources suggest that Couplet's information is incorrect. The Annual Letter of 1638 records Yuandu's conversion, which means that he was certainly still alive at that time (see João Monteiro, "Annua da Viceprovincia da China de 1638," s.l., 20 September 1639, ARSI, Jap. Sin. 121, 142r–193r, 171r). While the annual letters remain silent about Yuandu's year of death, it is probable that Fang Hao was correct in dating it to 1653 (Fang, *Zhongguo tianzhujiaoshi renwuzhuan*, vol. 2, 65–66), since Candida's activities as benefactress of the Jesuits (which befitted a widow much better than they did a married woman) become visible from the 1660s onward.
54. For the missionaries' description of Songjiang, see Manuel Dias Jr., "Carta Annua da Missam da China do anno de 1618," Macao, 7 December 1618, BA-JA 49-V-5, 232v–264v, 261v. On the establishment of Songjiang as a center of Chinese Catholicism, see PST, 273r. The importance of Songjiang is also illustrated by a contemporary map of Catholic communities in the region made by a Jesuit (probably Francesco Brancati). This map placed Songjiang in the center, grouping other important cities like Shanghai and Jiading around it. See Golvers, "Jesuit Cartographers."
55. Annual letters partly testify to this situation, rendering stories of women who became increasingly "cold" in matters of the religion. See, e.g., anon., "Carta Annua da China, dos annos 1651 e [16]52," s.l., s.d., ARSI, Jap. Sin. 117, 69r–146v, 143r–143v, and Pedro Marquez, "Missao da Ilha Haynam," Hainan, 20 May 1635, BA-JA 49-V-11, 239r–245v, 240v.
56. See anon., *Shengti huigui*, 263.

57. Couplet, *Histoire*, 11–12.
58. For similar findings on nineteenth-century Chinese Catholicism, see Sweeten, *Christianity in Rural China*, 189–90.
59. See Bossler, "'A Daughter,'" 97; Judd, "Niangjia"; and Gallin, "Matrilateral and Affinal Relationships."
60. See Menegon, *Ancestors*, 179–80, passim; Zürcher, "Un 'contrat communal,'" 12; and Laamann, *Christian Heretics*, 44.
61. See Kendall, *Shamans*, 168.
62. See Chau, "Modalities of Doing Religion," 552.
63. We know that the Xu ladies had a good level of literacy. See João Monteiro, "Annuae Sin[ae] 1639," s.l., 8 October 1640, ARSI, Jap. Sin. 121, 221r–313r, 275r.
64. See Thomas-Ignatius Dunyn-Szpot, "Historia Sinarum Imperii, 1641–1687," ARSI, Jap. Sin. 103, 204v, and Couplet, *Histoire*, 10.
65. See Thomas-Ignatius Dunyn-Szpot, "Historia Sinarum Imperii, 1641–1687," ARSI, Jap. Sin. 103, 206r.
66. Couplet, *Histoire*, 11.
67. See Chau, "Modalities of Doing Religion," 552. On Chinese Christian meditation, see also Standaert, "The Spiritual Exercises," 75.
68. On the popularity of sutra chanting among gentry women, see Mann, *Precious Records*, 190–91.
69. On motherhood and virginity as positive aspects of Chinese femininity, see Sangren, "Female Gender," 12–14.
70. Da Rocha had administered baptism to Xu Guangqi in 1603 and had subsequently acted as Xu's spiritual adviser (see Pfister, *Notices biographiques*, 68–69). For a translation of the whole text into German, see Qu, "*Song Nianzhu Guicheng*," 209–20.
71. See Lin, "Seeing the Place," 197.
72. See Francesco Brancati, "Annua da Residencia de Xam hai do anno de 1659 Xun Chi ano 16," s.l., s.d., BA-JA 49-V-14, 551r–565v, 561v.
73. Pictures of The Heart Consecrated to the Loving Jesus series seem to have been quite popular in China. See Menegon, "Jesuit Emblematica," 395–417. Monica was not the only Xu lady who had a preferred holy image. Candida Xu is said to have possessed an image of St. Francis, which had the power to heal people from evil influences (see Francesco Brancati, "Annua do anno 1643 de Cum Chim da Residencia de Xam Hay," Shanghai, March 1644, BNP, CÓD. 722, 237r–252v, 242r–242v), and her sister Felicitas especially cherished an image of the Holy Virgin (see João Monteiro, "Annua da Viceprovincia da China de 1638," s.l., 20 September 1639, ARSI, Jap. Sin. 121, 142r–193r, 170r–170v).
74. See Vagnone, *Tianzhu shengjiao shengren xingshi*, *juan* 6, 38v. On St. Catherine's penance, see 36v–38v.
75. See Thomas-Ignatius Dunyn-Szpot, "Historia Sinarum Imperii, 1641–1687," ARSI, Jap. Sin. 103, 6v.
76. See João Froes, "Annua da Provincia da China do anno de 1631," s.l., s.d., BA-JA 49-V-10, 1r–32v, 23v (on patron saints' days), and Couplet, *Histoire*, 79 (on saints of the month). On how "saints of the month" were selected, see Brockey, *Journey*, 383.

77. These dreams and visions are reported in the following sources: Francesco Brancati, "Annua do anno 1643 de Cum Chim da Residencia da Xam Hay," Shanghai, March 1644, BNP, CÓD. 722, 237r–252v, 240v; idem, "Annua da Rezidencia de Xam hai do anno de 1648," s.l., s.d., BA-JA 49-V-13, 473r–479v, 474r; idem, "Annua da Residencia de Xam hai do anno de 1659 Xun Chi an[n]o 16," s.l., s.d., BA-JA 49-V-14, 551r–565v, 559v–561v; Thomas-Ignatius Dunyn-Szpot, "Historia Sinarum Imperii, 1641–1687," ARSI, Jap. Sin. 103, 6r; and Couplet, *Histoire*, 130–31.
78. See Couplet, *Histoire*, 130–31. Couplet's cautionary attitude toward Candida's dreams might be explained by the fact that mystical and prophetical models of sanctity, which had been of crucial importance during the European Middle Ages, started to be stigmatized as a "pretense of holiness" after the Council of Trent, when the Holy Office initiated a number of legal processes against female mystics (see Zarri, "Female Sanctity," 194–97, and Schutte, *Aspiring Saints*).
79. Thomas-Ignatius Dunyn-Szpot, "Historia Sinarum Imperii, 1641–1687," ARSI, Jap. Sin. 103, 6r. The same dream is also rendered in Francesco Brancati, "Annua do anno 1643 de Cum Chim da Residencia da Xam Hay," Shanghai, March 1644, BNP, CÓD. 722, 237r–252v, 240v. For a complete rendering of the dream story in English, see Hsia, "Dreams," 123.
80. See Francesco Brancati, "Annua da Rezidencia de Xam hai do anno de 1648," s.l., s.d., BA-JA 49-V-13, 473r–479v, 474r.
81. See Jacques Le Faure, "Relaçam da Missam de Huquam," s.l., s.d. [ca. 1662?], BA-JA 49-V-15, 133r–148v, 138v. The romanized version of the Chinese phrase from Candida's dream was "Mai yuan Kia ti fam gui hao," which probably corresponds to "Mai Yuan jia difang [geng?] hao."
82. See Hsia, "Dreams."
83. See Ko, *Teachers*, 202. In accordance with Ko's assessment, Hsia found an even balance of female (twenty-nine) and male (twenty-eight) dreamers in the Chinese Catholic dream stories collected from annual letters. See Hsia, "Dreams," 113.
84. See Lackner, *Der chinesische Traumwald*.
85. See Ko, *Teachers*, 197.
86. Cited by Hsia, "Dreams," 231.
87. See Hsia, "Dreams," 119.

8. A Widow and Her Virgins

1. On female monasticism in Tridentine Europe, see van Wyhe, *Female Monasticism*.
2. See Zhang, *Guanfu*, 271–91; Menegon, "Child Bodies"; and idem, *Ancestors*, 301–56 (numbers cited on 327, 331).
3. For references to Agnes Yang in printed literature, see Pfister, *Notices biographiques*, 140, 159, 257.
4. See Menegon, *Ancestors*, 312–16.
5. See Menegon, *Ancestors*, 312.
6. See Menegon, "Child Bodies," 177–88, and Mann, *Precious Records*, 10. Note, however, that regional traditions of marriage resistance existed in South China. See Topley, "Marriage Resistance."

7. For a general analysis of Vagnone's *Biographies of the Saints* and its European sources, see Li, "Shengren, mogui, chanhui," esp. 206–9.
8. It is worth noting that, while sexuality was irrelevant to the structuring of the biographies of male saints (the latter subsumed under the categories "apostles," "church leaders," "martyrs," "non-monastic religious," and "monastic religious"), sexual abstinence was the single criterion applied to female saints.
9. Vagnone, *Tianzhu shengjiao shengren xingshi, juan* 6, 1a.
10. Martyrdom after marriage resistance was suffered by Catharina of Alexandria, Agatha, Lucia, Agnes, Barbara, Dorothea, and Thecla. Christina of Bolsena suffered martyrdom for resisting her father's plan for her to serve heathen gods as a consecrated virgin; Caecilia lived in a Josephite marriage and was martyred together with her husband.
11. Voragine, *Legenda Aurea*, 113–14. For the identification of *The Golden Legend* as source of Vagnone's *Biographies of the Saints*, see Li, "Shengren, mogui, chanhui," esp. 206–9.
12. Vagnone, *Tianzhu shengjiao shengren xingshi, juan* 6, 23a–23b.
13. See Huang, *Negotiating Masculinity*, chapter 4.
14. See Vagnone, *Tianzhu shengjiao shengren xingshi, juan* 6, 36a.
15. On the relationship between *beatas* and their native families, see Menegon, *Ancestors*, 332–33, and Zhang, *Guanfu*, 287–89.
16. See Menegon, *Ancestors*, 331, 327.
17. See Tiedemann, "Controlling the Virgins." An assumption of growth in the numbers of virgins in the Catholic communities of the Jesuits during the eighteenth century is also reasonable given how Jesuit presence disappeared from these communities after the prohibition of Catholicism issued by the Yongzheng emperor in 1724.
18. See Menegon, *Ancestors*, 302.
19. See Menegon, *Ancestors*, 330.
20. João Froes, "Annua da V[ice]provincia da China do anno de 1633," s.l. [Hangzhou?], 20 September 1634, BA-JA 49-V-11, 1r–99v, 13v.
21. João Monteiro, "Annua da Viceprov[inci]a da China do anno de 1637," s.l., 16 October 1638, ARSI, Jap. Sin. 115 II, 369r–435v, 425r–425v.
22. João Monteiro, "Annua da Viceprov[inci]a da China do anno de 1637," s.l., 16 October 1638, ARSI, Jap. Sin. 115 II, 369r-435v, 425r–425v.
23. See Strasser, *State of Virginity*, 175.
24. See Conrad, *Zwischen Kloster und Welt*, and Rahner, Introduction to *St. Ignatius of Loyola*.
25. See Menegon, *Ancestors*, 332. The difference between Dominicans and Jesuits has also been noted in Boxer, *Mary and Misogyny*, 109.
26. The fact that Agnes's husband left her considerable property is crucial, because widow chastity "was literally unaffordable for many widows" (Sommer, *Sex, Law, and Society*, 183), and poverty was the main factor forcing widows into remarriage.
27. João Froes, "Annua da V[ice]provincia da China do anno de 1633," s.l. [Hangzhou?], 20 September 1634, BA-JA 49-V-11, 1r–99v, 44v.

28. João Froes, "Annua da V[ice]provincia da China do anno de 1633," s.l. [Hangzhou?], 20 September 1634, BA-JA 49-V-11, 1r–99v, 44v.
29. Francisco Furtado, "Novas da China," Nanchang, 10 July 1638, BA-JA 49-V-12, 199r–216r, 200r.
30. See anon., "Pontos da annua da Caza de Ham cheu de 1648," s.l. [Hangzhou], s.d., BA-JA 49-V-13, 609r–612v, 609v.
31. João Froes, "Annua da V[ice]provincia da China do anno de 1633," s.l. [Hangzhou?], 20 September 1634, BA-JA 49-V-11, 1r–99v, 44v.
32. See Francisco Furtado, "Novas da China," Nanchang, 10 July 1638, BA-JA 49-V-12, 199r–216r, 200r.
33. See de Gouvea, *Cartas Ânuas*, 233–85, 265. On the sacrifice to the Silkworm Deity, see Bray, *Technology and Gender*, 251.
34. Francesco Furtado, "Annua delle Provincie della Cina spettanti al Norte del 1643," Beijing, 10 August 1643, ARSI, Jap. Sin. 119, 21r–38r, 37v.
35. See Thomas-Ignatius Dunyn-Szpot, "Historia Sinarum Imperii, 1641–1687," ARSI, Jap. Sin. 103, 21v–22r.
36. See Francesco Furtado, "Annua delle Provincie della Cina spettanti al Norte del 1643," Beijing, 10 August 1643, ARSI, Jap. Sin. 119, 21r–38r, 37v. Furtado's mention of statutes contradicts Paul Bornet's hypothesis that the virgins of the early years of the mission were not subjected to a formal rule (see Bornet, "Les vierges institutrices," 434).
37. See Pfister, *Notices biographiques*, 140.
38. See de Gouvea, *Cartas Ânuas*, 366, and Francesco Furtado, "Annua delle Provincie della Cina spettanti al Norte del 1643," Beijing, 10 August 1643, ARSI, Jap. Sin. 119, 21r–38r, 37v.
39. See Thomas-Ignatius Dunyn-Szpot, "Historia Sinarum Imperii, 1641–1687," ARSI, Jap. Sin. 103, 90r–90v, and Pfister, *Notices biographiques*, 140. On intact dead bodies as signs of sanctity both in China and in Europe, see Harrison, "Rethinking Missionaries and Medicine," 134–38.
40. On powerful virgin deities in China, see Boltz, "In Hommage to T'ien-fei"; Reed, "The Gender Symbolism of Kuan-yin"; and Sangren, "Female Gender." On the Virgin Mary as a divine intercessor in early modern Catholicism, see Strasser, *State of Virginity*.
41. See Sommer, *Sex, Law, and Society*, 167.
42. Especially wealthy widows often appeared as patronesses of religious institutions and pious endeavors. See Ingendahl, *Witwen*, 23–37.
43. The last reference to Agnes Yang that I have been able to find dates from 1647. See de Gouvea, *Cartas Ânuas*, 366.
44. See Waltner, "T'an-Yang-tzu," and idem, "Life and Letters."
45. See also Sommer, *Sex, Law, and Society*, 191.

9. Fabrics of Devotion

1. The idea of a "domestic Catholicism" practiced by Chinese women corresponds well with the observation that various versions of Chinese Catholicism existed in different social milieus. See HCC, 634–38.

2. See Francisco Pimentel, "Breve relação da jornada que fez a Corte de Pekim o Senhor Manoel de Saldanha Embaxador extraordinario del Rey de Portugal ao Emperador da China e Tartaria," s.l., s.d. [1670], BA-JA 49-VI-62, 715r–732r, 730r–730v.
3. See Jerónimo Rodriguez to Mutio Vitelleschi, Macao, 1 November 1620, ARSI, Jap. Sin. 121, 116r–131v, 124r, and Francisco Furtado, "Novas da China," Nanchang, 10 July 1638, BA-JA 49-V-12, 199r–216r, 200r.
4. See João Froes, "Annua da V[ice]provincia da China do anno de 1633," s.l. [Hangzhou?], 20 September 1634, BA-JA 49-V-11, 1r–99v, 5r–5v; Francesco Furtado, "Annuae Sinae et Cochinchina[e] 1618," Macao, 1 November 1620, ARSI, Jap. Sin. 114, 220r–233r, 228r; and anon., "Breve Relacão da Christandade da Corte de Pekim," s.l. [Beijing], s.d. [1692], BA-JA 49-V-22, 140r–145r, 143r.
5. See Rublack, *Dressing Up*, chapter 3, and Picaud and Foisselon, *Sacrées soieries.*
6. Mann, *Precious Records*, 159. See also Ko, *Teachers*, 172–73; Fong, "Female Hands"; and Li, "Embroidering Guanyin." Also note the sewing basket in the Annunciation scene depicted in João da Rocha's *Rules for Reciting the Rosary* (see figure 5.3).
7. See Mann, *Precious Records*, chapter 6; Ebrey, *The Inner Quarters*, chapter 7; and Bray, *Technology and Gender*, part 2.
8. See Manuel Dias [Jr.?], "Annua 1626," s.l., s.d., ARSI, Jap. Sin. 115 I, 93r–118v, 111r. On how traditional Chinese songs were, time and again, substituted by Christian ones, see Chaves, "Gathering Tea for God."
9. A letter by Jerónimo Rodriguez mentions embroidered floral patterns, whereas the Annual Letter of 1640 refers to embroideries of the mysteries of the Rosary. See Jerónimo Rodriguez to Mutio Vitelleschi, Macao, 1 November 1620, ARSI, Jap. Sin. 121, 116r–131v, 124r; Gabriel de Magalhães, "Littera Annua [1640]," s.l. [Beijing], s.d. [30 September 1641], BNP, CÓD. 722, 79r–108r, 88v. These embroideries may have been modeled on the illustrations of João da Rocha's *Rules for Reciting the Rosary.*
10. Besides these two examples, other liturgical textiles from eighteenth-century China exist. For an embroidered panel showing St. Anthony of Padua, see Clunas, *Pictures and Visuality*, 138. For an embroidered chasuble possessed by the Vatican, see *Mostra tesori*, no. 181. For an embroidered antependium possessed by an Antwerp church see *Anders gekleed*, 24–25.
11. The family was a benefactor of the Hofje van de Zeven Keurvorsten, a Catholic almshouse in Amsterdam, which possessed the chasuble until 1954. The family can be identified by its crest at the lower end of the chasuble (see Stam and Blerk, "Borduurkunst," 20–21).
12. See Stam and Blerk, "Borduurkunst," 21.
13. See Stam and Blerk, "Borduurkunst," 24–25.
14. Tuuk Stam and René van Blerk point out that, instead of the three young pelicans that are often found in European depictions and symbolize the three cardinal virtues, the antependium shows five young pelicans, probably alluding to the Confucian Five Constants (*wuchang*) (Stam and Blerk, "Borduurkunst," 25).
15. See Golvers, *François de Rougemont*, 592.
16. The Malayan-Portuguese term *tael* refers to the Chinese measurement *liang*, which equaled one ounce of (uncoined) silver. The exchange rates of taels into copper

cash varied greatly during the seventeenth century (see von Glahn, *Fountain of Fortune*, 106–9). Curiously, although the tael was always a measurement for silver, the Jesuits often translated the term as *aureus* or *écus d'or*, which, strictly speaking, referred to gold. See Golvers, *François de Rougemont*, 557.

17. See Golvers, *François de Rougemont*, 291.
18. See Golvers, *François de Rougemont*, 292, and Vermote, "The Role of Urban Real Estate," 291–94. On the problem of the delay and loss of European pensions, see Alden, *The Making of an Enterprise*, 325–29.
19. See PST, 272r–275v.
20. That Justa was a Manchu noblewoman and, indeed, the wife of a viceroy is suggested in a 1649 relation. See Ludovico Buglio and Gabriel de Magalhães, "Relaçao do que socedeo na Corte de Pekim ao P[adre] Fr[ancesco] Furtado Sup[eri]or do Norte para os P[adres] Luis Buglio, et Gabriel de Magalhães dos 20 de Fev[e]r[eir]o de 1648 os 25 de Outobro de 1649," s.l. [Beijing], s.d., ARSI, Jap. Sin. 142, 89r–106v, 104v.
21. See PST, 274v. The catalog does not mention all Chinese patrons of Catholic churches. For instance, it does not record Candida Xu's patronage of a church on Chongming Island, near Shanghai, and her establishment of around thirty smaller churches in the environs of Shanghai (see Couplet, *Histoire*, 69, 124), nor does it list Justa Zhao's and Agatha Tong's funding for a church in Hangzhou (see Thomas-Ignatius Dunyn-Szpot, "Historia Sinarum Imperii, 1641–1687," ARSI, Jap. Sin. 103, 114v, and Pfister, *Notices biographiques*, 259). No mention is made, furthermore, of a certain Monica Min, who is known to have sponsored a church in Zhejiang (see Pfister, *Notices biographiques*, 316).
22. See Feliciano Pacheco, "Carta Annua da Viceprovincia da China do anno de 1660," China, 19 July 1661, BA-JA 49-V-14, 702v–719r, 703r.
23. See Couplet, *Histoire*, 26.
24. See Adrien Greslon, "Litterae Annuae Viceprovincia Sinicae Annorum 1669 et 1670," s.l., 20 October 1670, ARSI, Jap. Sin. 120, 184r. In addition to the patronage directed toward the Jesuits, Candida Xu also provided financial support to Dominicans whenever they passed through Songjiang. See Couplet, *Histoire*, 128.
25. See Philippe Couplet to Charles de Noyelle, Macao, 24 April 1681, ARSI, Jap. Sin. 163, 120r–121r, 121r–120v [*sic*]. See also Golvers, *François de Rougemont*, 591, note 96. My estimate that this sum would have covered the daily expenditure of all Jesuits in China for almost ten years is based on two assumptions: that one missionary's annual expenditure amounted to roughly 230 taels (see Golvers, *François de Rougemont*, 627) and that, on average, twenty-five Jesuits were living at any one time in China between 1625 and 1690 (see HCC, 307).
26. See Brook, *Praying for Power*, 188–91, quotation 190.
27. See Naquin, *Peking*, 58, 156–58, and Liu, "Visualizing Perfection."
28. See Valone, "Piety and Patronage"; Zarri, "La Compagnia di Gesù"; and Kirkham, "Laura Battiferra."
29. On noblewomen's decreasing importance as benefactresses after the Society's founding period, see Hufton, "Altruism and Reciprocity," 329–31. On patronage by noblewomen in the eighteenth century, see Hsia, *Noble Patronage*.

30. On the uncertain financial basis of the mission under the Portuguese Padroado, and especially during the second half of the seventeenth century, see Golvers, *François de Rougemont*, 627–30.
31. See Brook, *Praying for Power*, 188–91.
32. On women's property rights in late imperial China, see Bray, *Technology and Gender*, 94, 139.
33. See Golvers, *François de Rougemont*, 590–91.
34. See Bray, *Technology and Gender*, 139.
35. Bernardus Regius, "Annuae ex V[ice]provincia Sinarum An[no] 1629," s.l., s.d., BA-JA 49-V-8, 608v–627v, 611r. *Juren* degree holders were successful candidates of the triennial provincial exams.
36. On the Songjiang women, see Couplet, *Histoire*, 125–26. On the Beijing women, see José Soares, "Annuae Litterae Collegii Pekinensis. Ab Exitu Julii Anni 1694 ad Finem Usque Julii Anni 1697," Beijing, 2 July 1697, ARSI, Jap. Sin. 116, 277r–301v, 277v.
37. See Manuel Dias [Jr.?], "Annua da Missao da China dos annos de [1]616 e [1]617," Macao, 14 January 1618, ARSI, Jap. Sin. 114, 13r–51v, 40r.
38. On the financial situation of Xu Guangqi's family, see Brook, "Xu Guangqi."
39. Couplet, *Histoire*, 24. It is noteworthy that much of Candida's patronage of the mission falls in the period of the Kangxi depression (from the 1660s to the 1690s). Since it must have been difficult to become rich through trade during the depression, it is possible that Candida had made her fortune before the 1660s (although evidence either way is lacking). On the depression, see von Glahn, *Fountain of Fortune*, 211–15.
40. See King, "The Family Letters," 14–26, passim. See also King, "Candida Xu," 55.
41. See Bray, *Technology and Gender*, 223–25.
42. It is not entirely clear what sort of tissues the women under Candida's aegis wove. Gail King's hypothesis that they (also) wove cotton cloth is a reasonable one given how Songjiang was the dominant center of cotton production of that time (see King, "Candida Xu," 55, note 34).
43. Couplet, *Histoire*, 24.
44. See Bray, *Technology and Gender*, 236–72; on the raising of silkworms, see 248–49. The proto-industrial revolution of Jiangnan's textile production was closely intertwined with the influx of foreign silver into China from circa 1550 to 1650. It was a major source of Jiangnan's proverbial wealth. See Atwell, "Notes on Silver," 6. On China's "silver century," see von Glahn, *Fountain of Fortune*, 113–41.
45. See, for instance, João Froes, "Annua da V[ice]provincia da China do anno de 1633," s.l. [Hangzhou?], 20 September 1634, BA-JA 49-V-11, 1r–99v, 75v, and Bernardus Regius, "Annuae ex V[ice]provincia Sinarum An[no] 1629," s.l., s.d., BA-JA 49-V-8, 608v–627v, 611r.
46. See Couplet, *Histoire*, 75–77, 133.
47. See Couplet, *Histoire*, 57, 78.
48. See Couplet, *Histoire*, 124.
49. See King, "Christian Charity," 24.
50. See PST, 272r–275v.

51. See Ko, *Teachers*, 119–224.
52. On Candida's support for construction work, see anon., "Ex Residencia Nancham pro Annua," s.l. [Nanchang], s.d. [ca. 1662?], BA-JA 49-V-15, 38v–40r, 39r. On the farewell given to Candida by the Nanchang Catholics, see Jacques Le Faure, "Relaçam da Missam de Huquam," s.l., s.d. [ca. 1662?], BA-JA 49-V-15, 133r–148v, 134v.
53. See Jacques Le Faure, "Relaçam da Missam de Huquam," s.l., s.d. [ca. 1662?], BA-JA 49-V-15, 133r–148v, 134v.
54. See Feliciano Pacheco, "Carta Annua da Viceprovincia da China do anno de 1660," s.l., 19 July 1661, 702v–719r, 703r–704r.
55. Anon., "Ex Residencia Nancham pro Annua," s.l. [Nanchang], s.d. [ca. 1662?], BA-JA 49-V-15, 38v–40r, 39r.
56. Jacques Le Faure, "Relaçam da Missam de Huquam," s.l., s.d. [ca. 1662?], BA-JA 49-V-15, 133r–148v, 134r.
57. Jacques Le Faure, "Relaçam da Missam de Huquam," s.l., s.d. [ca. 1662?], BA-JA 49-V-15, 133r–148v, 135v.
58. On the chapel in Chongqing, see Dehergne, "Études," 258. On Chengdu and on Tong Guoqi's funding initiatives, see PST, 272v, 274r.
59. See Brook, *Praying for Power*, 188–89.
60. That Candida actively supported the idea of a Chinese Church is also evident from her eagerness to receive news of distant Chinese Catholic communities. She received Catholic travelers for this purpose (see Couplet, *Histoire*, 102).
61. See Heijdra, "The Socio-Economic Development," 555–56, and Miyazaki, *China's Examination Hell*, 89.
62. Indeed, Couplet recorded only one gift by Candida that was not destined for the Society: her sponsored purchase of four hundred Chinese Catholic books printed by the Jesuits, to be given to various Roman libraries (see Couplet, *Histoire*, 126–27). On these books, see Golvers, *Building Humanistic Libraries*, 64.
63. Chinese women's awareness of the global dimension of Catholicism is also apparent in a letter written by Fujianese *beatas* to the nuns of a French convent in the late seventeenth century. See Menegon, *Ancestors*, 338. For Chinese Catholic women signing a statement on the rites controversy addressed to the Holy See in 1700, see Standaert, *Chinese Voices*, 195, 301, 418.
64. The Jesuits' attempts to further this awareness materialized in a regular prayer at congregational meetings, where Chinese Catholics prayed for the well-being of the pope. The same prayer also included a section addressing the well-being of the Chinese Church. See Couplet, *Histoire*, 80–81.

Conclusion

1. Duteil, "L'évangélisation," 246.
2. On this view of Chinese women, which imagined the latter's existence in the premodern era as "cloistered, crippled, and subservient," see Ko, *Teachers*, 3. See also Holmgren, "Myth, Fantasy."
3. Catholicism has been described as a global institution by Luke Clossey (Clossey, *Salvation*, esp. 9). However, Clossey exclusively focuses on European missionaries.

4. Couplet, *Histoire*, 102.
5. See Couplet, *Histoire*, 148.
6. On the female supporters whom I mention, see Couplet, *Histoire*, 148–49. See also von Collani, "Die Förderung," 98.
7. See Burrus, *Kino Writes*, 41, 48.
8. On the Lomellini family, see Grendi, *La repubblica*, 36.
9. See Golvers, "The XVIIth-Century Jesuit Mission," 173.
10. Louis Le Comte dedicated parts of his *Nouveaux mémoires* to these two duchesses (see vol. 1, 72–75, 311–13).
11. See Hsia, *Noble Patronage*, 63, and von Collani, "Die Förderung," 98.
12. The most noteworthy female patrons of the eighteenth century were two ladies of the Wittelsbach court in Munich, who do not refer to Candida Xu in their writing (see Hsia, *Noble Patronage*, 42, 113).
13. Foundation deed by Elisabeth, Maria Anna, and Clara Johanna de Prince, Antwerp, 16 December 1692 (translated by Philippe Couplet from Flemish into Latin), ARSI, Jap. Sin. 165, 278r. I would like to thank Noël Golvers for sharing with me his knowledge of the de Prince sisters and of Couplet's Antwerp connections.
14. On the public nature of early modern Catholicism, see Hersche, *Muße und Verschwendung*, vol. 1, 432–35, passim. On how public religiosity distinguished post-Tridentine Catholics from Protestants, see Forster, "Domestic Devotions," and Holzem, "Familie und Familienideal." Domestic piety did, however, play an important role in Renaissance Italy. See Howard, "Exploring Devotional Practice."
15. On Catholic clandestine churches (*schuilkerken*) in Holland, see Kaplan, *Divided by Faith*, 172–97. For a study of an English Catholic elite family's religious life, see Questier, *Catholicism and Community*. On how these Catholic minorities developed a tradition of family devotions, see Forster, "Domestic Devotions," 113.
16. On the fact that the implementation of Tridentine norms was all but a smooth and unidirectional process, see Forster, *The Counter-Reformation*, and Holzem, *Religion und Lebensform*.
17. See Županov, *Missionary Tropics*, 269–70, and Heyberger, *Les Chrétiens*.
18. See Standaert, *The Interweaving of Rituals*, and Menegon, *Ancestors*.
19. On Catholic women and gender relations in the Americas, see the contributions to Jaffary, *Gender, Race, and Religion*, part 2, and Leacock, "Montagnais Marriage." For case studies on Asia, see Županov, "Lust, Marriage, and Free Will" (on South India), and Ward, *Women Religious Leaders* (on Japan).
20. A first attempt has been made by Wiesner-Hanks, *Christianity and Sexuality*.

BIBLIOGRAPHY

Abbreviations

ARCHIVES AND SIGNATURES

ACDF Archivio della Congregazione per la Dottrina della Fede, Rome

S.O., St. St. Sanctum Officium, Stanza Storica

APF Archivio Storico della S. Congregazione "De Propaganda Fide," Rome

Acta Acta Sacrae Congregationis

Acta CP Acta Congregationis Particularis super rebus Sinarum et Indiarum Orientalium

CP Congregazioni Particolari

SC Scritture riferite nei Congressi

SOCG Scritture Originali riferite nelle Congregazioni Generali

SOCP Scritture Originali della Congregazione Particolare dell'Indie Orientali e Cina

ARSI Archivum Romanum Societatis Iesu, Rome

F.G. Fondo Gesuitico

Jap. Sin. Japonica Sinica

Opp. NN. Opera Nostrorum

ASV Archivio Segreto Vaticano

BA-JA Biblioteca da Ajuda, Lisbon, "Jesuítas na Ásia" collection

BAV, Borg. Lat. Biblioteca Apostolica Vaticana, "Borgia Latino" collection

BNCR Biblioteca Nazionale Centrale di Roma

BNP Biblioteca Nacional de Portugal, Lisbon

CÓD. Códice

REFERENCE WORKS AND EDITIONS

Fonti Ricciane D'Elia, Pasquale M., ed. *Fonti Ricciane: Documenti originali concernenti Matteo Ricci e la storia delle prime relazioni tra l'Europa e la Cina.* 3 vols. Rome: La Libreria dello Stato, 1942.

HCC Standaert, Nicolas, ed. *Handbook of Christianity in China.* Vol. 1, *635–1800.* Leiden: Brill, 2001.

PQD Pallu, François. "Praxes quaedam discusse in pleno Coetu 23. Patrum Missionariorum Chinae, quorum nomina in fide describuntur, statue et directe ad observandam inter eos uniformitatem." October 1669, APF, Fondo di Vienna 21.

PST Couplet, Philippe. "In Provincia Sinensi Templa, Collegia inchoata, Residentiae, Missiones et primo saeculo erecta à Patribus Societatis Jesu [appendix to the 'Litterae Annuae Vice-Provinciae Sinicae ab 1677 ad 1680,' s.l., s.d.]." ARSI, Jap. Sin. 116, 272r–275v.

Archival Sources

LISBON

Arquivos Nacionais, Torre do Tombo
Armario Jesuitico, no. 28
Maços, nos. 1–23, 36, 90, 97
Biblioteca da Ajuda
Jesuítas na Ásia (vols. 49-IV-61 to 49-IV-66, 49-V-3 to 49-V-22, and 49-V-25 to 49-V-26)
Biblioteca Nacional de Portugal
Códices 722–23
Manuscritos 29

ROME

Archivio della Congregazione per la Dottrina della Fede
Stanza Storica: D 4 a; D 4 e; E 4 f; Casanate H 5 e; L 5 d; L 6 a; LL 4 h; O 3 e; OO 5 a; OO 5 f–h; PP 1 a–o; PP 2 a–f; PP 3 a–c; PP 4 a–d; PP 5 f; PP 5 h; QQ 1 b–d; UV 10; UV 19; UV 47; UV 50–51; UV 58; UV 74; De Baptismate (D.B.) 1–2
Archivio Segreto Vaticano
Armaria XLIV 2, 13
Carte Theiner 12
Epistolae ad Principes, Registra 60
Fondo Albani 231, 246, 263
Fondo Bolognetti 124, 323
Fondo Carpegna 55, 69, 71bis
Missioni 102
Segreteria di Stato, Principi 78–79
Segreteria di Stato, Vescovi 63
Archivio Storico della S. Congregazione "De Propaganda Fide"
Acta Congregationis Particularis super rebus Sinarum et Indiarum Orientalium 1A–1B
Acta Sacrae Congregationis
Congregazioni Particolari 20
Fondo di Vienna 21, 72
Informazioni 118, 120, 134, 156–58, 162–67
Scritture Originali della Congregazione Particolare dell'Indie Orientali e Cina 2–25
Scritture Originali riferite nelle Congregazioni Generali 192–93, 432
Scritture riferite nei Congressi 1A-11
Archivum Romanum Societatis Iesu
Fondo Gesuitico: vols. 721 II-1, fasc. E; 722 1–24; 723
Japonica Sinica: vols. 1–199 II
Opera Nostrorum: vols. 147–48

Biblioteca Apostolica Vaticana

Borgia Latino: Ms. 93; Ms. 201; Ms. 245; Ms. 253; Ms. 450; Ms. 508; Ms. 510; Ms. 523; Ms. 543; Ms. 553

Vaticano Latino: 7348, 7373–74, 7403–4, 7406–7, 7488–89, 8272, 8463

Biblioteca Casanatense

650, 916, 1014, 1016, 1615–17, 1627–28, 1632, 1639–48, 1656, 2420, 2431, 2457–58, 2617, 3178

Biblioteca Nazionale Centrale di Roma, Fondo Gesuitico

1248: 85, 87

1251: 1–2, 9

1254: 1–2, 11–12, 18, 20, 23, 28, 31, 33

1256: 5–8, 10, 12–13, 14–15, 19, 22–21, 24–26, 34, 40–41, 48–49, 54

1305

1383: 1, 9, 11, 15, 19, 23

1495: 40, 54

Printed Primary Sources

Aleni, Giulio. *Dizui zhenggui lüe* 滌罪正規略 (The right rule for washing away sin). 1630. Reprinted in *Yesuhui Luoma dang'anguan Ming Qing tianzhujiao wenxian* 耶穌會羅馬檔案館明清天主教文獻 (Chinese Christian texts from the Roman Archives of the Society of Jesus), vol. 4, edited by Nicolas Standaert, 337–580. Taipei: Lishi xueshe, 2002.

Andersen, Jürgen, and Volquard Jversen. "Orientalische Reise-Beschreibung." In *Des welt-berühmten Adami Olearii colligierte und viel mehr vermehrte Reise Beschreibungen bestehend in der nach Musskau und Persien. Wie auch Johann Albrechts von Mandelslo Morgenländischen und Jürg. Andersens und Volq. Yversens Orientalischen Reise . . .*, edited by Adam Olearius, part 7. Hamburg: Zacharias Herteln and Thomas von Wiering, 1669.

Anon. *Shengti huigui* 聖體會規 (Statutes for the Congregation of the Eucharist). Beijing, late seventeenth or early eighteenth century. Reprinted in *Faguo guojia tushuguan Ming Qing tianzhujiao wenxian* 法國國家圖書館明清天主教文獻 (Chinese Christian texts from the French National Library), vol. 20, edited by Nicolas Standaert, Adrian Dudink, and Nathalie Monnet, 253–81. Taipei: Ricci Institute, 2009.

Augery, Humbert. *Shengmu huigui* 聖母會規 (Statutes of the Holy Mother's Congregation). [Hangzhou?], ca. 1660. Reprinted in *Yesuhui Luoma dang'anguan Ming Qing tianzhujiao wenxian* 耶穌會羅馬檔案館明清天主教文獻 (Chinese Christian texts from the Roman Archives of the Society of Jesus), vol. 12, edited by Nicolas Standaert, 439–62. Taipei: Lishi xueshe, 2002.

Bartoli, Daniello. *Della vita e dell'istituto di S. Ignazio, Fondatore della Compagnia di Gesù*. 5 vols. Milan: Presso Santo Bravetta Tipografo, 1834. First edition 1650.

———. *Dell'historia della Compagnia di Giesu. La Cina. Terza parte dell' Asia*. Rome: Stamperia del Varese, 1663.

Bernard, Henri. *Lettres et mémoires d'Adam Schall S.J.: Relation historique, texte latin avec traduction française du P. Paul Bornet S.J.* Tianjin: Hautes Études Tientsin, 1942.

Boxer, Charles, ed. *South China in the Sixteenth Century: Being the Narratives of Galeote Pereira, Fr. Gaspar da Cruz, O.P., Fr. Martín de Rada, O.E.S.A.* Nendeln, Liechtenstein: Klaus Reprint, 1967.

Boym, Michael. "Briefve relation de la Chine et de la notable conversion des personnes royales de cet estat . . . le 29. Septembre de l'année 1652." In *Relations de divers voyages curieux . . .*, edited by Melchisédec Thévenot, n.p. Paris: Jacques Langlois, 1664.

Brancati, Francesco. *Tianshen huike* 天神會課 (Rules for the Congregation of Angels). Ca. 1673. Reprinted in *Faguo guojia tushuguan Ming Qing tianzhujiao wenxian* 法國國家圖書館明清天主教文獻 (Chinese Christian texts from the French National Library), vol. 20, edited by Nicolas Standaert, Adrian Dudink, and Nathalie Monnet, 1–162. Taipei: Ricci Institute, 2009.

———. *Tianzhu shijie quanlun shengji* 天主十誡勸論聖迹蹟 (Explanations and miracles concerning the Ten Commandments of the Lord of Heaven). Shanghai: Cimu tang, 1904. First edition 1650.

Burrus, Ernest J., ed. *Kino Writes to the Duchess: Letters of Eusebio Francisco Kino, S.J., to the Duchess of Aveiro; An Annotated English Translation, and the Text of the Non-Spanish Documents.* Rome: Jesuit Historical Institute; St. Louis: St. Louis University, 1965.

Cao Xueqin. *The Story of the Stone; or, The Dream of the Red Chamber.* Translated by David Hawkes. 5 vols. Bloomington: Indiana University Press, 1979–87.

Chen Houguang 陳侯光. *Bianxue chuyan* 辨學芻言 (My views on heresy). Reprinted in *Po xie ji, juan* 5, edited by Xu, 1a–9b.

Chen Menglei 陳夢雷 and Jiang Tingxi 蔣廷錫, eds. *Gujin tushu jicheng* 古今圖書集成 (The complete collection of illustrations and writings from ancient and modern times). Shanghai: Zhonghua shuju, 1934.

Collectanea S. Congregationis de Propaganda Fide seu Decreta Instructione Rescripta pro Apostolicis Missionibus. Rome: Typographia polyglotta, 1907.

Constitutiones Apostolicae, Brevia, Decreta etc. pro Missionibus Sinarum, Tunquini etc. Paris: C. Angot, 1676.

Couplet, Philippe. *Histoire d'une dame chrétienne de la Chine, où par occasion les usages de ces peuples, l'etablissement de la Religion, les manieres des Missionnaires, & les Exercices de piété des nouveaux Chrétiens sont expliquez.* Paris: Estienne Michalet, 1688.

de Gouvea, António. *Asia Extrema.* Edited by Horácio Peixoto de Araujo. 3 vols. Macao: Fundação Oriente, 1995–2005.

———. *Cartas Ânuas da China.* Edited by Horácio Peixoto de Araujo. Macao: Istituto português do Oriente, 1998.

D'Elia, Pasquale M., ed. *Fonti Ricciane: Documenti originali concernenti Matteo Ricci e la storia delle prime relazioni tra l'Europa e la Cina.* 3 vols. Rome: La Libreria dello Stato, 1942.

Dias, Manuel, Sr. "Litterae Annuae 1619, Macao." In *Histoire de ce qui s'est passé és Royaumes de la Chine et du Japon, Tirées des lettres escrites és années 1619, 1620 & 1621, Adressées au R.P. Mutio Vitelleschi, General de la Compagnie de Jesus,* 1–95. Paris: Sebastien Cramoisy, 1625.

———. "Litterae Annuae 1625." In *Histoire de ce qui s'est passé au Royaume de la Chine, en l'année 1624, Tirée des lettres écrites & adressées au R.P. Mutio Vitelleschi, General de la Compagnie de Jesus*, 108–90. Paris: Sebastien Cramoisy, 1629.

Du Jarric, Pierre. *Histoire des choses plus mémorables advenues tant és Indes Orientales, que autres païs de la decouverte des Portugais, en l'establissement & progrez de la foy Chrestienne & Catholique; Et principalement de ce que les Religieux de la Compagnie de Iesus y ont faict, & enduré par le mesme fin. Depuis qu'ils y sont entrez jusqu'a l'an 1600*. 3 vols. Bordeaux: Millanges, 1610–14.

Fan Ye 范曄. *Houhan shu* 後漢書 (Standard history of the later Han). Beijing: Zhonghua shuju, 1965.

Gonzales de Mendoza, Juan. *Historia de las cosas mas notables, ritos y costumbres del gran reyno de la China*. Rome: B. Grassi, 1585.

Greslon, Adrien. *Histoire de la Chine sous la domination des Tartares*. Paris: Jean Henault, 1671.

Guerreiro, Fernão. *Relaçam annal das cousas que fezeram os Padres da Companhia de Jesus nas partes da India oriental e no Brasil, Angola, Cabo Verde, Guine, nos annos de 1602 e 1603*. Lisbon: J. Rodrigues, 1605.

Gumppenberg, Wilhelm. *Atlas Marianus: Quo Sanctae Dei Genitricis Mariae Imaginum Miraculosarum Origines Duodecim Historiarum Centurijs Explicantur*. Munich: Jaecklin, 1672. First edition 1655.

Kircher, Athanasius. *China Monumentis, Qua Sacris qua Profanis, Nec non variis Naturae et Artis Spectaculis, Aliarumque rerum memorabilium Argumentis Illustrata*. [*China Illustrata*.] Amsterdam: Meurs, 1667.

Kirwitzer, Wenzel Pantaleon. "Litterae Annuae 1620." In *Histoire de ce qui s'est passé és Royaumes de la Chine et du Japon, Tirées des lettres escrites és années 1619, 1620 & 1621, Adressées au R.P. Mutio Vitelleschi, General de la Compagnie de Jesus*, 96–158. Paris: Sebastien Cramoisy, 1625.

———. "Litterae Annuae 1624." In *Histoire de ce qui s'est passé au Royaume de la Chine, en l'année 1624, Tirée des lettres écrites & adressées au R.P. Mutio Vitelleschi, General de la Compagnie de Jesus*, 1–102. Paris: Sebastien Cramoisy, 1629.

Las Cortes, Adriano de. *Le voyage en Chine d'Adriano de las Cortes S.J. (1625), traduction, présentation et notes*. Edited and translated by Pascale Girard. Paris: Chandeigne, 2001.

Launay, Adrien, ed. *Lettres de Monseigneur Pallu, écrites de 1654 à 1684*. Paris: Les Indes savantes, 2008.

Le Comte, Louis. *Nouveaux mémoires sur l'état présent de la Chine*. 3 vols. Paris: J. Anisson, 1696–98.

Legge, James, trans. *The Lî Kî (The Book of Rites)*. Parts 1–2. Oxford, UK: Clarendon Press, 1885.

———, trans. *The Works of Mencius (The Chinese Classics: With a Translation, Critical and Exegetical Notes, Prolegomena, and Copious Indexes)*. Vol. 2. London: Trübner, 1895.

———, trans. *The Yî King*. Oxford: Oxford University Press, 1882.

Lettres édifiantes et curieuses, écrites des missions étrangères, par quelques missionnaires de la Compagnie de Jésus. 34 vols. Paris: [various subsequent publishers], 1703–76.

Li Can 李璨. *Pixie shuo* 劈邪說 (Dividing heresy). Reprinted in *Po xie ji, juan* 5, edited by Xu, 23a–27a.

Li Zhi 李贽. *Fen shu, Xu fen shu* 焚书, 续焚书 (Book to be burned and sequel to Book to be burned). Beijing: Zhonghua shuju, 1975.

Magalhães, Gabriel de. *Nouvelle relation de la Chine, contenant la description des particularitez les plus considérables de ce grand Empire, . . . traduite du Portugais en François par le Sr. Bernou*. Paris: Claude Barbin, 1668.

Martini, Martino. *Novus Atlas Sinensis*. 3 vols. Edited by Giuliano Bertuccioli. Trent: Università degli Studi di Trento, 2002.

Mish, John L. "Creating an Image of Europe for China: Aleni's Hsi-Fang Ta-Wen, Introduction, Translation, and Notes." *Monumenta Serica* 23 (1964): 1–87.

Navarrete, Domingo. *Tratados historicos, politicos, ethicos, y religiosos de la monarchia de China. . . .* Madrid: Imprenta Real, 1676.

Nieuhof, Johan. *Die Gesandschaft der Ost-Indischen Gesellschaft in den Niederlanden an den Tartarischen Cham und nunmehr auch Sinischen Keiser. Ber. durch . . . Peter de Gojer u. Jacob Keiser mit 150 Kupferstükken*. Amsterdam: Moers, 1666.

Nolarci, Vigilio. *Compendio della vita di S. Ignatio di Loiola, Raccolto con fedeltà, e con brevità da quanto n'hanno provatamente stampato in un secolo gravi Autori, per opera di don Vigilio Nolarci, e con maggior diligenza corretto in questa nuova impressione*. Venice: Presso Combi, e La Noù, 1680.

Padberg, John W., ed. *The Constitutions of the Society of Jesus and Their Complementary Norms*. St. Louis: Institute of Jesuit Sources, 1996.

Pantoja, Diego. "[Letter to] Ludovicus Guzmanus, Provinciae Toletanae Praepositum." Dated 7 March 1602. In *Litterae Societatis Iesu, Anno MDCII et MDCIII e Sinis, Molucis, Iapone Datae Progressum Rei Christianae in Ijs Oris, Aliaq[ue] Memoratu Iucunda Complexae*, 1–124. Munich: Balthasari Lipii, 1607.

———. *Qike* 七克 (Seven victories). Ca. 1610–15. Reprinted in *Tianzhujiao dongchuan wenxian* 天主教東傳文獻 (Documents related to the spread of Christianity in the East), vol. 2, edited by Wu Xiangxiang 吳相湘, n.p. Taipei: Xuesheng shuju, 1965.

———. *Relatione dell'entrata d'alcuni Padri della Compagnia di Giesu nella China*. Rome: Bartolomeo Zannetti, 1607.

Perceval, A. P. *The Roman Schism Illustrated from the Records of the Catholic Church*. London: J. Leslie, 1836.

Ricci, Matteo. *Lettere (1580–1609)*. Edited by Francesco D'Arelli, with a preface by Filippo Mignini. Macerata: Quodlibet, 2001.

———. "Litterae Annuae 1606–1607." In *Litterae Iaponicae anni MDCVI Chineses Anni MDCVI & MDCVII, Illae & R.P. Ioanne Rodriguez, Hae a R.P. Matthaeo Ricci, Societatis Iesu Sacerdotis, Transmissae ad Admodum R.P. Claudium Aquavivam, Eiusdem Societatis Praepositum Generalem*, 131–301. Antwerp: Officina Plantiniana, 1611.

———. *On Friendship: One Hundred Maxims for a Chinese Prince*. Translated by Timothy Billings. New York: Columbia University Press, 2009.

———. *The True Meaning of the Lord of Heaven (T'ien-chu Shih-i)*. Edited and translated by Douglas Lancashire and Peter Hu, revised by Thierry Meynard. St. Louis: Institute of Jesuit Sources, 2016.

Roy, David Tod, trans. *The Plum in the Golden Vase, or, Chin P'ing Mei.* 3 vols. Princeton, NJ: Princeton University Press, 1993–2006.

Ruggieri, Michele, and Matteo Ricci. *Dicionário Português-Chinês / Pu-Han cidian / Portuguese-Chinese Dictionary*, edited by John W. Witek. Lisbon: Biblioteca Nacional Portugal and Instituto Português do Oriente, 2001.

Schall von Bell, Johann Adam. *De Ortu et Progressu Fidei Orthodoxiae in Regno Chinensi.* Regensburg: Augustus Hanckwitz, 1672.

Semedo, Alvaro. *Histoire universelle de la Chine, par le P. Alvarez Semedo, Portugais. Avec l'Histoire de la Guerre des Tartares . . . Traduites nouvellement en François.* Lyon: Hierosme Prost, 1645.

———. *Imperio de la China i cultura evangelica en èl por los religios de la Compañia de Iesus. . . .* Madrid: Juan Sanchez, 1642.

Shen Que 沈㴶. *Faqian yuanyi hui zoushu* 發遣遠夷回奏疏 (Memorial to the throne [petitioning for] the deportation of the foreign barbarians). Reprinted in *Po xie ji, juan* 2, edited by Xu, 1a–4a.

Shi Nai-an. *The Water Margin: Outlaws of the Marsh (Shuihu zhuan).* Translated by J. H. Jackson. Tokyo: Tuttle Publishing, 2010.

Shi Bangyao 施邦曜. *Fujian xunhai dao gaoshi* 福建巡海道告示 (Proclamation by the maritime inspector of Fujian). Reprinted in *Po xie ji, juan* 2, edited by Xu, 30a–35a.

[Soares, José?]. *Shengmu lingbao huigui* 聖母領報會規 (Statutes of the Association of the Annunciation to Mary). Beijing, 1694. Reprinted in *Faguo guojia tushuguan Ming Qing tianzhujiao wenxian* 法國國家圖書館明清天主教文獻 (Chinese Christian texts from the French National Library), vol. 20, edited by Nicolas Standaert, Adrian Dudink, and Nathalie Monnet, 213–51. Taipei: Ricci Institute, 2009.

Sun Shangyang 孫尚揚 and Xiao Qinghe 肖清和, eds. *"Duo shu" jiao zhu* 《铎书》校注 (An annotated critical edition of the *Duoshu*). Beijing: Huaxia chubanshe, 2007.

Trigault, Nicolas. "Lettera Annua della Cina del 1610, Cocino, Maggio, 1613." In *Due Lettere Annue della Cina del 1610 e del 1611 scritte al M.R.P. Claudio Acquaviva Generale della Compagnia di GIESU*, 3–66. Milan: P. Pontio and G. B. Piccaglia, Stampatori Archiepiscopali, 1615.

———. "Lettera Annua della Cina del 1611, Nanjing, Agosto, 1612." In *Due Lettere Annue della Cina del 1610 e del 1611 scritte al M.R.P. Claudio Acquaviva Generale della Compagnia di GIESU*, 67–221. Milan: P. Pontio and G. B. Piccaglia, Stampatori Archiepiscopali, 1615.

———. "Litterae Annuae 1621." In *Histoire de ce qui s'est passé és Royaumes de la Chine et du Japon, Tirées des lettres escrites és années 1619, 1620 & 1621, Adressées au R.P. Mutio Vitelleschi, General de la Compagnie de Jesus*, 159–384. Paris: Sebastien Cramoisy, 1625.

———. "Litterae Annuae 1621." In *Lettere annue del Giappone dell'anno MDCXXII e della Cina del 1621 & 1622: al molto rev. in Christo P. Mutio Vitelleschi, Preposito Generale della Compagnia di Giesu*, 150–232. Milan: Giovanni Battista Cerri, 1627.

Vagnone, Alfonso. *Qijia xixue* 齊家西學 (Government of the family in the West). 1625–30. Reprinted in *Xujiahui cangshulou Ming Qing tianzhujiao wenxian* 徐家匯藏書樓明清天主教文獻 (Chinese Christian texts from the Zikawei Library), vol. 2, edited by Nicolas Standaert, Adrian Dudink, Huang Yi-long, and Chu Ping-yi, 491–598. Taipei: Ricci Institute, 1996.

———. *Shengmu xingshi* 聖母行實 (Biography of the Holy Mother). 1631. Reprinted in *Tianzhujiao dongchuan wenxian sanbian* 天主教東傳文獻三編 (Documents related to the spread of Christianity in the East, 3rd Series), vol. 3, edited by Wu Xiangxiang 吳相湘, 1497–1503. Taipei: Xuesheng shuju, 1972.

———. *Tianzhu shengjiao shengren xingshi* 天主聖教聖人行實 (Biographies of the saints of the holy teaching of the Lord of Heaven). Hangzhou (Wulin): Chaoxing tang, 1629.

Vives, Juan Luis. *De Officio Mariti: Introduction, Critical Edition, Translation and Notes.* Edited by Charles Fantazzi. Leiden: Brill, 2006.

Voragine, Jacobus a. *Legenda Aurea: Vulgo Historia Lombardica Dicta.* Edited by Johann Georg Theodor Graesse. Dresden: Arnold, 1846.

Wang Zheng 王徵. *Qiqing jiezui qigao* 祈請解罪启稿 (A draft prayer for obtaining absolution). 1637. Reprinted in *Tianzhujiao dongchuan wenxian sanbian* 天主教東傳文獻三編 (Documents related to the spread of Christianity in the East, 3rd Series), vol. 2, edited by Wu Xiangxiang 吳相湘, 833–37. Taipei: Xuesheng shuju, 1972.

Xu Caibai 許采白. *Xu taifuren zhuanlüe* 許太夫人傳略 (Biography of the honorable mother Xu). Shanghai: Tou se we, 1882.

Xu Changzhi 徐昌治, ed. *Po xie ji* 破邪集 (Collection [of writings] destroying heresy). 8 vols. Mito: Kodokan, 1856. First published 1639.

Xu Congzhi 徐從治. *Huishen Zhong Mingren Zhang Cai deng fan* 會審鐘鳴仁張菜等犯 (Trial for the crimes [committed by] Zhong Mingren [Sebastian Fernandes], Zhang Cai, and others). Reprinted in *Po xie ji, juan* 2, edited by Xu, 13a–20b.

Xu Dashou 許大受. *Shengchao zuopi* 聖朝佐闢 (Guide to confutation of the Holy Dynasty). Reprinted in *Po xie ji*, edited by Xu, *juan* 4, 2b–42b.

Xu Yunxi 徐允希. *Yi wei Zhongguo fengjiao taitai* 一位中國奉教太太 (A Chinese Christian woman). Shanghai: Tou se we, 1938.

[Yu Chunxi 虞淳熙 ?]. *Po Li yi jian tian wang shi* 破利夷僭天罔世 (Refuting the barbarian Ricci who usurps heaven and deceives the world). Reprinted in *Po xie ji, juan* 5, edited by Xu, 15a–16a.

Zheng Xuan 鄭玄, ed. *Liji* 禮記. 6 vols. Beijing: Zhonghua shuju yingyin, 1992.

Zürcher, Erik. *Kouduo richao: Li Jiubiao's Diary of Oral Admonitions; A Late Ming Christian Journal Translated, with Introduction and Notes.* 2 vols. Nettetal: Steyler Verlag, 2007.

Electronic Resource

Dudink, Adrian, and Nicolas Standaert. *Chinese Christian Text Database.* www.arts.kuleuven.be/sinologie/english/cct.

Secondary Works

Ahern, Emily M. "The Power and Pollution of Chinese Women." In *Women in Chinese Society*, edited by Margery Wolf and Roxane Witke, 193–214. Stanford, CA: Stanford University Press, 1975.

Alden, Dauril. *The Making of an Enterprise: The Society of Jesus in Portugal, Its Empire, and Beyond, 1540–1750*. Stanford, CA: Stanford University Press, 1996.

Amsler, Nadine. "'Ein *yin*, ein *yang*'? Monogamie und die Konkubinenfrage im chinesischen Christentum der späten Ming-Zeit." In *Individualisierung durch christliche Mission?* edited by Martin Fuchs, Antje Linkenbach, and Wolfgang Reinhard, 293–304. Wiesbaden: Harrassowitz Verlag, 2015.

———. "Fromm, aber unfrei? Weibliche Tugenden und *agency* in der jesuitischen Darstellung der chinesischen Christin Candida Xu (1607–1680)." *Saeculum* 66, no. 2 (2016): 289–309.

———. "'Sie meinen, die drei Sekten seien eins': Matteo Riccis Aneignung des *sanjiao*-Konzepts und ihre Bedeutung für europäische Beschreibungen chinesischer Religion im 17. Jahrhundert." *Schweizerische Zeitschrift für Religions- und Kulturgeschichte* 105 (2011): 88–93.

Anders gekleed, anders gedragen: Drie Antwerpse kerken openen hun kleerkast. Exhibition catalog. Antwerp: Toerismepastoraal Antwerpen, 2001.

Anon. "Une pratique liturgique propre à la Chine: Le ji jin 祭巾 ou bonnet de messe." *Bulletin catholique de Pékin* 11 (1924): 376–77, 404–6.

Atwell, William S. "Notes on Silver, Foreign Trade, and the Late Ming Economy." *Late Imperial China* 3, no. 8 (1977): 1–33.

Bailey, Gauvin Alexander. *Art on the Jesuit Missions in Asia and Latin America, 1542–1773*. Toronto: University of Toronto Press, 1999.

Bake, Kristina. *Spiegel einer Christlichen und friedsamen Haußhaltung: Die Ehe in der populären Druckgraphik des 16. und 17. Jahrhunderts*. Wiesbaden: Harrassowitz Verlag, 2013.

Bamji, Alexandra, Geert H. Janssen, and Mary Laven, eds. *The Ashgate Research Companion to the Counter-Reformation*. Farnham: Ashgate, 2013.

Baptandier, Brigitte. *The Lady of Linshui: A Chinese Female Cult*. Translated by Kristin Ingrid Fryklund. Stanford, CA: Stanford University Press, 2008.

Barthes, Roland. "Histoire et sociologie du vêtement." *Annales: Histoire, Sciences Sociales* 12, no. 3 (1957): 430–41.

Baudiment, Louis. *François Pallu, principal fondateur de la Société des Missions étrangères*. Paris: Beauchesne, 1934.

Bays, Daniel H. "Christianity and the Chinese Sectarian Tradition." *Ch'ing-shih wen-t'i* 4, no. 7 (1982): 33–55.

———, ed. *Christianity in China: From the Eighteenth Century to the Present*. Stanford, CA: Stanford University Press, 1996.

Berg, Daria. *Women and the Literary World in Early Modern China, 1580–1700*. London: Routledge, 2013.

Berling, Judith. *The Syncretic Religion of Lin Chao-en*. New York: Columbia University Press, 1980.

———. "Taoism in Ming Culture." In *The Cambridge History of China*, vol. 8, part 2, *The Ming Dynasty, 1368–1644*, edited by Denis Twitchett and John K. Fairbank, 953–86, Cambridge: Cambridge University Press, 1998.

Bernhardt, Kathryn. "A Ming-Qing Transition in Chinese Women's History?" In *Remapping China: Fissures in Historical Terrain*, edited by Gail Hershatter, Emily

Honig, Jonathan N. Lipman, and Randall Stross, 42–58. Stanford, CA: Stanford University Press, 1996.

Bettray, Johannes. *Die Akkommodationsmethode des P. Matteo Ricci S.I. in China.* Rome: Universitas Gregoriana, 1955.

Bilinkoff, Jodi. *Confessors and Their Female Penitents, 1450–1750.* Ithaca, NY: Cornell University Press, 2005.

Boltz, Judith Magee. "In Homage to T'ien-fei." *Journal of the American Oriental Society* 106 (1986): 211–32.

Bornet, Paul. "L'apostolat laïque en Chine aux XVIIe et XVIIIe siècles." *Bulletin catholique de Pékin* 35 (1948): 41–67.

———. "Les vierges institutrices et catechistes en Chine au XVIIIe siècle." *Bulletin catholique de Pékin* 29 (1942): 434–42.

Bossen, Laurel, and Hill Gates. *Bound Feet, Young Hands: Tracking the Demise of Footbinding in Village China.* Stanford, CA: Stanford University Press, 2017.

Bossler, Beverly Jo. "'A Daughter Is a Daughter All Her Life': Affinal Relations and Women's Networks in Song and Late Imperial China." *Late Imperial China* 21 (2000): 77–106.

Boxer, Charles. *Mary and Misogyny: Women and Iberian Expansion Overseas, 1415–1815: Some Facts, Fancies, and Personalities.* London: Duckworth, 1975.

Bray, Francesca. *Technology and Gender: Fabrics of Power in Late Imperial China.* Berkeley: University of California Press, 1997.

Brendecke, Arndt. *Imperium und Empirie: Funktionen des Wissens in der spanischen Kolonialherrschaft.* Cologne: Böhlau Verlag, 2009.

Brockey, Liam M. *Journey to the East: The Jesuit Mission to China, 1579–1724.* Cambridge, MA: Harvard University Press, 2007.

———. *The Visitor: André Palmeiro and the Jesuits in Asia.* Cambridge, MA: Harvard University Press, 2014.

Broggio, Paolo, Charlotte Castelnau-L'Estoile, and Giovanni Pizzorusso, eds. *Administrer les sacrements en Europe et au nouveau monde: La curie romaine et les Dubia circa sacramenta.* Rome: École française de Rome, 2009.

———. "Le temps des doutes: Les sacrements et l'Église romaine aux dimenions du monde." In *Administrer les sacrements*, edited by Broggio, Castelnau-L'Estoile, and Pizzorusso, 5–22.

Brokaw, Cynthia J. *The Ledgers of Merit and Demerit: Social Changes and the Moral Order in Late Imperial China.* Princeton, NJ: Princeton University Press, 1991.

Brook, Timothy. *The Confusions of Pleasure: Commerce and Culture in Ming China.* Berkeley: University of California Press, 1998.

———. *Praying for Power: Buddhism and the Formation of Gentry Society in Late-Ming China.* Cambridge, MA: Council on East Asian Studies, Harvard University, 1993.

———. "Xu Guangqi in His Context: The World of the Shanghai Gentry." In *Statecraft and Intellectual Renewal*, edited by Jami, Engelfriet, and Blue, 72–98.

Brownell, Susan, and Jeffrey N. Wasserstrom, eds. *Chinese Femininities / Chinese Masculinities: A Reader.* Berkeley: University of California Press, 2002.

———. "Introduction: Theorizing Femininities and Masculinities." In *Chinese Femininities / Chinese Masculinities*, edited by Brownell and Wasserstrom, 1–42.

Brunner, Paul. *L'euchologe de la mission de Chine: Edition princeps 1628 et développements jusqu'à nos jours (Contribution à l'histoire des livres des prières)*. Münster: Aschendorff, 1964.

Bynum, Caroline Walker. *Christian Materiality: An Essay on Religion in Late Medieval Europe*. New York: Zone Books, 2011.

Carlitz, Katherine. "Desire, Danger, and the Body: Stories of Women's Virtue in Late Ming China." In *Engendering China: Women, Culture, and the State*, edited by Christina K. Gilmartin, Gail Hershatter, Lisa Rofel, and Tyrene White, 101–24. Cambridge, MA: Harvard University Press, 1994.

Castelnau-L'Estoile, Charlotte de. "Le mariage des infidèles au XVIe siècle: Doutes missionnaires et autorité pontificale." In *Administrer les sacrements*, edited by Broggio, Castelnau-L'Estoile, and Pizzorusso, 95–121.

Chaix, Gérald. "De la piété à la dévotion: Le conseiller de Cologne Hermann Weinsberg entre mère et belle-soeur (1518–1597)." In *La religion de ma mère: Les femmes et la transmission de la foi*, edited by Jean Delumeau, 157–72. Paris: Edition du Cerf, 1992.

Châtellier, Louis. *L'Europe des dévots*. Paris: Flammarion, 1987.

Chau, Adam Yuet. "Efficacy, Not Confessionality: On Ritual Polytropy in Chine." In *Sharing the Sacra: The Politics and Pragmatics of Intercommunal Relations around Holy Places*, edited by Glenn Bowman, 79–96. New York: Berghahn Books, 2012.

———. *Miraculous Response: Doing Popular Religion in Contemporary China*. Stanford, CA: Stanford University Press, 2006.

———. "Modalities of Doing Religion and Ritual Polytropy: Evaluating the Religious Market Model from the Perspective of Chinese Religious History." *Religion* 41, no. 4 (2011): 547–68.

Chaves, Jonathan. "Gathering Tea for God." *Sino-Western Cultural Relations Journal* 24 (2002): 6–23.

Chen, Pi-yen. "The Chant of the Pure and the Music of the Popular: Conceptual Transformations in Contemporary Chinese Buddhist Chants." *Asian Music* 35, no. 2 (2004): 79–97.

Chen Yunü. "Buddhism and the Medical Treatment of Women in the Ming Dynasty: A Research Note." *Nan Nü* 10 (2008): 279–303.

Chow, Kai-wing. *Publishing, Culture, and Power in Early Modern China*. Stanford, CA: Stanford University Press, 2004.

Chu, Pingyi. "Scientific Dispute in the Imperial Court: The 1664 Calendar Case." *Chinese Science* 14 (1997): 7–34.

Clarke, Jeremy. *Catholic Shanghai: A Historical, Practical, and Reflective Guide*. St. Louis: Institute of Jesuit Sources, 2012.

———. *The Virgin Mary and Catholic Identities in Chinese History*. Hong Kong: Hong Kong University Press, 2013.

Classen, Constance. *The Deepest Sense: A Cultural History of Touch*. Urbana: University of Illinois Press, 2012.

Clossey, Luke. *Salvation and Globalization in the Early Jesuit Missions*. Cambridge: Cambridge University Press, 2008.

Clunas, Craig. *Pictures and Visuality in Early Modern China*. Princeton, NJ: Princeton University Press, 1997.

———. *Superfluous Things: Material Culture and Social Status in Early Modern China*. Urbana: University of Illinois Press, 1991.

Cohen, Paul Andrew. *China and Christianity: The Missionary Movement and the Growth of Chinese Antiforeignism, 1860–1870*. Cambridge, MA: Harvard University Press, 1963.

Colombel, Auguste M. *Jiangnan chuanjiao shi* 江南傳教史 (History of the mission in Jiangnan). Vol. 1, translated by Zhou Shiliang 周士良. Taipei: Fuda chubanshe, 2009.

Connell, R. W. *Masculinities*. Cambridge, UK: Polity Press, 2010.

Conrad, Anne. *Zwischen Kloster und Welt: Ursulinen und Jesuitinnen in der katholischen Reformbewegung des 16./17. Jahrhunderts*. Mainz: Philipp von Zabern Verlag, 1991.

Crossley, Pamela Kyle. "The Conquest Elite of the Ch'ing Empire." In *The Cambridge History of China*, vol. 9, part 1, *The Ch'ing Empire to 1800*, edited by Willard Peterson, 310–59. Cambridge: Cambridge University Press, 2003.

———. *A Translucent Mirror: History and Identity in Qing Imperial Ideology*. Berkeley: University of California Press, 2007.

Cummins, James Sylvester. *A Question of Rites: Friar Domingo Navarrete and the Jesuits in China*. Aldershot: Scholars Press, 1993.

Dalgado, Sebastião Rodolfo. *Glossário luso-asiático*. 2 vols. New Delhi: Asian Educational Services, 1988.

Dauncey, Sarah. "Illusions of Grandeur: Perceptions of Status and Wealth in Late-Ming Female Clothing and Ornamentation." *East Asian History* 25–26 (2003): 43–68.

de Bary, William Theodore. "Individualism and Humanitarianism in Late Ming Thought." In *Self and Society in Ming Thought*, edited by William Theodore de Bary, 145–247. New York: Columbia University Press, 1970.

Dehergne, Joseph. "Études de géographie missionaire: La Chine du Sud-Ouest; Le Szechwan, le Kweichow, le Yunnan." *Archivum Historicum Societatis Iesu* 42 (1973): 246–87.

———. "Les tablettes dans le culte des ancêtres en Chine confucéenne." *Recherches de science religieuse* 66, no. 2 (1978): 201–14.

———. *Répertoire des Jésuites de Chine de 1552 à 1800*. Rome: Institutum Historicum Societatis Iesu, 1973.

Dikötter, Frank: *The Discourse of Race in Modern China*. London: Hurst and Company, 1992.

Dinges, Martin. "Von der 'Lesbarkeit der Welt' zum universalisierten Wandel durch individuelle Strategien: Die soziale Funktion der Kleidung in der höfischen Gesellschaft." *Saeculum* 44 (1993): 90–112.

Dowdall, Joseph. "A Study of the Ritual of Baptism." *Studies in Pastoral Liturgy* 1 (1961): 62–78.

Dudbridge, Glen. "Women Pilgrims to T'ai Shan: Some Pages from a Seventeenth-Century Novel." In *Pilgrims and Sacred Sites in China*, edited by Susan Naquin and Yü Chün-Fang, 39–64. Berkeley: University of California Press, 1992.

Dudink, Adrian. "*Nangong shudu* (1620), *Poxie ji* (1640), and Western Reports on the Nanjing Persecution (1616/1617)." *Monumenta Serica* 48 (2000): 133–265.

———. "The *Sheng-ch'ao tso-p'i* (1623) of Hsü Ta-shou." In *Conflict and Accommodation in Early Modern East Asia: Essays in Honour of Erik Zürcher*, edited by Harriet Zurndorfer and Léonard Blussé, 94–140. Leiden: Brill, 1993.

———. "*Tianzhu jiaoyao*, the Catechism (1605) Published by Matteo Ricci." *Sino-Western Cultural Relations Journal* 24 (2002): 38–50.

Duhr, Bernhard. *Geschichte der Jesuiten in den Ländern deutscher Zunge*. 4 vols. Freiburg im Breisgau: Herder Verlag, 1907.

Durand-Dastès, Vincent. "Désirés, raillés, corrigés: Les bonzes dévoyés dans le roman en langue vulgaire du XVIe au XVIIIe siècle." *Extrême-Orient, Extrême-Occident* 24 (2002): 95–112.

Duteil, Jean-Pierre. "L'évangélisation et les femmes en Chine au XVIIe siècle: L'adaptation et ses limites." *Mélanges de sciences religieuses* 51, no. 3 (1994): 239–53.

Duyvendak, Jan Julius Lodewijk. Review of *Le origini dell'arte Cristiana Cinese (1583–1640)*, by Pasquale M. D'Elia. *T'oung Pao* 35 (1940): 385–98.

Ebrey, Patricia Buckley. "The *Book of Filial Piety for Women* Attributed to a Woman Née Zheng (ca. 730)." In *Under Confucian Eyes: Writings on Gender in Chinese History*, edited by Susan Mann and Cheng Yu-Yin, 47–69. Berkeley: University of California Press, 2001.

———. "Gender and Sinology: Shifting Western Interpretations of Footbinding, 1300–1890." *Late Imperial China* 20, no. 2 (1999): 1–34.

———. *The Inner Quarters: Marriage and the Lives of Chinese Women in the Sung Period*. Berkeley: University of California Press, 1993.

Edwards, Louise. "Women in *Honglou meng*: Prescriptions of Purity in the Femininity of Qing Dynasty China." *Modern China* 16, no. 4 (1990): 407–29.

Eibach, Joachim. "Das offene Haus: Kommunikative Praxis im sozialen Nahraum der europäischen Frühen Neuzeit." *Zeitschrift für historische Forschung* 38, no. 4 (2011): 621–64.

Eibach, Joachim, and Inken Schmidt-Voges, eds. *Das Haus in der Geschichte Europas: Ein Handbuch*. Berlin: De Gruyter Oldenbourg, 2015.

Elman, Benjamin A. *A Cultural History of Civil Examinations in Late Imperial China*. Berkeley: University of California Press, 2000.

Elvin, Mark. "Female Virtue and the State in China." *Past and Present* 104 (1984): 111–52.

Entenmann, Robert E. "Christian Virgins in Eighteenth-Century Sichuan." In *Christianity in China*, edited by Bays, 180–93.

Fairchilds, Cissie. *Women in Early Modern Europe, 1500–1700*. London: Pearson Education, 2007.

Fang Hao 方豪. *Zhongguo tianzhujiaoshi renwuzhuan* 中国天主教史人物傳 (Biographies of personalities from Chinese Christian history). 2 vols. Hong Kong: Xianggang gongjiao zhenli xuehui chuban, 1970.

Findlen, Paula. "Early Modern Things: Objects in Motion, 1500–1800." In *Early Modern Things: Objects and Their Histories, 1500–1800*, edited by Paula Findlen, 3–27. New York: Routledge, 2013.

Fong, Grace S. "Female Hands: Embroidery as a Knowledge Field in Women's Everyday Life in Late Imperial and Early Republican China." *Late Imperial China* 25, no. 1 (2004): 1–58.

Fong, Grace S., and Ellen Widmer, eds. *The Inner Quarters and Beyond: Women Writers from Ming through Qing*. Leiden: Brill, 2010.

Forster, Marc R. *The Counter-Reformation in the Villages: Religion and Reform in the Bishopric of Speyer, 1650–1720*. Ithaca, NY: Cornell University Press, 1992.

———. "Domestic Devotions and Family Piety in German Catholicism." In *Piety and Family in Early Modern Europe: Essays in Honour of Steven Ozment*, edited by Marc R. Forster and Benjamin Kaplan, 97–114. Aldershot: Ashgate, 2005.

Foss, Theodore N. "The European Sojourn of Philippe Couplet and Michael Shen Fuzong, 1683–1692." In *Philippe Couplet, S.J. (1623–1693): The Man Who Brought China to Europe*, edited by Jerome Heyndrickx, 121–42. Nettetal: Steyler Verlag, 1990.

Frank, Jill. *A Democracy of Distinction: Aristotle and the Work of Politics*. Chicago: University of Chicago Press, 2005.

Freedman, Maurice. "Ritual Aspects of Chinese Kinship and Marriage." In *The Study of Chinese Society: Essays by Maurice Freedman*, edited by G. William Skinner, 273–95. Stanford, CA: Stanford University Press, 1979.

Friedrich, Markus. "Circulating and Compiling the Litterae Annuae: Towards a History of the Jesuit System of Communication." *Archivum Historicum Societatis Iesu* 77 (2008): 3–39.

———. *Der lange Arm Roms? Globale Verwaltung und Kommunikation im Jesuitenorden, 1540–1773*. Frankfurt am Main: Campus Verlag, 2011.

———. "Government and Information-Management in Early Modern Europe: The Case of the Society of Jesus." *Journal of Early Modern History* 12 (2008): 539–63.

Furth, Charlotte. *A Flourishing Yin: Gender in China's Medical History, 960–1665*. Berkeley: University of California Press, 1999.

———. "The Patriarch's Legacy: Household Instructions and the Transmission of Orthodox Values." In *Orthodoxy in Late Imperial China*, edited by Liu, 187–211.

Gallin, Bernard. "Matrilateral and Affinal Relationships of a Taiwanese Village." *American Anthropologist* 62, no. 4 (1960): 632–42.

Gates, Hill. "The Commoditization of Chinese Women." *Signs* 14 (1989): 799–832.

Gélis, Jacques. *Les enfants des Limbes: Mort-nés et parents dans l'Europe chrétienne*. Paris: Audibert, 2006.

Gentilcore, David. *Healers and Healing in Early Modern Italy*. Manchester: Manchester University Press, 1998.

Gernet, Jacques. *Chine et christianisme: Action et réaction*. Paris: Gallimard, 1982.

Girard, Pascale. Introduction to *Le voyage en Chine*, by Las Cortes, 7–34.

———. "Les descriptions qui fâchent: La 'Relación' du Jésuite Adriano de las Cortes en Chine (1626) et le déni de la Compagnie." In *L'empire portugais face aux autres empires*, edited by Francisco Bethencourt and Luiz Felipe de Alencastro, 167–84. Paris: Maisonneuve et Larose and Centre culturel Calouste Gulbenkian, 2007.

Golvers, Noël. *Building Humanistic Libraries in Late Imperial China: Circulation of Books, Prints and Letters between Europe and China (XVIIth–XVIIIth Cent.) in the Framework of the Jesuit Mission*. Rome: Nuova Cultura, 2011.

———. "Distance as an Inconvenient Factor in the Scientific Communication between Europe and the Jesuits in China (17th/18th Century)." *Bulletin of Portuguese Japanese Studies* 18–19 (2009): 105–34.

———. *François de Rougemont, S.J., Missionary in Ch'ang-shu (Chiang-nan): A Study of the Account Book (1674–1676) and the Elogium*. Leuven: Leuven University Press, 1999.

———. "Jesuit Cartographers in China: Francesco Brancati, S.J., and the Map (1661?) of Sungchiang Prefecture (Shanghai)." *Imago Mundi* 52 (2000): 30–42.

———. "The XVIIth-Century Jesuit Mission in China and Its 'Antwerp Connections' (I): The Moretus Family (1660–1700)." In *Ex Officina Plantiniana Moretorum: Studies over het drukkersgeslacht Moretus*, edited by Marcus de Schepper and Francine de Nave, 157–88. Antwerp: Vereeniging der Antwerpsche Bibliophielen, 1996.

Goossaert, Vincent. "Irrepressible Female Piety: Late Imperial Bans on Women Visiting Temples." *Nan Nü* 10, no. 2 (2008): 212–41.

Goossaert, Vincent, and Valentine Zuber. "Introduction: La China a-t-elle connu l'anticléricalisme?" *Extrême-Orient, Extrême-Occident* 24 (2002): 5–16.

Gould, Peter, and Rodney White, eds. *Mental Maps*. Boston: Allen and Unwin, 1986.

Grant, Beata. *Eminent Nuns: Women Chan Masters of Seventeenth-Century China*. Honolulu: University of Hawaii Press, 2009.

———. "Women, Gender, and Religion in Premodern China: A Brief Introduction." *Nan Nü* 10 (2008): 2–21.

Grant, Beata, and Wilt L. Idema. *Escape from Blood Pond Hell: The Tales of Mulian and Woman Huang*. Seattle: University of Washington Press, 2011.

Grendi, Edoardo. *La repubblica aristocratica dei genovesi: Politica, carità e commercio fra Cinque e Seicento*. Bologna: Il Mulino, 1987.

Harrison, Henrietta. "Rethinking Missionaries and Medicine in China: The Miracles of Assunta Pallotta, 1905–2005." *Journal of Asian Studies* 71, no. 1 (2012): 127–48.

Heijdra, Martin. "The Socio-Economic Development of Rural China during the Ming." In *The Cambridge History of China*, vol. 8, part 2, *The Ming Dynasty, 1368–1644*, edited by Denis Twitchett and John K. Fairbank, 417–578. Cambridge: Cambridge University Press, 1998.

Hellman, Lisa. "Using China at Home: Knowledge Production and Gender in the Swedish East India Company, 1730–1800." *Itinerario* 381, no. 1 (2014): 35–55.

Hersche, Peter. *Muße und Verschwendung: Europäische Gesellschaft und Kultur im Barockzeitalter*. 2 vols. Freiburg: Herder Verlag, 2006.

Heyberger, Bernard. *Les chrétiens du Proche-Orient au temps de la réforme catholique (Syrie, Liban, Palestine, XVII*[e]*–XVIII*[e] *siècles)*. Rome: École française de Rome, 1994.

Hinsch, Bret. "The Origins of Separation of the Sexes in China." *Journal of the American Oriental Society* 123, no. 3 (2003): 595–616.

———. *Passions of the Cut Sleeve: The Male Homosexual Tradition in China*. Berkeley: University of California Press, 1990.

Höllmann, Thomas O. "Ein Zeichen von übernatürlicher Kraft und Tapferkeit: Vom Bart und seiner Bedeutung in China." In *Und folge nun dem, was mein Herz begehrt: Festschrift für Ulrich Unger zum 70. Geburtstag*, edited by Reinhard Emmerich and Hans Stumpfeldt, vol. 1, 329–41. Hamburg: Hamburger Sinologische Gesellschaft, 2002.

Holmgren, Jennifer. "Myth, Fantasy, or Scholarship: Images of the Status of Women in Traditional China." *Australian Journal of Chinese Affairs* 6 (1981): 1–27.

Holzem, Andreas. "Familie und Familienideal in der katholischen Konfessionalisierung: Pastorale Theologie und soziale Praxis." In *Ehe—Familie—Verwandtschaft: Vergesellschaftung in Religion und sozialer Lebenswelt*, edited by Andreas Holzem, 243–83. Paderborn: Ferdinand Schöningh, 2008.

———. *Religion und Lebensform: Katholische Konfessionalisierung im Sendgericht des Fürstbistums Münster, 1570–1800*. Paderborn: Ferdinand Schöningh, 2000.

Howard, Deborah. "Exploring Devotional Practice in the Italian Renaissance Home." *Scroope: Cambridge Architecture Journal* 24 (2015): 64–80.

Hsia, Florence. *Sojourners in a Strange Land: Jesuits and Their Scientific Missions in Late Imperial China*. Chicago: University of Chicago Press, 2009.

Hsia, Ronnie Po-chia. "Dreams and Conversions: A Comparative Analysis of Catholic and Buddhist Dreams in Ming and Qing China: Part II." *Journal of Religious History* 24, no. 2 (2010): 103–33.

———. "From Buddhist Garb to Literati Silk: Costume and Identity of the Jesuit Missionary." In *Religious Ceremonials and Images: Power and Social Meaning (1400–1750)*, edited by José Pedro Paiva, 143–54. Coimbra: Palimage, 2002.

———. *A Jesuit in the Forbidden City: Matteo Ricci 1552–1610*. Oxford: Oxford University Press, 2010.

———. *Noble Patronage and the Jesuit Missions: Maria Theresia von Fugger-Wellenburg (1690–1762) and Jesuit Missionaries in China and Vietnam*. Rome: Institutum Historicum Societatis Iesu, 2006.

———. *The World of Catholic Renewal, 1540–1770*. Cambridge: Cambridge University Press, 2005. First published 1998.

Huang, C. Julia, Elena Valussi, and David A. Palmer. "Gender and Sexuality." In *Chinese Religious Life*, edited by David A. Palmer, Glenn Shive, and Philip L. Wickeri, 107–23. Oxford: Oxford University Press, 2011.

Huang, Martin W. "Male Friendship in Ming China: An Introduction." *Nan Nü* 9 (2007): 2–33.

———. *Negotiating Masculinities in Late Imperial China*. Honolulu: University of Hawaii Press, 2006.

Huang, Xiaojuan. "Christian Communities and Alternative Devotions in China, 1780–1860." PhD dissertation, Princeton University, 2006.

Huang Yinong 黃一農, ed. *Liangtoushe: Mingmo Qingchu de diyidai tianzhujiaotu* 兩頭蛇: 明末清初的第一代天主教徒 (The two-headed snake: The first generation of Chinese Christians in the seventeenth century). Xinzhu: Qingda shubanshe, 2005.

———. "'Liangtoushe zu' de suming" 「兩頭蛇族」的宿命 (The fate of the "two-headed snake" people). In *Liangtoushe*, edited by Huang, 463–82.

———. "Rujiahua de tianzhujiaotu: Yi Wang Zheng weili" 儒家化的天主教徒。以王徵為例 (Christians with Confucian culture: The example of Wang Zheng). In *Liangtoushe*, edited by Huang, 132–74.

Hucker, Charles O. *A Dictionary of Official Titles in Imperial China*. Stanford, CA: Stanford University Press, 1985.

Hufton, Olwen Hazel. "Altruism and Reciprocity: The Early Jesuits and Their Female Patrons." *Renaissance Studies* 15 (2001): 328–53.

Idema, Wilt L., and Beata Grant, eds. *The Red Brush: Writing Women of Imperial China.* Cambridge, MA: Harvard University Asia Center, 2004.

Ingendahl, Gesa. *Witwen in der Frühen Neuzeit: Eine kulturhistorische Studie.* Frankfurt am Main: Campus Verlag, 2006.

Iseli, Andrea. *Gute Policey: Öffentliche Ordnung in der Frühen Neuzeit.* Stuttgart: Eugen Ulmer, 2009.

Jaffary, Nora E., ed. *Gender, Race, and Religion in the Colonization of the Americas.* Aldershot: Ashgate, 2007.

Jami, Catherine, Peter Engelfriet, and Gregory Blue, eds. *Statecraft and Intellectual Renewal in Late Ming China: The Cross-Cultural Synthesis of Xu Guangqi (1562–1633).* Leiden: Brill, 2001.

Jensen, Lionel. *Manufacturing Confucianism: Chinese Traditions and Universal Civilization.* Durham, NC: Duke University Press, 1997.

Jia Jinhua, Kang Xiaofei, and Ping Yao, eds. *Gendering Chinese Religion: Subject, Identity, and Body.* Albany: State University of New York Press, 2014.

Johnson, Trevor. "Blood, Tears and Xavier-Water: Jesuit Missionaries and Popular Religion in the Eighteenth-Century Upper Palatinate." In *Popular Religion in Germany and Central Europe, 1400–1800*, edited by Trevor Johnson, 183–202. London: Macmillan, 1996.

Jordan, David K. "The Glyphomancy Factor: Observations on Chinese Conversion." In *Conversion to Christianity: Historical and Anthropological Perspectives on a Great Transformation*, edited by Robert W. Hefner, 285–303. Berkeley: University of California Press, 1993.

———. *Gods, Ghosts, and Ancestors: The Folk Religion of a Taiwanese Village.* Berkeley: University of California Press, 1972.

Judd, Ellen R. "Niangjia: Chinese Women and Their Natal Families." *Journal of Asian Studies* 48, no. 3 (1989): 525–44.

Kang Zhijie 康志杰. "Lun Ming Qing zhiji lai Hua Yesuhuishi dui Zhongguo naqie hunsu de piping" 論明清之際來華耶穌會士對中國納妾婚俗的批評 (Discussing the Jesuits' criticism against Chinese customs of marriage and concubinage in the Ming and Qing periods). *Jidujiao yanjiu* 基督教研究 (Research on Christianity), no. 2 (1998): 172–77.

Kaplan, Benjamin. *Divided by Faith: Religious Conflict and the Practice of Toleration in Early Modern Europe.* Cambridge, MA: Belknap Press of Harvard University Press, 2007.

Kelleher, Teresa. "Confucianism." In *Women in World Religions*, edited by Arvind Sharma, 135–60. Albany: State University of New York Press, 1987.

Kelly, Edward Thomas. *The Anti-Christian Persecution of 1616–1617 in Nanking.* Ann Arbor: University Microfilms International, 1982.

Kendall, Laurel. *Shamans, Housewives, and Other Restless Spirits: Women in Korean Ritual Life.* Honolulu: University of Hawaii Press, 1985.

King, Gail. "Candida Xu and the Growth of Christianity in China in the Seventeenth Century." *Monumenta Serica* 46 (1998): 49–66.

———. "Christian Charity in Seventeenth-Century China." *Sino-Western Cultural Relations Journal* 22 (2000): 13–30.

———. "Couplet's Biography of Madame Candida Xu (1607–1680)." *Sino-Western Cultural Relations Journal* 18 (1996): 41–56.

———. "The Family Letters of Xu Guangqi." *Ming Studies* 1 (1991): 1–41.

———. "The Gospel for the Ordinary Reader: Aspects of Six Christian Texts in Chinese from the Late Ming Dynasty." *Monumenta Serica* 57 (2009): 167–94.

———. "Spaces for Belief: Christianity, Women, and Accommodation in Seventeenth-Century China." *Sino-Western Cultural Relations Journal* 35 (2013): 17–34.

———. "The Xujiahui (Zikawei) Library of Shanghai." *Libraries and Culture* 32, no. 4 (1997): 456–69.

King, Michelle T. *Between Birth and Death: Female Infanticide in Nineteenth-Century China*. Stanford, CA: Stanford University Press, 2014.

Kirkham, Pat, and Judy Attfield. Introduction to *The Gendered Object*, edited by Pat Kirkham, 1–11. Manchester: Manchester University Press, 1996.

Kirkham, Victoria. "Laura Battiferra degli Ammannati benefattrice dei Gesuiti fiorentini." *Quaderni storici* 104, no. 2 (2000): 331–54.

Klein, Thoralf. *Die Basler Mission in Guangdong (Südchina) 1859–1931: Akkulturationsprozesse und kulturelle Grenzziehungen zwischen Missionaren, chinesischen Christen und lokaler Gesellschaft*. Munich: Iudicium Verlag, 2002.

Ko, Dorothy. *Cinderella's Sisters: A Revisionist History of Footbinding*. Berkeley: University of California Press, 2005.

———. *Teachers of the Inner Chambers: Women and Culture in Seventeenth-Century China*. Stanford, CA: Stanford University Press, 1994.

Kürzeder, Christoph. *Als die Dinge heilig waren: Gelebte Frömmigkeit im Zeitalter des Barock*. Regensburg: Schnell und Steiner, 2005.

Laamann, Lars Peter. *Christian Heretics in Late Imperial China: Christian Inculturation and State Control, 1720–1850*. London: Routledge, 2006.

———. "Von Bodhisattva Guanyin zur Jungfrau Maria: Einige Aspekte zur Inkulturation des Christentums im China des 18. und frühen 19. Jahrhunderts." *Spirita* 1 (1998): 4–11.

Lach, Donald F., and Edwin J. Van Kley, eds. *Asia in the Making of Europe*. 3 vols. Chicago: University of Chicago Press, 1965–93.

Lackner, Michael. *Der chinesische Traumwald: Traditionelle Theorien des Traumes und seiner Deutung im Spiegel der Ming-zeitlichen Anthologie Meng-lin hsüan-chieh*. Frankfurt am Main: Peter Lang, 1985.

Laqua-O'Donnell, Simone. *Women and the Counter-Reformation in Early Modern Münster*. Oxford: Oxford University Press, 2014.

Laven, Mary, ed. "The Jesuits and Gender: Body, Sexuality, and Emotions." Special issue, *Journal of Jesuit Studies* 2, no. 4 (2015).

———. *Mission to China: Matteo Ricci and the Jesuit Encounter with the East*. London: Faber and Faber, 2011.

Leacock, Eleanor. "Montagnais Marriage and the Jesuits in the 17th Century." *Western Canadian Journal of Anthropology* 6, no. 3 (1976): 77–91.

Le Gall, Jean-Marie. "La virilité des clercs." In *Histoire de la virilité*, vol. 1, *L'invention de la virilité: De l'Antiquité aux Lumières*, edited by Alain Corbin, Jean-Jacques Courtine, and Georges Vigarello, 213–30. Paris: Edition du Seuil, 2011.

Levy, Evonne. "Jesuit Identity, Identifiable Jesuits? Jesuit Dress in Theory and in Image." In *Le monde est une peinture: Jesuitische Identität und die Rolle der Bilder*, edited by Elisabeth Oy-Marra and Volker R. Remmert, 127–52. Berlin: Akademieverlag, 2011.

Li, Ji. *God's Little Daughters: Catholic Women in Nineteenth-Century Manchuria*. Seattle: University of Washington Press, 2015.

Li Sher-shiueh 李奭學. "San mian Maliya: Lun Gao Yizhi 'Shengmu xingshi' li de Shengmu qiji gushi de kuaguo liubian ji qi yiyi" 三面瑪利亞: 論高一志《聖母行實》裏的聖母奇蹟故事的跨國流變及其意義 (A Ming lady with three faces: Mary as seen in Alfonso Vagnone's *Shengmu xingshi*). In *Yishu*, edited by Li, 151–203.

———. "Shengren, mogui, chanhui: Gao Yizhi yi 'Tianzhu shengjiao shengren xingshi'" 聖人 • 魔鬼 • 懺悔: 高一志譯《天主聖教聖人行實》 (Saints, demons, and penance: Alfonso Vagnone's "Biographies of the saints of the holy teaching of the Lord of Heaven"). In *Yishu*, edited by Li, 205–53.

———, ed. *Yishu: Mingmo Yesuhui fanyi wenxuelun* 譯述: 明末耶穌會翻譯文學論 (Transwriting: Translated literature and late Ming Jesuits). Hong Kong: Xianggang zhongwen daxue chubanshe, 2012.

Li Sher-shiueh, and Thierry Meynard, eds. *Jesuit Chreia in Late Ming China: Two Studies with an Annotated Translation of Alfonso Vagnone's Illustrations of the Grand Dao*. Bern: Peter Lang, 2013.

Li, Xiaorong. *Women's Poetry of Late Imperial China: Transforming the Inner Chambers*. Seattle: University of Washington Press, 2012.

Li, Yuhang. "Embroidering Guanyin: Constructions of the Divine through Hair." *East Asian Science, Technology and Medicine* 36 (2012): 131–66.

Lin, Xiaoping. "Seeing the Place: The Virgin Mary in a Chinese Lady's Inner Chamber." In *Early Modern Catholicism: Essays in Honour of John W. O'Malley, S.J.*, edited by Kathleen M. Comerford and Hilmar M. Pabel, 183–210. Toronto: University of Toronto Press, 2001.

Lin Zhongze 林中澤. *Wan Ming zhongxi xinglunli de xiangyu: Yi Li Madou "Tianzhushiyi" he Pang Diwo "Qike" wei zhongxin* 晚明中西性倫理的相遇: 以利馬竇 《天主實義》 和庞迪我《七克》為中心 (Eastern and Western gender ethics in the late Ming: Matteo Ricci's "Tianzhushiyi" and Diego Pantoja's "Qike"). Guangzhou: Guangdong jiaoyu chubanshe, 2003.

Liu, Kwang-Ching, ed. *Orthodoxy in Late Imperial China*. Berkeley: University of California Press, 1990.

Liu, Kwang-Ching, and Richard Shek, eds. *Heterodoxy in Late Imperial China*. Honolulu: University of Hawaii Press, 2004.

Liu, Xun. "Visualizing Perfection: Daoist Paintings of Our Lady, Court Patronage, and Elite Female Piety in the Late Qing." *Harvard Journal of Asiatic Studies* 64, no. 1 (2004): 57–115.

Liu Yunhua 刘耘华. "Xu Guangqi yinqin mailuo zhong de Shanghai tianzhujiao wenren: Yi Sun Yuanhua, Xu Leshan er jiazu wei zhongxin" 徐光启姻亲脉络中的上海天主教文人： 以孙元化、 许乐善二家族为中心 (The Catholic literati in Shanghai along the line of marriage of Xu Guangqi: A case study of Sun Yuanhua's and Xu Leshan's families). *Shijie zongjiao yanjiu* 世界宗教研究 (Studies in World Religions) 1 (2009): 98–107.

Logan, Anne-Marie, and Liam M. Brockey. "Nicolas Trigault, SJ: A Portrait by Peter Paul Rubens." *Metropolitan Museum Journal* 38 (2003): 157–67.

López Gay, Jesús. *El matrimonio de los Japoneses: Problema, y soluciones según un ms. inédito de Gil de la Mata, S.J. (1547–1599)*. Rome: Libreria dell'Università Gregoriana, 1964.

Louie, Kam, and Louise Edwards. "Chinese Masculinity: Theorizing *Wen* and *Wu*." *East Asian History* 8 (1994): 135–48.

Lowe, Hsing-yuan. *The Adventures of Wu: The Life Cycle of a Peking Man*. 2 vols. Princeton, NJ: Princeton University Press, 1983.

Lu, Weijing. *True to Her Word: The Faithful Maiden Cult in Late Imperial China*. Stanford, CA: Stanford University Press, 2008.

Lutz, Jessie, ed. *Pioneer Chinese Christian Women: Gender, Christianity, and Social Mobility*. Bethlehem, PA: Lehigh University Press, 2010.

Madsen, Richard. *China's Catholics: Tragedy and Hope in an Emerging Civil Society*. Berkeley: University of California Press, 1998.

Maihofer, Andrea. "Die Querelle des femmes: Lediglich literarisches Genre oder spezifische Form der gesellschaftlichen Auseinandersetzung um Wesen und Status der Geschlechter?" In *Geschlechterperspektiven: Forschungen zur frühen Neuzeit*, edited by Heide Wunder and Gisela Engel, 262–72. Königstein: Ulrike Helmer Verlag, 1998.

Mann, Susan. *Precious Records: Women in China's Long Eighteenth Century*. Stanford, CA: Stanford University Press, 1997.

Margiotti, Fortunato. "Congregazioni mariane della antica missione cinese." In *Das Laienapostolat in den Missionen: Festschrift Prof. Dr. Johannes Beckmann SMB zum 60. Geburtstag dargeboten*, edited by Johann Specker and Walbert Bühlmann, 131–53. Schöneck-Beckenried: Neue Zeitschrift für Missionswissenschaft, 1961.

———. "I riti cinesi davanti alla S. C. de Propaganda Fide prima del 1643." *Neue Zeitschrift für Missionswissenschaft* 35 (1979): 133–53, 192–211.

———. *Il cattolicismo nello Shansi dalle origini al 1738*. Rome: Edizione Sinica Franciscana, 1958.

———. "La Cina, ginepraio di questioni secolari." In *Sacrae Congregationis de Propaganda Fide memoria rerum: 350 Jahre im Dienste der Weltmission 1622–1972*, vol. 1, part 2, *1622–1700*, edited by Joseph Metzler, 597–631. Rome: Herder Verlag, 1971.

Maryks, Robert Alexander. *Saint Cicero and the Jesuits: The Influence of the Liberal Arts on the Adoption of Moral Probabilism*. Aldershot: Ashgate; Rome: Institutum Historicum Societatis Iesu, 2008.

Masakazu, Asami. "Solutions to the Chinese Rites Controversy Proposed by Antonio Rubino, S.J. (1578–1643), Visitor to Japan and China." In *Christianity and Cultures: Japan and China in Comparison 1543–1644*, edited by M. Antoni J. Üçerler, 126–41. Rome: Institutum Historicum Societatis Iesu, 2009.

McLaren, Anne E. "Women's Work and Ritual Space in China." In *Chinese Women—Living and Working*, edited by Anne E. McLaren, 169–87. London: Routledge, 2004.

McMahon, Keith. *Polygyny and Sublime Passion: Sexuality in China on the Verge of Modernity*. Honolulu: University of Hawaii Press, 2010.

Menegon, Eugenio. “Amicitia Palatina: The Jesuits and the Politics of Gift-Giving at the Qing Court.” In *Il liuto e i libri: Studi in onore di Mario Sabattini*, edited by Magda Abbiati and Federico Greselin, 547–61. Venice: Edizioni Ca’ Foscari, 2014.

———. *Ancestors, Virgins, and Friars: Christianity as a Local Religion in Late Imperial China*. Cambridge, MA: Harvard University Press, 2009.

———. “Child Bodies, Blessed Bodies: The Contest between Christian Virginity and Confucian Chastity.” *Nan Nü* 6, no. 2 (2004): 177–240.

———. “Deliver Us from Evil: Confession and Salvation in Seventeenth- and Eighteenth-Century Chinese Catholicism.” In *Forgive Us Our Sins*, edited by Standaert and Dudink, 9–101.

———. “European and Chinese Controversies over Rituals: A Seventeenth-Century Genealogy of Chinese Religion.” In *Devising Order: Socio-Religious Models, Rituals, and the Performativity of Practice*, edited by Bruno Boute and Thomas Småberg, 193–222. Leiden: Brill, 2013.

———. “The Habit Hides the Monk: Missionary Fashion Strategies at the Imperial Court in Early Modern China.” Paper presented at the workshop “Going Native or Remaining Foreign? Catholic Missionaries as Local Agents in Asia (17th to 18th Centuries),” Rome, May 2017.

———. “Jesuit Emblematica in China: The Use of European Allegorical Images in Flemish Engravings Described in the Kouduo Richao (ca. 1640).” *Monumenta Serica* 55 (2007): 389–437.

———. “Jesuits, Franciscans, and Dominicans in Fujian: The Anti-Christian Incidents of 1637–1638.” In *“Scholar from the West”: Giulio Aleni S.J. (1582–1649)*, edited by Tiziana Lipello, 219–62. Nettetal: Steyler Verlag, 1997.

———. “Popular or Local? Historiographical Shifts in the Study of Christianity in Late Imperial China.” In *Dongxi jiaoliushi de xinju: Yi Jidu zongjiao wei zhongxin* 東西交流史的新局: 以基督宗教為中心 (New developments of the history of exchange between East and West: Focusing on Christianity), edited by Ku Wei-ying 古偉瀛, 247–307. Taipei: Taiwan daxue chuban zhongxin, 2005.

———. “Yang Guangxian’s Opposition to Johann Adam Schall: Christianity and Western Science in His Work *Budeyi*.” In *Western Learning and Christianity in China: The Contribution and Impact of Johann Adam Schall von Bell, S.J. (1592–1666)*, edited by Roman Malek, vol. 1, 311–37. Nettetal: Steyler Verlag, 1998.

Metzler, Josef. *Die Synoden in China, Japan und Korea 1570–1931*. Paderborn: Ferdinand Schöningh, 1980.

———. “Orientation, programme et premières décisions (1622–1649).” In *Sacrae Congregationis de Propaganda Fide memoria rerum: 350 Jahre im Dienste der Weltmission 1622–1972*, vol. 1, part 2, *1622–1700*, edited by Josef Metzler, 146–96. Rome: Herder Verlag, 1971.

Meynard, Thierry. “Aristotelian Ethics in the Land of Confucius: A Study of Vagnone’s Western Learning on Personal Cultivation.” *Antiquorum Philosophia* 7 (2013): 145–69.

———, ed. *Confucius Sinarum Philosophus (1687): The First Translation of the Confucian Classics*. Rome: Institutum Historicum Societatis Iesu, 2011.

———. “Illustrations of the Grand Dao: A Book of Rhetoric and Morality in Late-Ming China.” In *Jesuit Chreia*, edited by Li and Meynard, 97–182.

———. Introduction to *Confucius Sinarum Philosophus*, edited by Meynard, 1–76.

Miles, Steven B. "Strange Encounters on the Cantonese Frontier: Region and Gender in Kuang Lu's (1604–1650) Chiya." *Nan Nü* 8, no. 1 (2006): 115–55.

Milhou, Alain. "Die Neue Welt als geistiges und moralisches Problem (1492–1609)." In *Handbuch der Geschichte Lateinamerikas*, vol. 1, edited by Walther L. Bernecker, Raymond Th. Buve, and John R. Fisher, 274–96. Stuttgart: Klett-Cotta, 1992.

Miller, Peter N., and François Louis, eds. *Antiquarianism and Intellectual Life in Europe and China, 1500–1800*. Ann Arbor: University of Michigan Press, 2012.

Mish, John L. "Creating an Image of Europe for China: Aleni's *Hsi-fang ta-wen*; Introduction, Translation, and Notes." *Monumenta Serica* 23 (1964): 1–87.

Miyazaki, Ichisada. *China's Examination Hell: The Civil Service Examinations of Imperial China*. Translated by Conrad Schirokauer. New York: Weatherhill, 1976.

Molina, J. Michelle. *To Overcome Oneself: The Jesuit Ethic and Spirit of Global Expansion, 1520–1767*. Berkeley: University of California Press, 2013.

Montrose, Louis. "The Work of Gender in the Discourse of Discovery." *Representations* 33 (1991): 1–41.

Moran, Joseph Francis. *The Japanese and the Jesuits: Alessandro Valignano in Sixteenth-Century Japan*. New York: Routledge, 1993.

Mostaccio, Silvia. *Early Modern Jesuits between Obedience and Conscience during the Generalate of Claudio Acquaviva (1581–1615)*. Farnham: Ashgate, 2014.

Mostra tesori d'arte sacra di Roma e del Lazio. Rome: Palazzo delle Esposizioni, 1975.

Mungello, Daniel E. *Curious Land: Jesuit Accommodation and the Origins of Sinology*. Stuttgart: Franz Steiner Verlag, 1985.

———. *Drowning Girls in China: Female Infanticide since 1650*. Lanham, MD: Rowman and Littlefield, 2008.

———. *The Forgotten Christians of Hangzhou*. Honolulu: University of Hawaii Press, 1994.

Naquin, Susan. *Peking: Temples and City Life, 1400–1900*. Berkeley: University of California Press, 2002.

Naquin, Susan, and Evelyn S. Rawski. *Chinese Society in the Eighteenth Century*. New Haven, CT: Yale University Press, 1987.

O'Malley, John W. *The First Jesuits*. Cambridge, MA: Harvard University Press, 1993.

O'Malley, John W., Gauvin Alexander Bailey, Steven J. Harris, and T. Frank Kennedy, eds. *The Jesuits: Cultures, Sciences, and the Arts, 1540–1773*. 2 vols. Toronto: University of Toronto Press, 1999–2006.

Oosterwijk, Sophie. "The Swaddling Clothes of Christ: A Medieval Relic on Display." *Medieval Life* 13 (2000): 25–30.

Osterhammel, Jürgen. *Die Entzauberung Asiens: Europa und die asiatischen Reiche im 18. Jahrhundert*. Munich: C. H. Beck, 1998.

Overmyer, Daniel L. *Folk Buddhist Religion: Dissenting Sects in Late Traditional China*. Cambridge, MA: Harvard University Press, 1976.

———. *Local Religion in North China in the Twentieth Century: The Structure and Organization of Community Rituals and Beliefs*. Leiden: Brill, 2009.

Paschoud, Adrien. *Le monde amérindien au miroir des "Lettres édifiantes et curieuses."* Oxford, UK: Voltaire Foundation, 2008.

Perera, S. G. *The Jesuits in Ceylon (in the XVI and XVII Centuries)*. New Delhi: Asian Educational Services, 2004.

Peterson, Willard. "Learning from Heaven: The Introduction of Christianity and Other Western Ideas into Late Ming China." In *China and Maritime Europe*, edited by Wills, 78–134.

———. "What to Wear? Observation and Participation by Jesuit Missionaries in Late Ming Society." In *Implicit Understandings: Observing, Reporting, and Reflecting on the Encounters between Europeans and Other Peoples in the Early Modern Era*, edited by Stuart B. Schwartz, 403–21. Cambridge: Cambridge University Press, 1994.

Pfister, Louis. *Notices biographiques et bibliographiques sur les jésuites de l'ancienne mission de Chine 1552–1773*. Shanghai: Imprimerie de la Mission catholique, 1932.

Picaud, Gérard, and Jean Foisselon, eds. *Sacrées soieries: Étoffes précieuses à la Visitation*. Paris: Somogy éditions d'art; Moulins: Musée de la Visitation, 2012.

Pizzorusso, Giovanni. "I dubbi sui sacramenti dalle missioni ad infideles: Percorsi nelle burocrazie di Curia." In *Administrer les sacrements*, edited by Broggio, Castelnau-L'Estoile, and Pizzorusso, 39–61.

Pomeranz, Kenneth. "Power, Gender, and Pluralism in the Cult of the Goddess of Taishan." In *Culture and State in Chinese History: Conventions, Accommodations, and Critiques*, edited by Theodore Huters, R. Bin Wong, and Pauline Yu, 182–204. Stanford, CA: Stanford University Press, 1997.

Qu Yi. "*Song Nianzhu Guicheng* (Die Anweisung zur Rezitation des Rosenkranzes): Ein illustriertes christliches Buch aus China vom Anfang des 17. Jahrhunderts." *Monumenta Serica* 60 (2012): 195–290.

Questier, Michael C. *Catholicism and Community in Early Modern England: Politics, Aristocratic Patronage, and Religion, c. 1550–1640*. Cambridge: Cambridge University Press, 2006.

Rahner, Hugo. Introduction to *St. Ignatius of Loyola: Letters to Women*, edited by Hugo Rahner. New York: Crossroad Publishing, 2007. First edition in German: Herder Verlag, 1956.

Raphals, Lisa. *Sharing the Light: Representations of Women and Virtue in Early China*. Albany: State University of New York Press, 1998.

Rapley, Elizabeth. *The Dévotes: Women and Church in Seventeenth-Century France*. Montreal and Kingston: McGill-Queen's University Press, 1990.

Rawski, Evelyn S. *Education and Popular Literacy in Ch'ing China*. Ann Arbor: University of Michigan Press, 1979.

Reed, Barbara E. "The Gender Symbolism of Kuan-yin Bodhisattva." In *Buddhism, Sexuality, and Gender*, edited by José Ignacio Cabezón, 159–80. Delhi: Sri Satguru Publications, 1992.

Reinhard, Wolfgang. "Gegenreformation als Modernisierung? Prolegomena zu einer Theorie des konfessionellen Zeitalters." *Archiv für Reformationsgeschichte* 68 (1977): 226–52.

Ropp, Paul. "Passionate Women: Female Suicide in Late Imperial China—Introduction." *Nan Nü* 3, no. 1 (2001): 3–21.

Rosenlee, Li-Hsiang Lisa. *Confucianism and Women: A Philosophical Interpretation*. Albany: State University of New York Press, 2006.

Rosner, Erhard. "Frauen als Anführerinnen chinesischer Sekten." In *Religion und Philosophie in Ostasien: Festschrift für Hans Steininger zum 65. Geburtstag*, edited by Gert Naundorf, Karl-Heinz Pohl, and Hans Hermann Schmidt, 239–46. Würzburg: Königshausen und Neumann, 1985.

Roth, Detlef. "*An uxor ducenda*: Zur Geschichte eines Topos von der Antike bis zur Frühen Neuzeit." In *Geschlechterbeziehungen und Textfunktionen: Studien zu Eheschriften der Frühen Neuzeit*, edited by Rüdiger Schnell, 170–232. Tübingen: Max Niemeyer Verlag, 1998.

Rowe, William T. "Women and the Family in Mid-Qing Social Thought: The Case of Chen Hongmou." *Late Imperial China* 13, no. 2 (1992): 1–41.

Rubiés, Joan-Pau. "Travel Writing and Ethnography." In *Travellers and Cosmographers: Studies in the History of Early Modern Travel and Ethnology*, edited by Joan-Pau Rubiés, 24–43. Aldershot: Ashgate, 2007.

Rublack, Ulinka. *Dressing Up: Cultural Identity in Renaissance Europe*. Oxford: Oxford University Press, 2010.

———. "Pregnancy, Childbirth and the Female Body in Early Modern Germany." *Past and Present* 150 (1996): 84–110.

Rule, Paul A. "From Missionary Hagiography to the History of Chinese Christianity." *Monumenta Serica* 53 (2005): 461–75.

———. *K'ung-tzu or Confucius? The Jesuit Interpretation of Confucianism*. Sydney: Allen and Unwin, 1986.

Sachdev, Rachana. "Contextualizing Female Infanticide: Ming China in Early Modern European Travelogues." *ASIANetwork Exchange* 18, no. 1 (2010): 24–39.

Sachsenmaier, Dominic. *Die Aufnahme europäischer Inhalte in die chinesische Kultur durch Zhu Zongyuan (ca. 1616–1660)*. Sankt Augustin: Institutum Monumenta Serica, 2001.

Sangren, P. Steven. "Female Gender in Chinese Religious Symbols: Kuan Yin, Ma Tsu, and the 'Eternal Mother.'" *Signs* 9, no. 1 (1983): 4–25.

———. *History and Magical Power in a Chinese Community*. Stanford, CA: Stanford University Press, 1987.

Schreiber, Georg. "Heilige Wasser in Segnungen und Volksbrauch." *Zeitschrift für Volkskunde* 44 (1934): 198–209.

Schüller, Sepp. *Die Geschichte der christlichen Kunst in China*. Berlin: Klinkhardt und Biermann Verlag, 1940.

Schurhammer, Georg. *Francis Xavier: His Life, His Times*. Translated by M. Joseph Costelloe. 4 vols. Rome: Jesuit Historical Institute, 1973–82.

Schutte, Anne Jacobson. *Aspiring Saints: Pretense of Holiness, Inquisition, and Gender in the Republic of Venice*. Baltimore: Johns Hopkins University Press, 2001.

Schwedt, Herman H. "Die römischen Kongregationen der Inquisition und des Index: Die Personen (16.–20. Jh.)." In *Inquisition, Index, Zensur: Wissenskulturen der Neuzeit im Widerstreit*, edited by Hubert Wolf, 89–101. Paderborn: Ferdinand Schöningh, 2001.

Scott, Joan W. "Gender: A Useful Category of Historical Analysis." *American Historical Review* 91, no. 5 (1986): 1053–75.

Sheieh, Bau-hwa. *Concubines in Chinese Society from the Fourteenth to the Seventeenth Centuries.* Ann Arbor: University Microfilms International, 1995.

Shi Xijuan. "The Christian Scholar Xu Guangqi and the Spread of Catholicism in Shanghai." *Asian Culture and History* 7, no. 1 (2015): 199–209.

Sieber, Dominik. *Jesuitische Missionierung, priesterliche Liebe, sakramentale Magie.* Basel: Schwabe Verlag, 2005.

Signori, Gabriela. *Von der Paradiesehe zur Gütergemeinschaft: Die Ehe in der mittelalterlichen Lebens- und Vorstellungswelt.* Frankfurt am Main: Campus Verlag, 2011.

Simmel, Georg. "Die Mode." In *Philosophische Kultur: Über das Abenteuer, die Geschlechter und die Krise der Moderne; Gesammelte Essays*, edited by Georg Simmel, 26–51. Berlin: Verlag Klaus Wagenbach, 1983. First edition 1911.

Sinha, Mrinalini. *Colonial Masculinity: The "Manly Englishman" and the "Effeminate Bengali" in the Late Nineteenth Century.* Manchester: Manchester University Press, 1995.

Smith, Joanna F. Handlin. *The Art of Doing Good: Charity in Late Ming China.* Berkeley: University of California Press, 2009.

Sommer, Matthew. "The Penetrated Male in Late Imperial China: Judicial Constructions and Social Stigma." *Modern China* 23, no. 2 (1997): 140–80.

———. *Polyandry and Wife-Selling in Qing Dynasty China: Survival Strategies and Judicial Interventions.* Berkeley: University of California Press, 2015.

———. *Sex, Law, and Society in Late Imperial China.* Stanford, CA: Stanford University Press, 2000.

Song, Gang. "Between Bodhisattva and Christian Deity: Guanyin and the Virgin Mary in Late Ming China." In *The Constant and Changing Faces of the Goddess Traditions of Asia*, edited by Deepak Shimkhada and Phyllis K. Herman, 101–20. Cambridge: Cambridge Scholars Publishing, 2008.

Song Geng. *The Fragile Scholar: Power and Masculinity in Chinese Culture.* Hong Kong: Hong Kong University Press, 2004.

Spence, Jonathan. *The Death of Woman Wang.* New York: Penguin Books, 1979.

———. *The Memory Palace of Matteo Ricci.* New York: Viking, 1985.

———. *Return to Dragon Mountain: Memories of a Late Ming Man.* New York: Penguin Books, 2008.

Staatliche Schlösser und Gärten Potsdam-Sanssouci, eds. *China und Europa: Chinaverständnis und Chinamode im 17. und 18. Jahrhundert.* Berlin: Verwaltung der staatlichen Schlösser und Gärten, 1973.

Stam, Tuuk, and René van Blerk. "Borduurkunst uit China." *Aziatische Kunst* 25, no. 2 (1995): 2–26.

Standaert, Nicolas. *Chinese Voices in the Rites Controversy: Travelling Books, Community Networks, Intercultural Arguments.* Rome: Institutum Historicum Societatis Iesu, 2012.

———, ed. *Handbook of Christianity in China.* Vol. 1, *635–1800.* Leiden: Brill, 2001.

———. *The Interweaving of Rituals: Funerals in the Cultural Exchange between China and Europe.* Seattle: University of Washington Press, 2008.

———. "The Jesuits Did NOT Manufacture 'Confucianism.'" Review article on *Manufacturing Confucianism*, by Lionel Jensen. *East Asian Science, Technology, and Medicine* 16 (1999): 115–32.

———. "The Spiritual Exercises of Ignatius of Loyola in the China Mission of the Seventeenth and Eighteenth Centuries." *Archivum Historicum Societatis Iesu* 81, no. 1 (2012): 73–124.

———. *Yang Tingyun, Confucian and Christian in Late Ming China: His Life and Thought*. Leiden: Brill, 1988.

Standaert, Nicolas, and Adrian Dudink, eds. *Forgive Us Our Sins: Confession in Late Ming and Early Qing China*. Nettetal: Steyler Verlag, 2006.

Stein, Rolf Alfred. "Les religions de la Chine." In *Encyclopédie française*, vol. 19, *Philosophie, religion*, edited by Gaston Berger, 54.3–54.10. Paris: Société de gestion de l'encyclopédie française, 1957.

Stollberg-Rilinger, Barbara. *Europa im Jahrhundert der Aufklärung*. Stuttgart: Reclam, 2006.

Strasser, Ulrike. "Cloistering Women's Past: Conflicting Accounts of Enclosure in a Seventeenth-Century Munich Nunnery." In *Gender in Early Modern German History*, edited by Ulinka Rublack, 221–46. Cambridge: Cambridge University Press, 2002.

———. "'The First Form and Grace': Ignatius of Loyola and the Reformation of Masculinity." In *Masculinity in the Reformation Era*, edited by Scott H. Hendrix and Susan C. Karant-Nunn, 45–70. Kirksville, MO: Truman State University Press, 2008.

———. *State of Virginity: Gender, Religion, and Politics in an Early Modern Catholic State*. Ann Arbor: University of Michigan Press, 2007.

Struve, Lynn A. *Voices from the Ming-Qing Cataclysm: China in Tiger's Jaws*. New Haven, CT: Yale University Press, 1993.

Stuart, Jan, and Evelyn S. Rawski. *Worshiping the Ancestors: Chinese Commemorative Portraits*. Washington, DC: Freer Gallery of Art, 2001.

Sweeten, Alan Richard. *Christianity in Rural China: Conflict and Accommodation in Jiangxi Province, 1860–1900*. Ann Arbor: Center for Chinese Studies, University of Michigan, 2001.

Taylor, Romeyn. "Official Religion in the Ming." In *The Cambridge History of China*, vol. 8, part 2, *The Ming Dynasty, 1368–1644*, edited by Denis Twitchett and John K. Fairbank, 840–92. Cambridge: Cambridge University Press, 1998.

Teng, Jinhua Emma. "An Island of Beautiful Women: The Discourse on Gender in Ch'ing Travel Accounts of Taiwan." In *Bodies in Contact: Rethinking Colonial Encounters in World History*, edited by Antoinette Burton and Tony Ballantyne, 38–53. Durham, NC: Duke University Press, 2005.

———. "The West as a Kingdom of Women: Woman and Occidentalism in Wang Tao's Tales of Travel." In *Traditions of East Asian Travel*, edited by Joshua A. Fogel, 97–124. London: Berghahn Books, 2006.

ter Haar, Barend J. *The White Lotus Teachings in Chinese Religious History*. Leiden: Brill, 1992.

Theiss, Janet M. *Disgraceful Matters: The Politics of Chastity in Eighteenth-Century China*. Berkeley: University of California Press, 2004.

Thibodeaux, Jennifer D. *The Manly Priest: Clerical Celibacy, Masculinity, and Reform in England and Normandy, 1066–1300*. Philadelphia: University of Pennsylvania Press, 2015.

Thoraval, Joël. "The Western Misconception of Chinese Religion: A Hong Kong Example." *China Perspectives* 3 (1996): 58–65.

Tian Haihua 田海華. "Mingmo tianzhujiao dui Zhongguo chuantong daode guannian de wenhua shenru: Yi fandui nagie wei li" 明末天主教對中國傳統道德觀念的文化滲入: 以反對納妾為例 (Acculturation of Catholicism to Chinese traditional morality in the late Ming: A case study on opposition to the custom of taking concubines). *Jidujiao yanjiu* 基督教研究 (Research on Christianity), no. 4 (2007): 172–77.

Tiedemann, R. Gary. "Controlling the Virgins: Female Propagators of the Faith and the Catholic Hierarchy in China." *Women's History Review* 17, no. 4 (2008): 501–20.

T'ien, Ju-kang. *Male Anxiety and Female Chastity: A Comparative Study of Chinese Ethical Values in Ming-Ch'ing Times*. Leiden: Brill, 1988.

Tippelskirch, Xenia. "Der Kleriker und die Leserin: Kontrollierte Lektüre im nachtridentinischen Italien." In *Das Geschlecht des Glaubens: Religiöse Kulturen Europas zwischen Mittelalter und Moderne*, edited by Monika Mommertz and Claudia Opitz-Belakhal, 257–82. Frankfurt am Main: Campus Verlag, 2008.

Topley, Marjorie. "Marriage Resistance in Rural Kwangtung." In *Women in Chinese Society*, edited by Margery Wolf and Roxane Witke, 67–88. Stanford, CA: Stanford University Press, 1975.

Touboul-Bouyeure, Frédérique. "Famille chrétienne dans la Chine prémoderne (1583–1776)." *Mélanges de l'École française de Rome—Italie* 101, no. 2 (1989): 953–71.

Valone, Carolyn. "Piety and Patronage: Women and the Early Jesuits." In *Creative Women in Medieval and Early Modern Italy: A Religious and Artistic Renaissance*, edited by E. Ann Matter and John Coakley, 157–84. Philadelphia: University of Pennsylvania Press, 1994.

van Wyhe, Cordula, ed. *Female Monasticism in Early Modern Europe: An Interdisciplinary View*. Aldershot: Ashgate, 2008.

Vareschi, Severino. "The Holy Office's Decree of 1656: The Question of the Chinese Rites and the Role of Martini." In *Martino Martini: A Humanist and Scientist in Seventeenth-Century China*, edited by Franco Demarchi and Riccardo Scartezzini, 353–66. Trent: Università degli Studi di Trento, 1996.

———. "Martino Martini S.I. e il decreto del Sant'Ufficio nella questione dei Riti Cinesi (1655–56)." *Archivum Historicum Societatis Iesu* 63 (1994): 209–60.

Väth, Alfons. "Die marianischen Kongregationen in der älteren Mission Chinas." *Die katholischen Missionen: Illustrierte Monatsschrift* 63 (1935): 117–20.

Verhaeren, Hubert. "Un livre inédit du P. Vagnoni, S.J. (1605–1640)." *Bulletin catholique de Pékin* 22 (1935): 36–40.

Vermote, Frederik. "The Role of Urban Real Estate in Jesuit Finances and Networks between Europe and China, 1612–1778." PhD dissertation, University of British Columbia, 2012.

Vigarello, Georges. "Le viril et le sauvage des terres de découverte." In *Histoire de la virilité*, vol. 1, *L'invention de la virilité: De l'Antiquité aux Lumières*, edited by

Alain Corbin, Jean-Jacques Courtine, and Georges Vigarello, 399–418. Paris: Edition du Seuil, 2011.

Vitiello, Giovanni. "Exemplary Sodomites: Chivalry and Love in Late Ming Culture." *Nan Nü* 2 (2000): 207–57.

von Collani, Claudia. "Die Förderung der Jesuitenmission in China durch die bayerischen Herzöge und Kurfürsten." In *Die Wittelsbacher und das Reich der Mitte: 400 Jahre China und Bayern*, edited by Renate Eikelmann, 92–104. Munich: Hirmer, 2009.

———. "Mission and Matrimony." In *Missionary Approaches and Linguistics in Mainland China and Taiwan*, edited by Ku Wei-ying, 11–31. Leuven: Leuven University Press, 2001.

von Glahn, Richard. *Fountain of Fortune: Money and Monetary Policy in China, 1000–1700*. Berkeley: University of California Press, 1996.

von Severus, Emmanuel. "Habit." In *Lexikon für Theologie und Kirche*, edited by Walter Kasper, vol. 4, 1128. Freiburg: Herder Verlag, 1995.

von Thiessen, Hillard. "Das Sterbebett als normative Schwelle: Der Mensch in der Frühen Neuzeit zwischen irdischer Normenkonkurrenz und göttlichem Gericht." *Historische Zeitschrift* 295, no. 3 (2012): 625–59.

———. *Die Kapuziner zwischen Konfessionalisierung und Alltagskultur: Vergleichende Fallstudie am Beispiel Freiburgs und Hildesheims 1599–1750*. Freiburg: Rombach, 2002.

Wakeman, Frederic, Jr. *The Great Enterprise: The Manchu Reconstruction of Imperial Order in Seventeenth-Century China*. 2 vols. Berkeley: University of California Press, 1985.

Waltner, Ann. "Demerits and Deadly Sins: Jesuit Moral Tracts in Late Ming China." In *Implicit Understandings: Observing, Reporting, and Reflecting on the Encounters between Europeans and Other Peoples in the Early Modern Era*, edited by Stuart B. Schwartz, 442–48. Cambridge: Cambridge University Press, 1994.

———. "Life and Letters: Reflections on Tanyangzi." In *Beyond Exemplar Tales: Women's Biography in Chinese History*, edited by Joan Judge and Hu Ying, 211–29. Berkeley: University of California Press, 2011.

———. "T'an-Yang-tzu and Wang Shi-chen: Visionary and Bureaucrat in the Late Ming." *Late Imperial China* 8, no. 1 (1987): 105–27.

Wang Gungwu. "Ming Foreign Relations: Southeast Asia." In *The Cambridge History of China*, vol. 8, part 2, *The Ming Dynasty, 1368–1644*, edited by Denis Twitchett and Frederick W. Mote, 301–32. Cambridge: Cambridge University Press, 1998.

Ward, Haruko Nawata. *Women Religious Leaders in Japan's Christian Century, 1549–1650*. Farnham: Ashgate, 2009.

Watson, James L. "Orthopraxy Revisited." *Modern China* 33, no. 1 (2007): 154–58.

———. "Standardizing the Gods: The Promotion of T'ien hou (Empress of Heaven) along the South China Coast, 960–1960." In *Popular Culture in Late Imperial China*, edited by David Johnson, 292–324. Berkeley: University of California Press, 1985.

Watson, Rubie S. "The Named and the Nameless: Gender and Person in Chinese Society." *American Ethnologist* 13, no. 4 (1986): 619–31.

Westphal, Siegrid, Inken Schmidt-Voges, and Anette Baumann. *Venus und Vulcanus: Ehen und ihre Konflikte in der Frühen Neuzeit*. Munich: Oldenbourg Wissenschaftsverlag, 2011.

Wicks, Ann Barrott. "The Art of Deliverance and Protection: Folk Deities in Paintings and Woodblock Prints." In *Children in Chinese Art*, edited by Ann Barrott Wicks, 133–58. Honolulu: University of Hawaii Press, 2002.

Widmer, Ellen, and Kang-i Sun Chang, eds. *Writing Women in Late Imperial China*. Stanford, CA: Stanford University Press, 1997.

Wiesner-Hanks, Merry E. *Christianity and Sexuality in the Early Modern World: Regulating Desire, Reforming Practice*. London: Routledge, 2000.

———. "Women and Religious Change." In *The Cambridge History of Christianity*, vol. 6, *Reform and Expansion, 1500–1660*, edited by Ronnie Po-chia Hsia, 465–82. Cambridge: Cambridge University Press, 2007.

Wills, John E., Jr., ed. *China and Maritime Europe, 1500–1800: Trade, Settlement, Diplomacy, and Missions*. Cambridge: Cambridge University Press, 2011.

Windler, Christian. "Uneindeutige Zugehörigkeiten: Katholische Missionare und die Kurie im Umgang mit 'communicatio in sacris.'" In *Konfessionelle Ambiguität: Uneindeutigkeit und Verstellung als religiöse Praxis in der Frühen Neuzeit*, edited by Andreas Pietsch and Barbara Stollberg-Rilinger, 314–45. Gütersloh: Gütersloher Verlagshaus, 2013.

Wolf, Margery. *A Thrice-Told Tale: Feminism, Postmodernism, and Ethnographic Responsibility*. Stanford, CA: Stanford University Press, 1992.

———. *Women and the Family in Rural Taiwan*. Stanford, CA: Stanford University Press, 1972.

Wu Hung. "Beyond Stereotypes: The Twelve Beauties in Qing Court Art and the *Dream of the Red Chamber*." In *Writing Women in Late Imperial China*, edited by Widmer and Chang, 306–65.

Wu, Pei-yi. "Self-Examination and Confession of Sins in Traditional China." *Harvard Journal of Asiatic Studies* 39, no. 1 (1979): 5–38.

Wu, Yi-Li. *Reproducing Women: Medicine, Metaphor, and Childbirth in Late Imperial China*. Berkeley: University of California Press, 2010.

Wunder, Heide. *He Is the Sun, She Is the Moon: Women in Early Modern Germany*. Translated by Thomas Dunlap. Cambridge, MA: Harvard University Press, 1998.

Xu, Dongfeng. "The Concept of Friendship and the Culture of Hospitality: The Encounter between the Jesuits and Late Ming China." PhD dissertation, University of Chicago, 2011.

Xu, Yunjing. "Seeking Redemption and Sanctity: Seventeenth-Century Chinese Christian Literati and Their Self-Writing." PhD dissertation, Washington University, 2014.

Yan, Rachel Lu, and Philip Vanhaelemeersch, eds. *Silent Force: Native Converts in the Catholic China Mission*. Leuven: Ferdinand Verbiest Institute, 2009.

Yang, Chi-ming. *Performing China: Virtue, Commerce, and Orientalism in Eighteenth-Century England, 1660–1760*. Baltimore: Johns Hopkins University Press, 2011.

Yang, C[hing] K[un]. *Religion in Chinese Society: A Study of Contemporary Functions of Religion and Some of Their Historical Factors*. Berkeley: University of California Press, 1961.

Yü, Chün-fang. *Kuan-yin: The Chinese Transformation of Avalokiteśvara*. New York: Columbia University Press, 2001.

———. "Ming Buddhism." In *The Cambridge History of China*, vol. 8, part 2, *The Ming Dynasty, 1368–1644*, edited by Denis Twitchett and John K. Fairbank, 893–952. Cambridge: Cambridge University Press, 1998.

———. *The Renewal of Buddhism in China: Chu-hung and the Late Ming Synthesis*. New York: Columbia University Press, 1981.

Yuan, Zujie. *Dressing the State, Dressing Society: Ritual, Morality, and Conspicuous Consumption in Ming Dynasty China*. Ann Arbor: UMI Dissertation Services, 2002.

Zarri, Gabriella. "Female Sanctity, 1500–1660." In *The Cambridge History of Christianity*, vol. 6, *Reform and Expansion, 1500–1660*, edited by Ronnie Po-chia Hsia, 180–200. Cambridge: Cambridge University Press, 2007.

———. "La Compagnia di Gesù a Bologna: Dall'origine alla stabilizzazione (1546–1568)." In *Dall'isola alla città: I gesuiti a Bologna*, edited by Gian Paolo Brizzi and Anna Maria Matteucci, 119–23. Bologna: Nuova Alfa Editoriale, 1988.

Zemon Davis, Natalie. "Women on Top: Symbolic Sexual Inversion and Political Disorder in Early Modern Europe." In *The Reversible World: Symbolic Inversion in Art and Society*, edited by Barbara A. Babcock, 147–90. Ithaca, NY: Cornell University Press, 1978.

Zhang Xianqing 张先清. *Guanfu, zongzu yu tianzhujiao: 17–19 shiji Fu'an xiangcun jiaohui de lishi xushi* 官府、宗族与天主教：17–19 世纪福安乡村教会的历史叙事 (The official, the lineage, and Catholicism: The history of the village church in Fu'an county, seventeenth to nineteenth centuries). Beijing: Zhonghua shuju, 2009.

———. "The Metaphor of Illness: Medical Culture in the Dissemination of Catholicism in Early Qing China." *Frontiers of History in China* 4, no. 4 (2009): 579–603.

Zhao Shiyu 趙世瑜. *Kuanghuan yu richang: Ming Qing yilai de miaohui yu minjian shehui* 狂歡與日常: 明清以來的廟會與民間社會 (Carnival and everyday life: Temple fairs and popular society since the Ming and Qing dynasties). Beijing: Beijing sanlian shudian, 2002.

Zhou Pingping 周萍萍. *Shiqi, shiba shiji tianzhujiao zai Jiangnan de chuanbo* 十七、十八世纪天主教在江南的传播 (The spread of Christianity in seventeenth- and eighteenth-century Jiangnan). Beijing: Shehui kexue wenxian chubanshe, 2007.

Zhou Yiqun. "The Hearth and the Temple: Mapping Female Religiosity in Late Imperial China, 1550–1900." *Late Imperial China* 24, no. 2 (2003): 109–55.

Županov, Ines G. *Disputed Mission: Jesuit Experiments and Brahmanical Knowledge in Seventeenth-Century India*. Oxford: Oxford University Press, 1997.

———. "Lust, Marriage, and Free Will: Jesuit Critique of Paganism in South India (Seventeenth Century)." *Studies in History* 16, no. 2 (2000): 199–220.

———. *Missionary Tropics: The Catholic Frontier in India (16th–17th Centuries)*. Ann Arbor: University of Michigan Press, 2005.

Zürcher, Erik. "Buddhismus in China, Korea und Vietnam." In *Der Buddhismus: Geschichte und Gegenwart*, edited by Heinz Bechert and Richard Gombrich, 215–51. Munich: C. H. Beck, 2002.

———. "Buddhist *Chanhui* and Christian Confession in Seventeenth-Century China." In *Forgive Us Our Sins*, edited by Standaert and Dudink, 103–27.

———. "Christian Social Action in Late Ming Times: Wang Zheng and His 'Humanitarian Society.'" In *Linked Faiths: Essays on Chinese Religions and Traditional Culture in Honour of Kristofer Schipper*, edited by Jan A. M. De Meyer and Peter Engelfriet, 269–86. Leiden: Brill, 1999.

———. "A Complement to Confucianism: Christianity and Orthodoxy in Late Ming China." In *Norms and the State in China*, edited by Huang Chun-chieh and Erik Zürcher, 71–92. Leiden: Brill. 1993.

———. "Confucian and Christian Religiosity in Late Ming China." *Catholic Historical Review* 83, no. 4 (1997): 614–53.

———. "The Jesuit Mission in Fujian in Late Ming Times: Levels of Response." In *Development and Decline of Fukien Province in the 17th and 18th Centuries*, edited by Eduard Boudewijn Vermeer, 417–57. Leiden: Brill, 1990.

———. "Un 'contrat communal' chrétien de la fin des Ming: Le *Livre d'Admonition* de Han Lin (1641)." In *L'Europe en Chine: Interactions scientifiques, religieuses et culturelles aux XVII*[e] *et XVIII*[e] *siècles*, edited by Catherine Jami and Hubert Delahaye, 3–22. Paris: Collège de France, Institut des hautes études chinoises, 1993.

———. "Xu Guangqi and Buddhism." In *Statecraft and Intellectual Renewal*, edited by Jami, Engelfriet, and Blue, 155–69.

Zurndorfer, Harriet. "Prostitutes and Courtesans in the Confucian Moral Universe of Late Ming China (1550–1644)." In *The Joy and Pain of Work: Global Attitudes and Valuations, 1500–1650*, edited by Karin Hofmeester and Christine Moll-Murata, 197–216. Cambridge: Cambridge University Press, 2011.

INDEX

S

CPSIA information can be obtained
at www.ICGtesting.com
Printed in the USA
BVHW030008121118
532805BV00001BA/1/P